Three to Ride

A Ride That Defied an Empire and Spawned a New Nation

John C. Redmond

Hamilton Books
A member of
The Rowman & Littlefield Publishing Group
Lanham • Boulder • New York • Toronto • Plymouth, UK

**Copyright © 2012 by
Hamilton Books**
4501 Forbes Boulevard
Suite 200
Lanham, Maryland 20706
Hamilton Books Acquisitions Department (301) 459-3366

10 Thornbury Road
Plymouth PL6 7PP
United Kingdom

Library of Congress Control Number: 2012932133
ISBN: 978-0-7618-5854-6 (clothbound : alk. paper)
eISBN: 978-0-7618-5855-3

Contents

Acknowledgments

The support and encouragement received from many friends and family members were essential in the writing of this work. The significant contributions by Colonel William D. Borum (US Army Retired) are gratefully acknowledged. Colonel Borum offered enumerable suggestions for improving the content and presentation of this important subject.

Prologue

Paul Revere has rightfully been honored for all of his momentous endeavors in abetting the American Revolution. He also gained a great deal of fame based on a poem by our preeminent American poet, Henry Wadsworth Longfellow—"The Midnight Ride of Paul Revere."

Without detracting from the role undertaken by Paul, it should be noted that famous ride to alert the patriots about the movement of British Regulars to Lexington and Concord, was not done by Paul Revere alone. There were two others who also carried the onus of spreading the consequential message. William Dawes and Paul Revere were dispatched on their charge by American revolutionary hero Dr. Joseph Warren; they were later joined by Dr. Samuel Prescott, the only one of the three to actually complete the mission.

This famous ride was the culmination of provocations which precipitated the rebellion of the American Colonies and heightened the intensity of their initial confrontations with the British military in their pursuit of independence.

Chapter One

Origins of Confliction

April 18, 1775, was the kind of invigorating early spring day that lifts the soul as a harbinger of a warm summer to come. However, in Boston and the surrounding towns and villages and farms, there was a disquieting apprehension in the air. It was felt by both the British military who occupied the city, and the local citizenry who populated the countryside. Both groups had intelligence that portended a confrontation between them which could lead to consequences neither side could foresee. The unease was palpable. The British had learned of a stockpiling of arms at Concord, which they perceived as a threat. The local citizenry had reports a British force was being prepared to march to Concord to confiscate any military stores found there, which they perceived as an invasion of their autonomy. It appeared a major encounter was about to ensue.

To understand how this confliction of attitudes came about between mainly British settlers and the British military representing the authority of Britannic rule, it is necessary to go back over two centuries to discern the reasons why a group of pioneers called Pilgrims decided to leave England in 1620 to sail to the New World where they could form a colony and practice their religion unhindered by English control. This group, like many others that followed, arrived with an attitude.

The problems they had with the monarchy in England had their origins in the Reformation in Europe; with Henry-VIII's break with the Roman Catholic Church in 1534, and the formation of the Church of England, the Anglican Church. It was a tumultuous time as powerful forces on different sides of the church-state issue maneuvered for control.

After Henry died, his son Edward's reign began in 1547 when he was only ten years of age. Too young to rule, he was aided by his uncle, Duke Edward Seymour, and Thomas Crammer, the Archbishop of Canterbury. Edward-VI's rule reinforced the break with the Catholic Church, and bolstered the legitimacy of the newly formed Church of England. After Edward died, there was an attempt to replace him with a protestant, Lady Jane Grey, but the English esteem for royal continuity prevailed, and another of Henry's children, Mary Tudor, the daughter of Henry's first wife, Katherine of Aragon, came to power as Mary-I. Mary was a Catholic and reestablished many of the ties with Rome that had been broken by her father and half-brother. However, her reign was a short five years, from 1553 to 1558.

Mary and her Spanish husband, Phillip, had no heirs, so Elizabeth, another daughter of Henry-VIII, and his second wife Ann Boleyn, took the throne. There was a great deal of disarray in the English realm at the time, caused by the recent succession of rulers with disparate religious outlooks. When Henry made his break with Rome, there followed persecution of those who would not accept the new church, and especially those who persisted in attending catholic services. These persecutions only increased in scope and intensity under Edward. However, when Mary became Queen, the roles were reversed, and the Protestants were the ones victimized. So much so that Mary became known to history by the enduring sobriquet "Bloody Mary."

It was into this environment that Elizabeth began her rule. In her attempt to bring order to the religious divisions she faced, she took a rather hard line. In 1559 she issued the Elizabethan Settlement. The Settlement had two Acts: The Act of Supremacy and the Act of Uniformity. In the first Act, Elizabeth was proclaimed "Supreme Governor of the Church in England." The Act required an oath of loyalty to the Queen, originally by the clergy, but later extended to many others.

The second act, the Act of Uniformity, defined how religious services should be conducted, including such things as what vestments should be worn, and dictated the use of the modified Book of Common Prayer in the services. The Act also made church attendance mandatory on Sunday, as well as on other holy days.

The settlement was supposedly a compromise that had something for all factions, even if pleased none. The Church of England, with the monarch as its head, was reaffirmed, and penalties were proscribed for recusants, but the church took on a look-and-feel much like the old Roman Church, so that it was more comfortable for ex-Catholics to attend and participate in the services.

While the settlement did satisfy many, there were a growing number who objected to the edict. The most vocal of these were later to be referred to as "Puritans," although they would not have called themselves by that name and would not have considered themselves as separate from the main body of the English church. However, they certainly had their differences. In general, they objected to the manner in which the Church of England was progressing—too much like the Roman Catholic Church. They disagreed with the need for ornate vestments such as the cope and surplice for the clergy, the presence of any idols, and certain rites and services that derived from, and were too close to, those of the Roman Church. They strongly felt an emphasis should be placed on the authority of the bible in determining how individuals should practice their religion and live their lives.

At the time of the Elizabethan Settlement, the Puritans views weren't the majority sense of the populace, but their views, articulated often, did sow the seeds of disagreement with the crown that grew in importance as the years passed. This sizable group of dissenters became more and more dissatisfied with the English Church and the monarchy which ruled it. Eventually they decided the restraints placed on their religious practices had become so burdensome it was imperative to separate themselves from the onerous restrictions.

Chapter Two

The First Settlement

At the start of the seventeenth century there were many in England who felt the country was not moving fast enough to settle the land they had claimed in North America. The Spanish were setting up settlements in the land they had claimed, while the French and Dutch were making moves to do the same. Thus, in 1606, King James had issued charters to the Virginia Company (The Virginia Company of London) and the Plymouth Company, both companies being stock companies which were established to make a profit for their investors by setting up settlements in the New World. The charters were written to provide a sort of spatial monopoly in the territory covered by the charter. The companies' directors and investors hoped to make a profit by giving patents to groups who would set up settlements that would engage in trades, such as fishing, trapping, logging, agriculture or some other means of producing a profit. When the Companies issued a patent it was with conditions that those receiving the patents would have to somehow serve the Companies profitability interests.

One of the dissident groups which disapproved of the path the English Church was taking was a congregation of a few men of standing, but mostly farmers and laborers, families and individuals, in Scrooby near Nottinghamshire, England. They were frustrated that the English Church did not aggressively continue its post-reformation path to purge itself of all vestiges of the Roman Church. The group's members were offended with the necessity of conducting their services clandestinely, as the Anglican Church leaders did not tolerate deviations from the church orthodoxy.

They could see no acceptable alternatives to satisfying their situation while remaining in England, so in 1608 they left the country and moved to Holland where there was a secular government. There, they were free to practice their beliefs without harassment from the religious authorities in England. It took them two tries to actually make the trip as leaving the country to escape the Church of England's precepts was illegal. On their second attempt they made it to Amsterdam, but later moved to Leiden where there were other likeminded groups.

Holland at the time had a strict separation of church and state, and many, desirous of practicing their religion unhindered, immigrated there. In addition to the separatist Puritans, there were many Huguenots from France who had escaped persecution from the French king, who was staunchly catholic and would not tolerate protestant services in his realm. The congregation from Scrooby, with the very likeable John Robinson as their pastor, and also including forceful men such as, William Brewster, John Carver, and William Bradford, grew in size as new members joined with them, ultimately numbering over three hundred.

These Puritans believed in the bible as the ultimate source of God's word. The Roman and Anglican churches included reverence to religious traditions; the Puritans would have none of it. These, "traditions" in their mind were really corruptions of the word of God made by men with less than pure motivations. They had no use for the embellishments of religion as evidenced by ornate altars and glistening roods, and little respect for Bishops or Archbishops or Popes. It was the bible, and the bible alone, that accurately held Jesus' words

After eleven years in Holland, there arose unease among the congregation's members as they became uncomfortable with their lot in the country. Not having special skills, many of the members, like émigrés throughout history, had to take menial jobs to survive. Also, like émigrés everywhere, their children were assuming more and more of the culture of the host country, and losing their ancestral ties. Going back to England was out of the question, thus began talk of moving to the New World where they would be free to practice their religion, and, also have a clean slate so to speak, for evolving their own society.

At issue at the time was where to go in the New World. Some favored going to the land controlled by the Virginia Company while others felt Guiana on the northeastern coast of South America would be more hospitable. These members argued that the weather there was essentially a perpetual spring where verdant growth provided sustenance aplenty without an excessive amount of labor. There was some concern the Spanish would try to impose rule over them, but those favoring Guiana pointed out the Spanish had not set up any settlements near where they would go.

Others favored Virginia, but worried they would be subject to the king's law and thus be hampered in the performance of their religion. These members thought Guiana too hot and harbored tropical diseases which would befall them. Also, there were many "noisome pests" in Guiana that did not exist in the temperate Virginia climate. They also feared that the Spanish would eventually come and treat them as they did the French in Florida.

Finally, they concluded they would settle on the Virginia Company land, but apart from any other settlement, and, also, plead with the King to allow freedom of religion within their confines.

To get things started, the congregation in Leiden applied for a patent from the Virginia Company in 1617 to set up a settlement in the land under their control. Even though there were questions about the religious tenets of the receiving group, a patent was finally issued on 19 June 1619,

Unfortunately, even with a patent, the congregation was unable to embark on their odyssey to the New World as the Leiden congregation simply did not have sufficient funds to support such an endeavor. In what they perceived as an act of providence, it was at this time that Thomas Weston entered into their acquaintance. Weston, an enterprising entrepreneur from London, had heard of their desire to establish a colony in the New World, and he informed them he represented a syndicate of investors who wanted to invest in a colony there as well.

Weston was probably sympathetic to the Puritans religious beliefs, and some of the people he represented, some of whom would also go along on the voyage, had similar views or were merely dissatisfied with the English Church and the path it was taking. However, it is not known if they were also separatists as were the members of the Leiden congregation. Weston promised funds and a ship to take them to the New World in return for the Puritans labor when they arrived there, to accrue profit for his investors. Weston was also a sort of wheeler-dealer who was not always consistent in his promises and there were numerous delays and disagreements within the two groups.

For whatever reason, the Pilgrim group did not utilize their original patent but instead, applied for another patent, this time in the name of John Peirce, which they received on 2 February 1620. It was this patent that was used when they sailed for the New World. It was for a settlement up Long Island Sound near the mouth of the Hudson River.

In spite of the difficulties they faced, and many disagreements among them, a plan was finally put together to sail to the New World. Not all of the Puritans in Leiden decided to make the trip, but about 125 of them did decide to go. They purchased a small 60–ton vessel, the Speedwell, to take them to Southampton, England to meet up with Weston. A limited number of them would use the Speedwell to travel across the ocean, while the rest would travel on the much larger ship Weston had commissioned, the 180–ton Mayflower. The Mayflower was a sturdy, three-masted sailing ship about 100–feet in length and 25–feet wide; it was over twice as long as the Speedwell.

The two vessels finally left Southampton together on August 5, 1620 but almost immediately ran into trouble; the Speedwell was leaking badly. The two ships had to return to England and put in at Dartmouth. Repairs were made and the crossing was attempted once again. However, the Speedwell continued to leak and the group put in at Plymouth. They finally ran out of patience with the Speedwell and it was sold. Many, but not all, of the Speedwell's passengers then boarded the Mayflower for the trip across the Atlantic, leaving on September 16, 1620. Of the 125 from the Leiden congregation who had voiced a desire to make the trip, only about 50 actually were on board, the rest decided they would come later when there was room on later ships. The ship was bound for the northern edge of the Virginia Company land near the mouth of the Hudson River with 102 passengers and a crew of about 25, captained by Christopher Jones.

The assemblage of personnel on the Mayflower was not the normal group of very early settlers to America. The group to be landed consisted essentially of families, with women and children aboard; in fact three of the women were pregnant; with one giving birth while at sea and another when the ship was anchored off Cape Cod. In addition to the families there were others aboard who would be needed because they possessed special skills, like John Alden, a cooper, Peter Browne, a carpenter, and Miles Standish, a soldier to provide security. Earlier groups sailing to the new world to set up colonies were mainly men, with only scattered women among them. But this aggregation was designed to form a self-sustaining colony from the start.

The 65 day crossing was not easy. According to an account by passenger William Bradford, one of the leaders of the Leiden congregation, *"they met with many fierce storms, with which the ship was shroudly shaken, and her upper works made very leaky, and one of the main beams in the mid ships was bowed and cracked, which put them in some fear that the ship would not be able to perform the voyage."* But the ship was skillfully repaired and the voyage continued. Two people died on the voyage, a passenger, William Butten, a servant to Samuel Fuller, and a crew member.

Navigation across the wide Atlantic Ocean in 1620 was difficult. While the latitude could be determined accurately using the ascension of the sun, or a star such as Polaris, determining the longitude was a sort of hit-or-miss proposition. The longitude could be determined using complicated astronomical observations and detailed computations, but more likely a ship's captain would judge his speed and direction each day and use dead reckoning to estimate how far he had come on the 2750–mile journey. With the length of time they had sailed and the storms they had endured, their east-west position off the New World was uncertain. So they were greatly relieved when they finally sighted land on November 19, 1620.

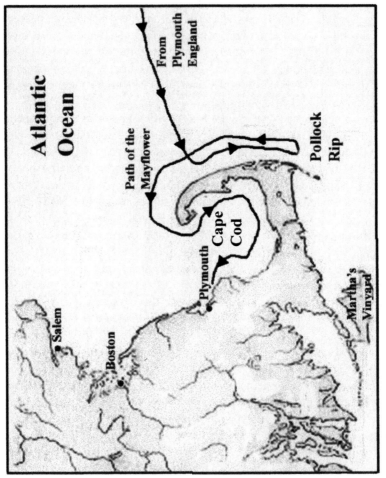

Figure 2.1.   Path of the Mayflower to Plymouth.

There was a problem though: They were not where they were supposed to be. According to their contract with the Virginia Company, they were obliged to set up their settlement on the northern edge of the Virginia Company land, near the mouth of the Hudson River. They were actually off of Cape Cod, substantially north of their intended target. The captain decided to make an attempt to sail south to reach the correct landing, but the ship came onto the dangerous shoals near Pollock Rip just past the Cape Cod elbow, and was in some serious trouble until the wind changed and they were able to backtrack north.

This episode is best described by the words from Brewster's account:

> After some deliberation had amongst themselves and with the master of the ship, they tacked about and resolved to stand for the southward (the wind and weather being fair) to find some place about Hudson's River for their habitation. But after they had sailed that course about half a day, they fell amongst dangerous shoals and roaring breakers, and they were so far entangled therewith as they conceived themselves in great danger, and the wind shrinking upon them withal, they resolved to bear up again for the Cape, and thought themselves happy to get out of those dangers before night overtook them, as by God's providence they did. And the next day they got into the Cape-harbor where they rid in safety.

With the winter closing in, Captain Jones decided it would be prudent to put into a safe harbor. But not arriving on land under the auspices of the Virginia Company meant they had no legal basis for governing in the new settlement. The contract that had been signed to get the Virginia Company's approval to disembark in their territory included agreeing to abide by the company's rules and regulations. Since, by landing at Cape Cod they were in violation of the contract, and its provisions were considered moot.

Without a formal government of some sort, there could arise disagreements among the settlers about such serious things as command and representation. Lack of agreed-to rules of governance had caused grave problems for other, earlier settlements. To resolve this problem they drew up the now famous, Mayflower Compact, which set the basis for the government they would establish when they landed. All forty-one of the adult male passengers agreed to, and signed, the contract. John Carver, one of the Pilgrims from Leiden, was elected the first governor of the colony, and on November 21, 1620 they dropped anchor near the tip of the cape (present day Provincetown).

The Mayflower Compact established the rules of government that would be used to elect leaders and promulgate laws. This was a very important step in the evolution of government in the New World. The concept, that the power of the government would be derived from the consent of the governed, was a major departure from the basis of governmental power in England. It set the stage for the desire for independence. Other, later colonies used this or a similar concept in constituting their governments.

The original Mayflower Contract has been lost, but William Bradford's hand written copy of it is still with us—in a vault at the State Library of Massachusetts—and we can appreciate its beauty.

> Having undertaken, for the Glory of God and advancement of the Christian Faith and Honour of our King and Country, a Voyage to plant the First Colony in the Northern Parts of Virginia, do by those presents solemnly and mutually, in the presence of God and one of another, Covenant and Combine ourselves together into a Civil Body Politic, for our better ordering and preservation and furtherance of the ends aforesaid, and by virtue hereof to enact, constitute and frame such just and equal Laws, Ordinances, Acts, Constitutions and Offices, from time to time, as shall be thought most meet and convenient for the general good of the Colony, unto which we promise all due submission and obedience. In witness whereof we have hereunder subscribed our names at Cape Cod, the 11th of November, in the year of the reign of our Sovereign Lord King James, of England, France and Ireland the eighteenth, and of Scotland the fifty-fourth. Anno Domini 1620.

The site at the Cape's tip was not deemed suitable for a permanent settlement, so they continued down the cape in search of better terrain. Cape Cod was named in 1602 by the English explorer, Bartholomew Gosnold, for the richness of the cod fishery in the vicinity. The cape was formed by glaciers during the last ice age, and it does provide shelter from the open ocean to the east, west, and south. But, it is large enough and open to the north, so that it can become turbulent even within its confines.

After they rounded the tip of the cape, the ship sailed south along the shore where they were hoping to find a suitable place to land the Mayflower's passengers, who were now very tired and desirous of setting foot on land. A small reconnaissance group was landed to inspect the terrain more closely. As the group made its way along the shore, several Indians appeared and shot arrows at them. The Pilgrims grabbed muskets, shot back, and chased them off. It was a small, brief encounter, likely by a small band of natives that was frightened by the intruders.

After this encounter with the Indians, they continued their search until they came upon a harbor on the west side of the cape that was out of the main body, and thus afforded some protection from wind and waves. While the waters were a little too shallow to bring the Mayflower close to the shore, and required ferrying the passengers ashore in small canoes, it was deemed an excellent harbor and well suitable for a settlement. It was the spot they had been looking for so, finally, the Matflower's passengers were landed on December 26, 1620. They called the site, which had been called Port St. Louis in 1605 when visited by Samuel de Champlain, "Plymouth," after the town in England from which they had left over two months earlier.

Prior to 1620 there had been several smaller attempts at setting up outposts in the New England area, but no real permanent towns. The Virginia Company had accomplished the establishment of a settlement at Jamestown, while the Plymouth Company had done virtually nothing. To overcome this inactivity, a revitalized Plymouth Company, with some new investors, petitioned for, and in 1620 was awarded, a new charter and acquired a new name: The Plymouth Council for New England. This charter covered land from the 40th parallel on the south to the 48th parallel on the north (generally Long Island Sound to New Brunswick).

When the Mayflower returned to England it carried a letter to Weston explaining that the settlement was now established within Cape Cod at Plymouth, on land under the jurisdiction of the Plymouth Council for New England. Weston conferred with Peirce and the latter then applied for a new patent from the Plymouth Council explaining the situation as it existed. The Council granted a new patent on June 1, 1621 (which currently hangs in the Pilgrim Hall Museum in Plymouth Massachusetts), thus legalizing the settlement. While Weston was glad to learn of the successful landing at Cape Cod, he was disappointed the Mayflower returned to England without any cargo that could be traded to recoup some of the investors' funds.

When Weston sent a small ship, the Fortune, back to Plymouth with thirty-five able-bodied men aboard to help with the manual work of setting up the settlement, he also sent a letter stating his displeasure at the lack of cargo on the Mayflower. When the ship was sent back to England it was, as Bradford states, *"laden with good clapboard, as full as she could stow; and two hogsheads of beaver and otter skins."* It no doubt pleased Weston and the investors.

The first year in their new settlement was extremely difficult. Travails beset them at every turn. Half of the settlers died due to starvation and disease, including their governor, John Carver. Fortunately, they had an able replacement in William Bradford.

In the spring after their arrival, the Pilgrims were very surprised with an encounter they did not expect. Some of the men had been working at a project near the settlement when their tools were stolen as they went for dinner. Previously, the men of the settlement had seen Indians at the peripheral of the encampment at various times, but they would run off when approached. As related in William Bradford's journal, this time was different: *"About the 16th of March a certain Indian came boldly among them, and spoke to them in broken English, which they could well understand, but were astonished at it.*" It seemed this Indian had had interaction with some earlier English explorers who had come to the area to fish. The Pilgrims were further astonished when the Indian told them of another Indian named Tisquanto, who had actually been in England and could speak the language well.

The workers gave the Indian some gifts and he left, only to return shortly with five others, who brought back the tools they had taken. After this encounter, a meeting was set up to meet with the great Sachem (Chief) of the Wampanoag (or Pokanoket), called Massasoit. The settlers and Massasoit agreed on a peace compact of six articles which stated neither side would harm the other. Tisquanto, who had come along as interpreter, remained, and was a very great service to the Pilgrims at Plymouth. He and other compassionate Indians showed them how to build huts tolerant of the local winter, and how to grow maize and other crops in the spring.

Tisquanto had an interesting tale to tell. He was captured in 1614 by earlier explorers and sold as a slave in Spain. Somehow, almost miraculously, he made his way to England, then back to North America, and finally to his home village on the cape, where he found the villagers had died due to disease. He must have been an extremely intelligent individual as the English he picked up in his travels was quite good. The settlers shortened his name and called him "Squanto."

Though their hardships were great, the Plymouth Colony persevered. Additional settlers arrived on later ships so by 1630 the colony had increased to about 300. The last of the congregation from Leiden arrived in May of 1630, but growth in the colony continued. Edward Winslow published his "Good Newes from New England" in London in 1624 extolling the merits of the Plymouth Plantation. The book, widely read, attracted many to the settlement.

The settlers maintained their strong religious beliefs, and their penchant for independence, which they passed on to subsequent generations, not a few of which were among those ready to confront British troops on that consequential day in April of 1775.

Chapter Three

The Massachusetts Bay Company

Puritans in England increased in number during the reign of James-I even though he persecuted all those not adhering to Church of England practices and rites. James was a major disappointment to those who were seeking reform in the English Church. Shortly after he assumed the throne in March 1603, he had agreed to attend the Hampton Court Conference in January of 1604, in which delegates presented a list of reforms to the Church. The reformers were hoping for reforms which would move the Church of England toward a Calvinist, bible-centered faith. However, they got very little of what they were after. The king did agree to a new translation of the bible (the King James Version), but little else of consequence. Ominously, he also warned the delegates not to oppose him or challenge his authority.

What James-I did, however, was mild compared to the havoc enacted by his successor, his son Charles-I, who became king upon James' death in 1625. Charles-I married Henrietta Maria of France, a catholic, and many were concerned with her influence on him, even though he staunchly supported the Anglican Church. The new king was abetted in his oppression of the Puritans by William Lund, the Bishop of London who would become the Archbishop of Canterbury. Lund was rigid in his beliefs and would not tolerate deviations from the edicts of the Church of England. He had absolutely no sympathy for the views of the Puritans.

Lund was an advocate of the Arminian doctrine, which was based on the theology of the Dutch scholar Jacobus Arminius. This doctrine professed a person's actions while living on earth determined their salvation, which disagreed with the Calvinist doctrine of predestination. Calvin taught that God was truly omniscience, that he knew who would be saved from the beginning of time and who would not. The Puritans accepted Calvinist theology which taught God "elected" only certain people for salvation at the beginning of time. This meant not all would be saved, no matter what they did in life. It was obvious to the early Puritans that certainly "evil" people were not among the elect. It was likewise obvious that the really "good" people were among the elect and would be saved. This understanding drove the basis for enforcing strict rules in admitting members to a congregation—a congregation of the elect.

Charles-I was a strong believer in the divine right of kings and had a disrespect of the parliament. He attempted to collect taxes without the approval of parliament, and later even disbanded the body altogether. He gave new life to two despised courts, the Court of High Commission and the Court of Star Chamber. These courts could elicit confessions through torture and require self-incrimination. It is not surprising there were multitudes who wanted to escape the country and its tyrannical king, and many did.

With the wealth of prospective émigrés desirous of leaving England, the leaders of the new Plymouth Council of New England were anxious to accommodate them and start new colonies in their charted land. Especially, since most of those wanting to leave were Puritans or Puritan sympathizers, who were honest, hard working Englishmen who could be counted on to make a determined effort to succeed. They did so by making land grants to groups who pledged to start settlements. The first of these was to a group of investors known as "The Adventurers," who formed the Dorchester Company. The company received a patent for a fishing settlement on Cape Ann that, unfortunately, failed after a few years.

However, an ensuing land grant (actually more a transfer of the Dorchester grant), did better. It was made to a group of investors, which included John Endicott and several from the original Dorchester Company. The grant to "The New England Company" encompassed land from the Merrimack River south to the Charles River including a swath three miles wide on the sides of the rivers, an area encompassing present day Boston and many of the surrounding towns.

Endicott wasted no time, and in 1628 he and his group of around sixty arrived in New England and settled in Naumkeap which was later renamed Salem. Encouraged by this success, the investors in England determined it was more secure to have a royal charter rather than a mere land grant. There was some confusion at the time regarding grant boundaries and legal precedents, and having a charter would help overcome any challenges that might be made against the new settlement. Charles-I was petitioned and a charter was granted in 1629. This new company was called "The Governor and Massachusetts Bay Company of New England." Endicott's settlement effectively merged with this new company.

In 1629 the new company sent another group of approximately 300 to join Endicott at Salem. But, even bigger plans were put in motion. At a meeting in Cambridge, England, the Company's General Court in October 20, 1629, elected John Winthrop, a prominent lawyer and investor in the Company, as governor of the Massachusetts Bay Company of New England.

Winthrop had been considering migrating from England for some time. He had thought first about going to Ireland, but later discarded that idea. He was having some financial troubles that he wanted to get away from, but what was likely more important to him was his feelings about England, and how the Church of England was failing in its progression under Reformation. He felt the English Church would feel the wrath of God for its misdeeds, and be severely punished. Winthrop wrote his feelings at the time, *"We have humbled ourselves not, to turn from our evil ways, but have provoked him more than all the nations round about us: therefore he is turning the cup toward us. I am verily persuaded God will bring some heavy affliction upon the land, and that speedily."* By going to the New World they would have the opportunity to set up a purified church, and be in favor with God; thus not be smitten.

On April 8, 1630, the first five of Winthrop's armada set sail from Yarmouth on the Isle of Wright. The remaining six ships followed soon after. In total, the convoy consisted of eleven ships with nearly a thousand new settlers to join those already there with Endicott. Winthrop's command ship, the Arbella, was a large 350–ton vessel, much larger than the 180–ton Mayflower the Pilgrims used. Winthrop made a speech either just prior to leaving England or while aboard his command ship. In this famous speech he exhorted his followers with the idea they would be setting an example for the world of how a religion should be followed: *"For we must consider that we shall be as a city upon a hill. The eyes of all people are upon us."*

It should be noted the puritans going with Winthrop were not the diehard separatists like the Pilgrims at Plymouth. The Massachusetts Bay puritans wanted to "correct" the Church of England, and shepherd it back on the path God had ordained—To set a shining example of a truly godly church for the world to see. While most of the settlers shared these views, there were some among them who were more interested in adventure and profit.

The area into which the settlers moved was nearly devoid of natives, who had suffered extensive losses as a result of disease, with smallpox the most deadly. Winthrop was not satisfied with the habitat around Salem and moved first to Charlestown on the north side of the Charles River, then, upon hearing about good water on the Shawmut Peninsula from William Blackstone, he moved his office there. He called his new town Boston (see maps in Chapters 30 & 31).

The Shawmut Peninsula, where Winthrop moved his colony's governorship, was a hilly promontory of only 789 acres. It was approximately three miles long and one mile wide. There were trees on the land, but not in great number; mostly oak, chestnut, hickory and dogwood. One settler, Anne Pollard, observed that the land was *"very uneven, abounding in small hollows and swamps, covered with blueberries and other bushes."* There were three main hills which, in later centuries, would be used to fill in the bays and ponds greatly increasing the land area. To reach the habitable land it was necessary to cross the Charles River from Charlestown (where a ferry was operated) or go around to the south, southwest to a narrow neck of land only a few hundred feet wide. A road was built along the neck, but at highest tide or in severe weather, it often overflowed with seawater.

Blackstone, who had informed Winthrop of the availability of a good spring on the peninsula, was a unique individual. An Anglican priest, he had come to the New World in 1623 as the minister of the Dorchester group. When that group failed and most sailed back to England in 1625, Blackstone stayed. He was something of a loner and moved south, ending up on the Shawmut peninsula, where he built a small house. He invited Winthrop to settle on the peninsula, but as more settlers joined Winthrop it became too crowded for Blackstone, and he moved on alone to be the first European settler in Rhode Island. The land he left on the Shawmut peninsula became Boston Common.

One of the most important provisions of the Massachusetts Bay Company charter, and one that somehow slipped through the king's advisors, was a dramatic proviso that had a consequential impact on history. The Virginia charter had a requirement that the seat of government of the company had to remain in England. Through an oversight by the royal administers, or a deliberate action by members of the Massachusetts Bay Company, the charter they were granted did not have that provision. Some of the Company's investors were nervous with moving the charter out of England since they would lose a great deal of control, but when John Winthrop left England he took the charter with him and set up the government of the colony as well as that of the Massachusetts Bay Company in the New World.

Many of the settlers spread out to start outlying towns such as Watertown, Lynn, Medford, and Cambridge. The first year was arduous with much sickness as the settlers found the winter much colder than in England and the summer much warmer.

Winthrop was acknowledged as a good leader, although his deputy Thomas Dudley thought him too lenient. Dudley was strict and intolerant, and a stark contrast to the governor. The charter they had received to start the colony dictated they form a General Court to establish laws and whatever was needed to govern. To accomplish this, the first year eight freemen, honorable, church-attending adult males, formed a Court of Assistants (to the governor) in August 1630 to appoint justices of the peace and to address other timely matters, such as setting town borders.

Those left out by this action protested, and, after reviewing the actual charter, discovered that all freemen should be members of the General Court. As a result, the next year 131 freemen made up the Court, essentially all of the adult male colonists. The freemen acquired the right to elect the members of the Court of Assistants as well as the Governor and Deputy Governor.

When it was first necessary to collect taxes for defense, there were vocal outcries from Watertown that this was taxation without representation. Sound familiar? In his memoirs of February 17, 1632, Winthrop discussed this important point.

> But understanding that this government was rather in the nature of a Parliament, and that no assistant could be chosen but by the freemen who had the power likewise to remove the assistants and put in others, and therefore at every General Court (which was to be held once every year) they had free liberty to confer and propound anything concerning the same, and to declare their grievances without being subject to question or, etc., they were fully satisfied.

However, those dissenters who complained about taxation without representation had a point. As the colony grew it soon became unmanageable to have all freemen involved as members of the General Court. For example, in 1633 and 1634 twenty ships arrived bringing many new settlers who established several new towns. Thus, in 1634, a representative form of government was established. The General Court would be made of two members from each town, elected locally, plus the Governor's Assistants, the Governor and Deputy Governor. With these actions, the Massachusetts Bay Company smoothly morphed from a commercial venture to a governmental polity. About the same time, the Plymouth colony, which had by then increased significantly in population residing in several towns, enacted a similar process.

Chapter Four

The Great Migration

Francis Higginson graciously welcomed his visitor, Mr. Jon Humfry, into his modest home in Leicestershire in Central England. Mr. Humfry had been sent by Isaac Johnson, the largest contributor to the Massachusetts Bay Company's stock, who was familiar with the ministerial adeptness Higginson had demonstrated with his local congregation. Humfry inquired of Reverend Higginson whether it was true he wished to travel to New England and serve as minister to a flock there. He did indeed, and an agreement was made between them. Higginson was given funds for the voyage and some additional as an advance on his salary. Arriving in 1630 Higginson was one of the first ministers to sail to New England, but was followed by over a hundred more during the next decade, some accompanied by their entire congregations.

That religion was of utmost importance to the organizers of the Massachusetts Bay Colony can be found in one of their early records which is still preserved in the Boston State House. The record is a simple list of the essentials that would be needed when setting up the colony in the New World. It is reproduced, in part, in Thomas Higginson's volume about Francis Higginson. It was entitled *"To provide to send for Newe England."* The following entries were on the list: *"Ministers; "Pattent under seale; " A seale; "Wheat. Rye. Barley, oats, a hhed (hogshead), of ech in the eare; benes, pease; "Stones of all sorts of fruits, as peaches, plums, filberts, cherries. "* After a number of other items, the list ended with: *"tame turkeys"* and *"copp. Kettells of ye Fch (French) making, without barrs of iron about them."* It is not surprising that "Ministers" was at the head of the list as the most important need in the new colony; for that was what the organizers felt was the most requisite ingredient in their burgeoning settlement.

From 1630 to 1640 there occurred what has been called "The Great Migration." During this decade approximately 80,000 Englishmen and Englishwomen left England to sail to the New World. Over 20,000 went to settle in New England, the remainder headed to Chesapeake Bay, other southern colonies or to the English territories in the Caribbean. The designation "Great Migration," however, refers only to those going to the New England colony. It is significant not because of the numbers involved, but rather because of the impact it had on the area to which they traveled.

At the start of this period, England was in turmoil. Charles-I ruled with a zest that greatly favored those who would support him unconditionally. His attitude of Royal Prerogative caused him to ignore prudent advice. He defiantly stated, "Kings are not bound to give an account of their actions but to God alone." His staunch support of the Anglican Church meant those who were in disagreement with him, such as the Puritans and Puritan sympathizers, Catholics and other religious persuasions, faced many obstacles in the practice of their creeds.

The king's rule was especially troublesome to the earls, dukes and other gentry, as well as the prosperous merchants, who were not accorded royal favor. They were frustrated that, with little access to nor influence with the royal court, they had no way to discourse their grievances. When the king finally dissolved the parliament their influence was decreased to essentially nil.

Ordinary citizens in England also suffered under the king. The economy was falling into disarray; the treasury was becoming bare due to the King's inept prosecution of the war with Spain. Trade decreased, affecting commerce in many areas, including the important cloth trade. And, as mentioned earlier, on the religious front the king was aided in his persecution of the Puritans by William Lund, Archbishop of Canterbury, who demanded strict adherence to the Church of England dogma. To many, it seemed the only recourse was to escape the country, and many did.

Those traveling to places like the Chesapeake or Caribbean were typically single men going to tobacco or sugar plantations for economic gain, or merely adventurers looking for a new life. The majority of those sailing to New England were family groups, many with children, looking for freedom to practice their religion unhindered by the royal and ecclesiastical authorities. These emigrants were generally well educated as most could read and write.

While the émigrés came from all parts of the English realm, there was a special concentration from East Anglia, where Puritan sentiment was twice that of England as a whole. In his book, "The Cousins War," Kevin Phillips, lists towns settled in the Massachusetts Bay Company land which were named for towns in East Anglia from which the immigrants had left. It was not an insignificant number; Phillips identifies over twenty such towns.

The inhabitants of East Anglia carried the blood of Anglo-Saxon invaders combined with the indigenous English stock, and they seemed to have a propensity of opposition to excessive external authority. They had participated in several earlier disagreements with their rulers, such as risings or rebellions in 1381, 1477, and 1548.

In her extraordinary work, "New England's Generation," V. J. Anderson examined, in detail, the lives of 693 emigrants to the Massachusetts Bay during the period 1630 to 1640. She did this by looking at the details of their person (sex, age, family relationships) and their station (trade, land ownership, social rank, etc.), before they left England, while they undertook the voyage and the whole of their lives in the New World.

As a result of her study she came up with some significant facts and statistics. The average age of the travelers was 37.4 years for men and 33.8 years for women. Ninety percent of them brought children, with the average number traveling with each family being slightly more than three. In England, as a whole, farmers outnumbered tradesmen (carpentry, leather, cloth, etc.) seven to one, while the ratio for the emigrants was one farmer for every two tradesmen. It is ironic that many of the newly arriving tradesmen became farmers as a means of achieving self-sufficiency in the new land. After their time in the New World, each of the settling families ended up, on average, with over seven children in the household.

The age at death was 71 years for men and 67 for women, both ages higher than the corresponding number for those who stayed in England. Seventeen percent of the emigrants were servants. It should be noted that being a servant was an advantage for many of the younger population. The master was obliged to pay the passage of his servants as well as feed and house them. The servants were usually indentured subjects, which meant they had signed up to serve for a set number of years (normally seven), after which they would be free. In fact, most of the servants became citizens of the colony.

An important feature of the totality of those making the migration is that none of the upper gentry made the trip because of their significant positions and land ownership in England, which they did not want to abandon during the chaotic reign of the King. Likewise, the very poor did not make the trip because they could not afford the passage nor the funding required to survive once there. Thus, there was a significant commonality if interest among the colony's population due to the homogeneity of the group, in part, because of the narrowed social spectrum.

When an immigrant family arrived in Massachusetts they did not remain long in the port town of their arrival, but moved to an outlying town where they could acquire property. Early in the settling of the area, the Massachusetts Bay Company allocated land based on a head right system; a family or an individual was given enough land to start a small farm which they would need for their subsistence—the more family members, the more land given.

However, a problem soon became evident with this form of land distribution. New arrivals wanted land they felt best suited for them individually, without regard to the need to form town centers which were needed for long-term survival of the colony. Towns were also necessary to form coherent religious congregations.

Thus, in 1634 the General Court began granting land to towns which, through proprietors, would grant land to town members. It became important for new arrivals to find a new town to settle in and to become one of the town's original proprietors, and thus enjoy the benefits of controlling the land distributions. The new system worked well and new towns sprang up in an orderly manner. Some towns actually became so populated they were closed to new settlers, requiring newcomers to start a new one further away.

While Boston, Salem, and Gloucester grew as many new arrivals stayed near the port of their landing, others moved away from the coast into the surrounding countryside, where a plethora of new towns were chartered, as such as: Medford, Mystic, Everett, Watertown, Cambridge, Ipswich, Concord, Newberry, Salisbury, and Braintree. Others, such as Lexington in 1642, followed soon after.

In addition to settling in the vicinity of Boston several groups migrated to the southern coast of Connecticut. Several of the Puritans from the Massachusetts Bay Colony started a settlement up the Connecticut River at Hartford in 1636. The leader of the group, Thomas Hooker, a former professor at Cambridge, England broke with Massachusetts and formed his own colony, appropriately called the Connecticut Colony. Other settlements, such as the one at New Haven, were made near the mouth of the river by others from Massachusetts. While the Dutch had previously established a settlement on the River, they were soon overwhelmed by the number of English and later abandoned the area.

One of the events occurring in 1636, only sixteen years following the landing of the Massachusetts Bay settlers, exemplified the significance these early settlers held for education and religious learning: the founding of a university in Cambridge near Boston. It was named for a young minister named John Harvard, who had left his library and half of his estate to the new institution. An early brochure from 1642 announced a rationale for the school, *"To advance Learning and perpetuate it to Posterity, dreading to leave an illiterate Ministry to the Churches."*

The end of the period of the Great Migration occurred rather abruptly as Oliver Cromwell, a Puritan supporter, took up the fight against King Charles-I thus obviating the main reason English were migrating to New England. While the stream of settlers from England to Massachusetts did not cease completely, it became a small portion of what it had been. However, the population of the area increased dramatically in future years due to the natural fecundity of the settlers. Large families were the rule, and without great wars or natural disasters the colony increased geometrically.

At the end of the Great Migration, 1640, the combined Massachusetts Bay and Plymouth Colonies had a population of approximately twenty-five thousand, and was an established and significant English settlement. With a hundred and thirty-five years to the 1775 confrontation with English Redcoats, there was sufficient time (over five generations) for the population to grow naturally to the five hundred thousand that then occupied the area.

These were the people, then, who gave the populace its fundamental character. They were solid, religiously devout to their congregational creed, hardworking and placed great emphasis on individual initiative. Over time other groups joined the cadre, French Huguenots, Dutch and Scottish settlers, and others, who contributed to the regions spirit, but the fundamental traits were implanted early and were sustained.

There was also an amendment to the Great Migration that should be noted. Although the stream of settlers to the New England colonies abated when Cromwell took control of England, there were many royalists who now felt uncomfortable remaining in the country. Thus, a mini-migration occurred with settlers who supported the monarchy, deciding the New World would be more hospitable to them. They generally avoided New England and went, rather, to New York and the southern colonies; with Virginia being a popular destination.

Chapter Five

Early Transforming Influences

The mien at both the expanded Massachusetts Bay and Plymouth colonies at the end of the Great Migration was still severe and faithful to their religious beliefs. The settlers adhered to the bible as the source of guidance for both religious and daily living habits. They had governments that were solidly theocratic and were intolerant of others who did not believe as they did. They did not accept change easily; however, several events occurred over time that did moderate their views. The first of these had occurred earlier and planted seeds of doubt in the strict thought process they clung to so fervently.

Roger Williams was born in Smithfield, England on December 21, 1603, and later became a brilliant theology student at Cambridge University, graduating in 1627. In late 1630 he and his wife sailed to Boston to join the settlement established by John Winthrop, arriving on the ship Lyon on February 5, 1631. Although ardent in his religious beliefs, Williams' views did not conform especially well to those in place in the colony.

The most startling of these differences, and one that placed him in immediate disparity with the populace, was a strict separation of religious and secular matters. He believed individuals should be free to believe in and practice their religion independent of the government, something he termed "Soul Liberty".

Even with these convictions he was such an imposing presence he was invited to become chaplain of the Boston congregation. However, after discussions with the leaders of the colony, he declined the offer, believing the Boston group was not "separated enough" from the Church of England, as were the Plymouth and Salem groups. Or as Winthrop would report, *"because they (the Boston congregation) would not make a public declaration of their repentance for having communion with the churches of England while they lived there."*

After his refusal of the Boston pastorship, the Salem congregation invited him to become pastor of their flock, but some in Boston, resenting his decline of their offer, and likely his opinions on religious freedom, complained to Endicott, the leader of the Salem settlement, expressing their disapproval of the offer. To further influence those at Salem, the Boston group offered to accede to Salem's claim to land at Marblehead if they acted, and thus the invitation was revoked. Not as influenced by the opinions of him in Boston, the Plymouth Colony acquired his services.

However, it didn't take long for Williams to become discordant with many at Plymouth. In his account of the Plymouth Plantation, William Bradford, the President of the Colony wrote about Roger Williams:

> Mr. Roger Williams, a godly and zealous man, with many rare qualities but a very unstable judgment, who settled first in Massachusetts, but owing to some discontent left there, came here where he was made welcome, according to their best ability. He exercised his gifts among them, and after some time was admitted as a member of the church; and his teaching was highly approved, and for the benefit I still bless God, and am thankful to him even for his sharpest admonitions and reproofs, so far as they agreed with the truth.

He added later,

> This year he began to hold some strange opinions, and from opinion proceeded to practice. This caused some controversy between the church and him, and in the end some discontent on his part, so that he left somewhat abruptly." And still later, "He is rather to be pitied and prayed for; so I shall leave to matter and desire the Lord to show him his errors and return him to the way of truth, and give him a settled judgment and constancy therein.

So what was the heresy that Williams preached? He objected to magistrates punishing offenders for religious infractions such as not properly observing the Sabbath or for liturgical blasphemy. He felt the settlers were not being fair with the Indians, and should not acquire their land without their approval and some form of compensation. He even voiced his belief that the king of England had no right giving away land belonging to the Indians, as it was not his land to give away. The most egregious of his opinions was that the forced conversion of the Indians was "monstrous and inhumane."

After a couple of years in Plymouth, Williams had outlived his welcome there and was asked to leave. He returned to Salem as assistant pastor, and was shortly given the pastoral position when the incumbent died suddenly. This placed him in a more prominent position where his openly articulated views on religion, which so inflamed many, caused him to be censured and exiled by law from Salem in 1635 as a dangerous influence, whereupon he was brought before the General Court of the Massachusetts Bay Colony in Boston.

The specific act that brought about Williams hearing before the Court and his eventual exile was the writing of a letter and sending it to the Governor and Assistants of the Massachusetts Bay Company. In his letter he questioned, as he had previously preached, the magistrates' authority to enforce compliance with religious decrees, even the ten commandants. There were three other passages in the letter which offended them. First, Williams charged King James with telling a lie because he stated he was the first Christian prince that had discovered the land on which New England was situated. Second, he charged the king with blasphemy for calling Europe "Christendom." And thirdly, that he applied to King Charles-I, three places in the Book of Revelations which were very despairing, for example, "the spirit of devils go forth unto the kings of the earth."

It is well to note here that, at this time, there were stirrings in England that the Massachusetts Bay Colony was behaving in ways that could offend the King, and some enemies of the Massachusetts Bay Company suggested he should revoke the colony's charter. Thus, the colony's leaders were sensitive to comments disparaging the monarchy that could be repeated in London.

At his hearing before the General Court in October 1635, Williams was given the opportunity to repudiate his transgressions, but he refused. He was further offered the opportunity to delay the hearing for a month, but again refused, demanding to address the complaint presently. As Winthrop tells it, *"A Mr. Hooker was appointed to dispute with him, but could not reduce him from any of his errors."* Thus, the Court exiled him from their jurisdiction demanding he leave within six weeks.

Williams, ever forceful, was not deterred from openly expressing his beliefs before the six weeks were up. He was a continuing thorn in the side of the colony's elders, and they decided to capture him and place him on a boat bound for London. Learning of their plot, he escaped and fled into the dense forests to the south. It is interesting to note Williams was alerted to the effort to deport him by none other than John Winthrop, the first governor of the Colony, who always had a somewhat benevolent feeling for him even as he disagreed with his views. As Williams himself wrote, *"That ever honored Governor Winthrop privately wrote to me to steer my course to the Narragansett Bay Indians."* which Williams did hastily.

After much wandering, in June of 1636, Williams moved to the site of Providence in present day Rhode Island, where he established a settlement with other followers who had moved with him from the Boston area. The governance of the settlement was based on a strict separation of church and state. In England, the church and the government, in the form of the monarchy, were closely related. One was used to promote and protect the other. Rebellious views against the government were perceived as attacks on the church and vice versa. Although not as clear as in England, the coupling of government and church in the new settlements was similarly strong as only approved church members in good standing could serve in government positions. In a truly secular settlement, the churchly and governmental influences were decoupled; government officials were held to standards of their governance and not how they practiced their religion. This was how the government at Providence was instituted.

The free-thinking Williams became a Baptist in 1639 when he was baptized by a Mr. Holyman from Salem. However, being a strong believer in the supremacy of the bible, Williams soon questioned the authority of those who advocated the baptism of believers and not of infants, since he could not find specific direction for it in his bible. Therefore, he decided he would belong to no specific church and pray with all regardless of their churchly affiliation.

In 1643 Williams was granted a charter for his Providence Plantation by the puritan government then in a position of power as Charles-I was under siege by the parliamentary army opposing his rule. Later, in 1647 the colony at Rhode Island joined with the Providence colony to effectively create what became the state of Rhode Island.

The joined colonies became a haven for those desiring religious freedom. The Quakers who were persecuted in Boston, the Baptists who were also not welcomed there, Jews and others came and settled. While his time in Boston was brief, and as much trouble as he caused for the authorities, there is no doubt his ideas and opinions had a significant influence on the populace, thus opening many minds to these revolutionary concepts. While most likely disagreed with him, they could not escape discussing his moderating influence. As much trouble as he created for the authorities of the settlements, there is no doubt his ideas were discussed frequently. In a sort of repentance by the Massachusetts Court, the law used to exit him was repealed the following year.

Another influence challenging the tenets of the religiously based Massachusetts government came shortly after Williams was evicted from the Massachusetts colony. Anne Hutchinson may or may not have been influenced by Williams, but her actions also inflamed resentment among the colony's leaders, and also caused many to rethink their basic beliefs. While the problems the hierarchy of the Massachusetts Bay Colony had with Roger Williams were difficult, they were, nevertheless, easy to understand. That was not the case with the problems they accrued shortly after they had removed him from their presence.

Anne Hutchinson was born as Anne Marbury on July 20, 1591, in Alford, England, where her father was a deacon at Christ Church in Cambridge. Although she did not attend university she was extremely intelligent and read extensively from her father's library. Her father agreed with the teaching of John Cotton, who questioned the path the Church of England was taking. His Puritan views were accepted by his daughter, as was his assertiveness.

When she was twenty-one Anne married William Hutchinson, a prosperous cloth merchant, who was in total agreement with her beliefs regarding the English Church. When Cotton left England in 1633 to sail to the Massachusetts Bay Colony, the couple, along with their eleven children, followed him the following year.

Upon arrival, they set up their home on a farm in Boston, becoming one of about two hundred families residing there. They joined Cotton's congregation and Will Hutchinson started his cloth business in their new home, while Anne became much in demand for her midwifely skills. At this time it was common for the men of the town to assemble to discuss both civic and religious subjects. Often they met to discuss the message a pastor may have preached at his last sermon. They would examine the ideas put forth and inspect the biblical passages that supported or disputed any conclusions drawn.

No women were invited to these discussions. In the Puritan society of New England, women were deemed to play the role of supporter for her husband and caretaker of the home. It was not thought proper for them to partake in open discussions of religious matters.

Anne Hutchinson was an intense reader of the bible and knew it intimately. She also inherited her father's outspokenness and was not reluctant to voice her opinions. She felt the omission of women from these religious discussions was a grave injustice that needed rectification. Accordingly, she began holding meetings in her home with other women to discuss religious matters, much as the men were doing.

If she had just conducted these meetings in a low profile manner and kept to the tenets of the time it is likely she would have been tolerated even though many of the colony's leaders would have disapproved of them.

But Anne went further than merely agreeing with the Puritan doctrine. She disagreed strongly with the Puritan interpretation of the story of Adam and Eve. In the Boston Puritan view, Eve accrued special blame for leading Adam astray resulting in mankind's original sin. The passage was used to support the dominant role of men in the society, which Anne did not agree with.

Anne was an eloquent, compelling speaker and her arguments threatened the hierarchy, both religious and civil. Her small meetings blossomed and many more, including some men, came to hear her speak, so much so, the meetings had to be moved from her home to a larger church. As some of the colony's male members began to point out, she did not follow Paul's declaration that women should be silent in public meetings; Anne was definitely not the silent type.

Some historians have attributed a misogynic attitude on the part of the colony's male members as the cause of her rejection, but this is too simplistic an apperception. It became evident that basic beliefs were being challenged. She preached that individuals could receive revelations directly from God, thus bypassing the pastors as necessary intermediaries. There were intricate interpretations of religious doctrine that were commonly examined that Anne disagreed with and so voiced her opinion. For example, a person could have the Holy Ghost indwell in him, but not, as Anne Hutchinson preached, have a personal union with the Holy Ghost.

John Winthrop first wrote in his journal in October 1636 about Anne: *"One Mrs. Hutchinson, a member of the church of Boston, a woman of ready wit and bold spirit, brought over with her two dangerous errors: 1. That the person of the Holy Ghost dwells in a justified person. 2. That no sanctification can help to evidence to us our justification."*

To the strictly ordered Puritans of the Massachusetts Bay Colony, her antinomian sentiments smacked of religious anarchy; and they were concerned her radical views could infect the "weaker" of the other colonists. She was finally brought before the Court in August 1637 for her crime of being a woman speaking, and even preaching, in public about religious matters. Her trial was not going well for Winthrop and the other magistrates as Anne skillfully deflected the charges they brought before her. Holding meetings to discuss the bible was common practice in England, she said, and was a proper thing to do. However, after two days of questioning, while this woman of fifteen children was required to stand, she finally doomed herself by declaring she received her knowledge of religious truth by direct revelations from God. To which Winthrop replied, *"I am persuaded that the revelation she brings forth is delusion."*

The Court determined her testimony was heresy, and at first put her under house arrest, but later a more formal religious trial was held in the Boston Church. John Winthrop was motivated to act as the main prosecutor as in his mind this was a serious matter that needed resolution. The schism in the Boston Church was deep and Winthrop felt if it continued and grew, the Colony was in danger of splitting over the issue of Anne Hutchinson and the beliefs she professed. She was not alone in these beliefs, and there was the danger the schism would grow and damage the fabric of government. There was no King to keep things in line and no rigid caste system as was present in England. They were on their own and vulnerable to disuniting. Anne Hutchinson was, unfortunately for her, an easy target. Discredit her and her heretical ideas would go with her.

After being exiled from Boston, Anne, her husband William, her children and a number of followers traveled to Providence and joined Roger Williams' settlement which was based on the separation of church and government; where religious freedom was the rule.

The group stayed at Providence for about four years before moving further south to settle in what is now Newport. When her husband Will died in 1642, Anne and her remaining children moved to the Dutch Colony of New Netherland in New York. The move was prompted by fears the magistrates at Boston might try to arrest her. Unfortunately, the Dutch had incurred a conflict with the local Indians who attacked the settlement where Anne had gone, and everyone there save one of Anne's daughters was massacred; the daughter survived because her red hair so marveled the Indians they kept her.

In an historical note, as a gesture of repentance, the State of Massachusetts placed a statue of Anne Hutchinson on the grounds of the State House in Boston in 1922, and in 1945 the legislature officially revoked her exile.

New concepts and ideas, especially if they sharply contradict long-held beliefs, have a gestation period before they are even acknowledged as worthy of discussion. Only after time can they be examined critically and as possibly having merit and thus affect beliefs and behavior. Roger Williams and Anne Hutchinson gave the New England settlers many issues to contemplate in both the civic and religious domains.

Roger Williams and Anne Hutchinson came from within the Puritan Church and had been staunch members of their congregational churches, but there were other thought provoking episodes that came to the colonies from without, and also caused internal soul searching.

When the Anabaptists, the word meaning again baptized arose in England in the sixteenth century most other religions, including the Catholics and Protestants, had serious issue with them. It was thought heresy to declare baptism was only for believers, and it was an egregious error not to baptize infants who were unable to profess their faith in Jesus. Infant baptism was one of the core beliefs of the Puritans that was done to cleanse the body of original sin.

The Anabaptists influenced the formation of the Baptists, but there are significant differences between the two denominations. In any case the Anabaptists had acquired a negative reputation among the other religions that carried over to the Baptists, and anyone professing Baptist views soon learned they were not welcome. Those Baptists who found their way to the Puritan colonies were not allowed to stay.

To formalize the Massachusetts Colony's opposition to having Baptists settle in their territory a law was passed on November 13, 1644. It read, in part:

> It is ordered and agreed, that if any person or persons within this jurisdiction shall either openly condomne or oppose the baptizing of infants, or to go about secretly to seduce others from their approbation or use thereof, or shall purposely depart the congregation at the administration of the ordinance, or shall deny the ordinance of magistracy, or their lawful right or authority to make war, or to punish the outward breaches of the fruit table, and shall appear to the Court willfully and obstinately to continue therein after due time and means of conviction, every such person or persons shall be sentenced to banishment.

It is obvious the civil leaders of the Colony were intent on keeping their Puritan beliefs "pure," but their efforts were not universally condoned. In March 1645, John Winthrop's son Steven, who was in London, wrote of *"great complaint against us for our severity against the Baptists."* Later in August of the same year, George Downing, the son of Winthrop's brother-in-law, wrote to John Winthrop, jr, *"The law of banishment for conscience makes us stink everywhere."*

The problem of keeping their Puritan "purity" was further complicated by what was happening in England at the time. Oliver Cromwell was conducting a successful civil war against Charles-I, and the titular leader of the Church of England's power was on the wane. Worse still for the Puritans, although Cromwell was a Puritan sympathizer, he was very tolerant of individual religious beliefs. Englishmen felt free to examine and practice their faith in accordance with their own conscience.

Some of the Baptists moved down to Providence where they were welcomed by Roger Williams and the other settlers there. Those remaining who held closet feelings for the Baptists or who felt the action was too severe just remained quiet. Some brave souls petitioned the governor to intercede and repeal the Baptist restriction law as well as another which required new arrivals to get the approval of the magistrates in order to remain in the Colony. The petition was brushed aside and rejected by the harsh Thomas Dudley, who was governor at the time, and a staunch supporter of the strict law.

As bad as the Baptists had it, their lot was relatively mild compared to how the group that followed them was treated. This group had acquired its well-known appellation when an English Justice tried one George Fox, who was brought before him in Derby, England in 1650. The honored official referred to Fox's group as "Quakers" because hey trembled at the word of god.

The Quakers acquired this reputation as a result of the manner in which they conducted their meetings. They believed in receiving God from within so the assembled faithful would wait in silence until one of them felt the spirit within him, and give voice to it. Waiting in the quiet, anticipating word from God was such an emotional experience for some they would tremble and quake, giving the name to their credo.

The Quakers were also an outgrowth of disagreement with the Church of England as were the Puritans, but they had their own brand of religious practice. They referred to themselves as The Religious Society of Friends. They believed in individual revelation from God from within. This meant they could disagree with some biblical passages, which was anathema for the Puritans. The Quakers were generally ascetic, believing in peace among all men to the degree they rejected fighting and war. That is not to say they were quiescence when espousing their faith on missionary missions, quite the contrary. They could be quite forceful and vociferous.

The Quakers felt it their duty to spread the word of their beliefs as missionaries traveled to many parts of the world; Italy, France, Holland, Turkey in Europe and many of the English colonies. Thus it became inevitable some would immigrate to the New World. Both the Massachusetts Bay and the Plymouth colonies were alarmed at the prospect of these "Friends" arriving, and possibly settling in their regions.

And arrive they did. The first were two women who arrived in Boston on July 11, 1656. The Deputy Governor, Richard Billingham had the two arrested and placed in a jail with the windows and doors boarded shut lest some citizens would come in contact with them. It was as if they carried some germs that could infect the local populace. After a short time in the jail they were placed aboard a ship bound for Barbados.

But the action did not resolve the Quaker invasion. Shortly after the two women were evicted, eight more Quakers arrived from London on the ship, Speedwell, so named after the vessel the Pilgrims tried to use in their journey to Plymouth. Like the two before them, the eight were placed in the Boston jailhouse where they were kept for several weeks before being sent back to England.

The governor at the time, John Endicott, thought the Quaker invaders were misguided and tried to exculpate them of their erroneous ways, even bringing one Mary Prince into his home and, working with two Puritan ministers, tried to cleanse her of her heretical beliefs. It didn't work; in fact, Mary was quite vociferous in her beratement of the Governor.

In a more formal effort to stem the arrivals, the Massachusetts Court passed a law setting a fine of one hundred pounds for the captain of any ship that landed a Quaker on their grounds. Further, any Quaker so landing would be beaten and jailed.

As Endicott failed with Mary Prince, the law did not deter other Quakers and more arrived. Several of the eight who had been expelled earlier, joined by others, returned to Boston. It was as if the Quakers now felt it a challenge to change the attitudes in the Puritan settlement. Massachusetts was not the only area that objected to Quakers arriving. Save for Roger Williams' Rhode Island, most other regions, including the Dutch settlement banned the Quakers as a disturbing influence.

In 1657, acknowledging the earlier law was not working, the Massachusetts Court, passed harsher laws, including penalties such as cutting off of a violators ear (two if caught a second time) or having their tongue pierced by a red hot iron. These stricter laws still didn't work. The Quakers were, it seemed, seeking to become martyrs to their faith. The Massachusetts leaders were frustrated and perplexed, and felt more extreme measures needed to be taken.

In October 1658, a law was passed that any Quaker, having been banished from the colony once, would be put to death if they returned. Many felt a law so harsh would finally prevail: no one would dare defy such a decree. However, true to the previous actions, several of the banished Quakers did return.

It was a situation that caused great consternation among the colonists. If they did not enforce the law they had written they could not expect the Quakers to believe they were serious. If they enforced the law they had to put the four violators they had in jail to death. The Boston authorities tried to reason with the condemned Quakers: They would be allowed to escape the gallows if they agreed to be banished and promised to stay away. They would not, and they were hung.

The hangings of what many knew were peace loving individuals so disturbed many of the colonists that the death penalty law was repealed in June 1661. It portended a change in attitude of the populace that moderated the harsh, unsympathetic attitude shown to others who did not believe exactly as they did.

The Quaker persecution, however, did not end immediately. The Massachusetts Court passed the Cart and Whip Act, which proscribed that any Quaker not leaving the area should be tied to a cart and whipped as they were escorted out of the colony's territory. Gradually, the impetus to punish Quakers waned, especially since several of the colony's settlers in Salem converted to the Quaker creed and remained as contributing and accepted members of the community.

The colonists had seen a number of governors who varied in their view of how the colony should be run. John Winthrop, the first governor was strict in his adherence to the law, but had a softer side that often moderated his views. Thomas Dudley and John Endicott were the hard liners, who rejected compromise. Their influence was strong during the early period of the settlement, but became less so as time passed. The settlers, at first struggling to survive in a strange environment, effectively cutoff from the home country by the vastness of the ocean, behaved defensively. As the settlements became more permanent the populace became more secure, and less fearful of outsiders and their influences. They could direct their lives to the betterment of their lot, to improve the land and look to a brighter future.

Chapter Six

Parliament Revolts

There were two important revolutions in England in the middle and latter half of the seventeenth century that had significant impacts on the Massachusetts Colony. The first of these was the aforementioned war between an army raised by parliament, led by Oliver Cromwell, and the king's army. Charles-I had been deprecating of parliament for some time. His belief in the absolute right of kings made him disdainful of parliament or anyone else who would be so presumptuous as to tell him what to do. He felt he was the divine ruler and all should acquiesce to his wishes.

Charles first found himself in serious trouble in 1639. The Church of Scotland wanted to institute a Presbyterian form of church governance, in which the church hierarchy would consist of members of the congregation elected as elders and deacons. Under Anglican (or Episcopalian) rules, the church hierarchy consisted of bishops and priests who were appointed by the higher ecclesiastical leaders. Thus, when the Church of Scotland leaders' refused to use the Anglican approach and, instead, adopted the Presbyterian, Charles acted. He entered into what has been called the first Bishops War. Defeated, he was forced to allow Scotland freedom to hold onto their Presbyterian form of church governance. More importantly for the king, the war was a financial drain. So much so he was forced to call parliament into session the next year to raise taxes to replenish the royal treasury. Parliament was willing to discuss the issue, but, in a quid quo pro, they wanted to tie the raising of taxes with changes in the king's rule, mainly to restrict his unilateral actions without Parliament's approval. Charles, still embracing his royal prerogative, cancelled the session after only a few weeks, thus labeling it "The Short Parliament."

Still not satisfied with his initial results in Scotland, and feeling he could do better the second time around, Charles entered into another armed conflict with the Scots, which, like the first, ended in October 1640 in a disaster for the king. His army was soundly defeated in the field and, after signing the Treaty of Ripon, he was obliged to pay Scotland expenses they had incurred in fighting him. Now, desperate for funds, Charles called Parliament back into session. The King did accede to several demands of Parliament, such as the arrest and execution of the King's Minister, Sir Thomas Wentworth, known in London's alleys as "Black Tom the Tyrant," and The Archbishop of Canterbury, William Laud. But, even as the king agreed to the demands, relations between the obstinate monarchy and Parliament did not improve.

Matters deteriorated further after an uprising in Ireland in October 1641, in which a number of English settlers were killed. Rumors spread of Charles complicity or possible foreknowledge of the action. The following month the House of Commons drew up a list of errors or reproofs in a formal act entitled the "Grand Remonstrance." While not directly attacking the king, the act left no doubt of parliament's disapproval of the King's rule, and no doubt to whom the act referred.

A sense of the depth of this dissatisfaction can be found in the statement naming those responsible for the country's ills: *"The root of all mischief we find to be a malignant and pernicious design of subverting the fundamental laws and principles of government upon which the religion and justice of this kingdom are firmly established."* The act went on to name the villains as: Jesuited papists, bishops and the corrupt part of the clergy, and such councilors and courtiers (who served their private ends). Parliament Member John Pym argued astutely and strongly for passage, and on November 22, 1641, the Grand Remonstrance passed by a vote of 159 to 148.

The triggering event for more serious hostilities occurred on January 4, 1642 when the king, with several hundred of his soldiers, stormed into the House of Commons intending to arrest five of the most bothersome members and charge them with high treason: John Pym, John Hampden, Denzil Holles, Arthur Hazelrig and William Strode. He was the first monarch to enter the chambers of the House of Commons during a session, which was considered a gross violation of protocol. He was likely provoked by a rumor that the House was going to impeach his wife, the catholic Henrietta Maria, and remove her from the country.

Upon entering and not finding his quarry he inquired of the Speaker, William Lenthall, where they were. The speaker's enduring reply was "May it please your Majesty, I have neither eyes to see nor tongue to speak in this place but as the House is pleased to direct me, whose servant I am here." The King's reply, "I see all the birds have flown," ended the intrusion and the King left humiliated.

Relations between the King and his Parliament had descended to the point the royalists felt threatened with overt action by Parliament and its activist leaders in a royal coup. Six days after the King had entered Commons, he and his supporters left London and moved to Oxford where they began to assemble an army to fight against any uprising, while his dutiful wife, Henrietta Maria, took the crown jewels and fled to Holland to raise funds for the oncoming battle. Parliament, remaining in London, did the same. The English Civil War began in earnest on October 26, 1642. It was a war Sir William Waller called, *"this war without an enemy."* The early battles were inconclusive as neither side was well organized, but as the war continued, the parliamentary army, led brilliantly by Oliver Cromwell, who had risen from commander of a modest cavalry troop to General of the Army, began to gain a decisive edge. A decisive battle took place June 14, 1645 at Nasby which was won decisively by the parliamentary army in which they took five thousand prisoners and much treasure.

Charles was finally forced to flee from Oxford, and escape to Scotland. The Scottish army, not quite knowing what to do with him, finally handed him over to representatives of Parliament. While in custody, Charles made several attempts to reorganize his forces. He made promises to the Scots which he likely could not keep, but with Scottish support, revitalized a part of his army and tried to continue the battle; but nothing really worked. Finally, the king was re-captured and placed in a prison in Hurst Castle before being moved to a more secure holding in Windsor Castle. There were a number of options discussed about what actions to take against the captured monarch. The most damaging action the king had taken was to rouse the Scots to another fight after he had been taken the first time, and many were incensed at this "dishonorable" action.

The makeup of parliament was soundly shaken when on December 6, 1648, Colonel Thomas Pride of Parliament's New Model Army surrounded the parliamentary buildings and refused entry to all royalists or those suspected of being royalists sympathizers. The ensuing session of the body, as a result of "Pride's Purge," voted to try the king for treason.

The king remained obdurate during the trial, stating they had no right to try him. As Robert Lacey wrote in his readable book "Great Tales from English History," the king voiced his objection to the proceedings, *"If power without law may make laws, I do not know what subject he is in England that can be sure of his life."*

His defense, though eloquent, was of no avail as the king was found guilty of high treason. Charles-I's head was chopped off on January 30, 1649. It was an especially cold day so the king had put on an extra garment so no one would see him shiver. While the death of the king meant the dissolution of the monarchy in England, not all of the kingdom followed this course. Almost immediately upon the death of the old king, Scotland proclaimed Charles-I's' son as king Charles-II of the Scots, which dictated unrest between the two nations. Oliver Cromwell, with his army intact, went on to conquer Ireland and Scotland, and the realm was ruled, albeit poorly, as a republic by a parliament, called by historians as "The Rump Parliament."

Even though the parliament, which had been purged of royalists, had agreement on opposition to a monarchy, they disagreed on nearly everything else. The many factions could not reach consensus on matters of governance. Cromwell, still wielding the power of army commander, became so disgusted with parliament's ineptitude that he dissolved the body by force on April 30, 1653.

There were further attempts to form a more relevant government but nothing worked. Finally, a member, John Lambert, proposed a new constitution which made Cromwell Lord Protector of the empire. Cromwell accepted the position and assumed the title on December 16, 1653. During his reign, Cromwell did preside over a period of stability which was welcomed by the populace. He ended the Dutch war and instituted religious reforms that allowed a degree of freedom of worship, excluding Catholics. It was quite an achievement for the man who had once considered sailing to New England to join the puritans there.

The war and the ultimate defeat of the royalists, and the installation of Cromwell as Lord Protector, was welcomed in the Massachusetts Colonies, especially since he had evidenced strong religious views that were in concordance with those of the puritans. His abhorrence of Catholicism was based on his perception of that religion's denial of the primacy of the bible while demanding adherence to papal authority. Something the colonists could relate to. With the upheavals in the mother country the colonists were left alone to grow, and establish commerce and trade on their own. They developed new industries that added to their independence. The success of the parliamentary army against the monarch further strengthened the settler's commitment to the rule of law over the whims of kings.

While the winds of war monopolized England, the colonists took the opportunity to enact their own laws. The Body of Liberties was written by one of Massachusetts' prominent settlers, lawyer and preacher Nathaniel Ward. It codified the laws of the colony. It was a remarkable document that became, after several revisions over the years, the basis for the later Massachusetts Constitution as well as having a decided influence on the Bill of Rights. It drew on the Magna Carta and common English law. It was progressive in that it described rights and liberties rather than defining restrictions and penalties, and thus was properly named.

This progressive secular approach taken by Ward was in contrast to the more ecclesiastical approach advocated by the minister, John Cotton and others, who felt the laws should be based on biblical teachings, and the colony should be governed more as a theocracy. The majority of the settlers disagreed with Cotton. While they were, in general, Congregationalists who believed in supremacy of the bible and the teachings of John Calvin, and took their religion very seriously, they also had a strong distaste for a government forcing religious decrees upon them. They had had their fill of that in England and had no desire to recreate a similar situation in their colony.

When the document came before the General Court for approval, the colony's first governor, John Winthrop, surprised many as he opposed approving it. He preferred a system that would adjudge disputes or crimes in a manner that each case would be judged on its individual circumstances. Thus a code of laws would evolve over time based on precedent. He attempted to stall approval of the Body of Liberties by stating their royal charter prohibited them from enacting any law that were "repugnant to the laws of England." While it was uncertain exactly what in the articles was really repugnant to the laws of England, the Court approved the document on December 16, 1641 no matter what England might think.

There was a list of about one-hundred articles in the Body that covered all manner of fundamental rights and obligations. There were those relating to individual rights, rites, rules and liberties relating to judicial proceedings, liberties of freemen, women, children, servants, and foreigners and strangers, and even brute creatures (animals). The article relating to the liberties of foreigners and strangers seemed to allow slavery, albeit in a specific manner:

> There shall never be any bond slavery, villeinage, or captivity amongst us unless it be lawful captives taken in just wars, and such strangers as willingly sell themselves or are sold to us. And these shall have all the liberties and Christian usages which the law of God established in Israel concerning such persons cloth morally require. This exempts none from servitude who shall be judged thereto by authority.

There were laws relating to capital punishment and religious liberties, although these were not strictly defined. The list concluded with an article stating the articles in the body should be deliberately weighed in the future by the General Court.

Being left to their own, the New England colonies increased their trade, grew their economies and became more self sufficient. Their main industries of timber, fish, and fur provided ample trade with England. Not having a replenishable cash crop like tobacco, which Virginia enjoyed, New England branched out and broadened their industrial base in such important industries as iron works and shipbuilding. In the next half-century Boston was destined to become one of the main ship building centers of the world.

After ruling for eight years, Cromwell died on September 3, 1658, likely of malaria he had picked up on his Irish campaign, complicated by a kidney infection. He was followed in the role of Lord Protector by this son, Richard, who proved to be a far less effective leader than his father. He had no real support among Cromwell's army or the Parliament and abdicated. His leaving left a vacuum in the leadership of the country with no obvious individual who could be put into the post and rule effectively. Many yearned for the familiarity and stability the monarchy provided in the past, even with its failings. The country was nearing anarchy as various constituencies vied for power.

Those in favor of the restoration of the monarchy were many noble men of power who benefited by having a friendly monarch. Also included were those who were subject to royal appointments such as customs officials. Those advocating a strong parliament were merchants and entrepreneurs who desired laws encouraging commerce.

Sensing the country was failing, the English Governor of Scotland, General Monck, took matters into his own hands to enforce a compromise solution. He marched his army to London and demanded Parliament hold elections. After a free election was held, the new Parliament, now including many royalists, was seated. They asked the thirty-year old Charles-II to return and assume the monarchy, but with conditions that included pardons for any who fought with parliament. To smooth old tempers and win over the remnants of the army, a provision was added that would pay soldiers the pay past due to them.

On May 25, 1660 Charles arrived in London to complete what the English call "The Restoration." He was coroneted at Westminster on April 23, 1661. However, it wasn't a completely smooth resumption of regal power. While there was some amnesty given to those who had supported Cromwell and deposed Charles-I, there was some retribution against others. Several were executed and, in a bizarre move, Oliver Cromwell's body was exhumed from its grave and beheaded. His head was placed atop a pole outside of Westminster Abbey where it stayed in full view until 1685.

A new parliament was elected, and it supported the king and the Church of England. In a near repeat of the Elizabethan Compromise, public officials had to swear allegiance to the king while the use of the Book of Common Prayer of the English Church was deemed compulsory for church service. These laws were part of a broader series known collectively known as the Clarendon Code, which was passed to re-establish the supremacy of the Anglican Church, and to effectively rid the country of Puritanism forever.

England at the time of the restoration was enveloped in a dynamic, uncertain environment. It was obvious to the king and his royalist supporters that they were not immune to unsettlement and a nervous anxiety pervaded the court. While Cromwell's supporters were subdued, they did not all disappear so the threat was always in their minds. They had shown the king could be disposed and the Scots still wanted their complete freedom to follow Presbyterian tenets.

On a broader scope there were new conflicts with the Dutch and the burgeoning involvement in India to consider, all within the milieu of an evolving Europe. Religious issues had dominated much of the actions taken by the English rulers, but now, economic issues became more important. While economic issues always required consideration, the rapidly expanding world economy created a nationalistic competitive environment. England, as well as the other European nations, had to defend itself against economic as well as military threats to the ends of their empires.

After the monarchy had been restored to the throne in the new king, Charles-II, the new king remembered, or was reminded, the Massachusetts Bay Company had taken their charter out of England, and, further, they were Puritans who had supported Cromwell in his overthrow of his father. To stop persecution of the Quakers in Massachusetts, the newly ensconced king issued a writ of Mandamus that no Quaker under threat of hanging or in prison, should be tried there, but should be returned to England. It wasn't that the king had any favor for the Quakers, but rather he was demonstrating his authority over the colony. And he didn't stop there.

In 1675 the king had established the Lord of Trade and Plantation, a committee of twenty-one prominent subjects which reported to the monarch's Privy Council on colonial matters. It was designed to administer the relationships between the colonies and England.

The Massachusetts Bay Colony was placed under closer scrutiny by the committee and assigned Edward Randolph as their representative in Boston. He went right to work and undertook a detailed evaluation of the colony's actions over the previous decade. After he completed his work he reported back to the committee. He reported the Massachusetts Bay Colony was in violation of their royal charter.

Specifically, there were thirteen articles of high misdemeanor against the colony. Among these were:

> They continue to exact an oath of fidelity to themselves, notwithstanding the King's orders to the contrary, and make such oath essential to the tenure of the office and even freedom of the Company.
> They have obstructed the execution of the Acts of Trade and Navigation, and have refused to recognize many of them.

They impose customs on goods imported from England, though this was judged by Sir Robert Sawyer to be illegal. They have found against the King in all causes for seizure of ships in the face of clear evidence.

They discountenance and discourage members of the Church of England, forcing them under penalties to attend their meetings, and accounting all others unlawful assemblies.

Not surprisingly, in 1684 the Court of Chancery, under Charles-II, invalidated the Massachusetts Charter. The action was intended to bring the colony back under close London rule.

Chapter Seven

The Pequot and King Philip Indian Wars

When the first explorers made it to the New England coast they espied numerous Indian villages with farms around them. In 1604 Champlain, sailing along the New England shore noted, *"All along the shore there is a great deal of land cleared up and planted in Indian corn. The country is very pleasant and agreeable, and there is no lack of fine trees."* In addition to corn many other crops were planted; vegetables such as, beans, squash, artichokes, and pumpkins; and fruits, including numerous berries and melons. The early explorers especially noted fine fields of strawberries.

In 1614 John Smith found *"The shores well populated."* He wrote in "*A Description of New England,*" that he observed forty villages as he cruised north from Cape Cod to Maine. The Indian villages were usually situated on high ground, with clearing of the forests around them to allow ample room for farms alongside. This arrangement also provided warning in the event the village was attacked. The Indian population was essentially agrarian, with fish a staple along the coast and game inland.

An Indian village was a semi-permanent assemblage of shelters crafted from the materials at hand. In addition to a main village, which was moved occasionally when the natural resources around them became depleted, the natives often set up temporary sites along the coast or a river to catch and preserve fish. In the Plymouth and Massachusetts areas, the living abodes were wigwams, single family residences, but in other areas, especially to the north, larger, multifamily structures were also being used.

All of the structures, large or small, used similar construction techniques. The supporting walls were made from poles of resident trees cleaned of branches. The poles were securely placed in the ground vertically. The ends were then bent inward and tied with willow or other twigs forming a rounded top for the single family wigwams or a quonset-like, elongated roof-line for the multi-family residences. The vertical poles were reinforced around the structure's circumference, at different heights, with suppliant twigs resulting in a grid arrangement that greatly strengthened the walls. The sides were then covered with bark, birch preferred if it was available, but bark from other trees were used as well. For single-family wigwams a single smoke hole was left at the top; in multifamily-family structures each family had its own hole in the top above their fire pit. An opening in a wall, covered by a drop cloth, most likely an animal skin, served as a door. With a fire in the center, the structure, as noted by one of the English settlers, was warmer than the English houses.

The size of an Indian village was highly variable, from about fifty or a hundred or so families, to larger towns of over a thousand. The wigwams were normally scattered around a cleared area, but in some cases where the inhabitants felt threatened, the villages were surrounded by a protective palisade. There were usually many dogs resident in the villages.

The tribes of the area were of the general Algonquin family, and thus shared a common language (or at least a common base to their language). Many of their customs were likewise derived from a common heritage. This relationship did not, however, preclude competition and conflict among the different tribes, including warfare.

When, in 1620, the Pilgrims came to the same area where in 1614 John Smith saw his forty villages, it was nearly devoid of Indians due to the disease brought by the earlier European visitors. Villages further inland had not suffered as much as those on the coast, but none of them really escaped. Even with suffering this calamity, the Indians the settlers first met were generally peaceful; and were even essential to the Pilgrims at Plymouth, helping them to survive their first year.

The tribes resident in the area included the Wampanoag in southeast New England, whose territory overlapped Plymouth and Boston. The Pawtucket lived along the coast north of Salem. The Narragansett's land was in Rhode Island along Narragansett Bay, including Providence and Newport. The Pequot were located in southeast Connecticut while the closely related tribe, the Mohegan, lived along the Connecticut River upriver to Hartford and beyond. The Niantic occupied the southern coast of eastern Connecticut and Rhode Island. The Nipmuck and the Pocumtuck were in central Massachusetts. North and west were the Mohawks and the Abenakis. Each tribe knew well the limits of their territories, but finding Indians of different tribes in other Indian areas was not unusual.

These major tribes often had sub-tribes that were known to the settlers by their own names. The Pokanoket, who welcomed the Pilgrims at Plymouth were a sub-tribe of the Wampanoag, and both names are used to describe them.

For a period after the original settlements were in place, there were only sporadic confrontations between the settlers and the natives. In the beginning the Indians had only bows and arrows, or spears, but after a few years they acquired muskets, powder, and shot from traders who gave them the guns so they would be able to gather more pelts for trade. Several minor attacks took place, but nothing major interrupted the peace of the settlements until a more serious confrontation occurred in 1637 called the Pequot War. The conflict was as much a conflict between traditional native enemies as it involved the settlers, but it was the settlers' involvement which decided the issue. Even before the settlers arrived, the Pequot had been aggressively harassing neighboring tribes in an effort to extend their sphere of influence over a greater territory.

Once the settlers became established, a great deal of trade commenced between the settlers and the natives. The Indians liked the metal tools and trinkets they could obtain for pelts or other trading goods. After a time, the tribes started to become protective of this trade; each tribe had places and settler groups where they felt a proprietary ownership. The Pequot felt this ownership of trade along the Connecticut River, and became at odds with the Mohegan and Narragansett over trading rights in the area. At one time a Pequot party attacked several Narragansett who were attempting to trade at Hartford, which the Pequot considered their exclusive territory.

Sometime around 1634 the Pequot became very enraged at the Dutch because they had killed a Pequot sachem under obnoxious circumstances—some Dutchmen had captured the sachem and demanded a ransom for his return. The Pequot paid the ransom but got their sachem back—dead. The tribe was thus angry at all white men, regardless of their European place of origin.

The trouble the Pequot had with the English settlers started the same year when a Captain John Stone of the Virginia Colony was murdered along with some of his men by a party of Pequot. In the past he had kidnapped Indian women and children to sell as slaves in Virginia, and the Pequot likely felt justified in dispatching the Captain.

When the Indians were confronted by the settlers over killing Stone they readily admitted it, telling John Winthrop,

> Captain Stone coming into the river took 2 of their men and bound them and made them show the way up the river, which when they had done, he (Captain Stone) with 2 others and the 2 indians (their hands still bound) went on shore, and 9 of their (Indian) men watched then, and when they were on sleep in the night they killed them.

However the Pequot rationalized the killing of Stone, to the Massachusetts settlers it was murder. While the Indians felt they were only acting in self-defense, the settlers did not like leaving loose ends in matters in which one of their number was killed, and wanted Stone's killers returned for a trial, but the Indian Sachem refused.

Tensions increased in July 1636 when a Massachusetts Colony settler, John Oldham was murdered aboard his small pinnace near Block Island. The Pequot were blamed, but it is just as likely that the perpetrators were Narragansett. The English were resolute in their retaliation. They felt they could not let a murder of one of their own go unanswered lest the natives be tempted to dare additional crimes against them. John Endicott led a group of ninety English volunteers, along with several warriors from the Narragansett tribe, and burned several Pequot houses and destroyed some of their crops.

In early 1637 the Pequot increased their attacks on English towns in Connecticut. A raid on Wethersfield resulted in nine settlers' deaths and two young girls taken prisoner. The war finally reached a climax on May 26, 1637 when the Pequot sachem, Sassacus, took a group of his braves to raid Hartford leaving his main village unguarded. A militia under a Captain John Mason, consisting of ninety Englishmen and seventy Mohegan, plus two hundred Narragansett, attacked the village which lay on the Connecticut shore between the Mystic and Thames Rivers. The two acre village consisted of a number of wigwams inside a ten-foot high fence of pales, a palisade. Inside were six hundred to seven hundred Pequot, mainly women and children.

The attack came as a surprise and the Pequot had little chance. In an infamous decision, Mason ordered the fence and the houses set fire, and to kill anyone trying to escape. Almost all of the Pequot inside the village died that day. Mason, in justifying his action, termed it an act of God. The Indians witnessing this genocidal act were astounded at the brutality of the English. In their wars they tended to avoid killing women and children, instead capturing them and incorporating them into their tribe.

There were a few other battles, but, as a result of the devastating attack, the Pequot were essentially eliminated from the area as a viable tribe. The remaining Pequot fled their villages in small bands, some hunted down by the English and Narragansett and Mohegan war parties. Survivors were made slaves of the Mohegan and Narragansett, or shipped as slaves to other English settlements in Bermuda or the Caribbean. Some even became household servants of the English settlers. The Pequot lands were distributed to the victors. The English settlers justified confiscating the Pequot land as booty in a "just war." The last Sachem of the Pequot, Sassacus, escaped with some of his braves to Mohawk territory in New York. The Mohawk, fearing the ferocity of the English, killed Sassacus and sent his head to the settlers in Connecticut. Much later, a small band of surviving Pequot was provided with a small reservation in Connecticut.

The Pequot War had a decided effect on the Native Americans, especially the Pequot, but had relatively little repercussions for the English settlers other than enhancing their apprehension of the vulnerability they faced with their Native Americans neighbors. In an effort to consolidate their forces against outside threats, the colonies formed the New England Confederation, consisting of the English colonies of Massachusetts, Plymouth, Connecticut and New Haven. The confederation was based on an agreement between the participants signed on May 19, 1643. It remained in effect when New Haven was incorporated into Connecticut in 1665.

The accord was written to provide "comfortable fruits of protection" for its members. It was strictly a defensive pact; each member retained their local sovereignty for all other matters. The agreement defined how each colony would provide men and funds for defense if they became involved in a war. The potential adversaries included the Indians, the Dutch and the French. Rhode Island, under Roger Williams, or "Rouge Island" as it was sarcastically labeled by the other settlements, was excluded from the confederation as that colony's approach was to avoid conflicts with the Indians in all situations.

The English colonists viewed the Indians as a people without knowledge of Christianity and thus could not be trusted to follow modes of behavior dictated by religious teachings; modes that were very meaningful to the colonists. If they could not depend on the Indians following familiar and sacred conduct in all aspects of interpersonal interaction, they had to stay on guard against unexpected repercussions in dealing with them.

The Indians had their own laws and means of enforcing them, but they were not as codified as the English code of jurisprudence. The English had strict rules for determining guilt and meting out punishment that precluded extemporaneous actions by those in power, even if they did not always follow them. The Indians likely were suspicious of the English trials and thus the sachems were reluctant to turn over members of their tribes suspected of a criminal act.

It was in this environment that the next confrontation with the tribes would occur, and it would not be so easy or unaffecting this time, to both combatants. As discussed earlier when Massasoit, sachem of the Wampanoag, welcomed the Pilgrims after their arrival, he helped them establish their colony. Massasoit gave the Pilgrims land for their towns and farms, and his subjects provided valuable guidance in building shelters and growing corn and squash. The Indians generosity was crucial to the settlers' survival, so the colony prospered. Other settlers arrived and soon the colony was well established.

As the settlers' numbers grew by immigration and internal population increases, Massasoit's consulars became concerned the colonists were becoming too numerous and too powerful. His consulars advised Massasoit to take action against them while they still had superior numbers. The sachem did not heed the warnings. He was impressed by the knowledge the English possessed to improve the soil, to raise cattle, and to grow many fruits. He resisted action against the settlers as they took more and more of his land, and grew even stronger.

In 1660, prior to Massasoit's death that year at over eighty years of age, his two sons were given English names by the Plymouth Court: The names were derived from ancient Macedonian leaders. Wamsutta, the eldest, was given the name of "Alexander," while his younder brother Metacomet was designated "Philip." Sometime later in the year Massasoit died and his eldest son Wamsutta became sachem. In 1662, two years after becoming chief, Wamsutta was summoned, somewhat forcibly, to appear before the Plymouth Court. He was brought before the court by Josiah Winslow, who had succeeded Miles Standish as head of security. Winslow, a Harvard educated, second generation Pilgrim, did not have the same view of the Indians the first generation had. The first generation settlers were grateful to the Indians and their sachem for the critical assistance they provided. Winslow, and others, had no such memories and considered the Indians more an obstacle to acquiring additional land, rather than critical friends.

Wamsutta was brought before the court because he was suspected of selling some of his land to other settlers in violation of the pact Massasoit had signed with the Pilgrims, in which he would only sell land to them. While at the court he became sick and died a few days later. He was succeeded by his younger brother Metacomet, who was suspicious of foul play in the death of his brother. While nothing was ever proved one way or the other, Metacomet brooded over his loss.

In his somber mood and distrust of the English, Metacomet began reviewing what the tribe's consulars had advised his father; if the settlers became too powerful they would dominate the tribes and take their land forcibly. He knew well of the settlers' insatiable desire for more land and had no doubt they would try to take what they wanted when they were able. He also was concerned with loosing the tribe's basic customs and ideals, especially in light of the settlers' penchant for converting the natives to Christianity; which many did. One of those converted had been one of Metacomet's interpreters, John Sassamon.

Metacomet realized his tribe alone was not strong enough to take on the English, so over the next decade he powwowed with the sachem of the other tribes to convince them to join him in his quest to defeat the English and remove them from their territory before it was too late. The message resonated with many in the other tribes.

In April 1671 Metacomet was humiliated before a meeting with representatives of both the Plymouth and Massachusetts Bay colonies. He was brought before them and accused of inciting a rebellion. For whatever reason, Metacomet signed a statement admitting his guilt. He was forced to surrender his tribe's weapons and powder, and to be subject to the English.

It was following this mortifying concession that the sachem seriously began preparing for war. He sold land and bought more muskets and powder. He increased his dialogue with the neighboring tribes and began preparation in earnest.

Upset that his chief was preparing to make war against the settlers, Sassamon was true to his conscience, and in January of 1675 he traveled to Plymouth where he met with Josiah Winslow, who had been elected governor of the colony. Sassamon warned the governor of Metacomet's plans for war. He also feared for his life as his warning the English would certainly be known to his tribe, so he pleaded with Winslow for protection. The Harvard educated Winslow was disdainful of the Indians in general, so he dismissed Sassamon, telling associates, *"One can hardly believe them."*

Sassamon was forced to leave Plymouth and his body was found the next February under the ice on a pond, murdered, most believed, because of his warning to Winslow. After a brief investigation, the Plymouth authorities arrested three of Metacomet's tribe for the murder, tried them, and hung them on June 8, 1675. The trial incensed many of the natives who thought it highhanded the settlers' disrespect of native rights.

The war started shortly after. A band of Indians attacked the Pilgrim settlement of Swansea, destroying the town and killing a number of the inhabitants. In response, the English invoked the articles of the New England Confederation and formed a militia to raid the Wampamoag village at Mount Hope in Rhode Island where Metacomet was staying.

Metacomet learned of the force against him and moved his tribe to a nearby swamp. The militia leader, James Cudworth of the Plymouth Plantation, felt he had Metacomet trapped and would wait him out. However, under the cover of night Metacomet and his warriors, and some other members of the tribe escaped and made their way north to join up with the Nipmuck.

The war spread quickly. A number of English settlements were attacked in July and August 1675; Middleborough, Dartmouth, Mendon, Brookfield, and Lancaster. In September attacks continued with sieges at Deerfield, Hadley and Northfield. The New England Confederation, which had come into existence as a result of the Pequot War, officially declared open war on the native tribes on September 9, 1675. The war was called "King Philip's War," using the English name given to Metacomet fifteen years earlier.

Settlements in Maine, New Hampshire and Connecticut were attacked as the Nipmuck and the Abenakis joined in the battle. The war was intense and odious. Both sides were malicious in their treatment of captives. The colonial army would burn wigwams with women and children inside, killing any who tried to escape. The Indians had always tortured their captives, even other Indians, and they remained true to their past. One Thomas Warner was captured by the Indians along with others. He related how his captors treated their prisoners, *"kill'd one of the Prisoners presently after they had taken him, cutting a hole below his Breast out of which they pulled his Gutts, and then cut off his Head."*

A militia of a thousand men was formed under Josiah Winslow and they moved against the Narragansett, even though it was not clear that tribe had joined with the Wampanoag in the fight. The foray culminated in a battle in a frozen swamp where the Narragansett had built a large fort. Three hundred of the natives were killed as were seventy of the colonists. The fort was burnt down and the natives stores, needed to survive the winter, were destroyed. The surviving Narragansett, now committed to the battle, moved north to join the other tribes.

The war continued through the winter of 1675 and spring of 1676, and it was bloody. On March 12, 1676 the Indians actually attacked Plymouth, but were repelled. The effect on the English settlers, however, was chilling, and many of the outlying settlements were abandoned.

The English had one significant advantage: they could be resupplied by sea from England and other colonies in Bermuda and the Caribbean. They didn't expect much help from the mother country except for what they paid for, but it was available. The Indians had no such backup supplier and began to suffer. Normally, they would have had a repository filled with corn, peas, dried fish and game, to carry them over a winter, but that had not been possible during the hostilities.

During the spring, the battle began going against the natives. Smaller settler patrols harassed the Indians wherever they could be found. A surprise attack along the Connecticut River let by Captain William Turner resulted in the death of over a hundred, and possibly over two hundred, natives. The Narragansett were decisively defeated in April 1676. An English victory at Hadley, Massachusetts was followed by another at Marlborough.

By summer it was obvious the Indians could not sustain a major effort; they had lost the war. Many surrendered and Metacomet found himself with only a small band of followers. He had tried to get help from the French, but received only token arms. He was finally cornered at Mount Hope in Rhode Island, and shot and killed by an Indian friendly to the English, named John Alderman. As the English did in London to arch enemies, he was decapitated and his head displayed in Plymouth impaled on a long pole.

King Philip's war was the bloodiest war in American history on a per capita basis, and bloody it was. In total, some three to five thousand natives had died, due to battle injuries or disease or starvation. Many were sold into slavery or fled the area to live with more distant tribes. Estimates of the reduction in Native Americans in the New England area run as high as sixty percent, while that may be high, the tribes were reduced to small enclaves which no longer threatened the colonists.

For the English, Plymouth suffered the most, but the devastation was felt all across the area. Approximately eight hundred men lost their lives in battle while many women and children were lost in attacks on the towns. Over fifty towns or villages were attacked with thirteen completely demolished. Thousands of cattle were killed and acres of cropland destroyed. The cost of the war was a serious burden for the settlers, and it would be many years before they regained the same level of financial stature they had prior to the conflict. Likely the most significant long-range impact of the war was the now available Indian land for expansion, which, due to the ultimate continuation of their growth, the settlers took full advantage.

Chapter Eight

England's "Glorious" Revolution

Charles-II died on February 6, 1685, and was succeed by his son James-II. The new king went even further in causing problems for the New England colonies by creating the Dominion of New England, which combined Massachusetts, New Hampshire, East and West Jersey, New York, Plymouth and Rhode Island in a new governmental entity. The king appointed Edward Andros as the dominion's governor.

Under the Dominion's rule many of the colonists' rights were suspended. The election of representatives to the colonial assemblies was replaced by Andros' appointees. Rights at court, such as bail and juries were restricted. The Church of England gained favor and Anglican services were held in the formerly puritan congregational churches. The Dominion's government claimed all undistributed land for itself, thus taking each town's common land. It was not surprising that Andros was much disliked. It would take another English revolution to return Massachusetts its charter; a revolution the English would term "Glorious."

Charles-II had definite catholic leanings, likely derived from his mother Henrietta Maria of France. He is supposed to have entered into a secret treaty with Louis-XIV of France in which the French king would support him financially as well as aid in the war with the Dutch. In return, the English King supposedly agreed to convert to Catholicism at some unspecified time in the future. In fact, he reputedly did make the conversion on his deathbed.

Charles' son, James as King James-II, was openly catholic. Upon taking the crown he proceeded to place Catholics in important posts in government, and the army and navy. Many converted to Catholicism to keep their positions, but many would not and were removed from office or restricted in their authority. Converting was a difficult dilemma for many prominent Englishmen. Many had a fundamental belief in the protestant religion and contravening their conscience did not set well with them. But, they also had an ingrained allegiance to the King that was likewise strongly felt.

James had little support from the majority of Englishmen. The high Anglican clergy tolerated James as he had only daughters, Mary and Anne from his first marriage to Anne Hyde, and they felt he was, at least, far removed from the puritans and the likes of Cromwell. Better yet, both of the daughters had been raised protestant by a directive by James' father, to mollify his Anglican critics. When James' wife Anne died, he married Mary, an Italian Catholic, the daughter of the Duke of Modena. She tried ten times to produce an heir, but ten times the child was either stillborn or died early in infancy.

At this time James, did two things that alienated his moderate Anglican supporters. First, he tried to enact laws that would ease restrictions on all religions. While this would ease pressure on Catholics and others such as Quakers and Puritans, it would detract from the grip the Anglican Church had on the country. Second, but much more important, Mary had a healthy son. Now, this son was the heir to the throne, not his protestant daughters. Many felt the birth of this son was a ruse, that the infant really was someone else's child.

Although these suspicions were strong and widely believed, nothing definite concerning the boy's illegitimacy was ever proved, and the child was grudgingly accepted as James' son, at least by a part of the realm. Thus, in England, Scotland, and Ireland, all religious factions except the Catholics came together to address this threat of a catholic being heir to the throne..

James' first daughter, Mary. had married William of Orange, a stadholder in Holland on November 4, 1677, when she was fifteen and he was twenty-seven. William had a strong dislike for France in particular and for Catholics in general. France was the most populous, most wealthy of the European countries as well as being the most catholic. William was very concerned that an alliance would be made between England and France which would threaten the Dutch in many ways.

When the twenty-one year old William had come to power in 1672 France had attacked the United Provinces of the Netherlands; made up of the states of Holland, Zeeland, Utrecht, Gelderland, Overijssel, Friesland and Groningen. The French would likely have conquered all of the Netherlands had resourceful Dutch not opened several critical dikes that sealed the French army from the main cities of Amsterdam and The Hague.

The English, under Charles, had also agreed to join with the French by sending ships and some troops. However, interest in the war by the general English populace was lukewarm at best, and parliament hesitated to provide funds for any navel action. The French were not successful in their invasion and had to retreat, eventually signing a peace treaty with the Dutch in 1678.

The invasion engendered a strong dislike and mistrust of the French in the future king of England. Bringing England into a war against the French was one of the primary motivations William had to pursue the English throne.

When James set upon a path to pack parliament with Catholics, a number of the nobility became alarmed. A letter was prepared by seven prominent nobles to be given to William. English Admiral Arthur Herbert, who had been dismissed by James-II for not agreeing to repeal the Test Act that barred Catholics from membership in parliament, was given the letter to deliver secretly to William, which he dutifully did at William's castle near the town of Appledoon in the Netherlands on June 30, 1688. The letter, signed by the nobles who opposed James, suggested that William assemble an invasion force to remove James from the throne. They promised their support, and indicated the effort would have the support of the majority of the English populace.

The main concern William, and those supporting him, had was what France would do if he took the throne in England by force. It was a real concern, but when France attacked Germany by crossing the Rhine, William perceived France would be too distracted to interfere in England, and he acted. He sailed with a massive armada of nearly five hundred Dutch ships carrying 15,000 men and 3000 horses. In the first attempt to sail, stormy weather forced them back. However, the weather turned and they again set sail for England. It was an impressive sight.

With a favorable wind the lead ships reached Dover at ten in the morning. The sight is described in K. M. Chacksfield's book The Glorious Revolution 1688.

> More than six hundred vessels, with canvas spread to a favorable wind, followed in his (William's) train. The transports were in the center. The men of war, more than fifty in number, formed an outer rampart. . . His fleet spread to within a league (about three miles) of Dover on the north and Calais on the south. The men-of-war on the extreme right and left saluted both fortresses at once. . . The troops appeared under arms on the decks. The flourish of trumpets, the clash of cymbals and the rolling of drums were distinctly heard at once on the English and French shores.

It was an imposing sight for all on shore to observe. As the ships continued west down the English Channel, offshore of England's southern coast, the Dutch ships sailed unchallenged by the English navy, which, due to unfavorable winds or a lack of desire, did not confront them. The fleet finally put in at Tor Bay in the southwest part of the country on November 5, 1688. The army disembarked and met no resistance; in fact, they were either warmly greeted or passively allowed passage. After landing, William calmly made his way to London.

William had prepared for the invasion well. He had printed 60,000 copies of a proclamation in which he assured the English population his aim was to preserve the protestant religion and to install a free parliament. Its title was: *"The Declaration of his highness William Henry of Orange of reasons inducing him to appear in arms in the kingdom of England."*

It became evident that, rather than treating William as a conqueror; he was being received as a savior by many in the general population and even much of the English army and navy. The overthrow of James' government proceeded rapidly. James was allowed to flee to France to join his wife and son, whereupon he would be deemed to have abdicated his crown. However, there was a bit of comic opera when some seamen captured James as he was ready to sail to France. The king was in disguise, but his capturers eventually recognized him and returned him to London. William had to "arrange" another escape for James, which was successful and he left the country.

William, now in control of the country, called a parliament of members of Charles-II's last parliament. Initially, the parliament was unsure what action to take with regard to William. Perhaps, some proffered, they could make William Regent, rather than king, a lesser title, but he rejected the offer. After William threatened to leave and take his army with him, thus leaving the nation in anarchy, they decided to act.

Some in England felt it would be more appropriate if there was a strong genealogical connection to the old royal line, which William, being the son of Charles-I's daughter Mary, met only thinly. Thus, after much negotiation, on April 11, 1689, both William and his wife Mary were crowned monarchs. William as King William-III and Mary as Queen Mary-II.

One of the many consequences of the change in royalty was the limiting of the monarch's power and concomitant increase in the power of parliament. It would be parliament who would make laws, levy taxes and control the army. However, the king kept the option of selecting his own ministers who would administer the country, and also to have control over the term of parliament's sessions.

In religion, the Act of Toleration granted freedom from persecution to all protestant sects not affiliated with the Church of England. The act did not, however, extend to Catholics. Being Catholic meant something different to those living in the seventeenth century than what we have today in the twenty-first century. It wasn't just a matter of religious beliefs and faiths, and following religious customs and teachings. A Catholic in 1688 owed some allegiance to the Pope, who, at the time had secular as well as religious authority. He had land, an army, and a treasury. He could demand an oath of loyalty as well as funds to support his reign. He could influence the choice of monarchs and other heads of state, and dictate appointments to the clergy hierarchy.

The matter went even further in England where, after reformation by Henry-VIII, catholic churches, monasteries, and church land was confiscated by the crown and distributed to titled English gentry whose descendents now owned the properties. A reversion to Catholicism would mean the loss of title and estate to many prominent nobles.

A Bill of Rights was passed by parliament in 1689 that codified the rights and liberties of English subjects and included, for example; freedom of royal interference on government, freedom to elect members of parliament, freedom of speech in parliament, freedom from royal taxes without parliament's approval. Other directives were established with regard to royal succession. One of the members of Parliament who made these decisions was the renowned scientist, a pre-knighted, Isaac Newton, who had been elected to the body in 1689.

When William and Mary became monarchs, the country's finances were in disarray. William was well aware of the important role the Wisswlbank of Amsterdam played for the Dutch. It was the banking system that was an important ingredient in the nation's success in becoming a leader in world trade. Accordingly, William started the effort to create a banking system in his new kingdom leading to the formation of the Bank of England in 1694. It was an action that helped propel England into a leading position in world trade.

The English refer to this changing of monarchs as the "Glorious Revolution" because of the lasting effect it had on the nation.. More religious freedom for all protestant religions was granted, and the elimination of the possibility of a catholic ever becoming a ruling monarch was established. The latter change easily surviving Jacobite uprisings in 1715, 1719, and 1745, which were efforts to place Bonnie Prince Charlie on the throne. But, the most important modification was the change that gave more power to the people through a freely elected parliament. The country was on its way to a full representative government of the governed.

The nations of the world, and especially in Europe, were making the transition from a feudal society, one led by kings, warlords, and popes to one of representative government by the nations' inhabitants. And, as time progressed, more and more of the populace would become eligible to participate in the process of governance. The Glorious Revolution was an important step in this evolution for all of Britain.

Chapter Nine

The Glorious Revolution's Impact on New England

In Massachusetts, the colonists took advantage of James-II's removal as an opportunity to dispose of the hated Governor Andros, who was captured by the colonists and sent back to England. The New England colonists pledged loyalty to William and Mary and asked the new rulers to restore the Massachusetts Bay Colony's original charter. They responded by agreeing to revoke the Dominion of New England and in 1691 gave the colony a new charter, albeit, not the original one.

In the new charter, The Massachusetts Bay Colony acquired The Plymouth Colony, Maine, Nantucket, and part of what is now Nova Scotia. More significantly, the crown retained the right to appoint the governor, which it promptly did. The new charter contained restrictions which disallowed provincial restraints on voting by non-puritan Protestants. The leaders of the Church of England in London had always felt, correctly, that the Puritan settlers in New England were opposed to the formation of Anglican congregations in their province. The new charter specifically directed that all male property owners, not just church members, were given the right to elect representatives to the governing bodies, thus making the colony much more secular. New Hampshire was remade a royal colony with a governmental arrangement similar to Massachusetts.

The Massachusetts Bay colonists found themselves governed by a royal governor appointed by the crown, but they had returned to them, after elimination of the Dominion of New England, their own local representative government they had had since the colonies were first formed. It was situation that persisted, in general format, right up to the American Revolution.

This was a decisive step forward for representative government in England as well as in the colonies. In England, parliament acquired a new freedom of operation and new powers that only grew in the future. In the colonies the settlers felt they had reacquired a local form of government that would allow them to set their own destiny. That there would be disputes concerning how much freedom their governments actually had with regard to the dominance of the crown, would be a source of discordance that would grow into defiance in the years ahead.

William-III had been faulted for his one-minded rationale for disposing James-II and assuming the English monarchy. While his main goal of using the power of the English military and strong English economy to make war with France did change the balance of power in Europe, his aborting of James-II's endeavors to establish a more autocratic, less representative form of government in both England and the North American colonies, may be the more enduring accomplishment

The Glorious Revolution did many positive things that enhanced England's future, but it did little for the English colonies who soon found they did not always enjoy the same rights and liberties as the Englishmen who resided in the home country. If the parliament in England was sovereign and independent, the North American colonists felt the sovereignty and independence they had in their local governmental bodies should be treated the same. Thus, if laws were passed in a colony it should not be subject to change or invalidation by an English monarch or governor, or even an English parliament. They would find that was not how they were treated.

William, like most of those in the English government, believed the English colonies had to pay their own way. The colonies were, after all, established to make a profit for their investors and likewise to contribute to England's wealth. This concept was a consideration in the establishment of the mercantile system as it applied to England's possessions. In the mercantile system, the world was envisioned as a zero-sum game where, with a fixed amount of wealth in the world, a country could gain wealth only at the expense of other countries.

To accomplish this accumulation of wealth, the English parliament had passed the Navigation Act in 1651, which controlled shipping and trade. This act, which was enacted initially to restrict Dutch shipping, was rewritten over the latter half of the seventeenth century to include similar restrictions on the English colonies. The acts had the effect of forcing the colonies to trade in a way that would benefit the mother country, and not necessarily be of advantage to them. In essence, the colonies were to provide the raw materials that England would use to manufacture finished products at great profit.

The acts dictated that in its import and export trade, a colony could use only English ships manned by a majority of English crews (later established at three-fourths). All trade from other countries bound for the colonies had to pass through England. For example a ship from Holland with cargo for

New England had to first put in at an English port where the cargo would be unloaded, inspected, reloaded on the ship and a fee imposed. This effectively restricted the purchase of manufactured goods to English suppliers, but because England reduced duties on shipments of English goods to the colonies, they were, at least, for many commodities, cheaper than comparable goods from a foreign supplier.

While the colonies were allowed some trade with foreign nations, certain "enumerated" commodities were defined that could only be traded with England or another colony. At first, these commodities included tobacco, sugar, rice, indigo, cotton, wool and several other minor products. Later, the list was expanded to include hemp, rice, molasses, and furs. In 1705 naval stores were added as their acquisition became a source of concern by the British naval fleet.

The northern colonies lacked the staple, self-replenishing products of tobacco, sugar and rice and chaffed at the restrictions placed on their manufacturing efforts. As reported by Hugh Egerton in his treatise *The Origin & Growth of the English Colonies*:

> It was the want of commodities to make returns for English Goods which, as Lord Cornbury, the Governor of New York, wrote, 'sets men's wits to work, and has put them on a trade which I am sure will hurt England in a little time, viz. the woolen manufacture on Long Island and Connecticut. These colonies, which are but twigs to the main tree, ought to be kept entirely dependent upon and subservient to England, and that can never be is they are suffered to go on in the notion's they have, that, as they are Englishmen, so they may set up the same manufactures here as people may do in England.

As the colonies grew and produced ever-greater commodities that were in demand by other nations, they resisted the controls placed on them by their English rulers and soon took to smuggling. To counter this, the crown set up Admiralty Courts in each colony in an effort to enforce compliance with the acts. The courts, however, were largely ineffective. It should be observed that the colonies had been used to trading with the Spanish colonies in South America for some time, and it was only after this trade was redefined as "smuggling" by England after they forbade it, that it became a problem.

The total export that the colonies made to England was less than the total imports received, so the debts the colonies had incurred in their need for finished goods, as well as debts incurred as a result of such circumstances as King Philip's War, were not being paid off, and were a source of strain between England and its American colonies.

It was the imposition of the mercantile system with its goal of increasing the wealth of England at the expense of its colonies that caused inevitable conflicts between England and her growing, ambitious, vibrant, American colonies. As Hugh Egerton perceptibility points out: *"The mercantile system, at worst, wrought pin-pricks on the sturdy frame of the youthful colonies, but pin-pricks are keenly felt and as keenly resented."*

The colonies felt constrained by a dominant, ruling England, yet had limited means to rectify the constraints. They wanted to undertake profitable ventures on their own they felt well capable of accomplishing, but the imposition by England of many controls on manufacturing and shipping, kept the colonies in a subservient position, and exacerbated the feeling of frustration. It was a position any proud, assertive gathering would rebel against.

The seventeenth century ended for the inhabitants of New England in an aberrant series of events known as the Salem Witch Trials. Between February 1692 and May 1693 over one hundred and fifty citizens of the settlement of Salem, Massachusetts and surrounding towns, were arrested for the crime of witchcraft.

The presiding judges were magistrates recently appointed by the new royal governor of the colony, William Phips. All of the judges, prosecutors and juries were of the Puritan conviction who strongly believed in the wicked, evil influence the Devil could impart to mortals.

The accused were a mix of upstanding church-members, servants, poor mendicants and a slave. Most were imprisoned, with twenty-nine convicted, and nineteen hanged; fourteen women and five men.

That the trials proceeded to their inhumane conclusions was a manifestation of the religious fervor of the colonists, and the degree to which they accorded to spiritual entities; actions or occurrences, many ordinary, commonplace events. A howling, damaging storm or severe drought was the embodiment of God's displeasure with something they had done that offended him. An action by an individual that caused displeasure to another could be construed as the action of the Devil. Individual idiosyncrasies such as tremors, seizures, or twitching could be construed as demonic possession.

Saner minds eventually prevailed and the trials ended in May 1693, but that was not the end of the matter. In the years following many voiced regrets and apologized for their role in the trials or for standing mute in the face of the disparagement of justice. A minister at the witchcraft trial proceedings, John Hale expressed sorrow: *"Such was the darkness of that day, the tortures and lamentations of the afflicted, and the power of former presidents, that we walked in the clouds, and could not see our way."* In referring to former presidents, Hale was referring to the prominent jurists who conducted the trials such as Lieutenant Governor William Stoughton and Thomas Newton, the Crown's attorney, and there were a number of others.

Eventually, those convicted were exonerated and some even received compensation for their travails or lost income. For all but a few diehards, the events at Salem became an embarrassment that never disappeared. It was not an experience of which most citizens were proud, but it did show the intensity with which the New Englanders took their beliefs. Their religion was an integral part, perhaps the most important part, of their everyday existence, doctrines they would fight fiercely for and, if need be, die for.

Chapter Ten

A New Century—
A New British Line

At the start of the eighteenth century the English discovered they faced a problem of their own making: After William of Orange invaded England and deposed King James II, and he and his wife, daughter of the deposed king, became King and Queen of England in the "Glorious Revolution," there arose the question of who would succeed them in the event they were childless. To resolve the issue, a section was added to the Bill of Rights, passed by Parliament in 1689, that defined the order of succession to the English crown after William and Mary. The added section named Mary's sister Anne, another of James' daughters, as the heir to the throne. Mary died of smallpox in 1694 while her husband William remained King until his death in 1702, whereupon Anne was anointed Queen of England, Scotland and Ireland. Anne is remembered in United States as being the namesake of Annapolis, Maryland.

Anne, a devout protestant like her sister, had married Prince George of Denmark on July 28, 1683. But after Anne became queen, there was great concern in the country as she failed to produce a viable heir. She was pregnant eighteen times, but had only one child survive infancy, a boy who died at eleven years of age in 1700, and that highlighted England's new problem: who would succeed Anne.

Anne was not an especially strong queen and, after the death of her husband, few conflicts developed between the queen and parliament. What conflicts there were actually strengthened parliament's resolve, so that when in 1708 Anne withheld "Royal Assent" to a bill parliament had passed; it was the last time an English monarch was able to exercise what past kings and queens had done routinely. It was a significant change for the governance of the realm.

Queen Anne's passive rule allowed parliament to be more forceful and greatly strengthened the body. As a result, disputes among parliament's members became more significant, and a new era in the governance of the country naturally evolved. While there had always been blocs of like-minded individuals maneuvering to attain some goal, the new paradigm was more about institutionalizing a modus operandi by the members of parliament, rather than the ad hoc efforts of the past.

As J. M. D. Meiklejohn very aptly describes it:

> The power of the crown hence gradually passed into the hands of the party that had a majority; and, as the power of the Crown grew less, the power of the dominant party in Parliament grew greater. And thus it gradually came to pass that Government by Party became the recognized means of managing the affairs of the country; and as this power fell into the hands of those who could command the most votes, the power of Government gradually passed into the hands of the voters.

(Note: the parties at the time were the Whigs, who generally favored a stronger parliament, and the Tories, who were strong supporters of the Church of England and, by association, the monarchy.)

This does not mean the monarch lacked power, because the king or queen still retained considerable authority. The monarch appointed the ministers who ran the various branches of government, he or she also controlled the actions of the military and could bring the nation into war—but it was the parliament's duty to raise the taxes necessary to support any conflict the country waged. The governors in the North American colonies likewise were an extension of the monarch's rule and followed the crown's directions.

When the 1689 Bill of Rights was passed with the added section naming Anne heir to the throne, it had been assumed she would have surviving children who would become monarch after her; but that assumption was not fulfilled. The old King James-II was still alive (he died in September 1701) as was his son, a catholic, who would be genetically disposed to become king if Anne was childless, a possibility that alarmed parliament. The disquietude in the country was sensible as the 1689 Bill of Rights was mute with regard to succession to the crown following Anne.

To avoid any disputes when Anne died, in 1701 parliament passed the Act of Settlement which named the Electress of Hanover, Sophia, or her progeny, as next in line for the English crown were Anne to remain childless. The selection of Sophia, the maternal granddaughter of James-I, as a potential English monarch was a convoluted way of eliminating any Catholics, and especially King James-II and his son, in the line of succession, even though the old line still had its adherents. Unfortunately for Sophia,, she died in May of 1714, several weeks before Anne, whereupon her son George became next in line for the English crown, which he assumed upon Anne's death of a stroke, as King George-I.

The Act of Settlement, although resolving England's problem, did not satisfy Scotland who felt the English unilateral action in determining their monarch was an affront to them. Thus, they passed their own act: the Act of Security, which allowed the Scottish parliament to choose their own ruler. After much negotiations and threats, the dispute was finally resolved when both countries approved the Articles of Union in 1707 that united them under one monarch, the combined state, thereafter called "Great Britain."

The governance of England when George-I was coroneted on October 20, 1714, was in an uncertain state. Over the previous century there had been many perturbations to the historical leadership of the country. Cromwell had taken over the nation and made it a republic for a short time before a new king, supported by many of the nobility and Church of England leaders, was restored, continuing the monarchy.

While parliament was somewhat subdued after the restoration, it soon began to increase its strength vis-à-vis the reigning monarch. After William of Orange and Mary became King and Queen they enhanced parliament's role, but retained significant power in the monarchy. However the momentum of history was moving in the direction of increased power to the people, and it was through parliament that the populace began demanding a greater voice in how they were governed. The relative roles of monarch and the body of parliament, especially the House of Commons was destined to evolve significantly well into the future.

Thus, for the players of political power as the new century unfolded, there was some uncertainty in how individuals could assert their authority and how much support any would have from the power brokers of the time. That political turmoil was raft in England then is evidenced by what befell Robert Walpole. Walpole was appointed to be a member of the Council of the High Admiralty, a minor post but one in which his talents could be displayed. This was followed by further appoints at higher, more prominent positions.

His outspoken views against the Tory party angered some to the extent that in 1712 he was accused of corruption and imprisoned in the Tower of London for a short period before being released due to the efforts of his supporters, who felt his trial unjust. He was also expelled from parliament only to be reelected the next year. When George-I was made king in 1714, Walpole was completely rehabilitated and made Paymaster General in the new government.

George was fifty-four when he became king of England. A small, retiring man, who spoke little English, was now the reigning monarch and head of the English church. Since King George had no personal relevance to England other than being king, he spent most of his reign in Hanover where he felt much more comfortable. His absences made it necessary for the leader of parliament, now Robert Walpole, to assume much more of a role in running the country. Thus was born the role of "Prime Minister" in England, the leader of the dominant party in the House of Commons. It might be noted there was no real title of "Prime Minister" in any government document, and Walpole referred to himself as "The First Lord of the Treasury."

After settling into his new role, Walpole sensed he was secure enough that he could settle some old scores with those who had a part in arranging his imprisonment. One, Lord Bolingbroke, fearing imprisonment or worse, fled England for France where he allied himself with King James son. Several others also fled the country or were imprisoned, and Lord Oxford was impeached.

That the English government was in a chaotic state is evidenced by the parliamentary election of 1715. It was a stormy affair, with riots and threats among those seeking office. It was at this time the Riot Act was passed which made it a felony for any group which refused to disburse after being read the act by a constable. With a new king, a foreigner who had a continuing battle with his son, a future King George-II, disrupting the harmony of the royal family, with remnants of support for the old line still being felt, and with the evolving role of the monarch-parliament power arrangement, the actions of any individual involved in politics had to be carefully considered, as any action might bring retribution.

The effect on the American colonies as a result of this turmoil in England was more neglect and inattention to the details of their governance, which they didn't seem to mind. Walpole even felt neglect of the colonies beneficial, as he stated, *"If no restrictions were placed on the colonies, they would flourish."* This English policy towards its North American Colonies was termed "Salutary Neglect" by a later member of Commons, Edmund Burke.

In Massachusetts, the colony from the beginning of their settlement, had desired to be as free from English influence as possible. It was, in fact, one of the reasons their settlers had come to the new land in the first place; to live a godly life in their own fashion and to control their own destiny. In the other colonies, the neglect not only allowed, but virtually forced the colonies to seriously govern themselves, a charge that was readily accepted. This appetite for independence from England was not as strong outside New England during the initial period of settlement in the new world, but it soon became a more accepted view by a growing percentage of the population as the local governments matured. The interest England did pay to the colonies continued to be concentrated more on commercial matters than anything else.

Chapter Eleven

The New Century in the English Colonies

The dawn of the eighteenth century found the New World significantly changed from the small coastal communities that had been established eighty or so years before. The population of the English settlements in North America exceeded 250,000 by 1700, and continued to grow geometrically as the years passed. Although there was still significant immigration, the population growth of the English citizenry in North America was mainly internally driven by the natural increase in the populace due to a high birth rate. In the southern colonies the importation of slaves to work the tobacco and sugar plantations was moderate at first but soon grew rapidly.

All of the colonies were under English control as New York and New Jersey had been taken from the Dutch by the Duke of York in 1664. Most were royal colonies or charter colonies wherein the colonies operated under a charter given by the crown, such as with Massachusetts in 1691. In the royal colonies the governor was appointed by the King and ruled in his stead. Maryland, Delaware and Pennsylvania were proprietary colonies, which meant a charter had been given to a "Proprietor," such as William Penn in Pennsylvania or Lord Baltimore in Maryland. In these colonies the governor was appointed by the Proprietor.

In effect, however, England ruled all of the North American colonies no matter what their legal definition. As Evarts Greene points out in his 1898 Harvard University doctoral thesis: *the crown's law office declared there was nothing in the charters which could "exclude your Majesty (who has a right to govern all your subjects) from naming a Governor on your Majesty's behalf, for those colonies at all times."* The declaration was made for an issue with Rhode Island and Connecticut, which were charter colonies, but the concept of King's rule obviously was universally applicable to all of the English colonies.

In New England the population had grown to 120,000 at the start of the century and continued its strong growth unabated. Women married in their early twenties, or sometimes in their late teens, and averaged eight surviving children, a gigantic geometric. The general health of the population was good, better than those residing in England, due in large part to the salubrious atmosphere of the new land. Many of the settlers lived their biblical fourscore and ten years, some even beyond; it was not rare to find individuals in their eighties.

The colonists, many now third- and even fourth-generation native New Englanders, felt very much at home in the territory their ancestors had settled. It was a beautiful land, moderate hills formed from rock laid down eons in the distant past and worked by magmatic and tectonic forces to produce the granite, gneiss and marble that outcropped on scenic ridges. The terrain was later scared by the massive Laurentide ice sheet that brought a glacial till covering of rocks and soil to the fields being farmed by the new inhabitants. The glaciers also carved out the lakes, ponds, and swamps that contrasted idyllically with the rising hills and mountains surrounding them. The glaciers continued the molding of the land by depositing drumlins, those elongated hillocks of rock and soil on the Shawmut Peninsula, becoming the hills of Boston.

The entire area was sheathed in a variety of native trees which provided material for dwellings, fences, and even ocean vessels. The stately American Elm, the massive red and white oaks, the latter of which yielded tasty acorns, were widespread. The red maples provided a striking display of deep red, and along with the yellows and oranges of the sugar maples, set the autumn hills aflame. The tall, straight white pines provided masts for many ships built to ply the oceans, but the reserving of the tallest, straightest of these for the British Navy led to resentment by the colonials.

The local governments of the colonies were, like New England's, mostly bicameral (Pennsylvania and Delaware excepted) with an upper house usually controlled by an English governor and a lower house of selectmen elected by the region's landowners, who represented a regions' (town, county, colony) interests and views. There was no doubt the English parliament had the right to establish laws the colonies would have to adhere to, and the colonial governors, under the control of the crown, could overrule any laws passed by the colonial governments, but the governors often lacked the power to actually force compliance. The colonists thought of themselves as Englishmen, but market competition between the colonies and merchants in Britain often caused problems. The governors had veto power on any act a colony might pass that was not in consonance with English law, but with communication with England taking weeks or months; it was difficult to get guidance from the mother country on a timely basis. Although the veto was scarcely used, the threat of its use hung over all of the deliberations in the colonial assemblies.

The bustling port town of Boston reached nearly 7,000, to become the largest settlement in the colonies, followed by New York at about 5,000. The towns in Massachusetts, such as Concord or Lexington, close to Boston, or towns more inland such as Worcester also experienced significant growth.

The majority of the colonists considered themselves loyal English subjects, but they were now infused with other immigrants such as French Huguenots, Scotsmen and protestant Irish, who did not share the same reverence for the English crown. In all, however, there was no lack of independent spirit in these closely-knit communities. The crown might be respected, but that governor, appointed by the King, who ruled over them, often did not have the same respect. The New Englanders well remembered the persecution they felt under the imperious Governor Edmund Andros who taxed by executive order, dispensed with their elected assemblies, and revoked all grants of land. They were thus suspicious of any governor from the King, who had power over them, and they rebelled at any attempt at tight English control.

The towns were similar in that each had a commons, a meeting house which also usually served as a church, and an orderly system of roads and trails. In New England the churches were still mostly Congregational, but Anglican, Episcopal, or Presbyterian were not uncommon. Church attendance was still a law that essentially all observed. New England's and especially Massachusetts' citizens retained the puritan ethic of their predecessors.

While the increased interest in economic growth and personal financial enhancement was now becoming important In New England, religious interests were still prevalent, albeit with a bit less ardor than the original settlers possessed. Many of the church leaders decried a decrease in religious intensity in their flocks. But, the third-generation settlers did not forget that their predecessors had come to the New World for religious freedom and religious matters still held a primacy of interest. This was in contrast to the southern colonies where the original settlers came with profit the primary driving force and thus were more influenced by actions from Britain which affected their commerce.

A number of years before, Increase Mather, a prominent Puritan minister, had begun railing his congregation with warnings and chastisements for not adhering to the biblical principles of the original settlers. *"There are manifold transgressions and mighty sins amongst us,"* he warned in a sermon, and added, *"We can now see little difference between church members and other men."* The New England settlers had indeed come to the new world to practice their religion uninhibited by the strictures placed on them by the English Church, a point not lost on Mather. *"The interest of New England was religion, which did distinguish us from other English plantations, they were built on a worldly design, but we upon a religious design, whereas now we begin to espouse a worldly interest."*

Mather, like many other clergymen to follow, emphasized the dominance of the church as being of critical importance in their lives, but realized the temptations of mercantilism was intruding. The settler's forefathers faced survival at every turn and the interdependence of each for the other and for their communal progression was readily apparent, and it was their common religious beliefs that kept them united. As the population grew and stratification of the society expanded, economic considerations became more obvious, and to many, more important. This was more visible in the larger towns, especially in the population centers such as Boston, where wealth was being accrued by a minority of the citizens.

By the turn of the new century, New England, had developed an extensive fishing fleet and shipbuilding capability, and was becoming a significant maritime force. In 1700, the area was turning out over four hundred ships annually, many being used by the British trade companies in the now thriving trade between the colonies, England and the Caribbean, including the infamous Triangular Trade Route in which a ship never had to leave a port with less than a full load.

Typically, on a triangular course, a ship would leave out of a port in the Caribbean or the southern colonies of North American loaded with sugar, molasses, indigo or tobacco from the plantations and farms, and sail to England. There, the cargo would be unloaded and manufactured goods would be taken aboard. The ship would then proceed to Africa where the goods were sold and slaves taken, usually into the hold, and transported to the original ports in the Caribbean or southern colonies they had started from and unloaded the slaves. As a result, by the start of the new century, over 250,000 slaves had been shipped from Africa to the Caribbean plantations and southern farms to provide the extensive labor required there. Blacks in these regions soon outnumbered white settlers.

While New England merchantmen did not use this well-known trade route, it did a great deal of commerce with these triangular ports as well as many others, and, as a result, New England became home to some slaves, but nowhere near the number further south, as New England did not have a critical need for cheap labor as did the southern plantations. From New England, furs, lumber, livestock, and whale oil or spermaceti candles from sperm whales, were shipped to England and manufactured goods and luxury items returned. The Caribbean and the southern plantations provided sugar and molasses that New England used to ferment rum which was shipped to numerous locations. While preparing for the trip from New England, the ship's captains had to assemble a cargo from whatever they could find that could be sold at their destination. An example of a ship's eclectic cargo is provided in David Hawke's book, *Early Life in Early America*:

> 5 horses, 56 hogs, 84 geese, 4,460 feet of lumber,1,900 staves,5,500 shingles, 11 barrels of fish, 7 barrels of apples, 1,700 pounds of cheese.

As discussed in the previous chapter, England restricted trade from its North American colonies to other countries, but it was impossible to stop the shipments completely, and illegal trade continued flowing in spite of the English directives. It would become a important point of dispute between England and her colonies in the years ahead that would grow in importance as by mid-century, New England would have over three hundred ships with over four thousand seamen plying the oceans.

Several prominent English leaders became concerned about the growth of the maritime capabilities in New England. Stephen Innes quotes an English Lord, Sir Josiah Child:

> Of all the American Plantations his Majesty has, none are so apt for the build-ing of Shipping as New England, nor none more comparably so qualified for the breeding of Seamen, not only by Reason of the natural industry of that people, but principally by reason of their Cod and Mackeral Fisheries: and in my poor opinion, there is nothing more prejudicial, and in prospect. More dangerous to any Mother-Kingdom, than the increase of Shipping in her Colonies, Plantations, or Provinces.

Away from the coasts, New England was overwhelming an agrarian society of small, 50 to 100 acre farms around many towns and villages. Corn, along with livestock, both cattle and hogs, were the staples as the rocky ground made growing wheat or rye, which was done in the open fields in Pennsylva-nia, extremely difficult in New England. The land was used efficiently. Corn was planted in small mounds six-feet apart with perhaps a fish placed in each mound for fertilizer, which resulted in about 1,400 plants to the acre. Beans were planted near the corn to use the stalks as support. Other plants, such as squash or pumpkins were planted in the spaces between the mounds.

Chickens were raised on every farm for the protein substance they pro-vided to the farmers and their families and servants. Fruit trees, especially apples, added a desirable ingredient to the diet. While the farming was of the substance nature, through sedulous effort, farmers could produce an excess over their subsistence needs which could be marketed in the larger towns, especially the seaports.

While the farms could provide complete dietary necessities in the rural ar-eas, there was still a need for metal tools and other manufactured equipment required to operate the farm, as well as things like cooking utensils needed in the kitchen. And, as always a consideration, there were luxuries such as fine clothes and furniture that seduced desire of ownership. Thus, once subsistence was satisfied, there was always motivation to increase output to provide for these desires.

These tastes for things manufactured influenced some entrepreneurs to start small shops to produce some products locally. Some, such as furniture, shoes and hat makers were successful, and antagonized the comparable manufacturers in Britain, who did not relish the competition and reacted to try to stifle the colonial ventures.

On June 11, 1727, King George-I died suddenly while on a trip to Hanover and his son George became King of Great Britain as George-II. The new king had not gotten along all that well with his father, opposing many of his decisions, but had been reconciled with him shortly before his death due to the intervention of Sir Robert Walpole, the Prime Minister (de facto) who had earlier became indispensible to Queen Anne and later to King George-I. However, the new king did not seem supportive of having Walpole continue in his powerful role. Many thought the king would name Spencer Compton, as he had him write his acceptance speech. Compton had cultivated the support of the king's mistress, Lady Suffolk. But, with the intrigue that was so ingrained in the higher hierarchy of the English government, it did him no good. Walpole had the ear of the king's wife, Caroline of Ansbach, who had much greater influence with the king in matters of government. Thus it was a surprise to many when Walpole was named to continue in his position. A remark heard in the streets concerning Walpole's naming was, "he got the right sow by the ear."

The new king was not a native-born Englishman, but, unlike his father, he at least spoke the language and seemed more at home in London. To support the continued growth of the English North American colonies he granted a royal charter in 1732 to James Oglethorpe for a colony in the southern sector of North America which, Oglethorpe wisely named, "Georgia" after his benefactor.

In the early part of his reign the King George-II did not become intimately involved in the running of the nation, rather he relied more and more on his first minister, Robert Walpole. Walpole had a view of the English colonies as being subservient to the home country, especially in matters of commerce. Walpole required the support of the members of Commons for his authority, and he listened carefully to their and their constituents, pleas. Accordingly, parliament passed several acts that were designed to aid merchants in Britain at the expense of merchants in the colonies, who had no vote in the selection of members of parliament.

The hat makers in New England had become so successful that parliament was prompted to pass the Hat Act in 1732. The act severely restricted the manufacture of beaver hats in the colonies, which had become the vogue in Britain. Instead, the beaver pelts were to be sent to England to be made into hats within the country. The act also restricted the number of workers a colonial hat manufacturer could use in his shop thus restricting their ability to compete with the merchants in Britain who had no such restrictions. Needless to say this did not engender positive feelings in the colonies toward their mother country.

As bad an affront the Hat Act was, it was minor compared to an act parliament passed the following year. In March of 1733, both houses of parliament passed the Sugar and Molasses Act which imposed a tax on sugar and molasses from non-British sources. The colonies had historically gotten their sugar and molasses from the French West Indies. The British West Indies were also producing and selling sugar and molasses, but their costs were higher and they were losing sales to their French competitors. The producers in Barbados especially had the ear of members of parliament, and had petitioned for the law. The act was especially harsh for the New England colonies as, previously mentioned, unlike the southern colonies, they had little export they could use to settle their balance of payments with Britain. The one product they did export at a considerable profit was rum which they made from the sugar and molasses they imported from the French islands; Boston alone produced more than a million gallons of rum the year the act was passed..

While the tax was not overly oppressive at six pence per gallon on molasses and five shillings per hundred weight on sugar, it was repulsive to the New Englanders and was largely ignored, as the New Englanders, with their extensive naval capability, just smuggled what was needed to the consternation of the British authorities.

In June 1750 the British parliament passed the Importation Act which was aimed at increasing the iron and steel manufacturing capabilities of Britain. The act allowed pig iron and bar iron, the raw materials for the mills in Britain, to be obtained free of duty, but it restricted the colonists from constructing and operating mills or steel furnaces that produced finished product.

There were a number of similar prohibitions placed on the colonies at various times; sail manufacture, linen production; even shoe making, were inimical irritants that Britain imposed on the colonists. It was obvious the mother country had her own interests that would be served even at the expense of her own colonies. From the colonists' perspective, Britain seemed to be siding with the local English and Scottish interests in the realm and against theirs. It was obvious to them that not having adequate representation in the British government was a serious disadvantage.

Chapter Twelve

Prelude to the French and Indian War

What is referred to as THE French and Indian War started in 1754 in the regions north and west of the British North American colonies, however, many consider that major war to be but a continuation of three similar, but smaller wars that preceded it. To fully understand the genesis of the war that shaped the boundaries within the North American continent, it is necessary to go back a bit to look at the earlier conflicts to fully understand how the final war in the series was conducted by the war's combatants and the final peace secured.

The settling of North America by the three European nations, Spain, France and England was executed in a different manner by each of them. The Spanish, the first to arrive, established missions and forts in Mexico, the southwestern part of the present United States, the eastern Caribbean, South America, and Florida. They were searching for the mythical city of gold (or any gold). Also important to many of the explorers and accompanying friars, was the conversion of heathen Indians to Catholicism, and thus the building of missions wherever they traveled.

When the French first started to inhabit North America they established plantations on islands in the Caribbean to grow sugar cane and other warm-weather crops in the tropical climate. On the continent, they concentrated on exploration and the fur trade rather than setting up colonies. It was only in the time after Louis-XIV assumed the monarchy in mid-1654 that the French realized they were falling well behind the English in establishing permanent settlements. The English, on the other hand, had taken an aggressive approach to establishing settlements all along the eastern part of North America from Hudson's Bay to Georgia, as well as plantations in the West Indies (Caribbean). Thus, at the start of the eighteenth century the English population in North America greatly exceeded the French, perhaps over ten-fold, and the discrepancy increased as the century progressed.

The inhabitants of the English colonies thought of themselves as Englishmen and a part of the mother country. Likewise, the French settlers considered themselves Frenchmen with an allegiance to France, and the Spanish settlers considered themselves citizens of Spain. As the English populations in New England and the French settlements to the north grew, inevitable skirmishes arose between them, especially as the two sides had very different views on religion. A similar situation with Spain faced the English in the south. When the mother nations became involved in wars in Europe, the North American colonies found themselves drawn into complimentary conflicts in their regions. The battles in the New World involved not only the European settlers and European troops, but also local Indian tribes who were recruited to fight for one side or the other. The battles were often conducted under Indian war rules, which were, to the Europeans, especially innocent settlers, barbaric.

The first of these conflicts in Europe, which had a component in North America involving the settlers and the Native Americans, occurred when the New English King William-III started his war against France soon after ascending the throne in London in1688. It was called the "War of Grand Alliance" or alternatively the "Nine Years War." Allied with the English were Austria, Spain, Holland and several parts of the Holy Roman Empire, all of whom, like England, were leery of France's expansionist ambitions.

The related war in North America, termed "King William's War" started in July of 1689 when a band of Indians allied with the French attacked Cocheco, New Hampshire (now Dover). It was a well-planned attack that exemplified the savagery of many of the confrontations that occurred in this and the following wars. Indian squaws showed up at the door of the town's garrison's houses and asked to spend the night. It was not an unusual request, as there had been a peace treaty with the Indians at Cocheco in 1676, and their request was granted. The commander of the town was Richard Waldron, a veteran of King Philip's War with a severe negative attitude towards Indians. After the end of that war he had sent a number of Indians into slavery. Now an aged octogenarian, he had settled in the town to set up a grist mill. He traded with the Indians and many of them considered him dishonest in his trades.

Just before dawn, the squaws rose and opened the garrison houses' doors and war parties of braves quickly entered. At Waldron's house he was quickly subdued with a blow to the head and placed on a table where they slashed him with knives. According to an account by C. Alice Baker in "True Stories Of New England Captives,"

They cut off his finger joints and threw them in his face with fiendish glee, 'How much will your fist weigh now, Father Waldron?' Finally as he fell fainting from his chair they held his own sword under him, and death came to his relief.

The savagery continued at the other garrison houses. At Richard Otis' place the old blacksmith was shot dead immediately, his daughter, two-year old Hannah, was murdered by smashing her head on the stairs. Otis' wife and three-month old baby were, with other captives, forced to march to Canada, while the town's houses were burned to the ground. The following month, the same fate befell Pemaquid, Maine, and at the start of 1690, Schenectady, New York was ransacked and its occupants murdered.

The colonies of New York, Connecticut, and Massachusetts, alarmed at the viciousness of the attacks, formed a coordinated plan to attack Montreal and Quebec, but their efforts were ineffective. With a mounting war debt the colonies pleaded with England for help, but England at the time had its own financial burden and it left the colonies to fight their own battles.

Over the next several years there were a number of, mostly minor, skirmishes and the two sides tired of the fight in both Europe and North America. A treaty was finally signed in 1697 at Ryswick in The Dutch Republic that ended both the war in Europe and the one in North America. The treaty addressed the conflicts in North America simply as: all places captured in North America to be restored (to the original possessors) within six months.

It only took the European nations four short years to go at it again, this time Spain joined France against a coalition that included England, Portugal, The Holy Roman Empire, and The Dutch Republic. The conflict this time was called the "War of Spanish Succession." King Charles-II of Spain had died without an heir and named Philip, d'Anjou, a grandson of Louis XIV, as his successor. The Holy Roman Emperor, Leopold, felt his line should be made Spanish King, not Philip. The war was waged to stop Philip, who would be closely allied with France, from succeeding the Spanish King Charles. Of equal importance, he would also be in line to succeed King Louis-XIV of France to the French throne.. The concern of the opposing European nations was that the monarch would then essentially be reigning over both France and Spain, and thus have greatly enhanced power. The same fear of France's aggressive desires for expansion that caused them to action in the previous encounter still prevailed, and so the conflict resumed.

The war eventually spilled over into the North American colonies where it was referred to as "Queen Anne's War" after the reigning monarch in England. In North America, the war started when the governor of South Carolina, James Moore, in 1702 sanctioned an attack on the Spanish fort of Saint Augustine and the surrounding settlement by colonial troops aided by their Chickasaw Indian allies. While the town was burned, the potent Spanish fort repelled the attack and the colonists left, destroying a number of Spanish Missions and some competing Appalachee Indian villages in their departure. The following year the Carolinians withstood an attack by a combined

Spanish-French force sent from Havana, ending in a stalemate between the adversaries. The tragedy of these conflicts was felt deeply by the Indian tribes in northern Florida like the Appalachee, Timuca, and Yamasee. Approximately ten thousand of the Indians who had been converted to Christianity were slaughtered, enslaved, or just fled the region.

In the north, French forces from Canada, assisted by their Indian allies, attacked several New England settlements. In 1703 the towns Wells in Maine and Falmouth in Massachusetts were overrun with more than 150 killed or taken prisoner. The next year Deerfield, Massachusetts was attacked by French supported Abenakis Indians; with the loss of another 150 inhabitants.

The New Englanders responded by sacking the French settlements of Minas and Beaubassin in Acadia in an effort to disrupt supplies to the Abenakis. After several unsuccessful forays by both sides, in 1709 the French, again with their Indian allies, destroyed St. John's in Newfoundland, which the English explorer Sir Humphrey Gilbert had claimed for England in 1583. The rejoinder followed the next year when over three thousand British troops and colonial militia captured Port Royal in Acadia, effectively taking control of the province.

After much fighting in Europe, where an estimated 400,000 died, a peace treaty was signed in Utrecht in 1713. The treaty ended both the war in Europe and the war in North America. Under terms of the treaty, the British acquired Acadia, which they renamed Nova Scotia (New Scotland) and Newfoundland. Britain also gained some control over Hudson Bay. This gave Britain entry into the region north of their North American colonies, but the boundaries of the new possessions were ill defined and set up conditions for further conflicts in the area.

It took a little longer this next time for the European nations to go at it again in a war that affected the North American colonies, but in 1740 they started the "War of Austrian Succession." It was somewhat like the previous war in that it had to do with succession in one of the royal houses of Europe, but spilled over into the colonies where the English again battled France and Spain.

It started when the Holy Roman Emperor and head of the Hapsburg dynasty, Charles-VI died without a male heir in 1740. In accordance with an agreement Charles-VI had negotiated with several other nations in the 1713 Pragmatic Sanction, his daughter, Maria Theresa, was to assume the monarchies in Austria, Hungry, and Bohemia and her husband, the Duke of Lorraine, was to be the new Holy Roman Emperor. However, ignoring the Pragmatic Sanction, Charles Albert of Bavaria asserted his right to the monarchies was greater than Maria Theresa's as she was a woman, and, according to Salic Law, ineligible for the stations. At the same time, King

Frederick of Prussia, also violating the sanctions, invaded Silesia (present southern Poland) with a view to annexing the region; an action that Austria was sure to oppose.

The French sided with Bavaria while the English and the Dutch allied with Austria and Maria Theresa. Spain also entered the conflict in loose partnership with France, but had its own territorial ambitions in Italy in what became a confusing assemblage of nations fighting one another on a number of fronts.

In North America, the war, like the two previous wars was called "King George's War" after the King on the throne in England. The first action began in 1740 when James Oglethorpe in the new colony of Georgia, assembled a force of over one thousand local volunteers, augmented with neighboring Indians, to attack Saint Augustine. However, the effort went for naught when Oglethorpe decided his force was no match for the Spanish garrison. After he retreated back to Georgia, the Spanish launched a counterattack on Georgia. The colonials redeemed themselves as fighters by thrashing the Spanish at the Battle of Bloody Swamp.

In 1744 the French, along with their Indian allies, attacked and destroyed Canso, a fishing settlement in Nova Scotia. The following year they killed over a hundred settlers in Saratoga, New York, causing the abandonment of English settlements north of the town.

The English colonists retaliated in 1745 when the governor of Massachusetts, William Shirley, assembled an army to attack the French Fort Louisbourg on Cape Breton Island at the entrance to the St. Laurence River. Three thousand men, some from Connecticut and New Hampshire, joined the Massachusetts contingent. The force was carried to Cape Breton Island by the British Navy, which also remained to isolate the fort. Seeing itself outmaneuvered, the fort capitulated on June 16, giving the New Englanders a stirring victory. The defeat was a difficult one for the French to take; losing what they considered to be an impenetrable fortress to a small fleet of English ships and only a few thousand New England farmers and fishermen.

The New Englanders were willing to volunteer for what was a dangerous mission, as they felt threatened by the minatory French and their pernicious Indian allies to the north. The Massachusetts House passed a bill in 1745 that placed a bounty on Indian scalps: one hundred pounds for a male and fifty pounds for a female (both had to be over twelve years of age). Many battles had taken place between the two adversaries over the years and the opportunity to inflict a distasteful defeat on the French appealed to them. At the same time, the British North American colonists were assuaged by the presence and support of the Royal Navy and British troops, which would provide aid in any hostilities.

The French desperately tried to recapture Fort Louisbourg. The French King sent two separate fleets to affect the mission; both were unsuccessful. Worse, and more humiliating, the second fleet was captured by the English.

The wars, both in Europe as well as the fighting in North America ended with the signing of a peace treaty by all sides on October 18, 1748 in Aix-la-Chapelle. The Europeans allowed Maria Theresa to assume the throne in Austria, but the new military power on the scene, Prussia acquired the region of Silesia.

In North America, the English colonists were incensed when Fort Louisbourg was returned to France as England traded the fort for some advantage somewhere else. Many New Englanders had lost their lives in the battle for the fort, and relations between the English settlers and the mother country worsened. The settlers had no voice in the writing or signing of the peace treaty, and felt betrayed by the authorities in London.

Britain felt she had expended a great sum in support of her colonies and were unsympathetic to their complaints. To the colonists, on the other hand, the treaty verified their view that they must look out for their own affairs and not be dependent upon a governing body far across the ocean in which they had no representation. They could not rely on the mother country which was more interested in her own interests. They had to become more self-reliant and assume charge of their own destiny.

The next French/Indian war was the largest and most impacting of all the conflicts for both England and France, as well as their colonies in North America. It would be only six more years before this nation-changing conflagration would begin.

Chapter Thirteen

The French and Indian War

In 1753 the land west of the Appalachian Mountains and extending all the way to the Mississippi River, and from the Great Lakes in the north to the Gulf of Mexico in the south, was known as the Ohio Territory. A vast land, it was sparsely occupied, harboring several Indian tribes, scattered fur trappers, and a few trading posts. This land of verdant hills and valleys of fertile soil was aplenty with game. It had rivers and streams flowing generally west and south, valuable pathways to the mighty Mississippi. Several of the Indian tribes, the Delawares, Shawnees and others, had moved there to escape the persecution of the mighty six-nation league of the Iroquois, which included the Mohawk, Oneida, Onondaga, Cayuga, Seneca, and Tuscarora.

The powerful Iroquois tribes' homeland was in the northeast, generally in what is now the state of New York, but they dominated the tribes throughout Pennsylvania, Virginia and the Ohio Territory. They were feared for their sudden and violent attacks. With impunity, they often traded land belonging to the other tribes whether they agreed or not. The Iroquois had learned early there were two main divisions of Europeans they had to deal with: the English and the French, and they maneuvered skillfully to maintain friendly contacts with both groups, often playing off one against the other. For example, during Queen Anne's War the Iroquois were supposedly allied with the English and fought with them on several occasions, but they also provided the French with information on English troop movements and plans of attack.

When the London Company received its charter from King James-I to settle in the new world in 1609, no one was really sure how far west the land went. The charter they received gave them land "from sea-to-sea" and thus Britain felt it had laid claim to all of the land west of the Appalachian Mountains. The French also felt they had a valid claim for the same land. Cavalier de La Salle had claimed the Mississippi River and its watershed (which included the Ohio) for France in 1683. Early French explorers, Marquette, Joliet and others had gone up the Mississippi all the way from New Orleans to its headwaters, and continued throughout the Great Lakes region. Other Frenchmen had crisscrossed the rivers of the Ohio territory to trap beaver and other pelts, and had set up several outposts in the area, with a permanent fort at Detroit.

The English settlements along the Atlantic coast, founded at the start of the seventeenth century, had, over the intervening one hundred and fifty years, experienced explosive growth. Settlers had moved inland from the sea and now faced the Appalachian Mountains in the west as the next barrier to overcome.

Several groups saw opportunity in this new western land, and in the 1740's, traders from Pennsylvania moved into passes in the mountains where they could contact the Indians in the Ohio Territory and participate in lucrative trade with them. They set up small trading posts around a small settlement in Pennsylvania named Pickawillany. The action did not go unnoticed by the French who became alarmed at this incursion into what they believed was French territory. As a result, in 1749 the governor of New France, the Comte de la Galissoniere, sent an adventurous military captain, Pierre Celoron, along with over two hundred infantry, on an intelligence mission through the Ohio Territory. When he found the trading posts, he ordered the Pennsylvania traders to leave as they were unlawfully in French territory. The Indians were anxious to trade at the English posts, and rejected his assertion that the territory belonged to France. As far as the Indians were concerned it didn't belong to either France or England; it was Indian Territory. In an effort to substantiate France's claim to the area, all along his trail he buried lead tablets in the manner of early explorers when arriving on virgin soil. Each tablet officially pronounced: this was French land.

As much as the forays by the Pennsylvanian traders had bothered the French governor upon learning of them on Celoron's return, it got much worse. A group of investors from Virginia had started the Ohio Company of Virginia in 1749, and the next year began sending out advance parties to explore the Ohio Territory with a view to acquiring land they would sell to settlers wanting to establish new settlements. The area the Virginia investors had their eye on was the land around the Forks of the Ohio (where the Monongahela and Allegany Rivers converge at present day Pittsburgh to create the Ohio). The Virginia legislature, based on their assumed ownership of the land, had granted three hundred square miles of the land to the Virginia Company. The Virginia Company sent a representative, Christopher Gist, to the territory to negotiate an agreement with the local Indians, and to set up a trading post on the path to the Forks of the Ohio. De la Galissoniere was disturbed by the news of this new incursion, but was cautious about taking action. In fact, he did nothing until his death in 1752. A new, aggressive governor, the Marquis Duquesne arrived from France and had an entirely different perspective of the situation. He immediately took action.

He was not about to watch passively as the land the French considered their own was occupied by the English, so a force of over two hundred French-allied Indians led by a half-breed Frenchman named Charles de Langlade, was dispatched to discipline the Indians trading at the trading post set up by the Pennsylvanians at Pickawillany. The post was destroyed and the Indian chief who had welcomed the English to the post was killed. The Pennsylvania traders, being peace-loving Quakers, this time took the French warnings seriously and hastily departed to return to a safe haven in their home colony.

The Marquis Duquesne did not stop there. He sent Celoron on another mission to establish a permanent presence in the Ohio Territory by building four forts, including one at the Forks of the Ohio. It was a massive undertaking in manpower and funds, and set New France inevitably on a path of war with the British. While the British felt they had a claim to the territory, they were willing to negotiate with the French; perhaps making the land neutral ground that both nations could develop in some manner together, but the presence of military forts altered the equations of entitlement.

Trouble between the French and British wasn't brewing only in the Ohio Territory. The New England colonists were worried about French actions taken to strengthen the fortifications at the recently returned Fort Louisbourg on Cape Breton, as well as manning it with additional infantry from France. In addition, the French were building other strategic forts in the region, such as Fort Beausejour, which guarded the boarder between Acadia and Nova Scotia. While Britain retained Acadia as a result of the treaty ending the last war, France was working against English efforts to assimilate the island's occupants into the British Empire. The combination of these actions portended trouble for the New Englanders who well remembered the savage attacks suffered by their northern settlements. It was a delicate problem faced by Lord Newcastle, the first minister, in London that was succinctly described by Dorothy Marshall in her study of eighteenth century England: *"how to protect the interests of the British settlers while doing nothing that would precipitate a new war in Europe."*

The situation was viewed with decided anxiety by the British king and his ministers: Did France want a war? In any hostilities, would France or Prussia attack Hanover, the king's homeland which the monarch felt so protective of? Would Austria and the Dutch support Britain? What would the German princes do? There were many unresolved issues haunting the leaders of the realm. In addition, Britain was involved in adventures in India and Africa that required men and funds, both of which needed to be carefully husbanded.

The French also had inconclusive issues and concerns about a war with Britain. How seriously should the country fight for its North American settlements? Furs and fish from New France were nice, but they were not as important to France as their possessions in the Caribbean, which produced sugar, molasses, indigo, and tobacco, and would be vulnerable to the powerful British navy. Another reason the French wanted to avoid hostilities at this time was the extraordinary effort they had started to upgrade the vessels in the French navy. They were well aware of the advantage Britain held in naval warfare and needed time to become competitive at sea. France also had ventures in India and Africa, which required men and funds. The governments of both nations were encumbered with complex questions about the actions to take in their dominions as well as in Europe.

To some in France the concept of linking New France (Canada) with Louisiana through the Ohio Territory was a grand plan that could justify a war. If they could establish settlements throughout the area they would have control of the entire mid-continent, which would isolate the British on the east coast. The British were also well aware the effect of linking the north and south French settlements and forts would have on their North American provinces. While many in London still wanted to avoid war if that were possible, French occupation of the Ohio Territory was a tipping point for others. The Commissioner for Trade wrote: *"unless some measures were speedily taken to put a stop to these proceedings and encroachments any further attempts of His Majesty's subjects to make settlements in the interior of America will be effectively prevented."* The British Foreign Office thus authorized Robert Dinwiddie, lieutenant governor of Virginia, to take a forceful, yet cautious approach to move into the disputed area and establish a British presence there.

In November 1753 he sent an emissary to confront the French, inform them they were on British land, and request they leave. A military man was selected for the task, a twenty-one year old major of the Virginia militia named George Washington, who would lead a small force and contact the French as soon as possible. He was accompanied by several local Indians and by the Virginia Company's representative from the area, Christopher Gist, who knew the area well and could communicate with the Indians.

Washington finally confronted the French at their Fort Le Boeuf on the Allegheny in December 1753. The French commander, Captain Jacques Legardeur, listened to Washington's message but refused to leave, citing French claims to the land. Upon returning to Dinwiddie, Washington relayed the French refusal, and also offered his opinion that the French were getting ready to build a potent fort at the Forks of the Ohio. The British reaction in London was to order the immediate construction of a fort at the Forks, and to man it with soldiers, including some British regulars.

Thus, early in 1754, Dinwiddie sent an advance party under Ensign Ward to the Forks to begin the fort's construction. Ward's men hadn't been at it long when they were overwhelmed by a much larger French force and forcibly made to withdraw. The French then took over the construction and built a stout fort they named Fort Duquesne.

Not knowing the French had usurped the advantage at the Forks, Dinwiddie then sent Washington, along with 200 militia, on a mission to support the troops there and secure the area for the British. On April 20, while on his mission, Washington learned of the defeat of his advance party at the Forks. He was deciding what action to take when some local Indians alerted him to an encampment of French troops bivouacked in a ravine. Dawn was just breaking making the small French contingent vulnerable. True to his charge of capturing or killing any French soldiers who refused to leave, Washington ordered an attack.

The French officer in charge, Joseph de Jumonville, although wounded himself, quickly appraised the situation he was in and surrendered. Jumonville told Washington he was surprised by the attack as he was on a diplomatic mission to find Washington and tell him to leave French territory.

Things might have been worked out between them, and more diplomatic efforts might have been followed by all participants, but, in a surprise move the Indian chief who had accompanied Washington, moved up behind the French commander and buried his tomahawk in his skull, killing him instantly. A chaotic scene followed when other Indians attacked the remaining wounded, killing all but one before Washington could stop the carnage.

Knowing the French would retaliate, he moved his contingent to Great Meadows and quickly assembled a makeshift fort he appropriately called "Fort Necessity." On July third the French attacked Washington's contingent, with a large force. After the loss of many men (as well as the desertion of many), he surrendered on July fourth. Washington and his men were allowed to leave, but the French kept two of his men hostage, and took them back to Fort Duquesne. Washington returned to Virginia in defeat. The British realized they would have to field a stronger army to displace the French from the territory.

In an attempt to coordinate the strategy of the British colonies a meeting was held in Albany New York in July 1754, with seven of the colonies attending (Massachusetts, Connecticut, Maryland, New Hampshire, New York, Pennsylvania, and Rhode Island). It was the first such meeting of the colonies in an effort to act in concert. However, there seemed to be little comity among the colonies, and the proposed Articles of Confederation, authored in part by Benjamin Franklin, although approved by the meeting's attendees, was rejected by the colonies' governments when it was presented to them. The colonists were not yet inspired to give up any local control to a higher North American authority, so the initiative for action fell to London.

Lt. Governor Dinwiddie appealed to London for regular British troops. King George-II did not approve of the request as he thought the colonials ought to fight their own battles. Others in the government, however, did not share his views. The first minister, Lord Newcastle and others, believed regular army troops were indeed needed. He stated, *"the colonies must not be abandoned, that our rights and possessions in North America must be maintained and the French obliged to desist from their hostile attempts to dispossess us."*

In February 1755, Major General Edward Braddock was sent to Virginia along with two regiments of regular army troops (about two thousand men). Parliament voted one million pounds to strengthen the military in preparation for another conflict with France, and fifty thousand pounds specifically for Braddock's troops. The arrival of British troops in North America provoked the French to do likewise, and they dispatched three thousand of their regular army troops to New France.

The British strategy for the year 1755 was to conduct a three-pronged attack on the French in especially sensitive locations. In the most difficult and significant of the battles, General Braddock was to retake Fort Duquesne at the Forks. The second prong was to take place in New York where a dual thrust was to occur: The governor of Massachusetts, William Shirley, who was also a General in the militia, was to raise two regiments in New England and capture the French fort at Niagara while Colonel William Johnson was to lead a contingent of New York volunteers along with some Mohawk Indians, against Fort Ticonderoga. The final prong was led by Colonel Robert Monckton, a regular British officer and veteran of the wars in Europe, who was to lead three thousand New England militia and two hundred regular army troops against Fort Beausejour in Nova Scotia.

The first action in the British strategy occurred when Monckton and his contingent sailed from Boston on May 26. They arrived near Fort Beausejour in June and spent some time clearing the area around the fort of French-sympathizing Acadians, while they prepared their artillery for attack. The French force at the fort was unprepared for the onslaught. The start of the assault and the immediate capitulation of the fort is aptly described by a Frenchman on the scene as reported in Daniel Marston's book: *"on the morning of the 16 an enemy bomb exploded on one of the casements to the left of the entrance (it) was enough to bring about the surrender of the fort because fire combined with inexperience made everyone in that place give up."* Fort Gapereau nearby also surrendered, isolating the major French military base, Fort Louisbourg on Cape Breton Island. The British had acquired Acadia during

Queen Anne's war in 1713 and had given the residents a mandate to pledge allegiance to England, but not many did so. Thus, during the occupation of the area in 1755 the British again demanded a declaration of loyalty. Those French-speaking Acadians who refused (over 6,000), were deported; many of whom ended up in Louisiana as present day Cajuns.

In Virginia, Braddock had drilled his men extensively before moving out on the trail to the Forks and Fort Duquesne. The fort was not strongly defended with only about three hundred regulars and militiamen, but the French had about a thousand Indians nearby who would fight with them.

The battle began in July as Braddock's army neared the fort along the Monongahela River. It wasn't the sort of battle Braddock was familiar with; Indians roaming in the woods at the sides of the British, sporadically firing into them inflecting heavy casualties. The battle lasted only hours, but over eight hundred British were killed or wounded, including General Braddock who died on the return to Virginia of the defeated troops. Washington, amazingly, was not hurt even though his uniform was riddled with bullet holes.

The New York prong of the strategy was only partially successful. Shirley's army was delayed waiting for supplies, so much so, that in September, after learning the French had strengthened Fort Niagara, he decided to return to New England and await another opportunity the following year. However, Colonel Johnson, defeated the French in a skirmish at the southern end of Lake George, which allowed the British some control over the Hudson River.

Back in London, the King was still fretting over the vulnerability of his beloved Hanover to either a French, or more likely, a Prussian attack. To forestall such an eventuality, in September 1755, Britain signed treaties with Russia and Hesse-Cassel in Germany in which they promised their aid if Hanover was invaded. The treaties required Britain to pay subsidies to solidify their support. The king and his first minister faced a problem: any payment of British funds required the approval of the House of Commons at their November meeting, and the Commons could be notoriously independent.

While the King was obdurate on the matter, and many of the Commons members wanted to satisfy him, no one could convince William Pitt, a highly regarded member of the House to support approval of the funds. The irascible Pitt, who had a coterie of supporters, disagreed with any effort to defend Hanover. As reported well in Dorothy Marshall's book: *"Geography, he argued, had made Hanover indefensible and what was needed were ships, not subsidies for troops; the only justification for war was the plight of the long injured, long neglected, long forgotten people of America."*

In spite of Pitt's oratorical skills in Commons, he lost the vote and the funds were approved. The following week, the King dismissed Pitt and his supporters from their administrative offices in his government. Pitt had held a modest position in the Pay Office, which he lost but retained his seat in Commons. The King's action, however, did not deter Pitt from keeping to his views with temerity; and, as skillful and forceful as ever, and he could not be ignored.

In an unusual and surprising turn of events, King Frederick, fearful of Russian troops aligned against him, agreed to a non-aggression pact with Britain. The pact relieved a burden for Britain since it effectively eliminated an assault by the Prussians on Hanover. The country could now follow Pitt's advice, and devote more effort to America. War between France and Britain was formally declared on May 17, 1756.

The year 1756 did not go well for Britain in North America. A new British commander, John Campbell, the Earl of Laudon, arrived in early summer. After the debacle at the Forks the year before, discordance had arisen between the British regulars and the provincial militiamen. The provincials were disparaging of the British officers and their ability to wage war in the forests of North America, while many senior British regulars viewed the provincials as poorly trained and undisciplined.

In a major battle in August the new French commander, the Marquis de Montcalm, who had only arrived in Canada in May 1756, unexpectedly swept up on Fort Oswego on the eastern edge of Lake Ontario with an army of French regulars and Indian warriors. After a heavy bombardment the fort surrendered; another humiliating defeat for the British.

Montcalm followed this victory the next year by leading a large army of over 7,500 French soldiers and their Indian allies against Fort William Henry at the southern end of Lake George above Albany. The well-constructed fort was defended by about 2,000 British. Following an initial skirmish on August 3, 1757, an intense battle ensued. The British were out manned and out gunned, and in the next week surrendered. The French won the battle, but the pyretic victory proved to be extremely costly for them. The terms of the surrender allowed the surviving British troops to march south to Fort Edwards at Albany with full military honors. The agreement left nothing for France's Indian allies, who were only in the battle for the plunder and scalps they could take, and they were incensed when the defeated troops were allowed to leave freely. In reprisal, the Indians set upon and killed the wounded soldiers left at the fort, and attacked the retreating column of troops picking off as many as they could. It was difficult for Montcalm to restrain his Indian allies, but he eventually did so. The Indians felt they were betrayed and many of them abandoned the French cause, becoming neutral observers.

Back in London, the defeats of the British in America, the loss of Minorca in the Mediterranean, and losses in India caused great consternation. Although the King still retained a strong dislike for Pitt, it was apparent to most he was the man to lead the government at this time of crisis. Pitt was not popular with many of his peers, but they also recognized his intelligence and logic, and tenacious adherence to his convictions in how the war should be run. As he forcefully stated: *"I know that I can save the country and that no one else can."* It was an outlandish statement, but many agreed with it. While Pitt's attitude could be construed as arrogance, it was more likely his frustration in the way the war was being conducted that provoked his anguished outburst.

After much negotiation, Pitt, on November 15, 1756, was asked by the King to become the Secretary of State (for the southern division), which he accepted. Essentially he ran the government, placing ministers he trusted in critical offices, and effectively prosecuted the war. In March 1758 Pitt replaced the British commander in America, Lord Loudon with General James Abercromby. He also established new policies for dealing with the American colonies such as eliminating the practice followed by the British regular army of de-ranking colonial officers who joined forces with the regular army. He also agreed to pay for part of the costs of maintaining the provincial militia. The colonial governments welcomed all of these actions.

The French and Indian War in North America would ignite battles across the globe in what historians would call the first truly world war. In addition to hostilities throughout North America, warfare would occur in Europe (misnamed the Seven Year War as it took nine years 1754–1763). Britain's ally Prussia, attacked Saxony who was allied with Austria, who was in-turn allied with France. France attacked the British colony on the Mediterranean island of Minorca. In response, the British attacked France at St Malo and other settlements on the Normandy coast. Other battles between Britain and France occurred in India and Africa. The Russians and the Swedes joined the fray by confronting the Prussian army who had advanced against Austria. The French and British navies fought on the sea with Britain generally prevailing. After Spain came to the aid of France, conflicts with Britain occurred in the Philippines and the Caribbean.

In the Ohio Territory, the British were having problems with the local Indian tribes, who generally favored the French, thus hindering efforts to capture the important Fort Duquesne at the Forks of the Ohio. To bring the tribes over to their side, in October 1758, the English convened a conclave in eastern Pennsylvania at Easton, Pennsylvania attended by over five hundred Indian representatives from the multitude of tribes in the region. The English sent a prominent delegation headed by the Governor of Pennsylvania.

A treaty was signed in which the Indians agreed not to support the French if the English attacked the fort. In return the English agreed to set up a trading post to replace the French, but more importantly, promised a prohibition on any white settlements or farms to the west of the Alleghenies. The

British General John Forbes thus felt confident in leading an army of five thousand to conquer Fort Duquesne. The French commander at the fort, Captain Le Marchand de Lignery knew that with only several hundred military, and without his Indian allies, his position was hopeless. On November 23, 1757, he placed explosives around the compound, blew up the fort and left. The French still felt they could return some day with a stronger force and contend for the site. However, that hope proved impractical and the British took control of the Ohio Territory. The British then set to the task of rebuilding the fort, naming it "Fort Pitt."

In the Northern provinces, the British continued, their victories, albeit with several setbacks, through 1757–1758. The British were generally aided by the Iroquois, but in a lukewarm manner in which the Indian nation could claim some sort of neutrality. This support changed in late 1758 when the Iroquois concluded the British were the stronger of the two European adversaries, and decided to throw the full weight of their support to the British. The French had allies in the Abenakis, Ottawas, and other Algonquin-speaking tribes of the north, but as the war went on they provided less support to the French, often at the bequest of (or threat from) the Iroquois. The year 1758 culminated with the conquest of the re-strengthened Fort Louisbourg on Cape Breton at the mouth of the Saint Lawrence River.

Using the renewed Iroquois support, the British contrived an ambitious plan to capture Fort Niagara, effectively blocking any attempt by the French to recapture Fort Duquesne, and, at the same time, setting up for a western thrust to Montreal. Traveling unimpeded up the Oswego River through Iroquois country to Lake Ontario, and then west down the southern shore, a British force of five thousand under General John Prideaux, laid siege to Fort Niagara on July 10, 1759. The fort capitulated on July 26th, when the fort's French commander, Captain Pierre Pouchot, learned a rescue force would not come to his aid. Unfortunately, the British commander Prideaux did not witness the victory as he had been killed on July 20th.

The next great battle, and a critical one for the French, began inauspiciously as General James Wolfe, fresh from his victory at Fort Louisbourg, cruised up the St Lawrence River with over twenty thousand British soldiers, marines and support personnel, and landed at the Ile d'Orleans, a small island in the St. Lawrence, just downstream from Quebec, on June 28, 1759. After his conquest of Fort Louisbourg, he had been given a new charge by William Pitt in London—capture Quebec, which would likely end the war in New France.

The French commander in Quebec, the Marquis de Montcalm prepared the city to repel any attack. Quebec stood on a promontory facing east, and it was the east walls that were strengthened. The city was guarded to the west by

large bluffs along the river that dissuaded any attackers from trying to scale
the cliffs while under the eye of the defenders.

Initially Wolfe just bombarded the city with artillery. He wanted Montcalm
to commit troops to battle as he felt he had superior forces. The cagey Montcalm, however, knew that if he could hold out until late fall or early winter,
Wolfe would have to leave the river before it froze. Then, in the spring, the
French navy would come to Quebec's aid and re-supply the city with additional men, munitions and provisions.

It was difficult to discern how the British could thwart Montcalm's plans
as Wolfe had tried an assault that ended in disaster. After several months in
which Wolfe's troops terrorized the farms in the area, Wolfe came up with
a plan he himself devised and did not share with any of his subordinates. He
had personally scouted the bluffs for a variance in the slope which would allow quick, shielded access to the top. Late on the night of September 12th,
with a section of his army in boats west of the city, Wolfe sent a detachment
of troops up the steep slopes at such an indentation in the cliff line. At the
top, they subdued a small detachment of French soldiers. All but one of the
defenders were killed; the lone survivor running to Quebec about a half-mile
away to warn of the breech.

Immediately six battalions of British soldiers climbed the cliff and formed
a conventional attack column on the Plains of Abraham, facing the now surprised fortress of Quebec. The battle was intense, but quick. Montcalm rushed
his army out of the city to face the well-trained British regulars, but as the
two sides engaged, many of the French, who were irregular militiamen, and,
not trained to European-style battle, broke ranks. The British won but General
Wolfe was killed during the engagement. Montcalm too was wounded and he
succumbed the following morning as the British took over the city.

The only thing the French could hope for now was the arrival of reinforcements and supplies when the river thawed in the spring. However, the battles
the two navies had fought in Europe, with the British navy prevailing, made
rescue by French ships virtually impossible. Now, of the major settlements
in New France, only Montreal was left, and it fell on 8 September 1760 to a
combined British force that was closing in on three sides.

Chapter Fourteen

A New King and a Challenge

The end of the French and Indian War resulted in major alterations to national boundaries throughout the entire world, but alterations that were most strongly felt by the inhabitants of North America. When on September 7, 1760, the governor of New France, the Marquis de Vaudreuil, surrendered to the British General Jeffrey Amherst, and gave up control of New France, he successfully negotiated conditions that eased the effect of the defeat on New France's settlers. Amherst agreed that any resident of New France who desired to return to France would be allowed to do so, but had to agree not to participate in the present war. Those who chose to remain in Canada could keep their property and, very important to them, could continue to retain their French language and practice their Catholic faith.

That Amherst agreed to these terms is not surprising as his position was not especially secure. He had elements of the French army ensconced in small forts throughout the Ohio Territory and over sixty thousand French-speaking settlers in the northern regions. In addition, there were about a hundred and fifty thousand Indians dispersed throughout the land, whose loyalty and disposition were uncertain. He did not relish trouble from within the country now under his control.

The fall of Canada to the British was euphorically received throughout the North American colonies as well as in Britain. When four months after the victory in Montreal, the British were also victorious in India, the euphoria only increased. The British navy had captured the important French Caribbean island of Guadeloupe the year before, so all the king's subjects, on both sides of the Atlantic, posited a sense of power and immense pride.

The North American colonies had contributed greatly to the victories in the new world. Even though many of the British military leaders had a disdainful view of the colonists' soldierly skills, the colonists themselves did not share that view. The significant effort by thousands of colonial militia in a number of important victories, such as the capture of Fort Beausejour in Nova Scotia by New England volunteers was as important as any battle in the war. The colonies, in fact, had contributed significant manpower, as well as supporting the effort with taxes in not insignificant sums.

Unfortunately the British monarch, King George-II, did not have long to savor the nation's conquests, as he succumbed to a heart attack on October 25, 1760, just over a month after Montreal's surrender. The King's son, Frederick, had died nine years before him; thus he was succeeded by his twenty-one year old grandson as King George-III.

The new king had been generally ignored by his grandfather, although, upon the death of his father, Frederick, he had been made Prince of Wales, the normal post for potential monarchs. It was as if both King Georges, I and II, resented the existence of the designated heir to their throne, and would not allow them to experience any facets of governance of the country.

The new king thus acquired his understanding of the role of the monarchy through distant veiled views, and, as a result, formed his conceptions of how a monarch should rule from others. Those "others" were mainly his mother, Augusta, and his tutor, The Scotsman, John Stuart, the 3rd Earl of Bute. Both of whom seem to have had a jaundiced perception of the intrigue they witnessed by those at the highest levels of the realm, such as the contentious collisions, often acrimonious, between William Pitt, Henry Fox and Lord Newcastle in the battle for power. They viewed these aggressive machinations of the nation's elite as corruption, even though it was normal posturing, as seen at the apex of most governments.

Augusta and Bute taught the new king to wield power as a benevolent monarch, one who would act with only the most noble interests of his subjects at heart, one who would not bow to the encroachments of regal power by parliamentarians seeking to satisfy onerous ends. In referring to the subject, George wrote, *"If I do not show them that I will not permit Ministers to trample me, then my subjects will in time come to esteem me unworthy of the crown I wear."* It was a naive, idealist interpretation of the role of the king that George-III held, one belonging to a far removed past.

The relative roles of the king and parliament had changed when William-III became king in the 1688 Glorious Revolution. The republican period under Cromwell had convinced the country that a king was necessary for the orderly management of the country, but the king's power could not be absolute. William had allowed the free election of parliament without interfering influence by the crown, which freed the elected members from dependence on regal approval.

The Declaration of Rights further solidified parliament's power to make laws and levy taxes, and limited the king's power to raise an army without parliament's approval. William did retain the important ability to name his ministers, such as the heads of State, Treasury, Admiralty, and others, who would actually run the country. He could appoint ministers he trusted and possessed the ability to perform the roles appointed, as heads of the nation's operating departments.

Even with his ministers running the various organizations that administered the country, the King needed the support of Parliament, which consisted of the House of Lords and the House of Commons. The members of the House of Lords usually assumed their positions hereditarily and generally went along with the King's wishes, while those in Commons were elected. The House of Commons, which was responsible for the critical charge of approving the expenditures of the realm, rigorously guarded the power given them, and could be independently minded. Thus, the king needed ministers, or at least one primary minister, who could get things done with the cooperation of Commons.

William was a strong monarch, but Queen Anne following him, ruled timidly, and the role of the ministers in the management of the country grew under her reign. The role of the leading minister, the so-called "Prime Minister", became, virtually, the ruler-in-fact. Anne was succeeded by George-I, who had only a casual interest in English politics, and thus the ministers' role in running the country became more ensconced. George-II, although more involved than his predecessor, generally followed along the same path and was comfortable with the status quo in the nation's rule.

Now, however, with King George-III's mistrust of the elitists in the previous king's government, he wanted ministers he felt were aligned with his noble ideals and goals, and not be so independent-minded and self-serving. Unlike the three monarchs who preceded him, George-III felt an obligation to become more involved in the management of the realm. He was, in his mind, the faithful, caring monarch, ruling with only the good of his subjects' best interests in mind, not like some of those corrupt ministers who had only personal gain or greater power as their guiding force.

An issue brought to the attention of the new activist king was how to pay the great debt the realm was accruing as a result of the war. The British taxpayer was going to have to assume the entire burden unless other means could be found to at least share the load. One means identified that could be employed to raise revenue without having to write new laws, was merely to enforce laws that were already on the books, but were being ignored. These were laws, written several years earlier, dictating custom duties for certain import/export transactions, but were not being collected because smuggling was thwarting efforts to enforce them. Of particular importance, was the smuggling of molasses from the French West Indies into Massachusetts, ignoring payment of lawful duties as dictated by the 1733 Molasses Act. In fact, it was pointed out, while it was costing the realm eight thousand pounds a year for salaries of the customs officers to collect the duties, only two thousand pounds a year was actually being collected.

To collect the lawful custom duties, government ministers in London determined it would be necessary to strictly enforce both the Navigation Laws and the General Writs of Assistance which had been passed previously by Parliament. The Writs could be used to search for and detect the illicit cargos while the Admiralty Courts, codified in the Navigation Acts, could confiscate any illicit cargos and sell them for revenue. The King readily agreed.

To enforce the Writs of Assistance first required each colony to reaffirm the law, as was required upon the ascension of a new monarch to the throne. In Massachusetts, that role fell to the Superior Court. Thus, the court ordered a hearing to verify the legality of the writs for February of 1761 in the Boston Old Town Hall. Many regarded the hearing merely a formality that would be dispensed with quickly, so the King's wishes could be satisfied.

Massachusetts in 1761 was a major source of rum, which was exported widely at great profit. To make the rum, the sixty or so distillers in the colony needed molasses which they had been getting (smuggling) from the French West Indies, even throughout the French and Indian War. If the writs were strictly enforced, that source of good, cheap molasses would be denied and the distillers would be forced to buy molasses from the British West Indies (and pay the duties), which was more expensive and of a poorer quality.

While customs agents had always had the authority to search ships for smuggled cargo, the writs of assistance went far beyond that. They were general search warrants that allowed virtually unfettered searches. With a writ, customs agents could authorize nearly anyone with the authority to go into warehouses, wharfs, even homes of suspected violators. The writs were greatly abhorred by the merchants, likely because violation of the custom laws occurred routinely and the illegal cargo would be discovered by unrestricted searches, but also by many others in the general population on the more fundamental issue of protection from illegal intrusions into an individual's person and property.

It was becoming apparent to many of the areas citizens that their prosperity and general well being did not need control (nor intrusive laws) by a king and a Parliament three thousand miles away. An ever deepening chasm was growing in New England between the loyalists to Britain and the now-termed "Patriots" who believed they could get along very well without British control, especially that annoying Parliament. The prickly issue of loyalty to Britain versus self-rule was being addressed at the time in careful, subdued discussions, as it could be construed as treason to openly denounce the King or Parliament. But, even with the threat of accusations of treasonable thoughts, the subject was being discussed widely.

Many of the colonials made the distinction between the King's rule and Parliament's law-making ability. While many accepted the King's right to rule, they objected to Parliament's passing laws affecting them as they had their own legislative bodies that did that. Thus, the Boston trial on the legality of the Writs of Assistance was of importance, not only to the merchants involved, but also to the entire colony as a sort of plebiscite on their acceptance of an edict they opposed by a British government they more often disagreed with.

The royal governor of the colony, Francis Bernard, and the chief justice of the Superior Court, who would preside at the proceedings, Thomas Hutchinson, were dedicated loyalists who openly and strongly supported the King and Parliament (Hutchinson was also the Lieutenant Governor). Bernard, forty-eight, was born in Brightwell, England and came to North America in 1758, initially to act as governor of New Jersey. It was well known that the post of royal governor could be financially rewarding and individual governors campaigned to be assigned to the more lucrative positions. In August 1760 Bernard wanted to move to the governorship of New York or Pennsylvania, but instead was assigned as governor of Massachusetts, replacing Thomas Pownall, who moved to the more profitable Carolina governorship.

The Lieutenant Governor, fifty-year-old Thomas Hutchinson was a native of Boston with deep roots in the Commonwealth. He was the great-great-grandson of the infamous Anne of the same name. Tall, staid and considered a serious, humorless sort of fellow, Hutchinson had a long history of involvement in Massachusetts' politics, having been elected as a representative to the General Court in 1753. The General Court, the legislative body of the Massachusetts Bay Colony, was bicameral with an upper chamber called the Governor's Council and a lower branch, the House of Representatives.

Hutchinson had gone to London in 1740 and made a favorable impression on members of the British government there. Returning to Boston he became the Speaker of the General Court. He had served as a delegate to the Albany Convention in 1754, and had advocated agreement of the plan for united colonial action against the French, authored by Benjamin Franklin; it was ultimately rejected by the colonial governments. In 1758 he was named Lieutenant Governor of Massachusetts, and in 1760, Chief Justice of the Superior Court. Coming from a privileged background, his friends were the wealthy and powerful members of the community.

To oppose the legality of the writs, merchants in Boston and Salem asked James Otis, jr, a portly thirty-five year old Boston lawyer to argue their side of the case. The year before, Otis had resigned his position as Advocate General because he strongly objected to the issuance of the writs. He believed they were a violation of an individual's common rights, and were therefore illegal. He accepted the merchants' plea and took the case without fee. He was gregarious, but could be goaded into volatile and abrasive behavior, a characteristic many discovered to their dismay.

The Otis family had a long history in the area. John Otis-I, the present Otis' great-great-grandfather left Glastonbury, England in 1630 and settled in the small village of Bear Cove (later called Hingham), several miles south of Boston. There were a number of other settlers from the English west counties that settled there as well as a number of east Anglicans. Unlike the Puritan east Anglicans, Otis was more interested in the economic opportunities in the new country rather than religious freedom. He was an independent sort as were his descendents who prospered in the New World.

James Otis jr's father John, sr, already a successful businessman, became a lawyer when he was asked by a neighbor to defend him in a court suit. He won and decided law was a profession in which he could do well, taking the legal oath in 1731. He prospered in this career, and became sought out in legal matters, especially those dealing with property.

As a successful lawyer and respected member of the community, in 1745 Otis, sr was elected Barnstable's representative to the Colony's House of Representatives. The Massachusetts Legislature at the time was represented by ten counties which contained 161 separate towns, a wide range of political views, but with a decided leaning toward conservative Puritan convictions. Seventy percent of the legislative membership defined their profession as "farmer". Otis, sr. was as successful in politics as he had been in business and soon found himself serving on important committees. During the French and Indian War he was made a Colonel in the army and helped by building whaleboats in Barnstable.

In 1756 he expected to be made a member of the Governor's Council, the higher body in the assembly, and gave up his seat in the House of Representatives. Unfortunately, he was thwarted by Thomas Hutchinson and the seat went to one of Hutchinson's associates. Otis then had to regain a seat in the lower house in the next election, which he did, and even became speaker of the body. His goal was to become a justice of the Superior Court and possibly, Chief Justice, when the next seat became available.

When Chief Justice Samuel Sewall died in September 1760, the position Otis, sr. coveted became open. While Otis' interest in the court was well-known, Governor Bernard, who would make the appointment, had his own persuasions. First, there was the matter of self-interest. Any smuggled cargo seized by the customs agents was to be sold, with the governor receiving one-third of the sale revenue. It was thus in his self-interest to appoint someone to the court who would support the legality of the writs. While he did not know the views of the senior Otis on the subject, he was well aware that the junior Otis opposed them as they adversely affected his mercantile clients.

The senior Otis sent his son to speak to Thomas Hutchinson and learn whether he was seeking the office. When he stated he was not, the son reported that message to his father. Unfortunately, there might have been some sort of misunderstanding as Hutchinson never said he would not accept the post if it were offered to him, only that he would not actively seek it. Meanwhile Bernard had learned Hutchinson was supportive of the legality of the writs and thus appointed him to the Chief Justice's post, creating significant hard feelings among the Otis clan against both of the colony's top officers.

The junior Otis had had another run-in with the royal governor when he filed suit against the Customs Office of Governor Bernard in December 1760. British law declared that any revenue accrued as a result of capturing smuggled goods was to be split three ways: One-third for the governor, one-third for the province where the capture occurred, and one-third for the officials (such as naval officers) who executed the capture. Informers who alerted authorities to an act of smuggling were given a reward. At the time, the reward was paid out of the Province's share. Otis filed the suit against Governor Bernard's Collector of Customs, Charles Paxton, in a specific case to recover Massachusetts' full one-third share of 475 pounds, as the law stated the informers reward was supposed to be paid out of the Governor's share instead of the Province's.

Otis won his case in the lower Court of Common Pleas, a result that greatly infuriated and embarrassed Governor Bernard. Paxton then appealed his case to the higher Superior Court with Thomas Hutchinson presiding as Chief Justice. The Superior Court reversed the lower court's decision on technical grounds, but some damage to Bernard's and Hutchinson's reputation was done.

James Otis, jr was well-prepared to oppose the writs of assistance. Born February 5, 1725, he entered Harvard in 1743 and, though convivial, was a serious student, with a talent for logic and Puritan thought. At his father's urging he entered into a practice of law in Plymouth. With only mild success in his law practice, young Otis moved to Boston in 1750 where he was readily accepted into the elevated social fabric of the city. In 1755 he married Ruth Cunningham, an heiress to a sizeable sum from her well-to-do merchant father. Otis, jr. had a penchant for opposing what he perceived as illegal or unauthorized actions by a government, fighting against over taxation of trading towns. He was made a justice of the peace in 1756 and in 1757, the royal governor, Thomas Pownall made him deputy advocate-general of the local Vice-Admiralty Court (the office from which he resigned in 1760), before leaving for the governorship of Carolina, and was replaced by Francis Bernard.

So, the court session to decide the legality of the Writs of Assistance began with a background of animosity between Otis, jr and the Chief Justice,

Thomas Hutchinson. The king's attorney prosecuting the case for the crown was Jeremiah Gridley, a mild, agreeable lawyer who, in the past, had been one of Otis' teachers, and was considered his friend. To start the case, Gridley simply and succinctly stated the crown's rationale for the legality of the writs.

The English Court of Exchequer could legally issue writs because they had been authorized by Parliament during the reign of Charles-II. The Superior Court of Massachusetts could likewise issue writs as the colonial courts had been authorized to do so during the reign of William-III. Further, and of great importance, a search warrant was needed to collect customs duties, which were being flagrantly avoided by illegal means. How else could the customs agents do their job? If intruding on the liberty of an individual occurred, it was a necessary inconvenience in the need to maintain a workable government.

Upon Gridley's completion of his arguments, Otis' co-counsel, Oxenbridge Thacker, gave a rebuttal to Gridley's declarations. The case, Thacker explained, was based on the inability of the Massachusetts Superior Court to issue the writs as they did not have the same legal basis as did the English Courts that could. It was more than a legal point as it pointed out the difference between the legal bases of the British and Colonial courts, and the separation of British as opposed to Colonial law.

When Thacker finished, Otis then stood and began his discourse. He took a far different approach than his co-counsel. No law, Otis averred, could be legal if it went against common rights. No one could legitimize a law where one man could challenge another man's right to life, liberty and property. Otis' words supporting his arguments were convincing and presented in a manner that kept the court spectators, which included a young, captivated John Adams, in rapt attention as he jotted in his notebook attempting to summarize Otis' argument that the writs were against the fundamental principles of law. In a lengthy oration Otis expanded on individual rights and the necessity to place limits on governments' actions where they conflicted with an honorable citizen's rights.

If he would have stopped here and ended his brief he would still have been regarded as a patriot fighting effectively for freedom and individual rights. However, Otis continued with words that reverberated throughout the countryside. As effectively written by John Walters, jr in *The Otis Family*, Otis forcefully said the writ was the:

> worst instrument of arbitrary power, the most destructive to English liberty, and the fundamental principles of the constitution." He declared that it was the very exercise of the kind of arbitrary power "which in former periods of English history, cost one king of England his head and another his throne.

Otis implored the court to *"demolish this monster of oppression and tear into rags this remnant of Starchamber Tyranny."*

In this skewed, challenging statement (possibly treasonous), he openly denounced the king's support of Parliamentary laws the colonists felt oppressive, Otis boldly brought the subject of British rule in general, and Parliament's authority to pass laws enforceable on the colonies in particular, into more open discussion. He articulated the view of the King, Parliament and their loyal agents as less than benevolent, mighty leaders. They could also be viewed as threats to the well being of the British Colonies and their individual members.

The court session ended with Hutchinson, concerned with Thacker's legal points and the effect Otis' arguments had on the judicial panel, stating he would have to contact London and gain clarification of their intent in enforcing the law. Until further guidance was received, the court would not rule on the case, likely for another year.

With the delay in a decision, the use of writs would continue, and Otis did not win his case. But, the blow had been struck! Wherever Otis appeared, he was congratulated for his elocution. Patrons in the basement of the Green Dragon Tavern in Boston's North End rang praises for Otis' eloquence. In the next election he was easily voted into a seat in the House of Representatives where he served admirably, if not erratically at times. His persistent support of colonial and individual rights was an important facet of the increased popularity of the Patriot (or Popular) Party in future elections to the Massachusetts Congress.

Since the inception of their colonies, the New England settlers had exhibited a less than infusive support for the crown. It had started with their Puritan beliefs and never really subsided, even through successive generations. Congregationalism was the dominant religion, and its adherents still followed beliefs that had guided their ancestors. New arrivals from Scotland and Ireland came into the area along with French Huguenots, some Germans and a scattering of others. None of these newcomers had any special reverence for the English crown and easily assimilated into the majority of Englishmen already there, and readily accepted the negative views of the British governance already prevalent in the colony. Thus Otis' words rang with special meaning for most New Englanders.

The threat to individual rights by the arbitrary issuance of the invasive writs was not lost on the citizens of the other colonies. The forced mercantile system was generally tolerated. It was an irritant for many, but accepted as a means of commerce. The writs though were more of an oppressive action that was perceived as unfair, and thus raised objections to absolute British rule. Although nothing was really resolved by the trial and Otis' defense, since the court put off a decision, and no ruling issued. The fundamental charge of raising revenue was not resolved, and would again become prominent in later encounters between the British Parliament and the American Colonies.

It is not surprising that no action was taken by the Massachusetts Court regarding the legality of the writs. Although the fighting in North America had subsided, the British Empire was still involved in a war with France and Spain in Europe, the islands and on the sea. It would be another two years before Britain would again be able to pursue reconciling the problem they faced with the debt from the war and the costs of protecting their North American colonies.

Chapter Fifteen

Peace and a Secure North America

One of King George-III's goals upon being named monarch was to achieve a peace with France and end the war; in his mind a grand and noble goal. The conflict in continental North America had been completed favorably for the British realm, and now it was time to cease hostilities in the other areas still battling. The King felt a peace could be made with France that would be acceptable to both sides. However, he ran into a snag.

The leading minister, carried over from King George-II's cabinet, was the commanding William Pitt, who was accorded credit for the great victories in North America, India and Africa. Pitt was glorified as one of England's greatest statesmen. He was considered an orator of such eloquence and skill as never before seen in the House of Commons; a man whose logic overwhelmed opposing positions and commanded regard from all. Pitt saw no reason to accept a peace with France except upon very favorable terms for Britain.

While peace with France was still being debated, Spain decided they could no longer stand aside and see France critically threatened. A compact between the two countries, with close relatives on their respective thrones, was signed, the contents of which were not made public. The signing of a pact at this point in the war was viewed as a threat by Britain, as it could very well mean Spain was preparing to enter the war and come to France's aid at a time and place of their choosing. Spain's action provoked Pitt to the point where he actively led an effort to declare war on Spain, threatening to resign if the king did not. Pitt, ever aware of even the most minute detail of an issue, wanted to declare war on Spain at this time as the Spanish treasure ships were sailing from the Caribbean on their way to Spain. If war were declared now, the British navy could intercept the Spanish ships and command their precious cargo. The new king, in a manner that provoked his prime minister, intentionally deferred a decision, whereupon Pitt submitted his resignation, which the king blithely accepted.

Pitt was likely depending on a process that had forced previous kings to submit to the wishes of parliament and its leading minister. In similar situations in the recent past, the ministers, acting in concert, would threaten to resign en-mass if the king did not accede to their demands, thus placing the king in the position of running the country, but not having competent ministers to actually do so. To avoid a total collapse of government, the king would capitulate to the ministers' charges, albeit usually with compromises. Pitt likely hoped this would happen if the king replaced him, but Pitt's autocratic rule finally caught up with him, and when he was removed, only Lord Temple resigned his ministerial position as Privy Seal. The remaining ministers were tired of the war and averse to continuing to spend great sums in its continuation. They felt Pitt was becoming too intractable in his objections to compromises with France, and would agree to peace with only onerous terms that France would never agree to.

The king named Earl Bute, his tutor, as Pitt's replacement and set about trying to negotiate a peace treaty with France. However, as much as the remaining ministers did not support Pitt, unlike the novice king and his neophyte prime minister, they did not countenance a peace with France at this time. They were concerned about the effect a French peace treaty would have on Prussia if France, freed from the conflict with Britain, could turn all of their might to the battles in Europe, to the great detriment of the British alley. As Pitt had declared earlier, *"America had been conquered in Germany."* He meant that had France, a much more populous country than Britain, not been occupied with fighting in Europe, they would have been able to send great numbers of troops to New France and successfully defend their North American colony. Thus, the ministers felt an obligation to Frederick-II because of his role of aiding the British cause.

As events unfolded, parliament became more and more concerned about Spanish intentions and demanded assurances from Spain that the compact they had signed with France was non-aggressive with regard to Britain. When Spain ignored the demand, the king was forced to declared war on Spain on January 4, 1762. Unfortunately, because of the delay, the Spanish treasure ships were safely in ports in Spain. It didn't take long after the declaration for the powerful and charged British military to make itself felt. A month after the declaration, the British navy completed its conquest of the remaining French islands in the Caribbean and turned its forces towards Spain's most treasured possession in the area, Havana, on the island of Cuba, which fell in August. The British also captured Manila in the Spanish Philippines, further enhancing the aura of British invincibility.

With all sides fatigued by the war, and the remaining fronts essentially stalemated, a first peace treaty was finally signed in Paris between the North American combatants on February 10, 1763. The provisions of the treaty, which greatly favored British interests, altered the world in ways that forever changed the face of the globe.

Britain took control of Canada and all of the land east of the Mississippi River. France was allowed to keep two small islands near Newfoundland, Saint Pierre and Miquelon, so they would continue to have access to the cod fishery in the area, which was extremely important to the fishing industry in Normandy and Brittany. France was very pleased with the reacquisition of Guadeloupe and Martinique in the Caribbean which they valued greater than Canada (the so-called "ice for spice" trade).

Britain gained Florida from Spain in exchange for returning Havana (and also Manila), thus Britain now controlled all of North America east of the Mississippi River. In compensation for losing Florida, France ceded New Orleans and the Louisiana Territory to Spain.

Five days after the treaty in Paris, a second treaty was signed in the Saxony town of Hubertusburg, ending the war in Europe where approximately a million had died. The treaty did what had been the norm for such war-ending pacts in Europe between royal families wherein the rulers were often close relatives—it generally reestablished the boundaries that had existed before the war.

The success of Britain in the French and Indian War has been attributed to a number of factors: powerful British navy, competent generals, colonial support, all of which no doubt played a role. One other that deserves mention is rarely acknowledged: the role played by the conformation of the British government that had evolved in their recent history. Most of the European nations at the time, including Britain's enemies France and Spain, were still being ruled by concepts that originated in their feudal past, where a hereditary monarch was virtually an absolute ruler. Britain, although certainly a monarchy, was further along in the transition to a republic. As previously discussed, its parliament had gained strength under the terms that William-III agreed to in his overthrow of James-II. The monarchs following William, Anne and the two Georges I and II, were, with few exceptions, content to let Ministers who could cooperate with Parliament, especially the House of Commons, run the country.

The Commons was a unique body, one in which issues of importance to the nation could be debated in detail. Almost any facet of a critical national issue, such as the prosecution of a war or the signing of a peace treaty, could be dissected, examined, and the pros and cons of any strategy opened for critique. Alternative approaches could be put forward which were likewise appraised in fine detail. In such debates, it also became apparent which members best understood the critical issues, and could offer solutions that possessed the most promise. It was in this gathering of elected members, where a man like William Pitt would accrue the confidence of his fellow members to the degree the King would be virtually forced to place him in charge of the nation in conflict. Thus, in Britain, a portion of the success in the war could rightfully be ascribed to the form of government they operated under. A form where the best path to success could be debated and identified, and the best man for leading the nation along that path could be appointed to do so.

France and Spain, monarchies with able men supporting the king, had no comparable body to publicly probe alternatives in such fine detail, and no monarch strongly forced to submit to the will of such an independently minded group. It was unfortunate for Britain that the new king did not use this capability for the continuing growth of the nation. Instead, he took a more active role in decision-making and ministerial appointments, negating the advantages that had accrued the nation in the positive evolution of its government.

With the end of the war and the signing of the peace treaty, the North American colonies perceived an immediate emendation of their environment. They no longer had to fear conflict with France, neither in the northern colonies nor with those abutting the Ohio Territory. However, a new obstacle to a peaceful existence for the settlers arose, as the Indian tribes in the Ohio Territory were not pleased with their post-war lot. The Indians had been promised no settlers would be allowed into the Ohio Territory if the British were successful; yet, here were colonial settlers continuing to hunt in the area. In late 1762, a number of tribes, including the Seneca, Delaware, Ottawa, and Huron, some of which had fought with the British and some with the French, rebelled and took over several of the smaller forts. The major forts Pitt, Detroit and Niagara were besieged, but not taken. Battles with the Indians continued throughout most of 1763. To ease the tension with the Indians, King George-III formally issued a Royal Proclamation on October 7, 1763. The start of which is as follows:

> WHEREAS we have taken into Our Royal Consideration the extensive and valuable Acquisitions in America, secured to our Crown by the late Definitive Treaty of Peace, concluded at Paris the 10th Day of February last; and being desirous that all Our loving Subjects, as well of our Kingdom as of our Colonies in America, may avail themselves with all convenient Speed, of the great Benefits and Advantages which must accru therefrom to their Commerce, Manufacture, and Navigation, We have thought fit, with the Advice of our Privy Council, to issue this our Royal Proclamation, hereby to publish and declare to all our loving Subjects, that we have, with the Advice of our Privy Council , granted our

Letters Patent, under our Great Seal of Great Britain, to erect, within the Countries and Islands ceded and confirmed to Us by the said Treaty, Four distinct and separate Governments, styled and called by the names of Quebec, East Florida, West Florida and Granada.

After a detailed description of the boundaries of the new governmental areas that were to the north and south of the present colonies, the proclamation continued with a granting of land in the new areas to the military who served in the French and Indian War, with higher ranks awarded greater acreage.

The British government wanted to induce military veterans to settle in the three new North American areas, as it would dilute the presence of Frenchmen in the north and Spanish in the south, and help secure the boundaries of the British territory.

For the Indians:

...the several Nations or Tribes of Indians with whom We are connected, and who live under our Protection, should not be molested or disturbed in the Possession of such Parts of Our Dominions and Territories as, not having been ceded to or purchased by Us, are reserved to them, or any of them, as their Hunting Grounds.

And for any settler who had ambitions of inhabiting or selling land given to the tribes:

And We do hereby strictly forbid, on Pain of our Displeasure, all our loving Subjects from making any Purchases or Settlements whatever, or taking Possession of any of the Lands above reserved, without our especial leave and License for that Purpose first obtained. And We do further strictly enjoin and require all Persons whatever who have either willfully or inadvertently seated themselves upon and Lands within the Countries above described or upon any other Lands which, not having been ceded to or purchased by Us, are still reserved to the said Indians as aforesaid, forthwith to remove themselves from such Settlements.

Also included was a provision that, no colonial government was permitted to grant land in the same area, as Virginia had already done in 1740. While the proclamation satisfied many of the Indians, and a peace treaty was agreed to by most of them, it angered the colonists, deepening a growing rift between the colonies and the government in London. It is likely the proclamation wasn't necessary to subdue the Indian uprising, as many of the Indian chiefs had already seen the future. They were no longer able to acquire large quantities of arms or ammunition from the French, and it was apparent they would soon be overwhelmed by new, well-armed settlers who had an inexorable thirst for new land. The King issued the proclamation with noble words but many suspected the main motivation for it was to avoid the costs of additional troops that would be needed to secure the area.

The provision disturbed men such as George Washington, who, after returning to his native Virginia at the end of his military service in 1758, had married the wealthy widow Martha Curtis and had set forth to become a plantation owner and farmer. He had speculated on land in the Ohio Territory by purchasing warrants from his former military comrades that had been awarded to those who had fought in the recent war. With twenty-five thousand acres accumulated in the area, Washington felt the proclamation was *"a temporary expedient to quiet the Minds of the Indians,"* and would soon be rescinded or ignored in the not too distant future. Almost no one believed British settlers would heed the proclamation, and would move into the Ohio Territories in large numbers.

That King George-III's reign began with peace treaties that ended wide-scale warfare around the globe belied the travails he would face in the future. He has been regarded by some as mentally unstable, but that is too harsh an assessment, especially for his early rule. He was, certainly, obstinate, egocentric, and infused with a strong, non-compromising moral righteousness imparted him by his mother from an early age that made dealing with him difficult at times. But, he was also intelligent, a student of the sciences; a benefactor of the Royal Academy. He was totally fluent in both German and English, as well as knowledgeable in French and Latin.

It has been suggested he was a manic-depressive, but while his mental state cannot be diagnosed with certainty, it is fairly certain he suffered from porphyria. This inheritable disease is marked by red or purple urine due to the overproduction of porphyins by the body. During attacks, sufferers can experience pain in the abdomen and extremities. Seizures and mental disturbances can occur, and at times be severe; leading to hallucinations, anxiety and paranoia. Unfortunately, although the condition had been known by mendicants even in the time of the Greeks, it was not described until late in the nineteenth century, and thus effective treatment not available to the physicians of George's era. Whatever the cause, the king's instability would increase as he aged and play a role in the American Revolution.

The end of the war required Britain to expend significant funds to control the new lands in Canada and Florida. These expenses, along with the subsequent use of British troops to protect the colonists from Indian uprisings, spawned a major debate in London. The war had resulted in Britain amassing a large debt of over 120 million pounds. This debt, as it was pointed out in Parliament, was due, in large part, to the necessity to send and maintain troops in North America for the colonists' protection. Wasn't it then logical to expect the American Colonies, who prospered during the war as a result of

British protection, to pay a part of the support they were receiving? Britain had ten thousand troops in the American Colonies; stationed there for protection from Indians and a potential French reprisal, the cost of which was over 200,000 pounds annually. It was a question, Parliament's answer to, would harden the inevitable path to revolution.

Chapter Sixteen

Stirrings in the Colonies

The governance of Britain was based on its "Constitution". It wasn't a single, unique document as such, but rather the assemblage of acts and agreements that had been written over the history of the nation, which defined the rights of its citizens, and how the country was to be governed. It included the Magna Carta through such documents as the Acts of Union, the Act of Settlement and the 1698 Bill of Rights. The British "Constitution" in 1763 allowed the King to name the ministers to manage the various departments of government, but it was Parliament which was now a real power by its authority to enact laws and levy taxes.

The levying of taxes by Parliament was a sacred "right," closely guarded by British citizens. The authority to tax the country's citizenry was only granted to the representatives of that same citizenry. No longer could a monarch demand payment for special assessments or a myriad of other charges; it was the Parliament's House of Commons' sacred duty and theirs alone.

Naturally, following the British model, the colonial governments of each of the American Colonies levied taxes only through action of their representative bodies; as they had been doing since their inception. The colonial citizens, like their British relations, passionately guarded this "right" to be taxed only with their approval as manifest by their representative bodies. In place of the King in Britain, each colony had a governor, whether appointed by the crown in the crown colonies, designated by a proprietor (such as the Penn family in Pennsylvania) in a proprietor colony, or elected in a corporate charter colony. And, as Virginia and Massachusetts had demonstrated, the colonial citizens would violently oppose any attempt by a governor to enact a tax without approval by their representative assemblies. They would certainly strongly rebuff any attempt by the British Parliament, where they had no representation, to levy a tax on them.

The majority of the colonies were royal colonies in which the governor was appointed by the king, but in the other colonies, the governors were under the control of one of the king's ministers, which made them also under the king's superintendence. Thus, the colonies were effectively removed from the direct control of Parliament. While Parliament could write laws, such as navigation and trade laws which the colonies would be subject, it was the governors under the king who would dictate compliance. Parliamentary laws concerning navigation and trade were one thing, but laws concerning the levying of taxes was quite another.

Early in 1763, while the colonists and British troops were battling Indians on the colonies' western front, the British Parliament was struggling with ways to reduce the massive debt the country had accumulated as a result of the war with France and Spain. The British debt was at an all time high of over a hundred and twenty-two million pounds. Worse, the figure was rising as the post war economy was in the doldrums, and taxable revenue was not keeping up with expenditures. Previously, Parliament had passed a tax on beer and wine, but had excluded taxing cider as it was considered a "home brew" even though it was commonly and widely sold. Now, however, in desperation to gain additional revenue, Parliament was debating a tax on cider, including perry, the cider equivalent that used pears instead of apples. Such a tax was projected to bring in 800,000 pounds annually, a significant sum.

It was a vigorous debate, with Prime Minister Bute strongly supported by the Secretary of State George Grenville, arguing for adoption of the new tax. There were a number of ministers in opposition in both the House of Commons and Lords, most notably, William Pitt in Commons, the acknowledged hero of the recent war with France and Spain. Pitt's objection with the law was the provision necessary for enforcement, which would require a large number of government collection agents, who would be sent to virtually every apple orchard in the country, and, in some cases, even into farmers' homes.

George Grenville was adamant in his support of the Cider tax bill. He felt, it was absolutely needed because of the perilous state of the country's finances. He was frustrated by Pitt's strong opposition to the law, but was reluctant to reproach the great commoner directly, so he posed a rhetorical question to Parliament, *"Why does he not tell us where to go, if not this source?"* Pitt then, in one of his risible moments, ridiculed Grenville by humming the well-known tune "Gentle Sheppard Tell Me Where," whereupon Grenville acquired the appellation "Gentle Sheppard" which he detested. It was humiliating to Grenville, but did not deter him from pushing ahead in his support of the bill.

The Cider tax was finally passed and it befell mainly on the fruit orchards in Devon, Somerset, Dorset and other, mainly western counties, even though they had strong representation in Parliament. However, there was an immediate outcry over the tax and the bureaucracy that was being set up to collect it; there were near revolts in some counties.

In April of the same year, shortly after passage of the Cider Tax, the king's favorite, Bute, was forced to resign as Prime Minister when he was assailed in earnest by his political enemies, and even felt threatened by unruly mobs who were incensed by Parliament's new Cider Tax. The King reluctantly had to find a replacement for the departing Bute and first asked Pitt to re-accept the position he had left only two years before. However, Pitt declined and his fifty-year old brother-in-law, George Grenville, a commoner lawyer, was appointed Lord of the Treasury, and thus Prime Minister. Thus it was Grenville, who, in his deliberate manner, now took up the challenge of reducing the large British debt in earnest.

Grenville was recognized for his administrative skills, and knowledge of governmental rules and parliamentary procedures, but he was humorless, lacked tact and could be difficult as he held to the letter of the law as he saw it. He had a definite disadvantage in that the king did not like him, and accepted him as the first minister only because he seemed to be the only choice available. As the King had stated of him, *"His opinions are seldom formed from any other motives than such as may be expected to originate in the mind of a clerk in a counting house."* The King also found Grenville's speeches boring, *"When he has wearied me for two hours he looks at his watch to see if he may not tire me for one hour more"*. Since one of the main essentials needed to operate a stable administration was Royal support, Grenville did not have an auspicious start to his ministry. In addition, Grenville did not have solid support from many in the administration, and that made his job much more difficult in the hectic, rough and tumble London political environment.

In the first year, revenue from the Cider Tax netted less than ten-percent of the anticipated goal, and the revolts intensified and spread to London (the onerous provisions of the tax was officially repealed in 1766). The widespread and vigorous opposition to the Cider Tax convinced Grenville and others in Parliament that British citizens were carrying too large a tax burden. Whether this was true or whether they just didn't like this "working man's" tax is not known, but Grenville then seriously took up the problem of finding other sources of revenue for the British treasury. As a part of the growing deficit was due to the support of troops stationed in the American Colonies to protect them, Grenville looked purposely to the American Colonies to require them to contribute to this cost.

In the past, a non-tax approach by Parliament had been attempted to have the colonies pay for support they needed from the mother country, namely, to have the governors of each colony request their colonial assemblies to raise a defined amount for their protection and management. However, this method had proved to be unreliable, and thus, Grenville and others in Parliament knew they would have to use the more direct methods of assessing duties on products of trade or, in a more aggressive approach, by a direct tax.

The issue of taxing the colonies was not new. When the prospect of taxing the American Colonies was proposed to Sir Robert Walpole during his appointment as Prime Minister under the reigns of Kings George I & II, he refused. He felt, as a result of the mercantile system, Britain was getting much more revenue from exports (mostly manufactured items) to the colonies by Britain's merchants, than they were losing due to imports of goods (mostly raw materials) from the colonies. Britain's balance of payments with the colonies was strongly positive. In reference to the profits the British merchants were gaining from trade with the colonies, Walpole remarked, *"This is taxing them more agreeably to their own constitution and ours."*

Walpole had a point. Although the prevalent view in Britain, where the costs of supporting the colonies was readily apparent, many in Britain neglected to consider the profits accruing to the nation because of their exports of manufactured goods to the colonies. The problem with the accrual of funds due to exports was one of visibility: the funds were flowing to the British merchants, and not directly into Britain's treasury. Many of the merchants who were profiting greatly from exports to the colonies likely were aware of this, but still lobbied with their representatives to avoid being taxed themselves.

When Grenville scrutinized the opportunities for procuring revenue from the American Colonies an obvious opportunity became immediately apparent: Enforce the duties that were legislated by the Sugar Act of 1733, which imposed a duty on sugar and molasses imported into the American Colonies from non-British sources. The act was expiring and a new act was being written. However, a problem with the old act, which would likely affect any new version of the act, was the extensive smuggling the colonists were employing to avoid paying the duties. Thus, the first step in enacting duties on the sugar trade was the necessity of enforcing the existing trade laws, and stopping the prevalent smuggling that had contravened collection.

Grenville's first action was to make the customs agents, whose sinecure-like job it was to enforce the trade laws, move from their comfortable offices in England and locate to the colonies where they should have been in the first place. These agents had collected a salary, but relegated the actual work of enforcing the laws to colonial agents, who took bribes rather than enforce the duties. He also strengthened the naval inspection of the colonial ports and bolstered the Admiralty Courts where a suspected smuggler could be brought to a trial without jury; the admiralty judge deciding the case alone. New rules allowed any customs agent to bring a suspected violator of the trade laws to such a court. To further validate the procedure, a new Admiralty Court was established at Halifax where Lord Colville, in charge of the navy in America, posted his flagship. It could be used in cases where a regional Admiralty Court was too indulgent to local offenders.

No longer could a colonial smuggler expect lenient treatment from a local common-law or friendly admiralty court, which often tolerated the activities which profited the colony. With these new procedures, any duties, extant or in the future, were much more likely to be collected to alleviate the debt Britain faced.

Grenville was an astute financier and realized the duties that would be raised by a new Sugar Act would only be in the range of tens of thousands of pounds a year, and that amount would be insufficient in addressing the large size of the British debt. Thus, he looked further for other means which would bring much greater revenue. So, what else was available from the colonies that could bring in the larger capital?

Another method that had been discussed in the past was extending the British stamp tax to the colonies. In Britain, any of a broad number of documents, such as licenses, certificates, etc., required a stamp to be impressed on the document before it became legal. A fee (tax) was imposed for the stamp, which varied with the type of document issued. Such a tax had been in effect in England since at least 1694. It was a relatively simple and effective method of accruing funds into the treasury as the cost of collecting it was low and the income could be great.. A number of times in the intervening years it had been suggested to appertain such a measure to the colonies, but each time it was proposed, the colonial representatives in London had objected so strongly, that the matter was dropped.

Grenville took to the idea, and ordered Thomas Whately of the Treasury Department to begin preparation of a potential Stamp Act for the colonies. It was an extensive assignment as Whately had to discern what documents were used in each of the colonies, and then assign a tax to each separate type of document. To assist him in his assignment he requested guidance from a number of people, both in Britain and in the colonies for information on document usage in the colonies, thus alerting them a Stamp Act was being written and could become law. When Whately presented Grenville with a preliminary rendition of the act in late 1763, he saw at once it was unsatisfactory. It was obvious more work would have to be done; mainly to learn more of what documents were in actual use in the colonies, and what the value of each was, so an appropriate tax could be ascribed.

While Whately was busily gathering detailed information on colonial documents, Parliament was debating the content of a new, replacement Sugar Act which would set duties on sugar and molasses (and other commodities). When news of the debate on a new Sugar Act reached the colonies there was an immediate, but mixed reaction. Thomas Cushing, a prominent colonial politician, opined, *"if the Parliament should think fit to lower the Duty to an half penny or a penny per gallon (of molasses) the Duty would be cheerfully and universally paid."* Cushing was likely thinking that the lower figure was similar to the bribes the smugglers were now having to pay the customs agents to land the molasses needed to distill rum, and thus could be easily tolerated.

However, even the very loyalist lieutenant- governor, Thomas Hutchinson opposed the proposed duties on fundamental principles, as he said, *"Will not this be introductory to taxes and duties upon other articles?* Would it not, he continued, contravene the *"much esteemed privilege of English subjects—the being taxed by their own representatives?"*

James Otis heartily agreed with Hutchinson, *"as it will be conceding to the Parliament having a Right to Tax our trade which we can't by any means think of admitting, as it would be contrary to a fundamental Principal of our Constitution vizt. That all Taxes ought to originate with the people."* It was unclear to many in London why so many colonists assumed this strong objection to the proposed act as it was actually just an extension of the previous act that had not previously incited such reactions, and it had been law for decades. But now, the colonists were viewing themselves in a different light. Now, they were identities themselves, worthy citizens with rights of their own, and not just subservient subjects to a dominant Britain.

On March 9, 1764 Grenville presented his proposals to Parliament for a new Sugar Act. There were fifteen proposals made, fourteen of which concerned the details of the Sugar Act. It was the fifteenth that would later cause widespread unrest in the colonies. Grenville was well aware of the colonial objections to a Stamp Act and thus brought the matter up innocuously. Grenville had two goals in mind to accomplish for this part of his presentation: broach the idea of a Stamp Act for the colonies, and, secondly, to solidify the resolve of Parliament to pass it.

He began his discussion of the fifteenth proposal with the financial problem the country was facing due to its large deficit, and pointed out that a part of the deficit was directly attributable to the support the realm was providing the Provinces. It was, he continued, only fair they pay at least a part of that support, and a fair way to accomplish this, he informed them, would be a Stamp Act such as was already in existence in Britain for its citizens abiding there. He pointed out that if the colonies, being so adverse to a Stamp Act, could come up with an alternative way to cover the costs of their protection, he would be amenable to their suggestions. In this manner, Grenville placed the burden of avoiding a colonial stamp tax by Parliament squarely on the colonies themselves. While Grenville seemingly was offering the colonies a way to avoid Parliament's tax, it is likely he did not believe there was any feasible way to raise the necessary funds, except enacting a colonial Stamp Act. He was careful to say he was not asking for any action from Parliament at this time, but perhaps in another year some action might be required.

Grenville then issued a challenge that would resolve the issue of Parliament's belief that they had a right to tax the colonies when he *"hoped that the power and sovereignty of Parliament, over every part of the British dominions, for the purpose of raising or collecting any tax, would never be disputed. That if there was a single man doubted it, he would take the sense of the House, having heard without doors hints of this nature dropped."* When no one voiced any disagreement with his strong statement, the issue of Parliament's right to tax the colonies was inarguably resolved—at least as far as Parliament was concerned.

Many in the colonies were confused as to what Grenville was proposing. Was there to be a Stamp Act or not? Could there be an alternative to it that the colonies would find acceptable? There were no answers, only questions, but, in any case, it would be another year before the issue would be considered, time to digest the consequences and develop a response—or so the colonists thought.

After Grenville's first fourteen proposals were formally written into a Sugar Act, and in spite of the colonial objections, the Sugar Act (also known as the American Revenue Act) was passed by Parliament on April 5, 1764. The new act defined duties and restrictions on a number of items, such as coffee, indigo, and some fabrics, but the major impacts on the colonies were two:

The first was the placement of a three-penny a gallon duty on molasses imported from non-British sources. Although the duty halved the six-penny duty of the 1733 act, the new duty was to be vigorously enforced by the navy, and, as the naval officers received a bonus for every illicit cargo captured, the enforcement would indeed be vigorous. The second dealt with the export of lumber from the colonies to Europe. The act restricted the export of lumber from the colonies bound for Europe, solely to British ports. While the lumber could then be reshipped to other European ports, the restriction effectively raised the price of the colonial lumber significantly, reducing export.

After the actual passing of the Sugar Act, Hutchinson, Otis and others increased their opposition on constitutional grounds. They believed it was illegal under British law dating back to the middle ages, for Parliament to tax the American Colonies without being represented there. Otis warned that if

"Parliament have an equitable right to tax our trade...they have as good a one to tax our lands, everything else." New York, Virginia, and North and South Carolina likewise strongly objected to Parliament's action; all stating it was their "right" to tax their citizens only through the actions of their representative bodies.

In May 1764, Bostonian lawyer, Richard Dana, with help from a committee which included Samuel Adams, was assigned by the Boston Town Meeting of preparing written orders to the town's four representatives to the Massachusetts legislature. Sam Adams had been making fiery speeches against Parliament's action, and many of his words were included in the orders. The instructions included several penetrating questions that would be used in opposition:

> For if our Trade may be taxed why not our lands? Why not the Produce of our Lands & everything else we posses or make use of? This we apprehend annihilates our Charter Right to govern & tax ourselves. It strikes at our British privileges, which as we have never forfeited them, we hold in common with our Fellow Subjects who are Natives of Britain. If Taxes are laid upon us in any shape without our having a legal Representation where they are laid, are we not reduced from the Character of free Subjects to the miserable State of tributary Slaves?

While the most vehement voices against the duties objected to the taxation without representation argument, the economic impact for a number of colonies was severe, and they vehemently objected to the duties imposed. This was especially so for the New England colonies and New York. For example, consider the case of Rhode Island as reported in Edmund and Helen Morgan's book *The Stamp Act Crisis*:

> Rhode Island—consumed 120,000 pounds sterling of British manufactures every year and herself produced little more than 5,000 pounds sterling worth of exports. Only the profits from the molasses trade enabled the colony to pay for her consumption of British goods. As the British sugar islands could supply less than a fifth of the molasses that poured into Rhode Island's thirty distilleries, the other four-fifths must be French and subject to duty, the collection of which would entail a prohibitive increase in price and put an end not only to the molasses trade but to the distilling industry, the African trade in rum, and the sale of fish and produce in the West Indies, and consequently to the profits which British manufactures were drawing from Rhode Island.

The other colonies had similar accounts.

While not disagreeing with the other colonies regarding the questionable legality of the duties being imposed, the governor of Pennsylvania was disturbed by the British navy's energetic inspections, which extended to small boats plying the shallow waters along the shore and in bays. He felt it was inhibiting intra-colonial trade. It was the sort of irritant which angered many colonists, and added to the aggravation that was building against Britain's colonial rule.

That Grenville was insensitive to the colonies' financial problems is not surprising. Many in Britain were well aware the colonies were initially established as profit-making investments for English investors, and later were viewed as instruments to increase profitable trade for Britain under the mercantile system.

Colonial newspapers reported on protest meetings by Boston merchants who agreed to cease the purchase of British goods, and called on the other colonies to do likewise. Prominent citizens clamored for efforts to increase colonial manufacturing to replace the same goods presently imported from Britain.

Some of the loyalists resident in the colonies, such as the Massachusetts royal governor, Francis Bernard, realized the British attitude toward the colonies could not be sustained without causing a backlash of significant proportions. He warned his superiors in London that control of the colonies, and especially the relationship between Parliament and the colonies, would have to be altered to maintain effective British control. His pleas, however, fell on deaf ears as the pressure to rectify the British deficit, and bringing the colonies to task, seemed to dominate the reasoning of the politicians in London.

The opposition to the Sugar Act was vocal, but there was not universal agreement that the act was imposing a direct tax. It was considered by some to be, in reality, just a duty under the navigation laws, which would be a permissible action by Parliament. Otis argued against that concept stating it was a tax, even though external. Others, however, differentiated between an external duty and an internal (direct) tax. It wasn't a major disagreement, but it had the effect of confusing the opposition to the act in several places.

The adverse objections to the Sugar Act, however, paled in response to Grenville's next move to tax the American Colonies. The Prime Minister knew, even as the Sugar Act was being passed, that it was expected to raise only about 45,000 pounds annually, which was only a small percentage of the 220,000 pounds needed to support the British troops in North America, and much less than the total deficit. Thus, the result of Parliament's next action, The Stamp Act that Grenville had obliquely referred to in his speech of March, would be universally and clearly recognized as an internal tax enacted by Parliament, with no ambiguity about it.

Chapter Seventeen

A Turning Point—
The Stamp Act

The reaction in America to Grenville's proposal in March 1764 of a Stamp Act for the colonies was subdued. It was a year off and the colonies conceivably had an opportunity to come up with an alternative to reduce Britain's debt that would be more acceptable to them. The Massachusetts representative in London, Jasper Mauduit, wrote back to the Massachusetts Assembly that the much-discussed stamp act had been put off for another year. He added, *"Mr. Grenville being willing to give to the Provinces their option to raise that or some equivalent tax, Desirous as he express'd himself to consult the Ease, the Quiet, and the Goodwill of the Colonies."* Thus the colonies were lulled into a belief that a stamp act was not a sure thing, that they had time to come up with some other recourse.

Benjamin Franklin, who was recently arrived in London, was asked whether to avoid the colonial objection to being taxed unilaterally by Parliament, the colonies would request the Parliament to enact such a tax, so it could be construed to be their idea and not be forced upon them by Parliament. Franklin's immediate and definite reply was that possibility would be extremely unlikely. But, perhaps, he continued, if the British government were to ask for a specific sum from the colonies to offset the troop's support, they might be receptive to such a request.

That Grenville only casually and, not formally, requested the colonies to come up with an alternative to the proposed tax is illuminating. Left to themselves, the individual colonies would have a difficult time deciding what each colony would have to contribute to make up the whole amount expected. And, what was that whole Grenville would find acceptable? He would never say. Since the colonies were governed independently, they had few resources to coordinate an action such as Grenville was suggesting. If the Prime Minister was serious about his offer, the rational approach would have been for a London Ministry, who had the necessary information, to dictate what the total should be, and how much each colony should contribute, but this avenue was never taken.

As the months rolled by after Grenville's March speech, a number of colonial leaders became more apprehensive about the possibility of a Stamp Act, especially with the strong negative reaction they were witnessing from their citizens. The colonial representatives in London requested a meeting with the Prime Minister to clarify his intentions. On May 17, 1764, Grenville did meet with them. He was, however, still evasive as to what amount he would find acceptable for the colonies to contribute. In fact, in a recondite response to the question of how much would be sufficient, he responded, as reported by Edward and Helen Morgan in *The Stamp Act Crisis,*

> But Grenville, rather that stating the sum he wanted from them, now proposed that they assent in advance to the Parliamentary tax and thereby set a precedent for being consulted about any future taxes! He also spoke strongly of the difficulties which 'would have' attended any scheme of letting them tax themselves, as though that issue was closed.

It became obvious Grenville, in spite of his propitiate manner to the colonial representatives, meant to have his colonial Stamp Act no matter what alternatives the colonies may come up with. Thus, many in North America became more alarmed at the prospect of its reality. Grenville felt strongly that Parliament needed to enforce its authority over the colonies. He realized, especially from the proposals he had received from such loyalists in North America as Francis Bernard, the governor of Massachusetts Colony, that a prevalent feeling in America was one in which they considered their relationship with Britain as one where both segments of the realm, Britain and the Colonies, had separate governments, but were loyal to one King. It was, in fact, how they had operated for their whole existence. The British government, on the other hand, viewed the colonies as dependent satellites of the mother country, which were completely subject to British rule.

When members of the British Parliament started receiving formal petitions from the North America colonies asserting the British Parliament did not have the authority to tax them, Parliament did not take the normal course of objecting to the petitions, but more emphatically, they disdainfully refused to even hear them. They felt the colonies were exhibiting extreme hubris that was insulting and definitely in error—as they would soon be emphatically shown.

Although Grenville was likely pleased by Parliament's rejection of the colonies rejection of their authority, what was developing was a serious adversarial relationship between the North American colonies and the British government in general, and Parliament in particular.

That adversarial relationship between the colonies and Parliament was further breeched when Parliament passed a Currency Act that went into effect on September 1, 1764. The Act forbade any colony from issuing paper currency, which many had been doing for years with a positive effect on the colonial economy. With this new act, only gold, silver, or some other commodity of value (such as Virginia anointing tobacco as legal tender) could be used in trade or to pay taxes. The act greatly reduced the colonial money supply with its concomitant negative effect on the economy. It caused widespread dissent, and greatly exacerbated the ability of colonies to pay for their imports from Britain. The effect of the Currency Act being imposed at the same time a stamp tax was being proposed set up a great outburst of animosity toward Parliament and Britain.

On February 2, 1765, the colonial agents in London decided to make one last effort to deter the Prime Minister from bringing the stamp tax bill before the House of Commons. They reiterated their willingness to tax themselves to raise the funds needed for their support. They advised Grenville they objected to Parliament passing a tax bill for the colonies as it would effectively subvert the colonial assemblies and remove their power to govern themselves. Grenville was cordial but dismissive of their concerns. Like many others, Ben Franklin believed opposition to the Stamp Act was futile. As he stated to a friend, *"We might as well have hindered the sun's setting."*

On February 6, 1765, Granville went before the House of Commons to begin the debate leading to a vote on the Stamp Act. The tone of the debate soon made obvious Commons' resolve to pass the Stamp Act. This feeling of the Commons' members toward the Colonies is exemplified by Charles Townshend's remarks during the debate, as reported in the Morgan's *The Stamp Act Crisis*, *"And now will these Americans, Children planted by our Care, nourished by our Indulgence until they are grown to a Degree of Strength and Opulence, and protected by our Arms, will they grudge to contribute their mite to relieve us from the heavy weight of that burden which we lie under."*

Although Townshend's sarcastic question represented the majority view of the body, a colonial supporter, Colonel Isaac Barré, who had fought in the French and Indian War, took it upon himself to refute Townshend. He disagreed, point by point with the assertions Townshend had made, stating the colonists went to America to avoid British tyranny; they were not nourished by Britain's indulgence, but rather were neglected and prospered on their own initiative. They were not protected by British Arms, but rather nobly took up arms in England's defense. He referred to the colonists as "Sons of Liberty" for their valiant effort in pursuing their freedom and liberty. The words Barré spoke were well publicized in America and the Colonel was deemed an American hero.

The bill was brought before Commons for its first reading on February 13, 1765. The second reading occurred two-days later. At this reading several colonial agents presented petitions against the bill, but they were denied a hearing, Parliament strongly asserting its authority to pass the tax bill. After the third reading, the Stamp Act became law on March 22, 1765; it would take effect on November first.

The act assigned a tax to a variety of colonial documents including attorney licenses, college diplomas, bonds, deeds, mortgages, leases, contracts, bills of sale, liquor licenses, playing cards, pamphlets, newspapers, and almanacs. All of these documents were now required to carry a stamp, the value of which varied with the type of document, and varied from a few shillings to ten pounds for attorneys' licenses. The list of documents which had to carry a stamp was so broad that the colonists would be reminded of its imposition constantly. The tax for the stamps had to be paid in sterling and, while, it was promised that all of the sterling would stay in the colonies and be used to purchase provisions for the British troops stationed there, the colonists were not mollified by this gesture.

There was one provision of the act which outraged the Congregationalists with Puritan histories in New England, but also was of concern to all non-Anglican colonial religious denominations. The act did not specifically call for the establishment of ecclesiastical courts, which in England were used to adjudicate probate matters and were presided over by an Anglican Bishop, but it did impose a tax on documents in such courts. Even allusions to such a possibility aroused the New Englanders, and seemed to substantiate the rumors that an Anglican Bishop was to be appointed to their colonies. It may or not have had any substance, but it was a highly emotional topic that was deeply ingrained into the psyche of many New Englanders, as rejection of the Anglican Church was an integral component of their Puritan history. It was, after all, why they had left England in the first place.

Another facet of the Act that greatly troubled the colonists was the provision that a prosecutor could choose to bring a violation of the Stamp Act before an Admiralty Court, where a judge would adjudicate a case alone, without a jury, rather than a common-law court which had the option of a jury. While this provision was a part of the Sugar Act, it made no logical sense to be included in the Stamp Act. The Sugar Act considered itself with navigation and trade, and a part of it was written specifically to reduce smuggling; but the Stamp Act had little to do with navigation and trade. The provision was thus viewed as a punitive measure by Parliament against the colonies for their refusal to accept Parliament's sovereignty over them.

The colonial response to the adoption of the Stamp Act was efficiently summarized by Dr. Joseph Warren of Boston after the first reading of the act. In a March 19, letter he wrote to his Harvard college classmate Edmond Dana, who had moved to England,

> Never has there been a time since the first settlement of America, in which the people had so much reason to be alarmed as the present. The whole continent is enflamed to the highest degree. I believe this country may be esteemed as truly loyal in their principles as any in the universe; but the strange project of levying a stamp duty, and of depriving the people of the privilege of trial by jury, has roused their jealousy and resentment. They can conceive of no liberty when they have lost the power of taxing themselves, and when all controversies between the Crown and the people are to be determined by the opinion of one dependent man, and they think that slavery is not only the greatest misfortune, but that it is also the greatest crime if there be a possibility of escaping it.

The enactment of the Stamp Act was only partially due to the collection of funds to balance the costs of British troops in the colonies. While Parliament tied the cost of maintaining a British force in North America to the act; there was a much larger issue involved. To Parliament, the imposition of a tax on the colonies was a way to validate their power over the entire British Realm. Parliament had, not so long before, gained significant power in the governance of the country, and was not about to relinquish any authority it felt it had gained only with great difficulty. No longer did Parliament play a subservient role to the wishes and whims of a dominate monarch. No longer did its members fear facing a monarchial judge and being placed in a tower cell. Parliament was now in charge of setting the rules by which the nation operated. It prided itself at being a representative democratic body, with only the best interests of the nation at heart, and it was not about to be cowed by an imprudent cabal of provincials who did not know their place.

The view in the colonies was also about power, but with a different perspective. Each colony had a governor who was under the supervision of a King's minister, but each had control of their own laws (and taxes) through their representative assemblies. If they acknowledged Parliament's sovereignty over their rule of law, their assemblies would become infertile bodies with no real power except over the most mundane of local issues. Parliament, where the colonies had no representation, could pass laws and the king's ministers, through the colonial governors, could force compliance with them. They would not be able to exercise independent action, and thus be no different than a lowly vassal or slave in controlling their own affairs. They were goaded by anger and fear, and relenting was unthinkable.

It didn't help Colonial-Parliament relations when Parliament passed another act opposed by the majority of the colonies. On March 24, 1765, three days after enactment of the Stamp Act, Parliament passed a new Quartering Act, replacing the war-time version which had expired (it was slightly amended in 1766, adding the requirement to billet the soldiers in unoccupied houses, or taverns or inns). General Gage, in charge of the British troops in America, had petitioned for the new act, but it went even farther than he had requested. In this new act, each colony was required to provide shelter and substance (food, etc.) to British Troops stationed within its borders, supposedly to protect them. The costs for the troops were to be paid by each host colony. The colonies understood the stationing of troops during wartime, but there was no real war now, only some Indian uprisings which, by this time, had been greatly reduced. Therefore many colonists were suspicious about Parliament's true intent.

An understanding of the colonists negative reaction to the passage of the Quartering Act is found in an earlier response by Colonel Eliphalet Dyer, a lawyer from Connecticut, who, while visiting in London, had written back to a friend in the colonies about the Stamp Act,

> Mr. Grenville moved the House of Commons for Liberty to bring in a Bill in order to provide a Fund for Defraying the Expenses of protecting, securing and defending America, which contains the several Article of Duties mentioned in the enclosed Resolves. But may it not be concluded that those Regiments destined for America, for the support of which those Methods are taking are not primarily for our Defense (as they are undesired by us) but rather as a standing Army, to be as a Rod and Check over the Colonies, to enforce those Injunctions which are to be laid upon us, and at the same Time to oblige us to be at the Expense of their Support.

The Quartering Act was a nuisance, but did not produce the anxiety the colonists felt about the Stamp Act. The Stamp Act was immediately challenged. John Adams declared the Stamp Act unconstitutional under British law and was, therefore, illegal. To Adams and others it was simple: the colonists in America could not be taxed by the British Parliament because they had no representation there.

Grenville and others in London argued that the colonies did have representation in Parliament but it was a "virtual" representation. The Americans, he argued, were in a position similar to the boroughs of Leeds and Birmingham which did not have representative members in Parliament, but they were virtually represented by parliamentary members from other, similar boroughs that had interests similar to theirs.

This argument was rejected in the colonies as pamphlets and newspaper articles pointed out that even Leeds and Birmingham had representatives in Parliament as each English County had two members, and both towns could avail these members to make their charges known, while the North American colonies had none. Therefore Parliament could not legally tax them.

The colonial newspapers reported extensively on the effects of the Act, decrying the abuses Parliament was inflecting on the colonial citizens. The merchants in the colonies organized boycotts of British goods and promoted the manufacture of products in America that were, by necessity purchased from Britain. While the actions of the merchants were peaceful, not all followed this path.

In the lower room of the Green Dragon Inn in Boston's North End, a group of able men, shopkeepers, artisans, skilled workers, had met often in the past to discuss politics, and now the discussions were on the Stamp Act, and what they should do about it. It didn't take long for them to come to the conclusion they would have to take an active role in opposing the law as the only viable option available to them, to make their strong displeasure known. Originally known as The Loyal Nine, they had to find a more appropriate name as their numbers grew. They adopted the sobriquet first uttered by Colonel Barré in his defense of the colonies during debate on the Stamp Act in Parliament, and called themselves the "Sons of Liberty."

The Sons of Liberty agreed absolutely with the Virginia House of Burgesses, led by Patrick Henry, which had taken an action widely reported in the newspapers termed the "Virginia Resolves." The legislation declared that only the Virginia legislature had *"the Sole Right and Authority to lay Taxes and Impositions upon it's inhabitants: And, That every attempt to vest such Authority in any other Person or Persons whatsoever, had a Manifest Tendency to Destroy AMERICAN FREEDOM."*

On August 14, 1765, the Sons of Liberty hand-picked an obstreperous rabble-rouser from Boston's South End, named Ebenezer McIntosh, to lead a mob of laborers, seamen and many unemployed workers, in a demonstration against the detestable Stamp Act. In their first act of defiance they hung an effigy of the Massachusetts Stamp Collector, Andrew Oliver, on a tree on Newbury Street—ever since known as the Liberty Tree. The mob, ever growing and incited for action, took the effigy and marched to Oliver's business on Kilby Street by the water, and demolished the building there. Still riled, the mob proceeded to Oliver's residence and wrecked it as well. The mob was so large and boisterous that the sheriff was helpless to do anything to stop the raging vandalization. As the general population was in general agreement with the violent actions, the next day, Andrew Oliver wisely and prudently resigned as Stamp Collector.

Ten days later, on August 26th, the mob was out again and destroyed the houses of the Deputy Registrar of the Admiralty Court, Mr. Story, the Comptroller of Customs, Benjamin Hallowell, and the Lieutenant Governor, Thomas Hutchinson. There were rumors that Samuel Adams, James Otis and even John Adams were active in promoting the riots, but nothing was ever proven.

In the aftermath of the wreckage caused in Boston by the Sons of Liberty, new chapters of the organization formed in other colonies, and other rampages against persons favoring, accepting, or promoting the Stamp Act occurred. Disturbances with violence occurred in Rhode Island and New York. More subdued, but still threatening demonstrations occurred in most of the rest of the colonies. As a result, virtually all of the stamp collectors resigned or became unavailable for duty.

On October 7, 1765, a formal meeting of nine of the thirteen colonies was held in New York in what was called the Stamp Act Congress. The missing colonies likely just didn't get word of the conclave in time to send a representative. It was significant that the colonies felt it important to act in concert. The Albany Congress held during the French and Indian War did not yield a cooperative course of action among the colonies, but this time all could see the importance of organizing and maintaining a united front.

After three weeks, the Stamp Act Congress issued a fourteen-part Declaration of Rights and Grievances. It stated that the colonies could only be taxed by their own representative assemblies, and also addressed their objection to the Vice Admiralty Courts. The Declaration ended with a request for repeal of the Stamp Act.

With the enforcement of the Stamp Act so muted by the opposition against it, neither businesses nor courts could operate. British merchants, who were owed money by the colonists, could not collect anything due to the stoppage of activity. They were losing revenue from the lack of exports, and could not collect the debts owed them from previous transactions. The level of support for repeal of the Stamp Act was growing decidedly stronger in both America and Britain.

At the time opposition to the Stamp Act was growing violent, King George-III was concerned with a matter that had nothing to do with the Stamp Act. He had become ill early in 1765, but later recovered. Parliament was concerned that should George-III die, he had only an infant son to succeed him, and thus wanted to pass a bill naming a Regent should the King become incapacitated. The King did not want to enter a name for a potential Regent in the bill at the time for personal reasons that had to do with his brother. Prime Minister Grenville, unfortunately, assumed the King wanted to name his mother to the position. His mother was romantically linked with the Earl of Bute, Grenville's predecessor as Prime Minister, so Grenville feared that if the King's mother were named Regent, she would dismiss him and put Bute back in as Prime Minister (although it is doubtful Bute would even have accepted the role). Grenville managed to convince the King to agree to an amendment to the bill that would exclude his mother. After a while, the King realized his mother was being slighted and changed his mind. He asked

Grenville to re-insert her name, but he refused. The King later asked a friend in Lords, Lord Northington, to make the change, which was done.

The King, who never was fond of Grenville, was now very displeased with him, not because of the Stamp Act which was causing so much turmoil in the kingdom, but because of Grenville's actions in the Regency Act, which personally affected him. The King then set in motion the actions necessary to form a new administration, replacing Grenville. After Pitt again declined the position, the Marques of Rockingham was anointed Prime Minister to head a new administration in July 1765.

When word of the colonial riots arrived in London, the reaction in Parliament was mixed. Grenville was no longer the Prime Minister, but maintained his seat in the House of Commons from which he could be a portent force. Grenville and Townshend, and their supporters, condemned the American resistance and argued for stricter controls, using force if necessary. Saner heads realized the impractically of such an action that would require dispatching great numbers of British troops to America, so when Grenville, in December 1765 moved to formally condemn the colonies, his motion was rejected.

In December 1765, in the midst of the turmoil over the Stamp Act, General Gage, the British military commander in America, moved 1,500 troops to New York and requested the colony to comply with the new Quartering Act, and provide his troops with shelter and supplies, such as candles, vinegar, cooking utensils, beer (or cider) and bedding.

The New York assembly perceived the request as another tax (without representation) and turned down allocating any funds for Gage's troops, although they did provide some limited supplies. In London, the New York denial was seen as another example of colonial defiance of a lawful request by one of the King's representatives, and was deeply resented by many there.

Even with the displeasure over New York's action and the abhorrence of the destructive mob violence by the Sons of Liberty, Rockingham, the new Prime Minister, was being lobbied intensely by British merchants for repeal of the act. Their position was more significant in that the country was still imbedded in a post-war depression that was affecting the whole population. The problem Rockingham faced was how to repeal the Stamp Act, and yet not accede to the colonial view that Parliament had no right to tax them.

When Parliament re-convened in January 1766, the King further confused the matter in his opening speech when he declared Parliament had a constitutional authority to legislate, but also that measures should be taken to revive colonial trade. By his first point the king seemed to be agreeing that Parliament did have the right to tax the colonies, but in the second part he was asking them to repeal the Stamp Act.

Rockingham wanted Pitt's support for repeal as having the concurrence of the great commoner would be a great advantage, but he was unsure of how Pitt felt about the matter. In answer, Pitt made a forceful speech in Commons that finally defined his position. Near the start he stated emphatically, *"The Americans are the sons of, not the bastards, of England."* During a pause in his speech Grenville voiced his belief the Stamp Act was being used as a pretext for the colonists to seek independence, and that Pitt was unwittingly aiding their cause.

Pitt then continued with the dramatics for which he was noted, *"Gentlemen, Sir I have been charged with giving birth to sedition in America. They have spoken their sentiments with freedom against this unhappy act, and that freedom has become their crime."* With regard to taxing the colonies to acquire funds for the treasury, he said, *"I will be bold to affirm, that the profits to Great Britain from the trade of the colonies, through all its branches, is two millions (pounds) a year. This is the fund that carried you triumphantly through the last war."* Pitt then gave his unequivocal opinion of the Stamp Act, *"the Stamp Act be repealed absolutely, totally, and immediately...because it was founded on an erroneous principle."* However he then added, *"At the same time, let the sovereign authority of the country over the colonies be asserted in as strong terms as can be devised, and be made to extend every point of legislation whatsoever."* Obviously he did not consider taxing the colonies a part of government and legislature. It was a fine point that was never really resolved in the minds of many in the British Parliament.

Grenville and many other hard-liners rejected Pitt's opinion; stating emphatically Parliament did indeed have a right to tax the colonies. Rockingham, in attempting to balance the two sides, asked Parliament to approve a Declaratory Act which was a reaffirmation of Parliament's sovereignty over the colonies. While the act did not (on purpose) mention taxation, it included the words *"in all cases whatsoever."* Whether this phrase meant Parliament had the authority to levy a tax on the colonies was open to interpretation.

With the Declaratory Act satisfying many of Parliament's members, Rockingham got his repeal of the Stamp Act on economic grounds, on February 22, 1766 by a vote of 275 to 167. Thus ended, at least for the moment, one of the most significant episodes in British-Colonial relations. Although repeal gave instant economic relief, the fundamental issues were not resolved.

Left unanswered was Parliament's right to tax the colonies, and, in the opinion of many of the colonists, whether Parliament even had the right to legislate for them. In the issue of taxation, it was uncertain whether there was a distinction between internal taxes, which are taxes to raise revenue for the treasury, and external taxes, which are duties or fees imposed for the regulation of commerce.

It should be noted that, at this time, most of the North American colonists were not advocating outright independence from Britain. Rather, they were advocating a relationship with Britain that would allow them freedom from direct control by Parliament, but they would still pledge allegiance to the King, and continue as a fundamental part of the British Realm.

The repeal of the Stamp Act was greeted with jubilance throughout the American Colonies. There was a grand ball in Virginia, free drinks at the bars in Philadelphia; in New York some imbibed citizens even advocated erecting a statue to King George-III. While South Carolina also pondered erecting a statue it was not of the King, but of William Pitt. Bells rang across Boston, and John Hancock provided wine from his mansion to the mass of revelers on Boston Common for toasting the great victory.

Hancock was so revered for his generosity that in the next election, with support from Samuel Adams he was elected to the Massachusetts House. Sam Adams had nurtured Hancock, winning over the prosperous merchant to his views on opposing British Parliamentary rule over the colonies. Upon Hancock being elected, Sam commented to his second-cousin John, *"This town has done a wise thing today; they have made that young man's fortune their own."*

Samuel Adam's protégé, John Hancock had come from modest puritan stock to a position of wealth and prominence in 1766 Boston. His great-grandfather, Nathaniel Hancock, a shoemaker in Cambridge of the Massachusetts Bay Colony, was undoubtedly proud of his son John (our John Hancock's grandfather), who was admitted to Harvard in 1689. Nathaniel had lived in Cambridge since his birth in 1638, and none of the family had yet achieved this high academic honor since the family had arrived in the New World. With their Puritan heritage it was with pride that the family found one of their own accepted for study at the renowned Congregationalist University.

After graduation, the elder John began an honored career as a successful minister in North Cambridge. He was so well regarded by everyone he was called "Bishop," even though that title was not used in congregational churches as it smacked too much of Anglicanism or, even worse, of Catholicism. But the title seemed to fit the distinguished clergyman.

"Bishop" John married Mary Clarke, a minister's daughter from a prominent family in Chelmsford. John was also modestly successful in financial matters so that the Hancock's led a comfortable existence. Together John and Mary had five children. The first in 1702 was named John after his father. A year later, another son, Thomas was born followed two years later by a daughter Elizabeth. After a short hiatus, Ebenezer arrived in 1710 followed in 1713 by their last child, Lucy.

The area in North Cambridge where John was living and preaching had grown significantly since he first arrived fifteen years before. The growth was significant enough that North Cambridge broke from its parent community and reincorporated in 1713 as the separate town of Lexington.

While son John was sent to Harvard, the second son, Thomas, took another career path. It is likely that having two sons in Harvard at the same time would have been a financial burden for a minister, so Thomas left for Boston to seek his fortune. After graduation, John jr. tried to obtain appointment as minister in Westborough, but was not offered the position. In Congregational doctrine there was no ecclesiastical hierarchy to appoint ministers to individual churches; instead each congregation hired their own minister. After John missed out on the ministerial position in Westborough he instead took a position as librarian at Harvard. When the minister of Braintree died unexpectedly, the parishioners began a search for his replacement. Braintree was a well-established community with prominent citizens such as the Adams and Quincys as residents. It did not take them long to settle on the Harvard librarian, and on November 2, 1720 John jr. began the role he had always desired as the church's new minister.

It was important, as minister in a small town, to have a wife, so on December 13, 1733, John married the widow, Mary Hawke Thaxter of nearby Hingham. The couple settled into the town while John performed his ministerial duties faithfully, including baptizing one young John Adams in October 1734. The Hancock's family started with the birth of their first child Mary in 1735, followed by a son, another John, named after his father and grandfather, on January 12, 1737. The last child, Ebenezer arrived on 1741.

While John enjoyed the pastoral life as minister in Braintree, his brother Thomas had taken a much different road. More aggressive and determined than his older brother, upon his arrival in Boston at fourteen, he began an apprenticeship to a bookseller named Samuel Gerish. Thomas stayed at the book shop for seven years, learning the art of printing and binding books as well as the business aspects of the trade. In 1724 he took a trip to London to establish contact with British merchants, and to better understand the intricacies of trade, exploring areas beyond just books. Returning to Boston he opened his own bookshop and was instantly successful.

In 1727 he used his new found knowledge of commerce to ship a load of goods he and a friend had assembled, to Albany, New York. The endeavor was successful and soon he was attempting additional trades. With the attitude of a good entrepreneur, he joined with several other prominent Bostonians in the establishment of a paper mill just outside the city.

With his reputation and businesses growing, Thomas decided to marry. The bride was Lydia Henchmen, one of his partner's daughters and a member of a prominent central Massachusetts family. Thomas also became involved in politics, being elected a Boston constable. His business activities expanded to land speculation, and his shipping business grew significantly. He became, in a relatively short time, wealthy and prominent in the burgeoning port city of Boston.

He decided to move from the now crowded inner city, and had a mansion built on Beacon Hill which dominated the area. It was a magnificent Georgian structure with gardens that stretched down the slope to the Boston Commons. As testament to the role he now played in the community, in 1739 he was elected one of Boston's selectmen. Alas, however, with a spacious mansion to call home the couple was childless.

While Thomas had prospered beyond all expectations, life was not so kind to his two brothers. Ebenezer died in 1741 and brother John, with his large family in Braintree, died suddenly in 1744. When a minister in a small Massachusetts town died, his family had to vacate the ministerial house the town provided so the new minister could move in. With no other place to go, Mary took her children and moved in with the senior Bishop John Hancock at his residence in Lexington.

At the time of his younger brother's death, Thomas had become more involved in shipping goods in a large scale throughout the world. While the earnings from his lawful business were substantial, there were rumors of large profits being made with smuggled cargos. At the time, smuggling was endemic to New England, and while no specific instances are found linking Thomas directly with smuggling, he was very likely a conscious participant.

Thomas had always helped his family and now, with his brother gone, he took in the eight-year old John Hancock to live in the mansion with him and his wife Lydia. Aunt Lydia welcomed the young man and treated him like her own, doting on his every need. The young man was sent to Boston's prestigious Latin School to begin his education. As he grew up, the young lad took to his privileged life. He watched and learned as his uncle participated in business and politics.

In 1750 he was sent to Harvard. He was a good student, and well-liked by his classmates. He did get into a bit of trouble when, with several of his classmates, he got a slave very drunk. Other than that episode, his academic years were uneventful. He acquired his Bachelor's Degree in July 1754.

While his birth mother would likely have wanted him to become a minister like his father, John had been exposed to the active, exciting life his uncle lived, and that was where he was going. The French and Indian War was profitable for the Hancock's business, and it was expanding as young John got more involved in the company's activities. He was sent to London in June 1760 to meet with prominent merchants and government officials.

He enjoyed the time there, frequenting the theater and taverns such as those at Covent Gardens. He spent funds lavishly, for which he was unapologetic when asked about it by Uncle Thomas.

George II died while John was in England, and there was talk about the young man remaining there for the coronation, but it was decided he should return to Boston in July 1761. Before he left he negotiated an important agreement with a prominent British government contractor named Mathew Woodford. The contract made Hancock's company the American contact for Woodford's business activities. Getting the agreement signed was well received by Uncle Thomas.

When he arrived back in Boston, John found his uncle, while not desperately ill, still not his old active self. John's business success in London and his continually growing involvement in Thomas' business activities greatly pleased the old man. With his ever-growing confidence in his young nephew, on January 1, 1763, Thomas made a formal announcement for all of Boston to notice: *"I have this day Taken my nephew Mr. John Hancock into Partnership with me having had long Experience of his Uprightness (and) great abilities for business."*

After this formal announcement, Thomas turned over more of the day-to-day operations to his successor, who readily accepted the responsibilities. On August 1, 1764, Thomas went to a meeting in the State House where he collapsed and died. Cash, some land, and assorted items were willed to other relatives, slaves, Harvard and charities, but the business and the components of it were given to John. The mansion on Beacon Hill was left to Lydia, but she gave it to John with the proviso she be allowed to live there for the rest of her life, a condition John willingly agreed to. Young John Hancock thus became one of the wealthiest citizens of Boston, and also a convert to Samuel Adams' convictions regarding colonial independence.

Chapter Eighteen

Challenge of the Townshend Acts

The feeling in the colonies following the repeal of the Stamp Act was one more of satisfaction than relief, and the boycott of British goods was ended. To most colonists the issue had always been the continued importance and relevance of their colonial assemblies. The defeat of the Stamp Act was a reaffirmation of the right of colonial citizens to be taxed only by their own representatives. They were well aware of the near simultaneous (and overwhelming) passage of the Declatory Act which affirmed Parliament's power to make laws and statues which would be binding on the American Colonies *"in all cases whatsoever."* However, they believed that act was merely a face-saving gesture by an embarrassed Parliament, and would be of little real effect on them. Although the colonists recognized the discontent of many of the parliamentary members such as George Grenville and Charles Townshend, they underestimated the depth of that discontent. Many in London were incensed by the manner in which the Americans defied parliamentary law, and won repeal through mob violence and intimidation of the stamp collectors.

Unaware or ignoring the animosity brewing in London's governmental offices, the colonists continued to defy or subvert British law in a number of, generally minor, instances that continued to unsettle relations on the two sides of the Atlantic. In addition to New York's denial of Gage's request for troop lodging and supplies under the Quartering Act, other controversies occurred. When the British Secretary of State, Henry Conway strongly requested (demanded?) the Massachusetts Assembly compensate the victims of the mob actions which destroyed their homes and businesses, the assembly willfully complied, but they added a clause in the statue giving a "free and general" pardon to all of the rioters. Since it was normally the crown's prerogative to show mercy in civil uprisings, the action was considered an insult.

In this discordant time the British government itself was undergoing a significant alteration that would cause further discord between Britain and her American Colonies. The repeal of the Stamp Act spelled the end of Rockingham's tenure as Prime Minister. The King had a perception of him as inept, and, like Grenville before him, the King had a personal dispute with his Prime Minister. George III had promised his brothers they would be given a tidy allowance. However, Rockingham told the monarch the matter could not be brought up until the following year because the extensive debate on colonial problems did not allow time to address it. George III was considerably upset with Rockingham as he stated, *"Rockingham wants me to break my word, which I cannot do."* Thus, the King formally dismissed him on July 9, 1766.

The King had always had a distorted view of what, to him, was a discordant Parliament. His view of the body was of cliques of disagreeing ministers who, in the King's opinion, seemed to have more loyalty to a political party or to some official they depended upon for patronage than they did to the realm. Without a strong Prime Minister to bring order to the government, the King believed, the country could not effectively address the important issues it faced, both internally and externally. It was why the King so desired the commanding William Pitt to agree to become Prime Minister. After many entreaties by George III, Pitt finally agreed to form a new government. While Pitt did agree to the King's request, he had several conditions to his service that only caused more problems.

Pitt was not in good health at the time, some even questioned his mental state. He agreed to form and run a new government, but he would do it not as First Lord of the Treasury, the office held by past Prime Ministers, as Pitt coveted a peerage. In a surprising move, the desperate King granted him a peerage and Pitt became Lord Privy Seal as Lord Chatham. He would now serve in Parliament in the House of Lords as Earl of Chatham, not in Commons as William Pitt. Removing himself from the Commons where he was considered a strong debater, and where he had exhibited considerable influence, he would now be in the House of Lords away from the more intense action of government.

As First Lord of the Treasury, the office previous Prime Ministers had held, Pitt (or Chatham) selected the young, relatively inexperienced, Duke of Grafton. In turn, Grafton wanted Charles Townshend as Chancellor of the Exchequer to manage the government's finances. Pitt-Chatham (this is how he will be referred to herein) was not overly enthusiastic about the appointment, but went along with Grafton's wishes. It was an assignation that was to prove disastrous for Britain, and difficult for the American Colonies. With Pitt-Chatham not in prime health it fell to Grafton to run the government. Unfortunately, he would do this from his position in Parliament's House of

Lords which would give Townshend more influence with his position in the House of Commons where tax laws originated.

As the new government took office, it became apparent almost immediately the King would not have as well controlled nor smoothly operating administration as he envisioned when he convinced Pitt-Chatham to form it. Pitt-Chatham's health problems worsened and he spent considerable time away from London in the spas at Bath. Grafton, as acting Prime Minister, proved inadequate to the task, being overwhelmed by Townshend and others.

Townshend was a tall and imposing figure, with a loud, confident voice and a hearty laugh. He was charming, and much sought out for social companionship. However, some considered him undependable and shallow. He so sought accolades from his colleagues that he would strive to satisfy what he thought they sought. Thus, with the strong resentment of many in Parliament to the repeal of the Stamp Act, he was inclined to take some action to appease these feelings.

Early in 1767, Townshend, as the minister in charge of the government's finances, presented his budget for the year to a session of Parliament. In his presentation he acknowledged the common view that Britain's landowners were being taxed excessively, but he felt a discussed reduction in the land tax from four shillings to three would have to be put off for another year as the deficit had to be reduced. However, George Grenville and the ex-Exchequer, William Dowdeswell, in a move they knew would cause problems for the new administration, offered the opinion that there was no real reason the reduction could not indeed be accomplished immediately, and called for a vote on the matter. Not surprisingly, since many in Parliament would benefit from the reduction in taxes, it passed by a vote of 204 to 188. The impact of the reduction would result in the loss of 500,000 pounds annually to the country's revenue and significantly increase the deficit. Pitt-Chatham was furious with Grafton and Townshend for letting the vote happen, but his health kept him from any stronger involvement. Townshend was therefore forced to look elsewhere for funds.

Charles Townshend was an acknowledged brilliant intellect, and a master debater in Commons. In May 1767, he is acknowledged to have given one of the wittiest, most compelling speeches the Commons had ever heard. Known as the "Champagne Speech" as it was purportedly given after Townshend and several others had finished some champagne just prior to a Commons session. It wasn't a speech directed to some essential aspect of governance, but did give Townshend the accolades he sought from his fellow parliamentarians. His speech of importance to the colonies occurred less than a week later when he presented his proposals for raising funds from the American Colonies to offset the loss of revenue from the land tax.

Townshend was insightful enough to recognize the strong revulsion the Americans had to "direct" taxes, but seemed to accept the premise that Parliament could impose "indirect" taxes such as was done to regulate trade. He thought himself clever as he couched his new revenue act as imposing "duties" or external taxes, which the colonies would find acceptable. The revenue from the new duties would only amount to 40,000 pounds for the first year, but Townshend argued that once the colonies became used to being taxed, additional levies would be made later, raising the total.

Townshend's plan was received with mixed reaction in Parliament. Many in the body were still angry over the manner in which the Stamp Act had been repealed and desired to force some sort of compliance from the colonies acknowledging Parliaments right to pass laws binding on them. Others were not so sanguine about the success of such an approach. Edmund Burke voiced the opinion that the Americans would not be fooled by the ploy of defining the taxes as external. George Grenville went even further stating *"The Americans will laugh at you."* Having learned from the problems with the Stamp Act, Grenville proposed that instead of the taxes Townshend was proposing, the colonies should be assessed 400,000 pounds to cover imperial costs of their administration, and require they decide how to raise the funds. However, on May 15, 1767, Parliament approved Townshend's plan by a vote of 180 to 88 allowing him to proceed with the writing of formal statutes which would be enacted into law.

The full measure of Townshend's plan was defined in three actions that would be employed against the colonies; although Parliament added a fourth that strengthened enforcement. The first of Townshend's acts was one that suspended the New York Assembly from enacting any laws until it complied with all provisions of the Quartering Act. The second was to pass a Revenue Act that would institute duties on items the colonies had to import from Britain. The third was to establish a tough new Board of Customs Commissioners in Boston to insure collection of the duties. The fourth action, taken by Parliament separately from Townshend's plan, was to create additional Admiralty Courts to prosecute violators who attempted to evade the duties.

The first section, The Suspending Act, stated:

…whereas the house of representatives of his Majesty's province of New York in America have, in direct disobedience of the authority of the British Legislature, refused to make provision for supplying the necessaries and in the manner required by the said act:…That from and after the first day of October, one thousand seven hundred and sixty-seven, until provision shall have been made…it shall not be lawful for the governor, lieutenant governor, or person presiding or acting as governor or commander-in-chief,…the making or passing of any act of assembly;…to pass or make any bill, order, or resolution…until provision shall have been made for supplying his Majesty's troops with necessities as aforesaid…

Knowing the Sustaining Act was about to be passed by Parliament in July 1767, on June 6, 1767 New York relented and voted to provide the required supplies to Gage's troops. Their intent was to comply with the Quartering Act by an act of their own legislature, before the Revenue Act was passed, thus avoiding any appearance that Britain's Parliament was legislating the action.

The second provision of Townshend's statutes was the measure that had the most impact on the colonies. The Townshend Revenue Act was passed by Parliament on July 2, 1767. It was to take effect on November 20, 1767. The act imposed duties on articles imported into the American Colonies from Britain: such things as tea, paper, paint, glass, and several other items. The act detailed a number of items that were to be taxed, for example: *"For every hundredweight avoirdupois of crown, plate, flint, and white glass, four shillings and eight pence."* Or *"For every hundred weight avoirdupois of pasteboards, mil-boards, and scale boards made in Great Britain, two shillings and three pence."* Between these two articles were sixty distinct items for which duties would be required.

The colonists' distinction between "internal" and "external" taxes was misunderstood in London. The colonists' view was that ANY tax, no matter how defined, which was imposed to raise revenue for the treasury, was constitutional only if enacted by their own representative assemblies. Thus, when Townshend's revenue act began with the statement: *"WHEREAS it is expedient that a revenue should be raised in your Majesty's dominions in America for making a more certain and adequate provision for defraying the charges of the administration of justice, and the support of civil government, in such provinces where it shall be found necessary..."* it was apparent this was a direct tax to raise revenue no matter how it was cloaked.

Since the act itself stated it was enacted to raise revenue, it was strongly and vocally opposed by the colonists in America. And, just raising revenue wasn't all that concerned the colonials. The act reiterated the use of writs of assistance that could be used to discover smuggled goods by stating explicitly,

> ... it is lawful for any officer in his Majesty's customs, authorized by writ of assistance under the seal of his Majesty's court or exchequer, to take a constable, headborough, or other public officer inhabiting near the place, and in the daytime to enter and go into any house, shop, cellar, warehouse, or room or other place, and, in case of resistance, to break open doors, chests, trunks, and other packages there...

The purpose of the Revenue Act, like the Stamp Act before it, was to acquire funds in the colonies for the support of troops stationed there for their protection. But another new clause in the act was especially disturbing to the colonists. It stated: *"...to cause such monies to be applied, out of the produce of the duties granted by this act, as his Majesty or his successors, shall think proper or necessary, for defraying the charges of the administration of justice, and the support of the civil government, within all or any of the said colonies or plantations."* It meant that the funds collected by the duties would be used to pay for royal appointees to the colonies, such as governors, lieutenant-governors, judges, and a myriad of other officials. In the past, funds for these appointees were granted by the colonial assemblies. It would be a serious loss of control by the colonial assemblies over those appointed to administer them.

The final two provisions were designed to insure compliance. Prior to the act, the customs administration in the colonies was handled by a team of four Surveyors-General acting under the supervision of a London-based Board of Commissioners. This arrangement did little to stop the widespread smuggling so prevalent in the colonies, especially in New England. Under the new act, a Board of five Custom Commissioners, acting under the superintendence of Britain's Lords of the Treasury, was to be established in Boston which would have far ranging power in the collection of the duties. It would hire the customs agents needed for enforcement, and they would be present at all major ports. They had the authority to open or close ports at will. They had the support of the navy, and could hire informants (who would be rewarded with a part of any smuggled goods confiscated) who could identify a suspected ship the navy would then intercept.

To prosecute violators of the act, new Admiralty Courts were to be established in Boston, Philadelphia and Charleston. Thus, serious transgressors would no longer be required to be brought before the Admiralty Court in Halifax, which had proven too distant to be effective.

It is sensible that Townshend knew full well the Americans would not accept the tax merely under the shallow pretext that this was an "external" tax. By explicitly stating in the act that is was for the purpose of generating revenue, and by the severe provisions for insuring collection with the new Board of Custom Commissioners and additional Admiralty Courts, it was obvious the members of the British Parliament had decided they would indeed force the American Colonists to comply with the new tax. That the act did not conform to the intent of the old mercantile system, which was set up to increase commerce for British merchants, is not surprising. In fact, it worked against such goals. It was a thinly disguised assertion of the British government's power over the American Colonies, and inherently defied them to resist.

Ben Franklin, resident in London when Townshend's plan was presented to Parliament, was very disturbed by the hostile temper he found, not only among Parliament's members, but also in the British press, and even among average Englishmen. Many Britons reading the papers of the day read accounts that declared they were being taxed heavily to support colonists, who selfishly declined to provide any financial assistance to the British treasury in return for that support. At the same time the Britons underestimated the Americans resolve to resist, ignoring accounts from royalists in America, such as New England's governor, Francis Bernhard, who warned of rebellious sentiments in his colony that were growing stronger and bolder.

In a curious twist of history, Charles Townshend never saw his infamous acts go into effect. On September 4, 1767, he came down with a fever, likely typhoid, and died suddenly, over a month before the law was to be enforced. Townshend was succeeded as Chancellor of the Exchequer by thirty-five year old Frederick North, who, like Townshend, would serve in the House of Commons. Lord North (his title was a courtesy) had a close resemblance to King George III, a not so flattering comparison. The resemblance led to rumors, unfounded, that the two were somehow related. The new Chancellor, by all accounts was an amiable, well-liked Member of Parliament. Knowledgeable, good-humored; he had exhibited financial skills in the past that suited him well in his new assignment. Most of his contemporaries approved heartily of his appointment. He was also well-liked by the King, who found him one of the few parliamentarians with whom he was comfortable.

With Townshend gone and Pitt-Chatham still unable to serve actively, the King was concerned about the stability of his government. In January 1768 he changed several of his ministers, trying to find some sort of harmony among the infighting going on by powerful individuals to protect positions they were in, or to win the best posts for friends who had the same views. The King, with no good options he could see, kept Pitt-Chatham as the Prime Minister, if in name only, as his health relegated him to the periphery of governmental activity. The King kept the Duke of Grafton, Pitt-Chatham's protégé as First Lord of the Treasury and ersatz Prime Minister. Many of the new ministers did not have the same respect for the acting Prime Minister as they had for the redoubtable Pitt-Chatham, nor his tractable views regarding the American Colonies. Of more importance to the king, since Grafton had proven incapable of strong leadership in the Commons, Lord North would be the king's man in that important body.

The administration of the American colonies was under Lord Shelburne, the Secretary of State for the Southern Department. In a highly political move that was done partially to remove Shelburne, a new ministry was created specifically for the American Colonies alone. Shelburne was a close ally of Pitt-Chatham, and held views regarding the colonies similar to his. Grenville, the Duke of Bedford and others advocated a stronger approach to governing the American colonies, and wanted to remove him from that post. With the king's approval, a new ministry was created, appropriately entitled the Secretaryship for the American Colonies. The incumbent of the old ministry, Shelburne, was given a lesser post, and the person appointed to head the new department was Wills Hill, an Irish peer known as Lord Hillsborough. Hillsborough was appointed to the position even though the King seemed to have a low opinion of him, saying on one occasion, *"never met a man of less judgment than Lord Hillsborough."* Hillsborough was considered haughty and elitist, but he was close to George Grenville, and shared his view that the colonies must be forced to accept Parliamentary laws.

Chapter Nineteen

Defiant Colonial Reactions

The Townshend Acts affected a new perception among many far-thinking Americans regarding their relationship with the mother country. Many, such as Ben Franklin and others, felt British sovereignty over America could not remain as it had been in the past in which the colonies were subservient to Britain in nearly all matters. With a broad, verdant territory to the west, which many colonists were already exploiting in spite of the Royal Proclamation of 1763 reserving the territory for the Native American tribes, and a vigorous, expanding population, there would come a day, many thought, when America would become more populous, and likely even economically stronger than the land-locked island nation that birthed them. There was a feeling of strength growing among the colonial populace that was generally unrealized in Britain.

Certainly the British merchant class was concerned that America was growing prosperous at a more rapid rate than the home nation. There was no doubt, in 1767, that Britain was much stronger economically and militarily than their American Colonies, but those who could see into the future, perceived changes that could alter the balance between them. It is probable there was even some envy in England with the robustness the colonials were exhibiting. In fact, for many years the colonials exhibited greater overall health and longer average lives that did the citizens in England.

It is often argued among historians whether the drive for independence by the American colonies was born of an inner desire to become free from Britain; to form a new nation with a unique character embodying laws unentangled with the restraints of the monarchy. Or, whether the colonists were driven to independence by unwise, oppressive actions by Britain's King and Parliament. For those advocating the latter, the Townshend Acts are one of the major evidences offered to make their point. Coming right after the colonists had rebuffed the imperious actions of the Stamp Act, the new laws were proof to many the mother country was not promoting the Americans' best interests.

It was Parliament's intent to force the colonists to bend to its will; the majority passing the acts in the belief it was necessary to take strong measures now or they would forever lose any hope of ruling their colonies. Parliamentary moderates were told that later, perhaps, after the colonies complied with the new laws, there could be a lessening of the iron grip. In the colonies, however, there was little talk of compliance. They had underestimated Parliament's dedication to forcing laws on them, and realized they would have to take action now or forever become, as many opined, merely slaves to Britain. There was, thus, a sense of urgency on both sides of the Atlantic.

Talk of Boycotts of British imports began as the new duties were about to be enforced upon the landing of the first goods after the November 20, 1767 enforcement date. At a Boston Town meeting on October 28, 1767 an agreement was prepared and passed that pledged all signers not to buy a list of articles made in Britain and, instead, make an effort to purchase goods produced in the colonies. Copies of the agreement was dispatched to all the other New England towns as well as the main centers in the rest of the colonies.. The agreement, however, was loosely applied, and did not include and did not address concordant action by the major merchants. It did, however, arouse notice by the merchants in Britain.

In addition to the boycott of British goods, a number of efforts were begun to increase the capabilities and capacities of American manufactures. In Boston, people diligently saved rags to be made into paper for the Boston Gazette. Other efforts were made in cloth, clothes, shoes, and a number of other commodities.

The five new royal customs commissioners arrived in Boston on November 5th, 1767 to prepare for collection of the new duties on goods imported from Britain, which would arrive after November 20th. Some of the local Bostonians advocated treating the new commissioners in the same manner as shown the Stamp Act Collectors, which included physical attacks on their person and residences. However, while the Stamp Act Collectors were local men, these new commissioners were representatives of the King. Many, like James Otis, advised against any violent action, *"to insult and tear each other to pieces was an act like madmen."*

The commissioners clearly perceived this hostility and asked Governor Bernard for protection. The threats, although never consummated were real. As Bernard reported to London, *"Mr. Burch* (one of the royal commissioners) *had a large Number of men with Clubs assembled before his Door great Part of the Evening, and he was obliged to send away his Wife & Children by a back Door."* Charles Paxton, a Boston native and one of the new commissioners was friendly with many of the members of Parliament, and had been close to Charles Townshend. Paxton and Bernard both wrote letters to Lord Hillsborough demanding protection. They also sent letters to General Gage and to Commodore Samuel Hood, who was stationed in Halifax with a part of the British Fleet.

While the commissioners were not physically accosted, they were certainly not cordially welcomed by most of the city's citizenry. To provide a warmer welcome for them, Bernard and other local high-ranking royal officials, held formal and semi-formal receptions and dinners for them. Some, such as John Hancock, refused to attend any function at which the commissioners were present. Since Hancock was a prominent elected official, his non-attendance was considered an insult to the royal commissioners.

While the commissioners were settling in to assume their duties, a seemingly innocuous series of articles, written by a Pennsylvanian named John Dickenson was published. In a series of magazine articles that first appeared on December 2, 1767 in *The Pennsylvania Chronicle and Universal Advisor*, Dickenson articulated the Americans rationale for strongly opposing the new revenue acts.

Dickenson was a well-to-do lawyer and politician whose family had estates in both Pennsylvania and Delaware. He had received an education of the privileged in Delaware before traveling to London where he spent four years studying law at the prestigious Middle School. It was in England where he acquired his deep respect for the English "constitution," that body of rights and duties of British citizens that were embodied in compacts between the monarchy, the parliament and the citizenry, which were written over many years. He also had a natural love of history and intently studied the relationships between a government and its citizens that had so impacted Britain throughout its evolution.

Upon returning to America he moved to Pennsylvania where he started a career in law, and became involved in politics, serving in Pennsylvania's assembly. He had become angry with Britain's Parliament for the passage of the Stamp Act as he thought it went against the principles of English law. He served as a Pennsylvania representative to the Stamp Act Congress that demanded repeal of the act, but his opposition to Parliament did not include independence for the colonies. He felt the best solution would be a lawful accommodation between the colonies and Britain that would insure constitutional rights for the Americans, yet acknowledge allegiance to the mother country and the monarchy.

With passage of the Townshend Acts, Dickenson was motivated to begin his series of articles which were entitled, *Letters from a Farmer in Pennsylvania to the Inhabitants of the British Colonies*. Twelve installments were published under the original title that were widely read in the American Colonies, in Britain, and even in foreign countries across Europe.

Dickenson began his narrative with humility, *"I am a farmer, settled, after a variety of fortunes, near the banks of the river Delaware, in the province of Pennsylvania....I believe I have acquired a greater share of knowledge in history, and the laws and constitution of my country, than is generally attained by men of my class."*

His first article addressed his concern with the Sustaining Act by which the New York Assembly was suspended. In this, as in all of his writing, his approach is directed to the legal intricacies of the act, and why it is not in accordance with British law.

> If the BRITISH PARLIAMENT has a legal authority to order, that we shall furnish a single article for the troops here, and to compel obedience to that order; they have the same right to order us to supply those troops with arms, cloths, and every necesiary , and to compel obedience to that order also; in short, to lay any burdens they please upon us....In fact, if the people of New-York cannot be legally taxed, but by their own representatives, they cannot be legally deprived of the privileges of making laws, only for insisting on that exclusive privilege of taxation.

Dickenson went on to suggest the matter could have been taken care of in a different manner. *"It was not necessary that this suspension should be caused by an act of parliament. The crown might have restrained to governor of New-York, even from calling the assembly together, by its prerogative in the royal governments."* His point is that he objects to the British legislature taking the action, which he considers against British law, but it might have been agreeable if the King had taken unilateral action. Parliament passing the law was, *"pernicious to American freedom, and justly alarming to all the colonies."*

In his adherence to the rule of law, he abhorred what he saw as improper behavior by the violence shown by the citizens of New England in general, and those in Boston in particular during the opposition to the Stamp Act. However, he also believed, as did many others in America, that the New Englanders were critical to the opposition to the new duties. After publication of his first article he wrote to James Otis in Boston,

> The Liberties of our Common Country appear to me to be at this moment exposed to the most imminent Danger; and this Apprehension has engag'd me to lay my Sentiments before the Public in Letters of which I send you a copy... Only one has yet been publish'd and what there Effect may be, cannot yet be known, but whenever the Cause of American Freedom is to be vindicated, I look

towards the Province of Massachusetts Bay. She must, as she has hitherto done, first kindle the Sacred Flame, that on such occasions must warm and illuminate the Continent.

His next letter dealt with the passage of the Revenue Act, and here there was no equivocation. *"There is another late act of parliament, which seems to me to be a destructive to the liberty of these colonies, as that inferred in my last letter....It appears to me to be unconstitutional."* With regard to the issue of the Revenue Act defining the taxes as duties, he concludes the duties could be imposed, *"to preserve or promote a mutually beneficial intercourse between the several constituent parts of the empire...but added... the raising of revenue thereby was never intended."* Dickenson thus called into question the right of Parliament to impose "duties" just to raise revenue. *"This I call an innovation; and a most dangerous innovation."*

He also addressed the lack of glass and paper manufacture in the colonies which would preclude its production locally. He expresses the distress the colonies must face either by not importing British glass and paper, or by admitting the legality of the act. He admits Britain's right to have some control in trade, navigation and manufacture, but not to tax them. Specifically, he warns,

> Here then, let my countrymen ROUSE themselves, and behold the ruin hanging over their heads! If they ONCE admit, that Great-Britain may lay duties upon her exportations to us, for the purpose of levying money on us only, then will have nothing to do, but to lay those duties on the articles which she prohibits us to manufacture—and the tragedy of American liberty is finished.

Dickenson ends this letter with a bit of dramatic flair.

> *The single question is, whether the parliament can legally impose duties to be paid by the people of these colonies, only FOR THE SOLE PURPOSE OF RAISING A REVENUE, on commodities which she obliges us to take from her alone; or, in other words, whether the parliament can legally take money out of our pockets, without our consent?*

In the rest of his letters, Dickenson argued for a rational settlement of the dispute between the colonies and Britain, which was in character for him as a strong advocate of British law and a citizen of the British colonies. He further emphasized the danger to their future liberties were the colonies to accept the duties, and decried the impertinence and disrespect for colonial citizens some in the British government had exhibited. He called for a unified action by all of the colonies to resist parliament's attempt to illegally tax them.

The articles were widely reproduced and read in all of the American colonies, having a significant influence on the populace. Even in Britain, they were read with interest and created some sympathy for the American objections to Parliament's action. While the articles were of great influence on both sides of the Atlantic, another action, two months after Dickenson's first article, taken this time in New England, by Samuel Adams, James Otis, jr. and several others, inflamed emotions in Britain against the Americans.

In response to the passage of the Townshend Acts, a committee of the Boston Town Meeting was held to draft a response. The meeting chaired by James Otis, jr, and attended by Samuel Adams, Thomas Cushing, and Thomas Hawley of the Massachusetts Assembly, prepared a polite petition to the king, entreating the monarch for relief from the Townshend Acts. In addition, with Sam leading the way, they prepared a letter which would be sent to all of the other colonies to explain the Massachusetts position and to elicit responses from the other colonies. The Massachusetts Assembly approved the petition to the King on January twelfth and it was dispatched to London.

Samuel Adams had already made a name for himself in his opposition to the Sugar and Stamp Acts, and had become well-known to the British. His opposition to both the Sugar and Stamp Acts had branded him a radical. In fact, by this time in his life Adams was likely one of just very few who had come to the conclusion that the American colonies had to become independent of Britain if they were to prosper. So it was no surprise when Adams, along with James Otis, jr., Thomas Cashing, and Joseph Hawley, created, what was seen in Britain as the notorious Circular Letter.

There was some friction between Otis and Adams as Otis claimed ownership of the letter by stating, *"I have written them all, and handed them to Sam Adams to quieuvicue* (edit) *them."* It was a dubious boast and many, such as John Adams were concerned with Otis' behavior, questioning his mental health. In his erratic ranting Otis, was, at times, voicing strong allegiance to Britain, while at other times relentless in his disparagement of Parliament and its members.

The purpose of the Massachusetts Circular Letter was to define the concerns Massachusetts had with the Townshend Acts in a manner that would allow all of the other colonies to address the issues, and to promote an open discussion. Adams asked the Massachusetts Assembly for approval to send the letter to the other colonies on January 21, 1768. Many of the delegates were apprehensive about issuing such a document, fearing a hostile reaction from London, and, as a result, the motion to send failed.

Working behind the scenes, Adams convinced most of the assembly members that it was time to take action, and respond to Massachusetts' Governor Bernard's directive to rescind the Circular Letter. Adams chose the timing for a vote on the matter well, as many of those who had opposed the letter earlier, had returned to their farms leaving the urban Bostonians, who agreed with Adams' sentiments, in a majority. Thus, on February 4, 1768 the assembly concurred, and the letter was sent to the other colonial assemblies. The letter began:

> The House of Representatives of this province have taken into their serious consideration the great difficulties that must accrue to themselves and their constituents by the operation of several Acts of Parliament, imposing duties and taxes on the American colonies. As it is a subject in which every colony is deeply interested, they have no reason to doubt but your house is deeply impressed with its importance, and that such constitutional measures will be come into as are proper. It seems to be necessary that all possible care should be taken that the representatives of the several assemblies, upon so delicate a point, should harmonize with each other.

The letter went on to discuss British citizen's unalienable rights to property and freedom under the British constitution. In addition, the letter reiterated the point that the colonists were not represented in Parliament, but went even further be stating that they NEVER could be represented there: *"This House further are of the opinion that their constituents , considering their local circumstances, cannot, by any possibility, be represented in the Parliament; and that it will forever be impracticable, that they should be equally represented there."*

The problem of having royal administrators receive their pay from Britain and not from the colonial assemblies also meant that the customs commissioners could make as many appointments of custom agents as they desired. The point was addressed forcibly by stating: *"...that officers of the Crown may be multiplied to such a degree as to become dangerous to the liberty of the people."*

The last paragraph of the letter stated independence from Britain was not the intent of the colonies and concluded with, *"This House cannot conclude, without expressing their firm confidence in the king, our common head and father, that the united and dutiful supplications of his distressed American subjects will meet with his royal and favorable acceptance."*

While the general tone of the letter was mild, the Massachusetts Circular Letter aroused many in Britain who dreaded the idea of the American Colonies acting in concert. The Stamp Act Congress of 1765 had occasioned a coordinated boycott of British goods that resulted in the act's repeal. If the colonies were again allowed to act together against British rule the results could be even worse.

Inflaming the situation, the Massachusetts Royal Governor, Francis Bernard had been sending worrisome dispatches to London about the disloyal actions of several of the Bostonians. In January 1768 he had written, *"It seems to me unavoidable that the whole power of the Government must be in the hands of the people before June next, unless some relief, I know not what, comes from England. I can't stand in this gap again, unless I am assured of being supported from Home."* Bernard was predicting rebellion in the colonies unless Britain sent troops to subdue the radical element, in which he included Sam Adams at the top of the list. It is interesting that Bernard used the words' *"some relief, I know not what,"* in asking for troops. He did not want to explicitly ask for troops so that he could state he did not. He was very concerned about his safety if the Bostonians learned it was he who sent for British troops.

It was no surprise Bernard singled out Samuel Adams as the leading trouble maker in Boston. Sam was acquiring quite a reputation in London for the effectiveness of his opposition to Parliament's attempts to force the colonies to accept their laws. While James Otis was an incendiary speaker who excited audiences with his firebrand delivery, Samuel Adams was logically persuasive. He was also unquenchable in his pursuit of colonial freedom from what he saw as unjustified oppression by Britain. His effectiveness in molding public opinion, and rousing men to action infuriated the royal governor, the customs commissioners, and others in the service of British rule.

Samuel Adams was the epitome of a New Englander of Puritan descent. The first of Samuel's ancestors to set foot in America was Henry Adams who left Somersetshire, England sometime in the late 1630's as a part of the Great Migration of those of Puritan belief, who wanted to escape the edicts of the Church of England. He settled in Braintree (now Quincy), Massachusetts with his wife and nine children, and was the progenitor of a large clan of likeminded descendents. One of Henry's grandsons, John, moved to the bustling seaport of Boston where he became captain of one of the many ships that plied the waters there. One of John's sons, Samuel, felt he had a better chance at success in business rather than following his father to the sea, and became a prominent merchant with a successful malting business.

In 1713 Samuel married Mary Fifield, the daughter of a successful Boston merchant. Samuel had purchased a large house on Purchase Street, at the edge of Boston's harbor where he took his new bride. The couple were devout Congregationalists who valued their Puritan ancestry. Sam became a deacon in the church and they started a family. After the first child died they had a daughter in 1717 they named Mary after the proud mother, followed in 1722 by a son, named Samuel after the proud father. Like many families of the time, only one other son, Joseph, survive infancy from a total of twelve births.

The senior Samuel deeply regretted that he had not had the opportunity for an education and was determined his son would not suffer the same fate.

Young Samuel was sent to Harvard at fourteen, his pious mother hoping he would go into the ministry. However, her son had developed a strong penchant for politics and achieved his master's degree from the institution in 1743. Sam had already found his calling in fighting what he saw as oppressive government actions, which violated an individual's freedom. His master's thesis was appropriately entitled, *"Whether it be lawful to resist the Supreme Magistrate, if the Commonwealth cannot be otherwise preserved."*

His antagonism to imperious governmental actions was more than an intellectual disagreement. His father had suffered both financially and emotionally when the British Parliament interfered in a land-bank currency scheme his father had a major part in promoting, along with many others in the rural area around Boston. In 1740, with a dire shortage of cash, the group had endeavored to create a useable currency baked by the value of their properties. A currency was needed to settle debts in an expeditious manner to avoid interest on an unpaid balance. Some wealthy merchants in New England and in Britain came up with a similar scheme based on sterling, but it was more restrictive in its availability to the farmers and smaller business owners. The merchants did not like the property-based currency; it took business away from them, and reduced the interest they could charge to debtors. At the urging of the royal governor who backed the wealthy merchants, Parliament simply outlawed the land-bank currency, plunging its value. Further, in what was obviously a punitive action, Parliament also ruled that any of the officers of the defunct land-bank plan would be held liable for any losses. Many thought Parliament should not have interfered in what was a colonial matter. The episode likely hardened the detestation of inequitable government action the young student was harboring.

Samuel junior's early business efforts were encouraged by his father, even to the extent of lending him 1,000 pounds, a considerable sum at the time, which he immediately lent to a friend, never to be repaid. He made several attempts at a business career, but they were generally unsuccessful. When his father died in 1748 he took over his father's malting business, but there were debts to pay that were carried over from the land-bank episode and, combined with Samuel's disinterest in business, it eventually failed.

Young Sam Adams was an intense, but very likeable fellow. He made an effort to become friendly with everyone he came in contact with, spanning the entire social order. He would meet with workers and deckhands at the local taverns and also with prominent Bostonians such as John Hancock, James Otis, jr., Dr. Joseph Warren and others. Samuel was not reluctant to express his political views which closely followed those espoused by the seventeenth century political philosopher, John Locke, who argued that an individual's freedom and property, earned with his labors, were natural rights that could not be arbitrarily taken by government. Locke had also denied the divine right of monarchs to rule, which had an effect leading to the Glorious Revolution of 1688. Importantly, Locke did not disavow revolution against an oppressive government; it was the right of the populace if no other recourse were available. Sam agreed absolutely with the Declaration of Rights issued by the British Parliament in 1689 which stated all men were born with natural rights which could not be abridged.

In the fall of 1749 Samuel proposed to the very devout Elizabeth Checkley, the daughter of the family's congregational church minister. Sam started earning a small salary by being named a tax collector in 1756, earning five percent of the taxes he collected. He was not, however, a very effective tax collector. If times were economically depressed, he often omitted collecting all that was due. In an event not unusual for the period, Elizabeth died in July 1757 after giving birth to her sixth child, only two of which lived past infancy.

It was another matter he faced the year following his wife's death, that would anneal his resolve to tribulations he would face the remainder of his life. The debts his father had accrued as a result of the land-bank action had never been paid, and a notice appeared in the Boston paper announcing that Sam's property would be auctioned off to pay the debt. Samuel was still angered with the government's earlier decisions, and was now enraged they would try to take his property. In Sam's mind it was a gross violation of the British Constitution.

When the sheriff presented the notice to move the auction, Samuel took action. First he fired off a letter to the sheriff stating the taking of his property was illegal, stating *"How far your determination may lead you, you know better than I. I would only beg leave, with freedom, to assure you, that I am advised and determined to prosecute to the law any person whomsoever who shall trespass upon that estate."*

On the day of the auction, Samuel showed up and threatened anyone who might have had a thought of offering a bid for the property. He would sue anyone, including the sheriff if they tried to even set foot on his property. Intimidated by Samuel, there were no bids made, and the estate remained in his hands. The lesson Samuel learned was that if you were going to fight against the government for an injustice they were advancing, your response had to be passionate and complete; no half-measures would do.

Samuel was elected to the Massachusetts House of Representatives in 1765 when Oxenbridge Thacher, who with James Otis, jr had argued against the hated Writs of Assistance, died suddenly. Like Thatcher, an ardent Whig and Puritan, Samuel Adams fit the mold of the sort of representative popular with the Boston voters. After serving out Thatcher's term, Samuel was reelected by a large margin (691 votes out of a total of 746) on his own in May 1766. With his popularity at a high level Samuel was selected as the House Clerk, a position of considerable importance. He kept the minutes of the House, and wrote much of its official correspondence. The position allowed Samuel to write letters in the name of the House, even when the body was not in session.

The Circular Letter that Samuel Adams, in his official position as House Clerk, sent to the other colonial assemblies effected a potent reaction. The Virginia House of Burgesses, upon receipt of the letter on April 15th, took immediate action. By unanimous consent, the Virginia House sent a petition to the King that mirrored the petition sent by Massachusetts requesting redress from the acts. Not stopping there, official communications were dispatched to both Houses of Parliament stating the taxes, levied on the American Colonies to raise revenue for the British treasury, were patently unconstitutional as they did not have representation there. In a final action, the Virginia House alerted the assemblies of the other colonies of the actions it had taken, stating all of them should, *"unite in a firm but direct Opposition to every Measure which may affect the Rights and Liberties of the British Colonies in America."*

The remaining colonial assemblies, upon receiving the Massachusetts Letter, were poised to take similar actions to that of Virginia, but before they could react, the letter was received in London causing a reaction further angering the colonies.

Chapter Twenty

British / Colonial
Relations Deteriorate

After Massachusetts' Circular Letter had been received in London the British Cabinet met to discuss what action would be appropriate in response. It was decided that the tone of the British reply should be soft for the immediate time, to keep relations non-confrontational until the obviously serious concerns of the colonies could be addressed in a rationale manner without escalating the issue. But, Secretary of State for Colonial Affairs, Lord Hillsborough, did not agree with the cabinet, and he acted aggressively; it was, after all, his ministry. As Secretary of State, for the colonies, the royal colonial governors were under his administration, and he had a more truculent reply prepared.

When shown the response Hillsborough had written, the Duke of Grafton, the acting Prime Minister, expressed disapproval, and reminded him that it was not what the cabinet had in mind nor approved, but Hillsborough had already shown his response to the King and the King had approved it. Thus, in what was one of the most provocative actions aggravating British/Colonial relations, it was sent. Hillsborough's directive was sent to the Royal Governors in all of the American colonies. In addition, he ordered the Massachusetts House to revoke the Circular Letter, and for Governor Francis Bernard to suspend the Massachusetts assembly if they did not. His letter to the Royal Governors of each colony is as follows:

"Circular Letter to the Governors in America; April 21, 1768
I have his Majesty's commands to transmit to you the enclosed copy of a letter from the speaker of the House of Representatives of the Colony of Massachusetts Bay, addressed by order of that House to the speaker of the assembly of each colony upon the continent of North America.

As his Majesty considers this measure to be of a most dangerous and factious tendency, calculated to inflame the minds of his good subjects in the colonies, to promote an unwarranted combination, and to excite and encourage an open opposition to and denial of the authority of Parliament, and to subvert the true principles of the constitution; it is his Majesty's pleasure that you should immediately upon the receipt hereof exert your utmost influence to defeat this flagitious attempt to disturb the public peace by prevailing upon the Assembly of your province to take no notice of it, which will be treating it with the contempt it deserves.

The repeated proofs which have been given by the Assembly of (name of colony) of their reverence and respect for the laws, and of their faithful attachment to the constitution, leave little room in his Majesty's breast to doubt of their showing a proper resentment of this unjustifiable attempt to revive those distractions which have operated so fatally to the prejudice of this kingdom and the colonies'; and accordingly his Majesty had the fullest confidence in their affections. But if, notwithstanding these expectations and your most earnest endeavors, there should appear in the Assembly of your province a disposition to receive or give any countenance to this seditious paper, it will be your duty to prevent any proceeding upon it by an immediate prorogation of dissolution.

While Hillsborough's directive was on its way across the Atlantic, several other colonial assemblies responded to the Massachusetts Letter. The New Jersey Assembly approved a petition to the King on May 6th stating *"Rights and Liberties vested in the People of this colony is the Privilege of being exempt from any Taxation but such as imposed on them by themselves or their Representatives."* Connecticut followed in early June with a similar petition of its own.

After several months collecting revenue dictated by the new laws, it became obvious to the members of the customs board that payment of the duties was being widely disregarded in the port of Boston, but they felt powerless to strictly enforce Parliament's laws due to the non-cooperation of local officials and courts who sympathized with the local shippers. The month previously, on April 6th, one of John Hancock's ships, the Lydia had arrived in Boston harbor and two representatives of the customs officials went on board to watch over the cargo which was being unloaded. One of the tidesmen, (customs employees) made the mistake of going below deck to inspect the cargo. When Hancock arrived at the wharf and learned they did not have proper writs of assistance that allowed them to go into the hold, he threw the inspectors off the ship, adhering to the advice of the ship's captain that he not physically hurt them lest he be prosecuted. The episode was not forgotten by the commissioners, but they felt insecure at that time about taking action against the prominent colonial loyalist, and bided taking action until such time as they could act forcefully.

They got their opportunity in early May, when another of Hancock's ships, the Liberty, had entered Boston Harbor with—so the customs agents were told—25 casks of wine from the Portuguese archipelago of Madeira. It was much less cargo than the ship could actually hold, and although suspicions were raised, the custom agents inspecting the ship said they found nothing arrears.

However, when Commodore Hood responded in late May 1768 by sending the HMS Romney, a fifty-gun warship along with two armed schooners to support the customs officers, the commissioners, bolstered by this show of force, were embolden to act. One of the customs agents, who had conducted the original inspection of the Liberty, now stated he was forced to remain silent while illegal Madeira wine was unloaded. He claimed, he was overpowered by the ship's crew and held against his will as the cargo was unloaded away from his view. He had been warned not to speak about the incident, but, with new bravery, he was coming forward at this time to tell the true tale. Thus, on June 10th, based on this new revelation, the customs commissioners decided it was time to take action against Hancock.

In the early evening the commissioners acted; they claimed there was a false declaration and Hancock was in violation of the Townshend Acts. The proper action by the customs officials was to stamp a notice on the ship's mast that would put it in quarantine until the court could decide what proceedings should be taken. Angry mobs gathered on the wharf as the customs agents boarded the ship, led by Benjamin Hallowell, the Comptroller of the Port and Joseph Harrison, the collector of duties for Boston. The matter might have ended there, but when Hallowell decided it was better to move the ship out to the protection of the Romney, the mob became angry, and more threatening. One of the mob shouted, *"You had better let the vessel lie at the wharf."* Leaving it in quarantine was the legal thing to do but Hallowell did not trust the owner, Hancock, and he wanted the ship moved to a place where the owner's men could not interfere with the proceedings against her.

The Romney immediately sent a contingent of troops to support the commissioners. *"I shall not,"* Hallowell, now with the protection of the Romney's marines, replied insolently to the man on the dock. He then ordered a dock hand *"cast her off."*

The leader of the marines from the Romney threatened, *"I'll split out the brains of any man that offers to reeve a fast, or stop the vessel."* The Liberty was then cut from her moorings, and towed out to the protection of the warship.

The mob was more than a few disgruntled citizens who just happened to be passing by. In the early evening when this was occurring, the docks were nearly always teeming with seamen, dockhands, and other workers. While the commissioners had planned their operation as the workers had left or were leaving, there were still many in the area who responded to the activity on the wharf. The mob, aroused, then attacked the tax agents on the scene.

In a letter to London, Massachusetts' Chief Justice (and also Lieutenant Governor) , Thomas Hutchinson (who was not there when the disturbance took place) described the situation that ensued,

> In the evening the Custom House Officers seized a Sloop belonging to Mr. Hancock...The Comptroller thot it best to move her under the Guns of the Romney which lay a quarter of a mile from the Shoar and made a signal for the man of war boats to come ashore. The people upon the warffe said there was no occasion: she would be safe and no Officer had a right to move her; but the master of the Man of War cut her moorings and carried her off. A mob presently gathered and insulted the Custom House Officers, tore their cloths and bruised and otherwise hurt them until one after another they escaped. The mob increased to 2 or 3,000 chiefly sturdy boys and negroes, and broke the windows of the Comptroller's house. The mob ended their fury by burning a boat belonging to Mr. Harrison.

This was not the only letter Hutchinson wrote to friends and officials about the disloyal acts of the Bostonians and urged action against them. This letter and others like it from a number of royalists in Boston, was the sort of continuous denunciation of the colony's inhabitants that turned public opinion in England almost solidly against the New Englanders.

The following day, four of the Boston customs commissioners fled to the Romney in a mild panic, and on June 13th, they also wrote a letter to the Customs Board in London, "*The Collector and Comptroller, with the son of the Collector* (Joseph Harrison's son, who was also a tax agent) *on their return from the wharf into town were attacked by a numerous and outrageous mob; Mr. [Thomas] Irving, Inspector of imports and exports, who happened to be passing by was likewise attacked by the mob, who cried out, He is a Commissioner, kill him, kill him; these persons were grossly insulted and much bruised, and escaped with utmost hazard to their lives.*"

With letters like these arriving in London, along with dire warning from the Massachusetts Royal Governor Bernard, it is not surprising the King's ministers in London, as well as many parliamentarians, were highly perturbed concerning affairs in the American Colonies in general, and in Massachusetts Bay in particular. As a result of the mob attack, Bernard allowed the customs officials to move to a safe haven on the fort on Castle William Island in Boston Harbor where they could be protected. It is probable the commissioners were in no real or immediate danger (one of their members did not even bother to retreat to the Castle); more likely they were adding some drama to add their request to the Lords of the Treasury in London for more troops from General Gage. They stated, "*that nothing but the immediate exercise of military power would prevent an open revolt of the town of Boston, and probably of the Provinces. "*

Justice Hutchinson added in a letter to the Under Secretary of State, Thomas Whately, *"unless they should have immediately two or three regiments, it was the opinion of all the friends to government, that Boston would be in Open rebellion. "*

Although the correspondences to London calling for troops were supposed to be secret, the Bostonians, through various means, were aware of them. They thought the requests were unnecessary, and a grave provocation. At a Boston meeting on June 17th, a few days after the commissioners retreated to their safe haven on Castle William, John Adams reflected on what were the sentiments of the city's leading citizens,

> After the repeal of the last American Stamp Act, we were happy in the pleasing prospect of a restoration of tranquility and harmony. But the principle on which that detestable act was founded continues in full force, and a revenue is still demanded from America, and appropriated to the maintenance of swarms of officers and pensioners in idleness and luxury. It is our fixed resolution to maintain our loyalty and due subordination to the British Parliament, as the Supreme Legislative in all cases of necessity for the preservation of the whole empire. At the same time, it is our unalterable resolution, to assert and vindicate our dear and invaluable rights and liberties, at the utmost hazard of our lives and fortunes; and we have a full and rational confidence that no designs formed against them will ever prosper.

"Every person who shall solicit or promote the importation of troops at this time, is an enemy to this town and Province, and a disturber of the peace and good order of both. " Many, or most of the colonists were still hopeful of avoiding a confrontation with Britain which would forever alter their relationship, and the use of British troops could well cause unforeseen circumstances that would do just that.

Shortly after the disturbance on the Liberty, Hillsborough's order directing the colonial governors to have the colonial assemblies ignore Massachusetts' Circular Letter, was finally received in America in mid June, the threatening tone of the directive did not sit well with most of the members of these colonial assemblies. After deliberations in their respective assemblies, Delaware, Maryland, Pennsylvania, Rhode Island, New Hampshire, North and South Carolina, and even the newest colony, Georgia rejected the letter, and sent petitions of their own to the King declaring the same premise as the earlier supplications: the taxation of the American colonies by the British Parliament was unconstitutional. New York delayed action while the issue was being debated, but the sense there was in concordance with the rest of the colonies.

Following instructions in Hillsborough's order, the Massachusetts Royal Governor, Bernard, directed the Massachusetts House of Representatives to rescind their Circular Letter. In addition to being infuriated with London's response, many Bostonians held the belief their royal governor was sending false reports to his government contacts in London that incited hostility toward the Massachusetts Colony. With this distrust of Governor Benard, the Massachusetts House of Representatives met to take up a response to the governor's demand that they rescind the Circular Letter.

During the meeting the fiery Otis, in a two-hour harangue, described the members of Britain's Parliament as, *"a parcel of button-makers, pin-makers, horse jockeys, gamsters, pensioners, pimps and whoremasters."* British spies took down the words which Bernard immediately dispatched to London. While Otis was flamboyant in his oratory, Sam Adams was deliberate in his determination to send a clear, strong message to Bernard and the Parliamentarians in London.

After the vote was recorded, the House's response was presented to the royal governor, *"We have now only to inform your Excellency that this House have voted not to rescent, as required, the resolution of the last House; and that upon a division of the question, there were 92 nays and 17 yeas."* Twelve of the seventeen who voted to rescind were in government positions to which they were appointed by a royal governor. The other colonies generally applauded Massachusetts action.

After receiving the defiant response, the following day Bernard terminated the House, scorning Sam Adams at the time. The seventeen who had voted to accede to Bernard's request to rescind the letter were openly castigated by the local populace. Their names were published in the Boston Gazette. and hung on the Liberty Tree.

The next month, July, Governor Bernard was worried about further agitating the citizens of Massachusetts by the continuing discussions in the Council about Parliament's right to tax the colonies. Massachusetts' Council, their upper house, was decidedly royalist, but often showed an independent bent. In a gesture of good-will, he thus seemingly offered to assist the colony. He told the Massachusetts Council he would assist them in endeavoring to obtain relief from the revenue acts if they would put off discussing the issue. He wrote a letter stating his support for relief, and showed it to several council members. At the same time, however, in a duplicitous act, he wrote another, secret, letter to Hillsborough arguing that the revenue acts should be kept as they were, with no reduction in their force.

With the colonies now solidly united in opposition to the Townshend Acts it was time to initiate more assertive steps to challenge the loathsome laws. They decided to employ a course of action which worked well in opposing the Stamp Act: an effective boycott of British goods. An agreement was written and signed by the Boston merchants who pledged to boycott British goods as long as the Townshend Acts were in force. This action by the leading merchants had a much greater impact than the improvised non-importation statements individuals had agreed to earlier. It was an action which received immediate attention in London. The merchants' non-importation agreement, was published on August 1, 1768, and reprinted widely:

> The merchants and traders in the town of Boston, having taken into consideration the deplorable situation of the trade and the many difficulties it as present labours under on account of the scarcity of money, which is daily decreasing for want of the other remittances to discharge our debts in Great Britain, and the large sums collected by the officers of the customs for duties on goods imported; the heavy taxes levied to discharge the debts contracted by the government in the late war; the embarrassments and restrictions laid on the trade by the several acts of Parliament; together with the bad success of our cod fishery this season, and the discouraging prospect of the whale fishery, by which our principal sources of remittances are like to be greatly diminished, and we thereby rendered unable to pay the debts we owe the merchants in Great Britain, and to continue the importation of goods from thence:
>
> We the subscribers, in order to relieve the trade under those discouragements, to promote industry, frugality, and economy, and to discourage luxury and every kind of extravagance, do promise and engage to and with each other as follows:
>
> That we will not send or import from Great Britain this fall, either on our own account, or on commission, and other goods than what we already ordered for the fall supply.
>
> That we will not send for or import any kind of goods or merchandise from Great Britain, either on our own account, or on commissions, or any otherwise, From January 1, 1769 to January 1, 1770, except salt, coals, fish-hooks and lines, hemp, duck bar lead and shot, wool-cards and card-wire.
>
> That we will not purchase of any factors, or others, any kind of goods imported from Great Britain from January 1, 1769 to January 1, 1770. That we will not import on our own account, or on commission, or Purchase from any Who shall import from any other colony in America, from January 1, 1769 to January 1, 1770, any tea, glass, paper, or other goods commonly imported from Great Britain.
>
> That we will not, from and after January 1, 1769, import into the province any tea, paper, glass, or painters' colours, until the Acts imposing duties on these articles have been repealed.

The Bostonians were joined by the merchants in Salem, but the New Englanders were not alone in their boycott. New York also published a non-importation agreement that was even more severe than Boston's as it included a proviso to boycott loyalist shops who continued to import British goods.

Likewise Virginia and the other colonies followed in varying degrees with similar actions. The impact on the merchants in Britain was to be strongly felt. The colonies had become, by far, Britain's largest trading partner, and now, the loss of a significant portion of that business, would wreck havoc among the British merchants as well as severely impacting the nation's economy, thus affecting the general populace.

In London Lord Hillsborough, The Lords of the Treasury, and many other royal officials were disturbed about what he was hearing from Governor Bernard and the customs commissioners concerning the increase in unrest they were witnessing in Boston. The mobs were threatening all in royal authority, especially tax collectors, and the upstart colonial leaders seem to be preaching sedition. He felt the colonials had to be subdued, and if it took a show of British might, so be it. He ordered General Gage to send some troops stationed in Halifax to Boston, and additionally ordered two additional regiments from Ireland to Boston.

When early in September 1768, two large British ships, The Senegal and the Duke of Cumberland, left Boston Harbor, Bernard discretely let it be known they were bound for Halifax to bring British troops to Boston. The incident absolutely convinced Samuel Adams that independence from Britain was the only viable option open to the colonies. He conversed with and explained to any and all in the city of the necessity of this action. He openly declared his disregard for the King. He reminded his Puritan neighbors they had come to America to escape from Kings' oppression and gain freedom.

The members of the Massachusetts House were perturbed by the knowledge of the ships departure, but since Bernard refused to allow the House to assemble, they were unable to formally address the threat. Instead, Otis, Adams and Warren met to plan a Town Meeting of the people of Boston. The meeting was called on September 12th at Faneuil Hall to discuss what action to take upon the troop's arrival. In a mild show of force, the town's cache of arms, four hundred muskets, was brought to the hall where they were placed on display in boxes for all to see. Standing over them Otis asserted, *"When an attempt is made against your liberties, they will be delivered."*

While Boston's citizens were meeting, Bernard remained in his residence, very concerned for his safety. He did not think the Romney would offer sufficient protection if the Bostonians became too defiant, and possibly two regiments of British troops might not be enough. While there he wrote to Hillsborough requesting the revocation of the Massachusetts Bay Charter.

The leaders of Boston's Town Meeting knew they would have to widen the debate to all of the citizens of the colony, and plans were made to do just that. The Town Meeting ended with a declaration that could be taken up by a broader assembly. The declaration stated, *"It is the first principle in civil so-*

ciety, founded in nature and reason, that no law of the society can be binding on any individual, without his consent, given by himself in person, or by his representative of his own free election." The meeting then issued a resolve, *"That the inhabitants of the town of Boston will, at the utmost peril of their lives and fortunes, maintain and defend their rights, liberties, privileges, and immunities."* In a specific definition of these rights, they voted, *"that money could not be levied, nor a standing army be kept up in the Province but by their own free consult."*

To gain the concordance of the rest of the colony, the Boston Selectmen, led by Adams, Hancock, Cushing, and Otis invited all of the colonies' towns to a convention in Faneuil Hall to discuss what action to take in the face of British troops arriving. On September 22, 1768 sixty-six Massachusetts towns heeded the call and assembled at Faneuil Hall. The meeting soon grew to ninety-six towns and eight districts, essentially the whole of the Massachusetts Bay Colony. It was, in the eyes of the royal governor, an anarchical action. It demonstrated the futility of the governor's edict rescinding the Massachusetts House, and verified the unified convictions the citizens of the colony shared. It also demonstrated they would take independent action if that was necessary.

The point was made and it greatly alarmed the royalists in the area. *"Treason,"* some called. *"Mutinous,"* General Gage exclaimed. The attendees at the convention elected the former leaders of the Massachusetts House to the same positions they held in the "official" House. For six days the representatives met and re-verified the measures taken previously, including the petition to the King, and the Circular Letter to the other American Colonies. Bernard, as expected, refused to receive a petition from the convention that called on him to call the Massachusetts Assembly together to consider means of stopping an unlawful military incursion into their civil territory. He was still fearful of his safety, and refused to condemn the convention stating, *"I dare not publish a proclamation against the Convention without first securing my retreat."*

After six days the convention disbanded after reaffirming their opposition to the unconstitutional taxation by Parliament, and against the use of a standing army camped in their midst.

The French Foreign Minister, the Duc de (Duke of) Choiseul made his own assessment of the relations between Britain and her American Colonies. Since France and Britain were the two major powers in Europe, the Duke felt it important to become familiar with the state of affairs of his rival, as it could well affect his countries actions with either Britain or the Americans. He thought the official proclamations by the British government and the articles in the London newspapers did not really reflect how the Americans felt about their mother country. To better understand the situation, Choiseul had the French minister in London seek out Benjamin Franklin to obtain his sense of the American attitudes. He also had agents read the colonial newspapers, examine correspondence from American merchants, and even listened to sermons delivered by Puritan pastors.

He came to the conclusion the Americans would not agree to a token representation in Parliament, and that there was *"no other method of concili-ation."* He believed that Britain would have to yield to American demands or use escalating measures of violence to control them. He also wisely noted *"The forces of the English in America are scarcely ten thousand men, and they have no cavalry, but the militia of the Colonies numbers four hundred thousand men, and among them several regiments of cavalry."*

With regard to the Americans' attitude, he concluded, *"The people are enthusiastic for liberty, and have inherited a republican spirit, which the consciousness of strength and circumstances may push to extremities. They will not be intimidated by the presence of troops, too insignificant to cause alarm."* It was a precise appraisal Choiseul made, one that affected the man-ner France would use in its relations and actions with both sides.

Spain was also concerned with the ongoing disputes between Britain and America, but their attitude was decidedly different from France's. The Span-ish foreign minister, Fuentes hoped, *"the English might master their Colonies lest the Spanish Colonies also catch the flame."*

Chapter Twenty-One

British Troops in Boston

The anticipated arrival of British troops created an unanticipated problem for Massachusetts Governor, Thomas Bernard. General Gage had written Bernard a letter informing him one of the regiments could stay at Castle William, but the other was to be encamped in Boston as desired by Lord Hillsborough. When Bernard told the Massachusetts Council that two regiments of British troops were coming from Halifax and they would have to find quarters for them, the Council pointed out to Bernard that the Quartering Act passed by Parliament required local civil officials to billet the military only if barracks were not available to house them. Since the crown facility at Castle William could hold all of the Halifax regiments, approximately one thousand men, the Council told Bernard they had no obligation to provide housing for them. They further pointed out the Act also specifically stated, *"that if any military officer should take it upon himself to quarter soldiers in any of his majesty's dominions in America otherwise than was limited and allowed by the Act, he should be ipso facto cashiered and disabled to hold any military employment in his Majesty's service."*

The members of the Massachusetts Council felt compelled to support the arriving troops, but they had no desire to alienate their neighbors by being overly supportive of the military's arrival. In an ironic twist of the law, they found a path that would allow them not to oppose the crown's action, but also avoid collaboration with it. They would insist on a strict interpretation of Parliamentary Laws, which meant Bernard could not legally comply with Gage's directive that some of the troops be camped in Boston itself.

Thus was the situation when the British troops arrived on September 28, 1768, just after the Massachusetts convention had ended. The potent British force included two regiments of field (infantry) soldiers and a unit of artillery. The troop's commander, Colonel Dalrymple, was dismayed upon arrival that no billets had been prepared for his men. When he approached Bernard about the discrepancy, the Governor weakly told him he could do nothing without his council's approval, and explained their position.

Completely dissatisfied with Bernard's explanation, on October first, Dalrymple, acting without civil approval, moved the ships to Boston's docks, and aimed the loaded on-deck cannon toward the town. It was an aggressive move meant to intimidate the populace. He then brazenly disembarked the soldiers, who came ashore carrying loaded rifles. No action was ever taken against Dalrymple for his illegal action.

To add to the drama, the troops marched into and through Boston with all flags flying and drums beating. For several hours they displayed their might before finally stopping on Boston Common. One regiment, the twenty-ninth had tents and field gear, and encamped on the Common grounds. Dalrymple ordered Faneuil Hall opened where a contingent of troops were quartered. Unfortunately, the town's arms were still there, and were confiscated by the British troops. Bernard then capitulated completely, and allowed use of the Boston Town House for some of the troops. After the rental of additional houses by the officers, negotiations allowed a commissary to be set up, and the troops settled in.

A guard station was set up opposite the State House where cannons were aimed at the very rooms where the colony's delegates convened. The royalists in the city were placated by the arrival of British troops, and felt more secure. *"No more wrecked houses,"* exclaimed one. But the views of the majority of Bostonians remained unchanged, and they despised what they viewed as the illegal presence of British troops. Even facing the menace of the encamped military in their midst, the Bostonians resolved never to give into the unconstitutional laws of Parliament. They were now more entrenched in their defiance than ever before.

Before the troops had arrived there had been boasts by several of Boston's citizens of armed resistance to any redcoats that dared to land, but after their arrival the mood in the town was subdued, even with the undertone of hostility. General Gage chided, *"a people who have been very bold in council but never remarkable for their feats of action."* One of his officers added, *"All of their bravadoes ended as may be imagined."* Lieutenant Governor Hutchinson observed, *"Men are not easily brought to fight when they know death by the sword, or the halter will be the consequence."*

Since the first arrival of settlers in the New World, it had been a requirement for every able bodied man to serve in a local defense force or militia. Every city, town, and settlement in every colony had a standing militia. It hadn't been that long since the war with the French, and battles with Indians, while greatly reduced, was still a potential threat. The various colonial militias were locally organized; with only cursory coordination on a broader venue. The little coordination that existed would not have permitted a viable opposition to the well-armed British force landing in Boston.

While no overt action was taken against the troops upon their arrival, they were treated as unwelcome invaders, and were made to feel the animosity the citizenry felt towards them. Soon many small incidents between the two sides occurred, keeping a strained tension in place.. For their part, the troops did not take measures to endear the population to their presence.

A series of newspaper articles known as the *Journal of the Times* (also known as the *Journal of Occurrences*) began to appear in the *Boston Gazette* and other colonial newspapers describing the abuses and malice the British troops were inflecting on the populace. Governor Bernard suspected Samuel Adams was in league with the journal's writers in New York and Philadelphia, but that suspicion was never verified. The journal reported rapes, assaults and disturbances of religious worship by swearing and blasphemies near church services by the occupying troops. Whether the tales were real or fabricated was never certain, but they made a decided impression on the colonists, amplifying negative impressions of the British troops and, by association, of the British government.

While the existence of British troops in Boston satisfied the customs commissioners, the hardened resolve of the colonists increased the effectiveness of the boycott of British goods. Although it was not evident at the time, Britain was at a critical point in their history. The dawning of the Industrial Revolution was causing a disruption of the agrarian economy which had prevailed in the past. James Watt had just patented his new steam engine, greatly improving its efficiency over the fifty-year old Newcomen design. The new engine ultimately allowed small engines to provide much of the work needed for industrial production. The development of the Abraham Darby blast furnaces for producing iron, the advanced spinning mills and carding machines to yield wool, and the general shift to factory from farm was having a decided effect. In this environment, the colonial boycott was being acutely felt in the industrial sectors as unemployment increased. The merchants were not trading as much with the colonies, and thus not ordering goods from the manufacturers and other suppliers.

Dislocations brought about by this upheaval were noted by Benjamin Franklin. While residing in London he observed in a spring letter to a friend in Philadelphia, *"a daily scene of lawless riot and confusion. Mobs patrolling the streets at noonday...coal heavers and porters pulling down the houses of coal merchants that refuse to give them more wages, sawyers destroying sawmills...."*

Making the problem especially bad in Britain at this time was a new reality: with a movement to the cities of agrarian workers, Britain now had to import grain and other foodstuffs to feed its growing population. It was the import of these commodities from the American Colonies in ever growing amounts that made relations between Britain and her colonies of significant importance. This new dependence of Britain was not lost on many of the more knowledgeable merchants and politicians in the country, but seemed of little accord to the monarch and many of his loyal ministers.

It was in this setting in the fall of 1768, that the King once again decided he was not satisfied with his ministers. He felt he still did not have a smooth-working government where party prejudices were subjugated to the betterment of the realm as he saw it. The King actually had a point in his assessment of Parliament. With no major war to bring them together, the members of Parliament concentrated on enhancing the security of their positions. Corruption was evident in the widespread buying of votes in the last election, and patronage decisions strongly affected the manner in which votes were cast in Parliament.

With his illness, Pitt-Chatham was of little help to the king in resolving disputes. Pitt-Chatham's chosen second-in-command, the Duke of Grafton, had proven unable to control Commons. Townshend had his revenue acts passed without Grafton's approval and Hillsborough had frustrated Grafton by issuing his aggressive rejoinder to the Massachusetts Circular Letter even though a cabinet meeting had agreed Britain's response should be mild. The King had gone to Pitt-Chatham and asked him to meet with Grafton to bolster his attitude and strengthen his will, hoping it would invigorate the Duke, *"Five minutes with you would raise his spirits for his heart is good,"* the King had said.

Reluctantly, Pitt-Chatham did meet; not only with Grafton, but with many of those in opposition to discuss the manner he and Grafton were guiding the nation. However, the negotiations proved fruitless and on October 14, 1768, Pitt-Chatham, in frustration or in anger, abruptly resigned using poor health as his reason, surprising (and angering) the King. Grafton was now the actual Prime Minister. He operated this role from his seat in the House of Lords, and did not have the command of Commons that Pitt-Chatham had held. Grafton's unassertive style allowed his opponents greater reign in the government, and significantly lessened his control. With Lord North in Commons, the king felt he had a kindred mind there, and thus did not make any significant changes to his ministers. However, the tenor of the government toward the American colonies had shifted with Pitt-Chatham's resignation, as those advocating a more stringent approach acquired more potency.

The King made a speech to Parliament on November 8th that confirmed his conviction a hard line must be used against the Boston colonists,

Boston appears to be in a state of disobedience to all law and government, and has proceeded to measures subversive of the constitution, and attended with circumstances that might manifest a disposition to throw off its dependence on Great Britain. With your concurrence and support, I shall be able to defeat the mischievous designs of those turbulent and seditious persons, who, under false pretences, have too successfully deluded numbers of my subjects in America.

Lord North, ever wishing to accede to the King's wishes, reflected his monarchs views, *"America must fear you before she can love you....I am against repealing the last Act of Parliament securing to us a revenue out of America; I will never think of repealing it until I see America prostrate at my feet."* At the time this was the prevalent feeling of many members of Parliament.

The customs commissioners were ardently pursuing the collection of duties dictated by the new law. Numerous agents had been hired, and there were over twenty customs cutters plying the waters of the eastern colonial coasts, along with many smaller boats patrolling the smaller rivers and bays. However much they sought to collect the taxes from the colonial importers, the revenue was far less than the Townshend Acts had expected to produce.

In November the two regiments Hillsborough had dispatched from Ireland, the 64th and the 65th finally arrived. Some were quartered, at the fort on Castle William Island in the harbor, and some in warehouses near the waterfront which Dalrymple had rented. As there had been no openly hostile confrontations between the troops and the colonials, their arrival was generally uneventful.

By the end of the year, all of the colonies had accepted the tenants of Massachusetts' Circular Letter, and either approved it or prepared one of their own, voicing similar sentiments. Even Pennsylvania, which had originally decided against supporting Massachusetts' position, finally agreed (after receiving Hillsborough's demand that all colonies reject it) with the provision that Parliament did not have the authority to tax the colonies.

As the year 1769 began, Hillsborough, with the King's blessing, asked Governor Bernard to send him evidence that could be used to bring Boston's agitators, including Samuel Adams, James Otis, and John Hancock, to London to be tried for treason and presumably executed there. The maneuver was based on an obscure law enacted during the reign of Henry the Eighth which allowed for prosecution of crimes against England committed out of the country. Try as he would, Bernard could not find evidence strong enough to convince Britain's legal authorities in London that a sufficiently strong case existed to extradite the men. The British Attorney General stated they were very close to treason, but had not yet crossed the threshold, and the matter was temporarily dropped. The threat, however, of trial and execution of the colonial leaders imparted a more severe consequence to their efforts to oppose Parliament's laws.

It became obvious to many in Parliament that the continued confrontation with the colonies and the effect the boycott was having on the British economy, was not worth the trouble the revenue laws were causing. Certainly the realm was not accruing much of the expected revenue from them, and considerable revenue was being lost due to the lack of trade. While the British troops had ended the overt mob rule that threatened the custom commissioners, there were still instances of abuse of their agents. It was apparent the troops were not welcome, and the tone of the press and speeches in the colonies was ever more intransigent toward British rule. So now, in 1769, serious talk of repeal began.

Somewhat surprising, it was Hillsborough who broached the idea of repealing the Townshend Acts to several of the colonial representatives in London. He stated that he never did like them, and repeal could pave the way for better colonial relations. He also told them; however, he believed strongly that any repeal had to be done in a manner that would substantiate Parliament's right to make laws which would be enforceable on the colonies, including tax laws.

While sentiment for repeal was growing, on April 19, 1769, Thomas Pownall, the respected former governor of the Massachusetts Bay Colony, and now a member of the House of Commons, rose to make a speech before Parliament explicitly calling for repeal. With a solid reputation on both sides of the Atlantic, Pownall's call for repeal had a significant impact. John Adams had described Pownall as *"a friend of liberty, the most constitutional governor, in my opinion, who ever represented the crown in this (Massachusetts) province."*

Pownall could see the damage the law was doing to colonial relations, and he feared a breach could occur which would be difficult to mend. He, Benjamin Franklin, and many others, envisioned a relationship between Britain and the American Colonies in which the colonial citizens would have the same rights as citizens in Britain, including representation in Parliament.

Lord North, the Chancellor of the Exchequer, agreed with both Pownall and Hillsborough that repeal was necessary, but while Pownall did not attach a caveat to his call for repeal, North agreed with Hillsborough that Parliament's right to tax the colonies must be secured. In a meeting of the British Cabinet, North offered his solution. It was to repeal most of the taxes dictated by the Townshend Acts, but retain the tax on tea. He reasoned that since the revenue acts taxed products manufactured in Britain, like paint, glass, lead and paper, tea was not grown or produced in Britain, and thus was of a nature more like an article of trade. Those opposed to the idea thought it best to just repeal all of the taxes to avoid any further conflict with the colonies. The retained tax on tea would not amount to much, and it would obviously be done to force the colonies to accept a tax they thought illegal and unconstitutional. They would be right back to where they were with the original Townshend Acts.

Those supporting North's recommendation to keep a tax on tea felt it necessary to validate Britain's right to legislate for the American Colonies. To the cabinet members supporting the tea-tax solution, like many other Britons, the tax was perceived almost as a testosterone test of manhood: they had to assert their dominance over the colonies who had challenged them. A vote was taken and the cabinet voted five to four for North's plan. News of the cabinet's decision reached the colonies, but since no formal action was taken, a wait-and see-attitude prevailed there.

During his time as Governor of the Massachusetts Bay Colony, Governor Bernard had written a great deal of correspondence to officials and friends in London. What he forgot, or was not aware of, was a parliamentary rule that allowed any member of Parliament to read and copy any correspondence that was received by members of the body. One of Parliament's members, William Beckford, was sympathetic to the American Colonies' cause and had copied many of the correspondences that had come into Parliament relevant to colonial issues. Among those were several that Bernard had sent which were deprecating of the New England citizens, their official and unofficial organizations, and even its Council. Some of his communications to Secretary Hillsborough were overtly duplicitous. He had believed these communications were secret and unavailable to his colonial cohorts. He found out otherwise.

Beckford passed some of Bernard's letters to a friend who saw to it they were sent to Boston where the letters were openly published. When the Massachusetts Assembly met in June of 1769, Sam Adams, along with James Otis and others presented a petition to the House that would be sent to the King requesting that Bernard be recalled. The petition was approved unanimously. Unknown to the members of the assembly, Hillsborough had already summoned Bernard to London, supposedly to report to the King on conditions in Boston, but actually to remove him as many British officials had reported negatively on Bernard's governorship. The King granted Bernard a baronet to ease the stigma of his removal, but it was a hollow award. He left for England on July 17, 1769 and was replaced by Lieutenant Governor Thomas Hutchinson, who acquired the title "Acting Governor."

About the same time Bernard left, General Gage felt confident enough in the situation in Boston that he sent the Irish regiments to Halifax, reducing by half the British troops stationed in the city.

Chapter Twenty-Two

Growth and Conflict

By the start of 1770, the population of the American Colonies had passed two million (2,210,000). There was vibrancy and a sense of adventure in the colonies that portended a bountiful future. The increase in population, along with the settlement of most of the good land in and around the coastal towns, led many to look away from the old populist settlements to the sparsely, or even, unsettled land north and west for their future. In New England many ventured to Maine, Vermont and New Hampshire. A number of pioneers from Connecticut even made the long trek to seek land in West Florida. Although Hillsborough wanted to restrict migration to the lands west of the present colonies, land speculators, corrupt government agents, and others just looking for adventure or a new life, soon fueled the movement westward.

In May of 1769 an intrepid woodsman named Daniel Boone, along with John Finley had moved through the Cumberland Gap into Kentucky, leading the way for others to follow. In November of 1769, the Indians of the Six Nations had signed at treaty at Fort Stanwix that ceded much of the extensive territory south of the Ohio to the British, and the rush to settle in this new land began in earnest.

In Boston and New York, having British troops stationed in their towns was a continuing irritant affecting both citizens and soldiers. In Boston, young boys would throw small stones or, in winter, snowballs at the soldiers. In passing on the streets, piqued soldiers were known to use the butt of their rifle or bayonet to shove citizens off the sidewalks. Taunting of the troops was common, as was the swearing replies by the soldiers. It was a caustic atmosphere compounded by newspaper articles, and orations from community leaders that railed against the illegal occupation.

The first serious encounter between the troops and the colonists occurred not in Boston, but in New York in an episode called the Battle of Golden

Hill, although it could scarcely be termed a "battle". The troops in New York had been there for some time, a remnant of the French and Indian War, but tensions between the military and the citizenry increased with the imposition of the Stamp and Quartering Acts. New York's initial refusal to provide housing and funds for the troops created a hostility between the two sides that continued even after New York acceded to a partial payment in early 1769.

In an act of celebration after repeal of the Stamp Act in 1766, the New York Sons of Liberty had erected the first "Liberty Pole" near Golden Hill to emblemize their triumph over the British Parliament. The site became a meeting place for patriots to assemble. Over time the poles on Golden Hill, so named for the field of wheat which grew there, became an object of disdain by the British Regulars stationed in nearby barracks. In early January 1770, some soldiers succeeded in cutting down the standing Liberty Pole arousing the New Yorkers. The Son's of Liberty put up replacement poles which were also cut down.

When, on January 18, 1770, two soldiers posted handbills at the site denouncing the Sons of Liberty, one New Yorker, Isaac Sears, with a growing mob supporting him, arrested the soldiers for a civil violation, and proceeded to march them to the office of the city's mayor. Other soldiers were alerted, and soon arrived to support their beleaguered comrades. A fracas erupted at which bayonets were drawn and clubs wielded. A number of New Yorkers were injured, with at least one stabbed seriously, while several soldiers suffered bruises and minor wounds. The hostile encounter is considered by some to be the first aggressive bloodletting in the conflict between British troops and her American Colonists. While it might have been the first, it wasn't the most serious; that would occur six weeks later in Boston.

At the same time discord was occurring in America between the British military and the local citizens, the British government in London was undergoing its own dissonance. Seven years before, in 1763, a British citizen, John Wilkes, had published an article in a newspaper in which he openly assailed the King for his speech at Parliament's opening. The King, enraged by the article, responded by ordering general warrants for Wilkes and others who had assisted him. Never one to be intimidated, Wilkes argued against the constitutionality of the warrants, and the authority of the King to have them issued. He also demanded immunity from any royal action because he was a duly elected member of the House of Commons. Wilkes was extremely popular with his constituents because of his iconoclast behavior towards the established government in general, and the crown in particular.

Sensing the inevitably of arrest, Wilkes fled to France after being found guilty of seditious libel by a London court. After running out of funds, and to avoid creditors in France, he returned to London early in 1768. In a slap at the British court he was immediately elected a member of Commons by the citizens of Middlesex. It didn't help as the British court sent him to prison for twenty-two months. The King's Bench Prison where Wilkes was sent was not severe, being used mostly for debtors. An inmate could procure the right to travel freely within the vicinity of the prison's walls, and have other privileges, which Wilkes took full advantage of; including visits by admiring women. He could write letters to his constituents, and even write newspaper articles which continuously aroused his followers.

Unruly mobs of workers, apprentices and unemployed laborers regularly prowled the London streets in support of Wilkes, while also protesting high costs and poor living conditions. Windows were often broken in prominent mansions. A protest supporting Wilkes outside of the King's Bench Prison turned especially ugly when troops were called in and shots were fired at the crowd, killing at least six.

The King approved of the action by the troops in quelling what he saw as an attempt at anarchy, but he was infuriated that Wilkes was still a member of parliament, and he voiced his displeasure to his ministers. The following February, to satisfy the royal wishes, Parliament got around to expelling Wilkes from the House of Commons. However, not to be outdone, the Middlesex' citizens immediately reelected him again. When the same series of events (Expulsion-Reelection) was repeated in April, Parliament decided it had had enough, and declared Henry Luttrell to be the winner of the next election in Middlesex, even though he had received only 296 votes while Wilkes received 1,143.

The Wilkes affair disturbed a number of members of Parliament as it brought back memories of royal abuses that commonly occurred before the Glorious Revolution. The heavy-handed treatment of John Wilkes, who had been properly elected to the House of Commons from Middlesex, but denied his seat because of the animosity of the King was disturbing. There was an introspective examination of their governance by several parliamentarians: Edmund Burke, an Irishman from Dublin, who was elected to the House of Commons in 1765 and quickly gained a reputation for his insightful intelligence, had written a pamphlet in 1769 entitled *Observations on a Late State of the Nation*. In it Burke defined a "political party" as *"a body of men united for promoting by their joint endeavors the national interest upon some particular principle in which they are all agreed."*

It was a positive definition as it defined group action which would enhance the national interest. It contrasted sharply with the political associations now predominant in Parliament which were based on personal loyalties and patronage. Burke was a leader, but was not alone in January 1770, in questioning the limits of power wielded by the King and his ministers in the running of the realm.

A number of prominent Whigs were dissatisfied with the manner in which the government and the monarchy were operating. Pitt-Chatham, Lord Chancellor Camden, William Beckford, the Lord Mayor of London and also a member of the House of Commons, as well as ex-prime minister, Rockingham and others were offended by the treatment shown Wilkes. Beyond that, they felt the government was drifting away from representing the needs of the people. They wanted more independence for the elected representatives in Commons and greater scrutiny and accountability of ministerial performance. There were motions made in Parliament for adding more representatives in Commons from the counties on the assumption they would be more independent than those from the boroughs. While no changes actually came about a simmering sentiment arose believing the monarchy was abusing its powers.

It was at this critical time the Duke of Grafton resigned his position as First Lord of the Treasury and Prime Minister. He was tired of the responsibilities he was under after Pitt-Chatham resigned, and put him in the lofty position. He was also tired of the attack he had been under by an anonymous writer named *Junius* in the *Public Advertiser*, the political tabloid newspaper, for his unsavory behavior in his pursuit of women, and attraction to gaming and horse racing.

The King was not at all dissatisfied to see Grafton leave and quickly installed Lord North as the new First Lord of the Treasury and Prime Minister. The new Prime Minister was a competent administrator, and well regarded for his financial acumen. He was generally well-liked by allies and opponents alike for his straightforward manner, and honesty in personal dealings. The King had a liking for North, who exhibited obsequious behavior toward the monarch. North saw his role as Prime Minister as one of striving to please the King, and running the government in a manner that would bring royal approval. It was a contrast to the more independent minded Prime Ministers who had preceded him. It was said a Prime Minister who could control Commons, and also have the strong support of the King, could guide the government in the direction of his choosing. North fit this model. Following the King's lead, North believed the American Colonies should be brought to subservience to Parliament, and he would use his position to ensure its occurrence.

With North as the Prime Minister operating out of the Commons the King felt more comfortable with his government. The sense of security North brought to the King was important to the monarch as he felt threatened. Those Whigs were causing problems with their malicious objections to the government, but that was not all. The same anonymous author, *Junius*, who had attacked the Duke of Grafton, had turned his ire on the King. In a startling article in the *Public Advertiser*, *Janius* warned the King directly, as reported in Christopher Hibbert's book *George III*:

You have still an honorable part to act. The affection of your subjects may still be recovered. But before you subdue their hearts, you must gain a noble victory over your own. Discard those little, personal resentments, which have too long directed your public conduct…Pardon this man [Wilkes]. Let it appear to your people that you can determine and act for yourself. Come forward to your people. Lay aside the wretched formalities of a King, and speak to your subjects with the spirit of a man and in the language of a gentleman. Tell them you have been fatally deceived…Remember that {the security of your title to the crown] was acquired by one revolution [in 1688]; it may be lost by another.

The reference to the King acting for himself was likely an allusion to the influence some felt he was still under from his mother and his former tutor, Lord Bute. But it was unlikely either was affecting his actions since his mother was seriously ill and Bute was traveling abroad. The inference may also have been a reference to the counsel he was receiving from members of his ministry. The threat, however, was clear, and may have contributed to the King's hardened attitude against all potential threats to his royal position, including those from across the Atlantic.

In early March of 1770 the Boston winter was still making life grim for members of the British troops bivouacked in the town. Being set among a hostile population, they were constantly reminded they were unwelcome intruders. The pay was poor, with little left over for personal items. Many of the soldiers, in their off hours would gladly take menial jobs from the merchants at less pay than the normal rate the town's laborers usually received, for which they were further resented.

One of the jobs the off-duty troops took was braiding rope that was used by the port's ships. On March 2, 1770 Patrick Walker, a soldier of the 29th regiment passed by John Gray's rope making shop where several laborers were working. Insults between Walker and the workers grew intense, and a fight broke out in which the trooper was beaten and had to flee. Back at his barracks he gathered several of his buddies, and returned to the shop with clubs to avenge his thrashing.

The workers, along with their apprentices, called out to others nearby, and repelled the soldiers. The fracas didn't end there as the scene was repeated, this time with more soldiers recruited to fight the laborers, but the result was the same. Additional brawls broke out at various locations as tempers were high on both sides.

News of the fight at the rope works quickly spread, and passing soldiers were insulted and taunted as cowards, which left them primed for confrontation. Soldiers passing citizens on the pathways used their cutlasses to temerariously rip at their clothes causing small cuts. Any soldier outside of the barracks would be pummeled with snowballs by young lads, further angering them.

Animosities simmered between Boston's workmen and the soldiers, and talk of further fights was widespread. In the evening of March 5th, as Private Hugh White was standing guard near the Customs House, a young lad, Edward Garrick, approached the soldier, and accused a British officer of not paying his master for service, thus impugning the troops' character. It shouldn't have been a serious matter, but the lad kept up the ridicule from outside White's sentry box.

White challenged the rude boy to show his face. When Garrick boldly stepped forward, the soldier struck him in the head with the butt of his musket. The boy, surprised, retreated, but White pursued him and struck him a second time. Other lads nearby heard Garrick's cries, and rushed over to join in taunting White. The commotion attracted an ever growing crowd of Bostonians.

As the crowd grew its behavior became more mob-like. They were incited by Edward Garrick, who was crying, tending his wounds, and pointing to Private White as the soldier who hit him. As the throng pressed forward toward White, he fastened his bayonet and loaded his musket. A bystander warned the soldier not to fire, but White grew very angry as some in the crowd pelted him with snowballs and pieces of icicles. As the throng grew, White's demeanor changed as he became more fearful for his safety, and he called for help from the Main Guard.

The officer of the guard, Captain Preston, appraised the situation, but was unsure of what action to take. Was the sentry in real danger, or were these just rowdy boys being troublesome. He finally gathered seven troopers with him to go to White's aid. It was later learned three of the rescue party had been in the fight at the rope works, and were still enraged from the humiliation they suffered there.

Arriving at the scene, the squad loaded their muskets. Captain Preston, sensing danger ordered the men, along with White, back to the barracks. However, the crowd was now so thick it was not possible for the men to move. Feeling threatened, Preston formed the squad in a semi-circle at a corner of the Customs House.

Many of Boston's citizens were familiar with the law which prohibited soldiers from firing their weapons without permission from a civil authority, and believed they would not fire as it would put them in jeopardy of being jailed. However, as the crowd became more unruly someone shouted "fire!" followed by others with the same order. Whether Captain Preston shouted "fire" is not for certain. Some witnesses said he did while others said he did not. Private Hugh Montgomery was struck by a solid piece of wood, knocking him to the ground. Furious, he rose awkwardly, raised his musket and fired into the crowd. A silent pause shocked the crowd as the sound reverberated off nearby buildings along King Street.

The other soldiers then also began to fire. One Crispus Attucks, a large, broad-shouldered former slave, but now a sailor, was hit by two of the lead balls, and died on the spot. Samuel Grey was hit in the head, and killed instantly.

As the firing continued several citizens fell to the street. Captain Preston ordered his men to stop firing. Cursing at the line of troops, he pushed their muskets back, repeating his order to cease fire. His action was too late as three citizens lay dead with two more succumbing to their wounds later. Several others sustained non-fatal injuries in what became known as the Boston Massacre.

As church bells resounded across the city, the dead and wounded were removed, leaving bloody footprints in the snow. The next morning a quickly called Boston Town Meeting was convened at Faneuil Hall where 3,500 to 4,000 citizens showed up. Samuel Adams, John Hancock, William Molineux and Deacon William Philips were empowered by the assemblage to demand that Hutchinson, the acting governor, remove the troops out of the city and relocate them to Castle William in the harbor. The city was decidedly on edge.

In the meeting with Acting Governor Hutchinson, the delegation from the Town Hall meeting demanded the immediate removal of all troops from the city. Adams emphasized the seriousness of the demand by stating, *"Nothing can rationally be expected to prevent blood and carnage, but the immediate removal of the troops."* His comment contained an implied threat of action by Massachusetts citizens outraged by the killings. In fact, a call had gone out to the surrounding towns to be prepared for some, as yet undefined, action. But, it is unlikely Adams and the others had a confrontation with the troops in mind, since their paramount aim was to have the troops removed by the royalist governor.

Hutchinson, however, recognizing the danger in Adams' comment, replied aggressively, *"If violence is the consequence of the illegal assembly of the people,* (since the Town Meeting had been called without a prior notice) *and an attempt should be made to drive out the King's troops, everyone abetting and advising would be guilty of high treason."* It was an overreaction, a specious threat which only served to strengthen agreement by all there, including members of the Massachusetts Council that the troops needed to go.

Hutchinson initially refused as he was unsure Lord Hillsborough would agree with their removal. In an attempt to avoid taking action, and thus draw disfavor from Hillsborough, he said aloud he did not know if he had the authority to remove the troops. When Colonel Dalrymple, who was in attendance at the meeting, stated he would abide by the governor's command, it placed Hutchinson in an awkward position. Since Dalrymple was implying Hutchinson did indeed have the authority.

In a compromise, Hutchinson declared he would remove only the offending 29th Regiment as it was their troops that had caused the disturbance. His proposal did not satisfy the town meeting representatives, and Samuel Adams demanded he remove of all of the troops. Hutchinson was again reluctant, again stating he was unsure of his authority. Adams reasoned, *"If you have the power to remove one regiment, you have the power to remove both."* Adams' logic was persuasive on the members of the Massachusetts Council present, who agreed all troops should be removed. Capitulating to the united voices, Hutchinson reluctantly ordered all troops to the fort on Castle William Island in Boston's Harbor; the 29th Regiment on March 10, the 14th the following day.

The deaths of ordinary colonists by British troops shocked all of the Americans, and were decried in newspapers in every colony. A vivid, colored print prepared by Paul Revere (some claim it was copied from a print originally prepared by Henry Pelham) was published widely. It depicted (inaccurately) the savagery of the shootings, and further inflamed sentiments against the British troops. The print even showed a musket firing from a window in the Customs House, substantiating a wild accusation that the Customs Commissioners or their agents somehow were involved. The picture provided a powerful visual impression, and alarmed many in colonial America; if it could happen in Boston, might each colony one day suffer a similar fate?

In an effort to show the troops in a favorable light, and the Boston citizens as instigators of the massacre, custom commissioner John Robinson took a sheath of dispositions from the military and royalist supporters to London for delivery to the colonial ministry there. A pamphlet was prepared from the documents, *A Fair Account of the Late Disturbances at Boston*, which was widely read and influenced opinion in Britain. Not to be out done, an opposing version of the events was prepared by patriots in Boston, and also sent to London where it was printed in British newspapers.

At the funeral procession of the victims of the shootings, ten thousand colonists marched behind the caskets, a reminder of the strength the Americans could muster. Fearing once again for their safety, the royalist custom commissioners removed themselves from Boston, thus verifying their contention that they could not conduct their normal duties without the support of British troops.

It is ironic that on the same day citizens were being killed in Boston, Lord North was before the House of Commons recommending the repeal of the Townshend Duties, except for tea. He stated his recommendation was not based on the mutinous acts in the colonies, but on a formal petition from the merchants and traders of the city of London, who were affected by the colonial boycott. Most in Parliament agreed with North; repealing the revenue acts would increase trade and improve British-Colonial relations. All were certain a viable trade would be resumed as the colonists needed British goods.

While improved colonial relations were expected by the removal of the duties, Lord North unnecessarily exacerbated the situation when he addressed the colonies option of creating manufactures of their own to avoid importing British goods with a veiled threat, *"The necessities of the Colonies and their want of union will open trade. There is an impossibility of their manufacturing to supply any considerable part of their wants. If they should attempt it and be likely to succeed, it is in our power to make laws, and so to check the manufactures in America for many years to come."*

The King had already made his feelings apparent by stating, *"There must always be one tax to keep up the right (to tax). And as such I approve of the tea tax."* In the debate that followed, Lord North, agreed with his King, arguing, *"The Americans have not deserved indulgence. The preamble to the Act and the duty on tea must be retained as a mark of Supremacy of Parliament and the efficient declaration of its right to govern the Colonies."*

The debate on repeal of the Townshend Acts continued into April 1770. When a last ditch attempt was made by a prominent group of parliamentarians to include tea in the repeal, the King became angry; he had stated his wishes, and objected strenuously to any action that would counter them. Finally, a vote was taken to repeal the Townshend duties, but retain the tax on tea. It passed on April 12, 1770.

It should be noted the statue to repeal the duties on imports did not affect two of the measures of the original act which were vigorously opposed by the colonies: the creation of the Board of Customs Commissioners in Boston, and the payment of the salaries of royal appointees in the colonies, independent of the colonial assemblies. The action of Parliament did not at all satisfy the colonists in America.

An insightful impression of the British King at the time is written in Volume IV of George Bancroft's mammoth *History of the United States.* Bancroft wrote,

> He did not rest on Colonial liberty or a people struggling towards more intelligence and happiness, the Crown was to him the emblem of all rightful power. He had that worst quality of evil, that he, as it were, adored himself; and regarded opposition to his designs as an offence against integrity and patriotism. He thought no exertions too great to crush the spirit of revolution, and no suffering or punishment too cruel or too severe for those whom he esteemed as rebels.

Chapter Twenty-Three

Trial and a Misleading Calm

Captain Preston and the soldiers involved in the shootings were arrested, but the trial was put off for six months, as the standing Superior Court judges were supposedly ill, and Hutchinson would not agree to appoint substitute judges. The delay allowed time for emotions to moderate, and for legal preparations to be initiated.

On March 6th, the day after the shootings, Captain Preston sent a messenger to John Adams asking for legal assistance in defending him at the upcoming trial. Thomas Hutchinson had recommended Adams, along with another patriot lawyer named Josiah Quincy, as counsels for Preston's defense. Hutchinson's reasoning in recommending two Sons of Liberty to act for the defense of a British officer, as well as the other troopers, is not known, but it did impart an aura of impartiality to the proceedings. Many believed the Captain was not in real danger, even if convicted. The crown had let it be known that, if convicted, Hutchinson was to delay sentencing until the King had an opportunity to grant a retrieve or a pardon.

The choice of John Adams to serve as counsel for the British soldiers was not especially surprising as he was regarded as an extremely honest man, as well as a very competent lawyer. John Adams was born in Braintree, Massachusetts on October 30, 1735, descended from a long line of Puritan ancestors. He shared his great-grandfather with his second cousin, Samuel Adams, thirteen years his senior. While Samuel's grandfather had moved to Boston, John's remained in Braintree (Quincy) to start his family. John's father, also named John, was a shoemaker and farmer; a deacon in the local Congregational church and a selectman of the town. His mother, Susanna Boyleston, an intelligent woman from nearby Brookline, also reflected the Puritan upbringing of her ancestors.

John Adams was well aware of his heritage, stating later in life, *"Neither my Father or Mother, Grandfather or Grandmother, Great Grandfather or Great Grandmother nor any other Relation that I know of or care a farthing have been in England these past 150 years. So that you see, I have not a drop of Blood in my veins, but what is American."*

The senior John Adams and his wife Susanna decided their oldest son would receive an education, so John, who had demonstrated a solid intellect, was sent to Harvard at sixteen; his parents hoping he would become a minister. After graduating in 1755, John taught Latin for a few years in Worcester, but found the experience boring. The law profession seemed to him a more interesting, challenging pursuit, and he gained an apprenticeship to a prominent Worcester attorney, James Putnam. In 1758, John was admitted to the Massachusetts bar, and began his legal career in earnest. After achieving a sustainable practice, on October 25, 1764 he married Abigail Smith, the daughter of a congressional minister, with whom he had six children.

While respecting his Puritan heritage, John did not embrace the Calvinist doctrine of predestination. He attended a congressional church presided over by a Unitarian minister, which seemed more agreeable with his religious views, including the importance of free-will as an essential attribute of human existence. John, as many entries in his diary show, was an introspective sort, who was often self-critical of his behavior in personal as well as business situations. He didn't dwell on any of the perceived shortcomings he identified; rather he strove to continually improve in manner and actions.

Attending James Otis' arguments in the Writs of Assistance trial in 1761, John was impressed with the logic put forth by Otis regarding basic human rights, which became a central aspect of his perception of the role of government. He was very vocal in opposing the British Stamp Act. In a meeting of the Massachusetts Council in 1765, he forcefully stated the act was, *"utterly void, and of no binding Force upon us; for it is against our Rights as Men, and our Privileges as Englishmen. A Parliament of Great Britain can have no more Right to tax the colonies than a Parliament of Paris."*

John's guiding principles were based on the *"dignity of human nature"* which included the right to govern only by the consent of the governed. With his profound respect for the law, and belief that every man had a right to a competent defense, Adams accepted the charge to defend Preston and the British troops. Quincy, following Adams' lead, also consented to defend the men. They would be joined by a loyalist attorney, Richard Auchmuty. None of the major patriot leaders like Samuel Adams or John Hancock objected to the assent of their patriot associates to defend the British soldiers, likely to show esteem for the proper application of the law. They were confident that Adams and Quincy would exercise a competent, fair defense which would serve as an example of the colony's respect for justice, contrasting the proceedings with overbearing British rule. The approval of the patriot leadership was substantiated when on June 6th; John Adams was elected to the Massachusetts House in a special election to replace a departing member.

As a result of the killings and woundings on King Street, the polarization between the loyalists to the crown and the patriots deepened, and life became more uncomfortable for those Bostonians professing allegiance to Parliament and King. Although there was little overt violence against the loyalists, there was still the occasional episode by the more rowdy Bostonians to keep the populace on edge.

In May 1770, a custom tidesman, Owen Richardson, who had been involved with the incident involving Hancock's ship *Lydia*, discovered some undeclared cargo (brown sugar) on the colonial schooner *Martin*. The customs official marked the cargo and the vessel with the King's mark, effectively seizing the boat. As it was becoming cool in the evening he returned home to get a warmer cloak. When he returned to the dock area, he was met by a mob yelling "an informer" at him. Although he fought back, he was overwhelmed. He was beaten and taken to the site of the shootings on King Street where he was stripped of his clothes, and tarred and feathered. None of the local Justices of the Peace dared interfere as the unruly crowd placed the unfortunate customs official in a cart, and paraded him about the streets.

However, Richardson's misfortune was not a common event in the city, and things were relatively quiet when the trial of the British soldiers finally began in the Queen's Street court in late October 1770. Captain Preston was to be tried first and alone, while the remaining troopers would be tried after the completion of the officer's trial. The troopers objected to this arrangement as their defense was partially based on their only following orders issued by their commander to "fire." If Preston were acquitted of giving the order to fire, where would that leave them? It was an uncomfortable position for Adams and Quincy to be in as they were defending all of the accused. However, the decision to go with the Captain's trial first was finally ordered by the court.

The selection of a jury of twelve men ended with a fair representation of both loyalists and patriots. The prosecution was led by Samuel Quincy, Josiah's brother, who, unlike Josiah, was a staunch loyalist.

Witnesses' testimony of events on King Street were confusing; conflicting descriptions of events and actions of those involved, the rule. There was further confusion because of the rumors that were being bantered about which purported to explain the motives behind the fray. One was that the troopers had planned the confrontation to pay the citizens back because of the defeat they had suffered at the rope works. Another stated the patriot leaders orchestrated the melee to inflame the populace against the troops' presence in the city. Still another was whispers of a secret plot to plunder the crown's colonial treasury which was kept in the Customs House.

It was difficult for the jury to separate fact from conjecture or outright lies. Probably the most telling testimony was given by Richard Palmes, a resolute Son of Liberty, who attested he had his hand on Captain Preston's shoulder, and was looking into his face when the order to "fire" was shouted. With Palmes' telling words, and the conflicting testimony of the other witnesses, Captain Preston was declared "Not Guilty" on October 31, 1770. He was quickly returned to Britain; in such haste he never thanked his defenders.

The trial of the other soldiers was delayed as the court took up other business, so the second phase of the trial did not begin in earnest until late November. The defense of the soldiers was based on two premises: The first, they were following a legitimate order of their officer to fire; and second, they were in immediate danger from the crowd.

The witnesses' testimony in this trial was as confusing as it had been in the earlier one, so it was difficult to ascertain the true facts of the episode. As a result Corporal Wemms, Privates Harrigan, McCauley, White, Warren, and Carrol were all declared "Not Guilty." However, there was a sense that someone must be guilty since citizens had been shot. Tensions were still high in the community, and it would be difficult to find all of the soldiers' guilt-free. Thus, Privates Mathew Kilroy and Hugh Montgomery, the two all agreed had fired their weapons, were found not guilty of murder, but guilty of manslaughter. While they could have faced the death penalty, they pleaded "benefit of clergy," employing a medieval English law that allowed them to be defined as clergy by reading a passage from the bible. They were thus sentenced to the reduced penalty of branding, which was done by a hot iron on their thumbs. In an epilog to the affair, Hugh Montgomery later admitted it was he who had yelled "fire" after being knocked down by a piece of wood thrown at his head.

With the repeal of the Townshend duties, a more normal trade resumed between Britain and the colonies, welcomed by merchants on both side of the ocean. Samuel Adams tried to keep the ire of the Bostonians focused on the nearby troops and the British government, but since the troops had left the city proper, and the Townshend duties were no longer a major irritant, the ardor of the town's anger slackened. The hiatus was short-lived, however, as hostile British actions soon had the colonists again aroused.

After the trial, the Massachusetts House elected sixty-four old Benjamin Franklin to represent their interests in London. He was appointed to present the colony's objections to Parliament's ability to tax them directly to the King and his ministers. The well-respected Franklin was already representing Pennsylvania, Georgia and New Jersey, where his son was the royal governor. Immediately after the vote appointing Franklin, Massachusetts Governor Hutchinson wrote to Colonial Minister Hillsborough, advising him of the election, and urging him not to accept Franklin's appointment as Hutchinson had not approved the appointment (actually he was not even consulted by the members of the House about the appointment). When Franklin, in December 1771, paid a courtesy visit to Hillsborough at his residence to inform him of his new duties, the Minister was extremely impolite, and stated he could not accept his charge to represent Massachusetts as he had not been approved by Massachusetts' royal governor. Franklin pointed out he was representing the Massachusetts House of Representatives, and not the royal governor. Franklin was not intimidated by the rejection, and continued performing in the role, effectively representing the colony.

In London at the end of 1770, the dire warnings of imminent revolt in the Massachusetts Colony related by Frances Bernard, the ex-governor of Massachusetts, who was now at Hillsborough's side, were augmented by similar reports from the present governor Thomas Hutchinson. Lord Hillsborough was sufficiently alarmed that he advocated further measures be taken against Massachusetts in general and Boston in particular. The colonial minister was convinced strong measures must be taken to prevent a move to independence by the colony which could envelope the entire British domain in America. While, in fact, there were such sentiments in the colony, convictions had not yet hardened for many to such an extreme path. It was the King and Hillsborough, with prodding from Hutchinson, who made moves which drove the populace to consider independence as a viable alternative.

Spurred by Hillsborough's warnings, the King's council developed plans to contain Boston by British military might. Additional naval ships were ordered to Boston Harbor where they would menace the city. Hutchinson was directed to turn over the fort on Castle William in the harbor to troops commanded by General Gage. The governor did this in an especially nefarious manner. The fort on the island in Boston's harbor had always been under the jurisdiction of the Massachusetts Colony. It was paid for and maintained with colonial funds, and the sentries on duty there were colonial militia. The replacement of the militia by British troops was a gross violation of the colony's charter.

Hutchinson, fully aware of the significance of the move, had hesitated before actually making it. But, as he still strongly curried Hillsborough's favor, he went ahead. It was a despicable provocation that was worsened by the manner in which Hutchinson acted. He had called the Massachusetts Council to discuss the action, and while they were at the meeting the British troops under Colonel Dalrymple took command of the fort. The reaction of the members of the Council, as well as other political leaders, when they learned of the subterfuge maneuvered by the governor, was outrage at his nefarious behavior. Hutchinson was so concerned by the reaction, and the hostility he felt, he spent the next week in the safety of the fort.

Hillsborough was now satisfied he had Boston contained. British troops controlled the strategic fort in the harbor, and British naval ships were positioned to take action against the city if its defiance expanded. Hutchinson wrote to Hillsborough, *"no measure could have been pitched upon more proper than the possession of the harbor of Boston by the King's troops and ships."*

Thomas Hutchinson had previously sent a letter to Lord Hillsborough earlier in 1770 resigning from his position as Acting Royal Governor, citing various reasons for leaving the post, but most likely was dissatisfied with the "Acting" in his title. Finally, in March 1771, Hillsborough responded. He requested Hutchinson remain in the position, but he would be Massachusetts' Royal Governor without the "Acting" appellation. Further, he would be paid an annual stipend of 1,500 pounds sterling, a mighty sum, and it would be paid directly from the crown, making him financially independent of the colonial assembly.

In his correspondence with Hillsborough, Hutchinson had advocated a complete revision of the Massachusetts Charter, replacing the original charter with one in which Britain would exercise effective control over all of the significant government functions. The King and his ministers, however, decided against a complete revision, opting instead for a change which would have the colony's Council, the upper house of the assembly, appointed by the King rather than elected by members of the Massachusetts House. The Council members' salary would also be paid by the crown. Such a move would have made the colony extremely subservient to the monarch and his government in Britain. Hutchinson, while still favoring a complete rewrite of the charter to insure subservience to the crown and Parliament, dutifully submitted names for potential council members who would serve the crown faithfully.

There was no doubt in Hutchinson's mind the citizens of the colony would object strenuously to such a drastic change, but with war ships in the harbor and troops in the castle, they would have little recourse to remonstrate.

The resumption of trade, and the lessening of overt disturbances seemed, in general (except for Boston), to bring a period of quiescence between Britain and her American Colonies. However, even with this more placid atmosphere, there was no slackening of the commitment of the colonies to control their own affairs. The concept of real independence was growing, not only in Massachusetts, but across the breadth of the colonial landscape.

Adams, like Franklin and many others, was coming to the conclusion the colonies were formed with (or grew into) the status of states which would tax and legislate their own governments, with no need or want of Parliament's involvement. Parliament's taxation of the colonies, and stationing of a standing army on their soil, was a violation of their sovereignty and, likewise, was even an abuse of the British Constitution.

With his obsession with subduing Boston and Massachusetts, Hillsborough, lulled by the reduction of overt hostile acts, overlooked the prevailing mood in the rest of the American colonies. The general reaction to Britain's threats to one colony angered and enflamed many in the others. He did not perceive the depth of asperity felt by all of the colonists to the menace they sensed to their liberty by Parliament's and the King's challenge to their own governance. In his arrogance, tempered with ignorance, the colonial minister continued to provoke animosity by actions sure to rile resistance.

In late 1771 the colonial assembly of Georgia elected as its new speaker, Noble Jones, an upstanding, well respected citizen. Georgia's Royal Governor, however, suspected Jones was *"a very strong Liberty Boy"* and would not allow him to serve. The legislature objected to the Royal Governor's interference, but Minister Hillsborough, true to his obstinateness, belligerent character directed the governor *"to put his negative upon any person whom they (the Georgia Assembly) should next elect for Speaker, and to dissolve the Assembly in case they should question the right of such a negative."*

In South Carolina, the Royal Governor, Lord Charles Greville Montagu, routinely irritated his colony's citizens by the arrogant manner in which he operated. Several judges were dismissed for actions objected to by the royal governor, and replaced with loyal Britons sent by Hillsborough from Ireland, Scotland and Wales. The governor also alienated South Carolinas' citizens by demanding the construction of a mansion for him to live in, as well as claiming he could appropriate funds for official use without the approval of the Colony's Council.

An especially poignant confrontation with the King and his government arose in Virginia over the continued importation of slaves from Africa. Even Thomas Jefferson, a slave owner, seemed to realize the inhumane and immoral practice of slave ownership. While keeping his present salves, he wanted to eliminate the importation of more. Or, as Virginian Patrick Henry would say in a similar vein, while acknowledging the inhumanity of slave ownership, *"I am drawn along by the general inconvenience of living without them."*

Of more immediate concern than the moral correctness of slave ownership, however, were situations arising where revolts against white owners were possible. In several towns slaves outnumbered the white settlers. Virginia had tried to legislate the cessation of slave imports in the past, but had been rebuffed by the British rulers. In December 1770, the King, influenced by the wealthy slave traders in London, who were accruing great profits from the business, had issued a resolve to the Virginia Assembly, *"upon pain of the highest displeasure, to assent to no law, by which the importation of slaves should be in any respect prohibited or obstructed."*

Now, in April 1772, the issue was revisited by the Virginia Legislature where a new petition to the King was prepared:

> The importation of slaves into the colonies from the coast of Africa hath long been considered as a trade of great inhumanity; and, under its present encouragement, we have too much reason to fear, will endanger the very existence of your majesty's American dominions. We are sensible that some of your majesty's subjects in Great Britain may reap emoluments from this sort of traffic; but when we consider that it greatly retards the settlement of the colonies with more useful inhabitants, and may in time have the most destructive influence, we presume to hope that the interest of a few will be disregarded, when placed in competition with the security and happiness of such numbers of your majesty's dutiful and loyal subjects.
>
> Deeply impressed with these sentiments, we most humbly beseech your majesty to remove all those restraints on your majesty's governors of this colony which inhibit their assenting to such laws as might check so very pernicious commerce.

A number of other colonies were of the same sentiment as Virginia, and similar petitions were discussed in Maryland, New Jersey, North Carolina, Pennsylvania and New York. Massachusetts had already addressed the subject.

Virginia's petition was deliberately ignored by the King, thus reaffirming his previous position the slave trade would continue unabated. The King's rejection was a manifestation of the monarch and his ministers impressing their will on the colonies in an area the colonists considered vital to their well-being. It was as if the government in Britain reacted negatively to any petition or redress from the American Colonies, as they considered the requests as challenges to their right to rule.

It was becoming clear that the colonies would not only not accept Parliament's authority to tax them, but would also refuse to accept Parliament's right to legislate for them as well. In a more consequential awareness, the right of the King's rule over the colonies was coming into dispute.

In Britain, the King and Parliament deemed themselves to be the overriding authority for all of the British Domain. To question that authority was tantamount to sedition. Thus, with this rigid, intractable persuasion of righteous dominance pervading the British government, and the new awakenings in the American Colonies of their right to govern themselves, and determine their own future, a line was being drawn and stiffened between the contradicting views, and no peaceful means were readily apparent to resolve the disputes as confrontations continued.

In May 1772, the Massachusetts House elected John Hancock to the Council which was composed of the more loyal citizens. Governor Hutchinson let it be known he would approve of the move. He was likely following Lord Hillsborough's earlier suggestion that he should curry favor with Hancock, who they thought seemed partial to positions of importance, and in the Council would be further separated from the influence of the more rabid Bostonians. Hancock was never influenced by any but his own apperceptions. He saw through Hutchinson's maneuver, and refused the position. Interestingly, the following month the House elected John Adams to the Massachusetts Council as he was commanding more respect in the colony's politics. Hutchinson, as expected, vetoed this appointment.

Naval vessels were commonly used in support of the customs commissioners in the enforcement of the duties established by Parliament, by stopping and searching colonial ships in an effort to find illegal cargo. One such naval officer, Lieutenant William Dudingston, commander of the schooner Gaspee, was extremely zealous in his enforcement efforts in the waters around Rhode Island.

New England was considered a hotbed of smuggling by the custom commissioners, with Rhode Island prominent even over the other colonies in the region. The Rhode Islanders had previously had clashes with British navy vessels, but in 1772 they were especially irritated by the actions of the Gaspee and its captain. The Rhode Island governor, Joseph Wanton, had sent a letter to Lt. Dudingston requesting to see the papers authorizing him to conduct his frequent searches of colonial ships. Dudingston, indignant, forwarded the letter to Admiral John Montagu, commander of the British fleet in America. The Admiral immediately wrote the Rhode Island Governor a scathing letter telling him to leave the Lieutenant alone, and not to question his orders.

Lt. Dudingston, more confident with the Admiral's support, on the late afternoon of June 9, 1772, spied a small sailing craft coming into Narragansett Bay. The craft was captained by a Rhode Island native, Thomas Lindsay, who was sailing from Newport to Providence. Irked at the approach of the Gaspee, Lindsay decided to run north in the bay, hoping to reach Providence before the Gaspee could catch him. The Gaspee immediately gave chase, intending to board the fleeing vessel, and search her for smuggled cargo.

Dudingston ordered a shot across the bow of the escaping ship, demanding it stop and be searched. Lindsay, however, was not deterred, and continued around Namquid Point a few miles south of Providence. At this maneuver, Lt. Dudingston saw an opportunity to close on the colonial ship by taking a shorter path closer to the shore. To the anguish of the Lieutenant, the Gaspee ran aground in the low-tide waters. Try as they might, her crew could not budge the schooner; it was tightly fixed to the sea bottom. Relief would come only on the next high tide at three the next morning.

When Lindsay arrived in Providence, he reported the grounding of the hated Gaspee, and described her helpless situation. A party of Rhode Island's Sons of Liberty saw an opportunity for revenge against the disliked Lieutenant and his troublesome Gaspee. An armed party was organized, and set out in several longboats from Fenner's Wharf, to find the trapped Gaspee.

Arriving at the Gaspee several hours later, the invaders were soon spotted by the British crew, and a fight broke out. Shots were fired, one wounding Lt. Dudingston, and the angry colonists quickly overwhelmed the outnumbered defenders. After tending to Dudingston's wound, he and his crew were moved to the shore near Warwick. The Gaspee was then set afire. As the combatants watched, the ship burned furiously before exploding, completely destroying it.

The Royal Governor, Wanton offered a five hundred pound reward for identification of the perpetrators of the raid, but no one came forward to identify a single individual. The saga would continue later when the King learned of the attack on a British naval vessel, and took actions that further angered the colonists.

While the affair of the Gaspee would soon have repercussions on British/ Colonial relations, Minister Hillsborough was further evoking strong negative reactions from the citizens of Massachusetts. According to the Massachusetts Charter, the Governor, with the consent of the Council, appointed the judges of the Supreme Court. While the judges effectively served at the pleasure of the crown through the Royal Governor, the Massachusetts House of Representatives had a strong influence on the jurists as they voted their salaries; and the vote was done annually. Hillsborough disrupted this arrangement when, on July 26, 1772, he ordered the British Treasury to begin paying the judges salaries. The Treasury complied, garnering the funds, *"from the Duties on Tea imported into America."*

Back in London at this time, Benjamin Franklin was helping to coordinate an effort to establish a new British Colony in the Ohio Territory. Investing in this endeavor was a number of prominent members of Parliament, who carried great weight in the English capitol. For unknown reasons, Hillsborough strongly opposed the venture, angering the prominent, potential investors. This opposition, combined with a general dissatisfaction of his superintendence of the American Colonies by numerous others in government, led to his dismissal from office in August 1772. The King replaced him as Minister for the American Colonies with William Legge, the second Earl of Dartmouth. Lord Dartmouth was Lord North's younger step-brother. Even with Hillsborough gone, however, Franklin never did get approval to start the new colony.

Dartmouth was liked by nearly everyone. He was the veritable opposite of the irascible, caustic Hillsborough. The new minister was considerate and mild in manner; adverse to contentious situations, he worked to resolve disputes without rancor. He was a philanthropist, granting large sums to establish an Indian School in the Connecticut Colony that later became a college bearing his name.

While advocating moderation in Britain's handling of the American Colonies, he was, however, a dutiful servant of the realm, and strictly enforced the King's decrees and Parliament's laws. The interactions between Dartmouth and the colonies were characterized by more civility than accorded by the Hillsborough ministry, but, fundamentally, nothing really changed with Britain asserting their domination over them, *"in all cases whatsoever."*

While Hillsborough was no longer involved, his action regarding the judges' salaries caused Samuel Adams to call a Boston Town meeting as the Massachusetts Assembly was not in session. The meeting, held on November 20, 1772, deplored the reduction of control over colonial judges by the Massachusetts House of Representatives, and approved the sending of a letter to all towns in the colony asking each to set up a standing committee of correspondence to coordinate the colony's reactions to British incursions on their liberty. With a mutual feeling of distrust of Britain's dominion over them, nearly all of the population centers in the colony responded quickly and favorably.

In town and villages across the province, meetings were held to debate the issue culminating in votes being taken, and referendums approved. In the village of Kittery they spoke plainly, *"We offer our lives as a sacrifice in the glorious cause of liberty."* The Cambridge assembly was, *"much concerned to maintain and secure their invaluable rights which were not gifts of Kings, but purchased with the precious blood and treasure of their ancestors."*

The people of Roxbury echoed the call, *"Our pious Forefathers died with the pleasing hope, that we their children should live free; let none, as they will answer it another day, disturb the ashes of those heroes by selling their birthright."* The people of Roxbury, like those in Cambridge and elsewhere, were referring to their Puritan ancestors who had left England to escape the rule of an unjust monarch. All across the colony towns joined in the chorus. From the fishermen of Gloucester to the farmers of Lenox, the exhortation for opposition against illegal British rule reverberated. The citizens of the small town of Pembroke came right to the point, *"if the measures so justly complained of were persisted in and enforced by fleets and armies, they must, they will, in a little time issue in the total dissolution of the union between the mother country and the Colonies."*

The formation of the Committees of Correspondence established a potent process for rapid, coordinated reaction to Britain's dictates. Governor

Hutchinson, in a letter to the colonial ministry in London, which was read by the King, referred to the organizers of the correspondence committees as *"blackhearted fellows whom one would not choose to meet in the dark."* The intensity of temper by the majority of the colonists to the perceived threat to their freedom was laid openly for all to see. These settlers were willing to forego their fortunes and lives to preserve their liberty; yet these convictions were not appreciated within the governmental halls in London. There, they clung to the comforting surety that the problems in the colonies were due to a few misguided malcontents, who, if properly quelled, would allow order to be reinstated and submission to British law restored.

The Committees of Correspondence were not official organizations authorized by the colonial charters, and thus were free of many legal restraints of British and Colonial law that dictated their activities. While the Massachusetts' committees were a strong enabler for coordinated action within that province; it took the King's wrath regarding the destruction of the Gaspee to expand the concept across all of the American Colonies. On December 19, 1772, the Providence Gazette reported the King was endeavoring to identify those responsible for destroying the Gaspee, and to bring them to England where they would be tried for treason, and presumably hanged. The King had enacted a Commission of Inquiry, which included the Rhode Island Royal Governor, along with the Chief Justices of New York, New Jersey, and Massachusetts, and also included the judge of the Admiralty Court in New England.

The threat of taking colonial citizens back to England for trial disturbed many Americans, as it engendered the repulsion many recalled of monarchial intrusion on individual liberties that were a malignancy in England's past. In Virginia, the Virginia House of Burgesses, acting in a manner similar to what was done in Massachusetts with their towns, formed its own Committee of Correspondence which included Patrick Henry and Thomas Jefferson.

The committee's purpose was defined clearly:

> whose business it shall be to obtain the most early and authentic intelligence of all Acts and Resolutions of the British Parliament, or proceedings of Administration as may relate to or affect the British Colonies in America, and to keep up and maintain a Correspondence and Communication with our sister Colonies, respecting these important Considerations...

The Virginia House directed its Speaker to send copies of their committee's purpose to all of the other American Colonies, and request they establish similar committees; which he did on March 19, 1773. All of the remaining colonies eventually did establish similar committees, adopting the same or a similar purpose to that enacted by Virginia. It affected a united colonial approach to

Britain which grew in importance as the now colonial-wide Committees of Correspondence could work together in their opposition to British rule.

In an epilog to the sinking of the Gaspee, the King's Committee of Inquiry could not find any competent witnesses to identify those who committed the destruction of the ship. In an official report to the King in June 1773, the committee verified the absence of any reliable witnesses, thus effectively ending the inquiry, to the great frustration of Admiral Montagu and many in the King's Privy Council.

Chapter Twenty-Four

Letters and Tea

In March 1773, Thomas Cushing, the Speaker of the Massachusetts House, had received a packet of letters sent to him by Benjamin Franklin, the House's London representative. Franklin had received the letters the previous December from a London friend who wanted to show him that much of the discord which existed between the British government and the Massachusetts Colony originated not in Britain's governmental offices in London, but, surprisingly, in the Massachusetts Colony itself. Franklin's friend asserted the discord was not the result of the British government's malicious desire to dominate the colony, but rather originated with high-ranking officials in the Massachusetts Colony, who had repeatedly sent inaccurate, damming reports about the colony's citizens who were accused of continuously abusing their freedom by felonious actions, and by denigrating the King and Parliament.

The packet contained nineteen letters, which had been written to Thomas Whately, a former Member of Parliament, and strong advocate of the Stamp Act, who had died the previous June. The letters had been written in the late 1760's by several important New England authors, including the present Massachusetts Colonial Governor, Thomas Hutchinson, and Lieutenant Governor, Andrew Oliver.

Franklin's friend wanted the colonial representative to show the letters to his patriot friends in America so they could see the damaging information that was being received in London from prominent colonial sources. It was these malicious ruminations, Franklin's friend alleged, which affected the corrosive atmosphere between Britain and America. If Franklin were to show the letters to his governmental friends in Massachusetts, they could see true source of the dissonance between the two governments, and, hopefully, mend the breach. The letters came to Franklin with several constraints: No copies could be made of them nor could they be published, they could be shown only to those of Franklin's acquaintances in America he felt would benefit from reading them, and lastly Whatley's name must be removed.

Upon reception in Massachusetts the letters were, at first, read by a selected few throughout Boston and the surrounding towns. John Adams had shown them in his travels outside of Boston, where they were seen by many, but only on an individual basis. Those viewing the letters wanted them available to a wider audience so all could see the duplicity of the authors, and chafed at the restriction on publication. Suddenly, in June of 1773, Samuel Adams stated he had come into possession of copies of the letters independently of those sent by Franklin, and thus could be published. John Hancock later admitted it was he who had given the letters to Adams after he had received them from an unnamed source on Boston Commons. To Franklin's dismay, as he was not duped by this self-serving maneuver, the letters were published in many colonial newspapers for everyone to read.

The letters from New England deplored the illegal mobs raging in Boston, threatening government officials in the performance of their lawful duties, and wrecking the homes and businesses of the same officials in an attempt to intimidate them. The letters' writers encouraged the sending of British troops to Boston to constrain the citizenry by force so they could be governed in an orderly, lawful manner. Perhaps, it was mentioned, it might be necessary to alter the Massachusetts Colony's charter to strengthen the King's control over the appointment of colonial officers, judges and legislators to insure the proper running of the government. One of the letters even went so far as to recommend the denial of Parliament's supremacy be made a capital crime.

Governor Hutchinson had penned six of the letters enunciating sentiments which caused him the most severe reprisals. He had written: *"I never think of the measures necessary for the peace and good order of the colonies without pain. There must be an abridgement of what are called English Liberties."* He added, *"I wish the good of the colony when I wish to see some further restraint of liberty rather than the connexion with the parent state should be broken; for I am sure such a breach must prove the ruin of the colony."*

Hutchinson did indeed have a genuine affection for his colony; he was a native Bostonian, being born to a prominent family in Boston's north end. He came from a long line of colonial ancestors, but the colony he desired was one subservient to Britain; one which would be bound by Parliament's laws and be subject to paying taxes levied against them. His membership in King's Chapel, an Anglican Church, was further evidence of his love for things British, and at odds with the puritan history of most of the local population, who attended Congregationalist Churches.

According to Hutchinson's defenders the letters were personal correspondences to a person the writer considered a friend, not official dispatches to a British government official. However, they were written by colonial government officials to a British government official, and in that vein were at least quasi-official reports. They did not really reveal anything new, as the opinions expressed in them had been voiced openly by these same writers. But, it was one thing for Hutchinson and Oliver to make their views known in speeches in Boston to the citizens there, and quite another to document similar thoughts to British authorities in London, especially when some of the letters implored the recipients to keep their contents secret, thus substantiating their deceitful intentions.

The patriot leaders in all of the American Colonies were outraged. Hutchinson was advocating a restraint of their liberties—the very cause they were vigorously championing against. On June 23, 1773 the Massachusetts House approved a petition to the King's Privy Council by a vote of 80 to 11 to remove both Hutchinson and Oliver from their posts. The petition did not accuse the men of any criminal conduct; rather they were denounced for losing the confidence of the colony's legislature. Hutchinson, himself, requested a leave of absence from his duties to sail to London to clear his name.

However, the crisis created with the publication of the letters in June 1773, although adding to the distrust between the two sides, was soon overtaken by events of substantially greater consequence.

The British East India Company was originally formed to compete with the Dutch in the East Indies, who had established a trade with the islands in Southeast Asia for spices and other tropical goods. The British company was formed as a joint-stock company with its charter granted by Queen Elizabeth in 1600. In the years following its inception, circumstances altered the direction of the company as it became more involved in India and China, where British conquests opened up lucrative trade opportunities in cotton, silk, indigo, opium, and, especially, tea. From the beginning, investors in the company came from the higher echelons of British society, including many powerful members of the government, which gave it special advantages.

The company had a tumultuous history, with periods of prosperity intertwined with periods of uncertainty and financial distress. In India it operated as a quasi-government, effectively ruling parts of the country, as well as managing most of its trade. In 1773, the company was at one of the lowest financial points in its existence. Troubles in Bengal, combined with the colonial boycott of tea, had put the company in a dire financial position, bringing it to the brink of bankruptcy.

The company had warehouses in England full of tea, but exports to America, where they consumed over a million pounds of tea annually, had come to a veritable standstill due to the effectiveness of the embargo on British tea by the colonies. The boycott was a problem, but another obstacle to the trade of tea from Britain was its significantly greater cost than tea from other sources. British law required the East India Company to bring its tea for export first to Britain, where a heavy duty was placed on it, before merchants could purchase it, and export it abroad. As a result, America was buying cheaper smuggled tea in large quantities. As the company was an important facet of Britain's economy, some in America thought the financial pressure on the East India Company, as a result of their boycott, would eventually force Britain to rescind the Townshend duty on tea. It became obvious to the government in London something had to be done.

In early 1773, Prime Minister North, believed things had calmed somewhat in the American Colonies since the repeal of most of the Townshend duties. There were, of course, the occasional disruption such as the burning of the Gaspee, and that unfortunate matter of the shooting of civilians by British troops, and even a few other episodes, but; they were minor, and much less troublesome than the mob riots inspired by the Stamp and Townshend Acts.

Lord North, with his financial acumen, came up with what he saw as an effective plan to solve several problems with a single action. In his plan, the East India Company would be allowed to ship tea directly to the American Colonies without having to store it in England, and not to have to pay any duty in Britain at all. Of course, the very meager (three pence per pound) duty from the Townshend Acts would have to be assessed upon landing the tea in America, but it was such a trifling amount that the East India Company tea would be available in America at considerably less cost than smuggled tea from the Dutch, French or privateers.

North thought his solution inspirational, even though he was told bluntly by a Member of Parliament if they didn't remove the Townshend duty from the tea, the Americans would not take it. North countered with the assertion that at such a low cost, the colonists would eagerly purchase the cheap tea. By so doing, the American Colonies would be acknowledging the right of Parliament to impose a duty on them that was for the purpose of raising revenue for the British treasury. *"Men will always go to the cheapest markets,"* he observed, avoiding consideration of the colonists strong aversion to being taxed in such a manner.

North's ideas, which the King strongly endorsed, were embodied in the Tea Act, which Parliament approved on May 10, 1773. The act also allowed the East India Company to appoint distributors of their own choosing, who would have a monopoly in their geographic markets to import and sell the tea. Since the acquisition of such a distributorship was expected to be very profitable, it could become a sort of patronage to reward loyal subjects in America, and be damaging to any merchant who did not pledge their loyalty to Britain.

Considerably lowering the price of tea was disastrous to many merchants on both sides of the Atlantic. Merchants, who were not designated as official distributors by the East India Company, who had purchased tea at the higher price with the expectation they could resell it with a profit added, now found their inventory worth much less than they had paid for it; a financial disaster for them. It was obvious to many of the merchants their interests were being subjugated to the desire of the British government to finally have a method of enforcing the colonies to pay a tax enacted by Parliament, and they added their voices in opposition to the Act.

One family which was not left out was the Hutchinson's. The Massachusetts Royal Governor had invested a considerable sum in the East India Company, and his two sons, Thomas and Elisha, and another relative, Richard Clarke, were among the five authorized agents to import, and sell tea in the port of Boston.

The King and his Ministers in Britain may have thought it was an excellent plan which would solve several of their more bothersome problems, but again, they completely misread the Colonial sentiments. Ben Franklin warned the tea company and the British Ministry the plan would fail as the American Colonists were firm in their intractable conviction no duty would be paid on the tea, whatever its cost. He wasn't aware what specific action the colonies would take to refuse the tea, but was certain it would be forceful. Lord North, with a bit of arrogance, replied, *"It is to no purpose making objections, for the king will have it so. He means to try the question with the Americans."* The King seemed to be daring them—to not comply would unleash an unsaid, but ominous reaction against them.

The American Colonies, however, were not deterred; to accept the tea would be to accept a menial role in the British Realm, which these proud settlers, whose ancestors had suffered so much to create a land where they could be free and now prosperous, was unthinkable. The passage of the Tea Act, and the colonial responses to it were momentous events. Upon learning of the British plan to sell cheap tea with the small tax added, the colonists' reactions were immediate and formidable. The Committees of Correspondence, which were now established across the breadth of the colonies, along with the Sons of Liberty, denounced the British tactic as a subterfuge designed to force compliance with Parliament's right to tax them, and plans were made to prohibit the landing of any of the tainted tea on their shores.

In August, as the East India Company received its official documents allowing it to export tea directly to the colonies, colonial newspapers took up the subject, printing warnings by colonial leaders, and branding the British Parliament as devious and untrustworthy. Samuel Adams called for a colonial congress to coordinate a response. Shouts for independence, only alluded to in the past, now became an open clamor. The Boston Gazette reported (likely at the urging of Adams) the need for a *"Congress of American States to form a Bill of Rights, or to form an independent state, an American Commonwealth."*

In mid-October, 1773, seven ships of the East India Company, laden with two thousand chests of tea, departed Britain bound for ports in America. The *Polly* was bound for Philadelphia, the *Nancy* for New York, the *London* for Charleston, and four ships, the *Dartmouth, Eleanor, Beaver* and *William* for Boston. Their reception in each of the cities was eventful.

Philadelphia: As the ship *Polly* under the command of Captain Ayers, began its voyage across the Atlantic bound for the port of Philadelphia, the citizens of that city, alerted to the ship's journey, held a town meeting at their State House October 16, 1773, attended by thousands. The outrage of the populace was palpable. After much debate and discussion, what became known as the "Philadelphia Resolves" were approved overwhelmingly. They were published in the Philadelphia Gazette on October 20, 1773:

1. That the disposal of their own property is the inherent right of freemen, that there can be no property in that which can, of right, take from us without our consent, that the claim of Parliament to tax America is, in other words, a claim of right to levy contributions on us at pleasure.
2. That the duty imposed by Parliament upon tea landed in America is a tax on the Americans, or levying contributions on them without their consent.
3. That the express purpose for which the tax is levied on the Americans, namely for the support of government, administration of justice, and defense of his Majesty's dominions in America, has a direct tendency to render assemblies useless and to introduce arbitrary government and slavery.
4. That a virtuous and steady opposition to this ministerial plan of governing America is absolutely necessary to preserve even the shadow of liberty and is a duty which every freeman in America owes to his country, to himself, and to his posterity.
5. That the resolutions lately entered into by the East India Company to send out their tea to America, subject to the payment of duties on its being landed here, is an open attempt to enforce this ministerial plan and a violent attack upon the liberties of America.
6. That it is the duty of every American to oppose this attempt.
7. That whoever shall, directly or indirectly, countenance this attempt or in any wise aid or abet in unloading, receiving, or vending the tea sent or to be sent out by the East India Company while it remains subject to the payment of a duty here, is an enemy to his country.
8. That a committee be immediately chosen to wait on those gentlemen who, it is reported, are appointed by the East India Company to receive and sell said tea and request them, from a regard to their own characters and the peace and good order of the city and province, immediately to resign their appointment.

In response to the last resolve, the committee so ordained, met the East India Company representatives authorized by the company to import and sell tea. Pointing out the detestability of importing the tainted tea, and the strong opposition to it, the committee requested they resign their positions. The implied threat of retribution, along no doubt with patriotic fervor by some, convinced them to comply, and within a few days all had done so.

When, in November, the Polly arrived at Chester in the Delaware River below Philadelphia, the citizens formed a "Committee for Tarring and Feathering," which went to the ship to meet with the Captain and present a message to him. In it they stated they realized the Captain was not from this place, and thus might not be aware of the strong displeasure of the citizens to the landing of his cargo.

They told him they appreciated he might not recognize the diabolical nature of the mission he was assigned, in which the British government schemed to tax them without their consent. They warned him of the possible consequences which might ensue if he was foolish enough to attempt to complete it. As reported by the committee, they inquired of him, *"What think you Captain, of a halter around your neck, ten gallons of liquid tar decanted on your pate, with feathers of a dozen wild geese laid over that to enliven your appearance?"*

After due consideration, the Captain agreed to turn back, and return to England without unloading his tea. In a gesture of friendship, the Philadelphia Committee agreed to let the ship take on new provisions for its return trip.

Charleston: The ship *London* arrived in Charleston, South Carolina on December 2, 1773 and, unlike Philadelphia, proceeded directly to a mooring at the city's dock. Before the ship arrived, the local Sons of Liberty had convinced all of the distributors appointed by the East India Company to sell the tea, to resign their positions, which all did. Thus, the tea sat in the *London's* hold unloaded.

There was a provision in the statues of commerce which allowed the custom commissioners to unload any cargo that sat on a ship in port for twenty days. When the twenty days passed, the tea was impounded by the commissioners, and stored in a warehouse. Without any merchants to take ownership of the tea to sell it, it remained safely locked away, unused. No duty was ever paid on the tea.

New York: At about the same time Philadelphia was approving its resolves, New York's citizens were deciding what action to take appropriate to the threat. On December 15, 1773, the New York Sons of Liberty wrote resolves that mirrored those promulgated by Philadelphia. The preamble to the resolves castigated Parliament for its diabolical project of enslaving America. It went on, *"they have chartered ships to bring tea to this country, which may be hourly expected, to make an important trial of our virtue. If they succeed in the sale of that tea, we shall have no property that we can call our own, and then we may bid adieu to American Liberty."*

The strong, forceful words went on, *"...and disposed to use all lawful endeavors in our power, to defeat the pernicious project, and to transmit to our posterity those blessings of freedom which our ancestors have handed down to us."* The formal resolves were then agreed upon, being in agreement with those issued by Philadelphia.

On December 27th, expecting the *Nancy* to arrive shortly, the East India Company agents were persuaded to write a message to the ship's captain, *"we can neither receive the tea or pay the duty,"* and added, *it will be most prudent for you to return as soon as you can be supplied with such necessaries as you may have occasion for on the voyage."*

The *Nancy*, under the command of Captain Benjamin Lockyer, ran into bad weather in its crossing and did not arrive at Sandy Hook below New York, until mid-April, 1774. The Captain, upon the advice of the pilot, who came aboard to guide the ship into port, decided to leave his vessel at anchor while he went into the city to gauge public sentiment. What he found so alarmed him he wisely decided to leave with the tea still aboard. He was sent off in a grand farewell with the sound of cannons reverberating in the air.

Boston: The strong opposition of the colony's citizens to the importation of the dutied tea, and the intractable position taken by the East India Company agents led by the Royal Governor, Thomas Hutchinson, resulted in a more dramatic resolution of the confrontation.

When news of the shipment of the tea to Boston was verified, its citizens were outraged. A meeting was held by the North End Caucus on October 23, 1774 in which it was decided no tea would be unloaded in Boston. The North End Caucus consisted of approximately sixty prominent lawyers, merchants, artists, and shippers, such as William Molineux, Samuel Adams, Dr. Joseph Warren, and Paul Revere. On November 2nd, in another meeting, held at the Green Dragon Tavern, a resolution was crafted which was to be read at the Liberty Tree the following morning, where it was politely requested the East India Company agents should appear and resign their positions. When they failed to appear, a committee headed by William Molineux and Dr. Joseph Warren were sent to confront them directly. The committee was received with hostility; the agents refusing to resign and return the tea to London. Upon learning of the brusque refusal, the agents were branded enemies of the people.

At a Boston Town Meeting a few days later John Hancock presided over a session which adopted the resolves published by Philadelphia, and vowed the tea should not be landed.

The effort to ban the tea was strengthened when at a meeting on November 22, the Committees of Correspondence from the nearby towns of Dorchester, Roxbury, Brookline, and Cambridge, joined the Boston committee to establish a plan for stopping the tea. The five-committee group also established coordination with other towns, which, in turn, offered their support.

From Newburyport came the declaration, *if an occasion should offer, a goodly number from among us will hasten to join you."* Charleston vowed support, *"at the risk of life and fortune,"* The committed from Lexington added forcefully, *"We trust in God that should the state of our affairs require it, we shall be ready to sacrifice our estates and everything dear in life, yea, and life itself in support of the common cause."*

On November 28th the *Dartmouth* finally entered Boston Harbor with its cargo of 114 chests of tea. The populace reacted. Everywhere, notices were posted announcing, *"Friends, Brethren, Countrymen. That worst of the plagues, the detested tea shipped for this port by the East India Company is now arrived in this harbor. The hour of destruction, or manly opposition to the machinations of tyranny, stares you in the face."*

As was common, a town meeting was called for the next morning. At the appointed time the turnout of citizens, over five thousand, exceeded the capacity of Faneuil Hall near the wharf, so the meeting was moved to the Old South Meeting House. There, the attendees, by acclamation, approved the declaration, *"the tea should be returned to the place from whence it came, at all events."*

The ship was tied up at Griffin's Wharf, and a committee appointed; including Paul Revere, to keep a constant vigil at the dock, to make certain no tea would be unloaded with the rest of the cargo.

At a continuation of the Town Meeting the next morning, Governor, Thomas Hutchinson, sent Sherriff Greenleaf to inform the assemblage their meeting was illegal, and they would have to disperse. The sheriff's order was ignored, with Samuel Adams denouncing the governor in extremely disparaging words.

An owner of the Dartmouth, young Francis Rotch, a Quaker from Nantucket Island, was called and asked to return the ship to London with the tea still aboard. Rotch, assessing the mood of the crowd agreed to the request. However, Governor Hutchinson would not let the ship leave as he insisted the tea would have to be unloaded first. The dilemma increased as on December 2nd, the ship *Eleanor* arrived with its 114 chests of tea. It was immediately tied up to the *Dartmouth*, to be followed on December 7th by the *Beaver*, with its 112 chests of tea. The remaining ship, the *William*, ran into trouble in the waters off Cape Cod, and never did arrive.

Time became important to resolve the issue. As in Charleston, there was a twenty-day restriction on ships in port with unloaded cargo. According to a provision in the *Acts of Trade*, if the cargo remained unloaded after the twenty days, the customs commissioners could impound the ship, tow it to the safety of the fort at Castle William Island, and unload the tea. Unlike Charleston, however, where the East India Company agents had resigned, the Company's agents in Boston had not resigned, so they could pay the duty, and try to sell the tea. The fateful twentieth day for the Dartmouth was to be December 17, 1773.

On December 15th the five Committees of Correspondence met to discuss what steps must be taken to prevent the tea from being unloaded. It is likely that definitive plans were discussed by the participants about what specific action would be taken to stop the tea from being landed, but, unfortunately, no meeting notes were taken and the meeting's official journal reported, *"No business transacted, matter of record."* What actions were discussed to prohibit the landing of the tea were not recorded.

On December 16th another Town Meeting was called, again attended by thousands. The tea agents had taken refuge at the fort in the harbor while Governor Hutchinson had retreated to his mansion in Milton, outside Boston. At the meeting Rotch was asked why he had not yet sailed his ship out of the harbor. Rotch pleaded he had previously requested permission to leave the harbor from the Custom Commissioners, but his request had been denied. In a last effort to have Rotch send his ship back to London with the tea still aboard, he was sent to Milton to see the governor, to obtain his permission to sail the ship out of the harbor. The meeting waited for Rotch to return with an answer.

The governor, however, was still adamant the ship could not leave, and so informed the hapless ship's owner. Hutchinson had had the canons at the fort loaded to challenge an attempt to run the ship through the normal passage to the ocean. He had also requested Admiral Montagu to post his naval ships at the less used passages out of the harbor, to cover all possible escape routes.

Hutchinson had come to the conclusion the patriots would abandon their effort to stop the unloading of the tea after they found all avenues of escape sealed. To save face, they could claim they did all they could to stop the tea from being unloaded, but eventually they must acknowledge defeat. The governor, had written a few days earlier to London to advise severe action be taken against Boston, and criminal proceedings be instituted against several of Boston's patriots. He was now reveling in what he thought was a victory over Samuel Adams, John Hancock and the rest of those disloyal subjects. He gloated, *"They find themselves in invincible difficulties."*

The large gathering at the Town Meeting waited for Rotch to return. Although anxious, the Bostonians' resolve was evident in the tense patience that permeated the hall. It was only a few hours until the twentieth day would be here, and there was tension in the hall. Rotch finally arrived about six PM, and reported the governor had again refused his request, Samuel Adams then rose, and solemnly pronounced, *"This meeting can do nothing more to save the country."*

At that, forty to fifty men dressed as Mohawk Indians appeared, and passed on their way to Griffin's Wharf with guttural grunts and loud war whoops. Their faces were blackened with burnt cork, soot or coal dust, and several had red or white war stripes painted on their cheeks and foreheads. A bright moon lit the scene enough to allow easy maneuvering of the "tribes." Landell Pitts directed three teams of warriors, one to each vessel. The action was efficient and precise. At each ship the first mates were asked to provide keys to the holds, so minimal damage to the ships would occur, which they gladly did.

With enthusiastic vigor, and imitation Indian war cries, the cases of tea were hauled to deck, broken open and dumped overboard; 340 cases in all. The scene was witnessed by many onlookers who were drawn to the scene, as well as by British Admiral Montagu who was visiting at a house near the harbor. While he had naval ships in the harbor he later stated, *"I could easily have prevented the Execution of the Plan but must have endangered the lives of many innocent People by firing upon the town."*

The aggressive action by the patriots likely caught Governor Hutchinson by surprise. He could have asked for help guarding the ships from Admiral Montagu, or he could have posted British Soldiers from Colonel Leskie's regiment on the wharf near the tea ships to prohibit any rebel maneuvers against the tea. Instead of his anticipated "victory" over the patriots, he suffered a crippling humiliation.

In just three hours it was over. Unlike the unruly mobs that raged after passage of the Stamp Act, and caused a great deal of damage to private property, The Tea Party participants were unduly careful to avoid causing damage to any of the ships. During the action, a lock was inadvertently broken on one of the ships. To the surprise of the ship's captain, a new one was later delivered to him.

There was celebration and numerous toasts in Boston's Green Dragon Tavern where the patriots exuberantly sang:

> Rally, Mohawks bring out your axes!
> And tell King George we'll pay no taxes
> On his foreign tea!
> His threats are vain—and vain to think
> To force our girls and wives to drink

His vile Bohea!
Then rally boys, and hasten on
To meet our Chiefs at the Green Dragon,
Our Warren's there, and bold Revere.
With hands to do and words to cheer
For Liberty and Laws!
Our country's Braves and firm defenders
Shall ne'er be left by true North-Enders.
Fighting Freedom's cause!
Then rally boys and hasten on
To meet our Chiefs at the Green Dragon

Paul Revere was sent on a mission to inform the patriots in New York and Philadelphia, where news of what had occurred in Boston was joyously received. John Adams, who was generally against mob violence wrote, *"There is a dignity, majesty, a sublimity, in this last effort of the patriots that I greatly admire."* In reference to his Bostonian friends, he also observed, *"they had passed the river and cut away the bridge."*

Word of the dumping of East India tea into the Boston Harbor reached London on January 20, 1774.

Chapter Twenty-Five

Intolerable Retaliation

The King's Privy Council got around to taking up the matter of Massachusetts' petition to remove Governor Hutchinson and Lieutenant Governor Oliver from office on January 29, 1774. Benjamin Franklin had previously admitted it was he who had obtained the damaging letters, and sent them to America. Franklin had made this confession in an honorable act to absolve two British citizens who had been unjustly implicated in taking the letters from the deceased Whately, and were being harassed for an act they didn't commit.

Word of the Boston Tea Party had arrived in London only several days before the session, and the whole of Britain was in an uproar over what was perceived as an illegal, insubordinate deed. The Privy Council, with an unusually large number (35) of Lords in attendance, was led by the irascible Solicitor General, Alexander Wedderburn. The atmosphere in the room was skewed with anger over the recent events in Boston.

Sixty-eight year old Benjamin Franklin, who had presented the petition on behalf of the Massachusetts Colony, was in attendance in a formal wig and full court dress. He stood erect, maintaining a stoic countenance, as Wedderburn, to the applause of the Lords and spectators, castigated him as a lowly thief who surreptitiously stole private correspondence from a deceased British peer, and malevolently maligned the letters' authors, while Hutchinson was praised as an outstanding jurist, innocent of any charges of malfeasance. The vituperative language used by Wedderburn was so invective that several prominent Londoners later apologized to Franklin for this indecorous attack on his character. He received no sympathy from the ministers, however, and was subsequently dismissed from his position as Deputy Post Master General for America, losing the three-hundred pound stipend it paid annually.

Franklin was dismayed, both by the treatment he received in the Privy Council and by Boston's aggressive action. He counseled Massachusetts to reimburse the East India Company for the destroyed tea in order to alleviate the hostility he perceived in London. He had thought an accord between the colonies and Britain could be agreed upon in which the colonies would acknowledge the sovereignty of the monarch, yet not agree to Parliament's right to legislate for them nor to tax them. In this arrangement, compacts could be written to allow preferential trade agreements, and treaties signed in which either side would come to the aid of the other in times of war. With the advantage of his position, Franklin could view the sentiments of both sides, and he was coming to the conclusion that the arrangement he had envisioned may not be possible. Britain's Parliament would not give up its dominance of the colonies, and the colonies were hardening their opposition to Parliamentary rule. Like many others, he was uncertain what the future would bring. Feeling his effectiveness as Massachusetts representative was at an end; he resigned the position, and was replaced by his deputy, Virginian Arthur Lee. Franklin did, however, volunteer to help the colony as a private person whenever asked.

The anger felt in Britain befell mainly on the Massachusetts Colony. They had committed an illegal and insubordinate act, and the leaders there were being branded as no more than common criminals. The rejection of the tea at the other ports was regrettable, but not considered as reprehensible as Boston's. In fact, if the East Indian Agents had resigned in Boston, the response there would have been the same, or similar to, the other ports. In New York, they had readied their own "Mohawks" for action should a ship with British tea reach a dock there with company agents willing to take it. When a private ship did arrive in New York, with several chests of tea hidden in the hold, it was discovered by the Sons of Liberty and unceremoniously dumped overboard.

Sentiment in Britain was for forceful action against the Bostonians. The London newspapers railed against the felonious colonials, urging severe reprisals against those in America who behaved so outrageously. It is not surprising the hostility was so intense against the Massachusetts Colony. With the alarming reports which had come into London from the last two royal governors and the uprisings after passage of the Stamp and Townshend Acts, dumping the tea into the harbor, cemented belief that strict action must be taken to keep the colony under British control. The King encouraged Lord North to have Parliament enact strong measures against the offenders.

General Thomas Gage had returned to London in the summer of 1773 leaving General Haldimand in New York in charge of British Forces in America.

On February 4, 1774, he had an audience with the King, who was striving to better understand the disposition of the American Colonies in general, and Boston in particular. The monarch was seeking counsel on what actions could be effected to bring about the restoration of the colony's submission to British rule. Gage's observations greatly impressed the monarch. In a note to his Prime Minister, the King wrote Gage had said, *"I am willing to go back at a day's notice, if coercive measures are adopted. They will be like lions while we are lambs; but if we take the resolute part, they will undoubtedly prove very meek. Four regiments sent to Boston will be sufficient to prevent any disturbance."* King George encouraged Lord North to meet with the General, calling him an honest and determined man.

In early March 1774, Parliament took up debate on measures to bring Boston to task for their insolent behavior. While it was agreed Boston would have to pay the East India Company for the tea it destroyed, nearly ten thousand pounds sterling, Lord North, reflecting the Kings wishes, stated firmly, *"obedience not indemnification will be the test of the Bostonians."*

Another Member of Parliament, reflecting the mood of the body, as well as the entire nation, declared, *"The town of Boston ought to be knocked about their ears and destroyed...You will never meet with proper obedience to the laws of this country, until you have destroyed that nest of locusts."*

On March 18th Lord North introduced the Boston Port Bill in the House of Commons where it met essentially no resistance. The intent of the bill was to shut down the port of Boston to all traffic entirely. No traffic of any kind, other than British Naval vessels, were to be allowed to enter Boston's harbor. Even one of the colonists' most ardent supporters, Isaac Barré, felt they had gone too far and stated, *"I like the bill, adopt it and embrace it cheerfully for its moderation."*

Later in the month, the bill was presented in the House of Lords, where several members did not share Barré's impression of its moderation. Past Prime Minister Rockingham felt the bill too severe. Others agreed, stating only if Boston was in an actual state of rebellion should the measures apply. Lord Dartmouth, who was generally sympathetic to the colonists' cause, tended to agree with Rockingham, and opined that the city was in a state of "commotion" not "rebellion". Disagreeing with Dartmouth, Lord Mansfield voiced the prevailing conviction, *"What passed in Boston is the last overt act of High Treason, proceeding from our overly lenity and want of foresight."*

Perhaps the most insightful and reasoned objection to the act was penned by Pitt-Chatham, the wise ex-prime minister, who had shepherd Britain successfully through the French and Indian War. In a letter on March 20, 1774 to his friend William Petty, the second Earl of Shelburne, he wrote:

Perhaps a fatal desire to take advantage of this guilty tumult of the Bostonians, in order to crush the spirit of liberty among the Americans in general, has taken possession of the heart of government. Boston, I hope and believe, would make reparation, for a heinous wrong, in the tea cargo; but to consent quietly to have no right over their own purse, I conceive the people of America will never be brought to do. Laws of navigation and trade, for regulation not for revenue I should hope and believe, America, once at ease about internal taxation, would also acquiesce under, and friendly intercourse be again opened; without which we, not they, shall be undone.

Pitt-Chatham, being out of favor with the King, was ignored.

The bill was then approved by both houses; the official record reading the votes in both houses of Parliament was unanimous. The King quickly assented, and the bill became law on March 31, 1774, with an implementation date of June 1, 1774.

The Act was explicitly written, *"to discontinue, in such manner, and for such time as are therein mentioned, the landing and discharging, lading or shipping, of goods, wares, and merchandise, at the town, and within the harbor, of Boston."* The act called for the complete shutdown of all activity in Boston's harbor, with allowances for military supplies, or fuel or food needed by Boston's citizens for survival. Penalties for violation of the act's provisions were severe.

The closing of the port would have an extreme impact on the economy of the area. Boston had been one of the busiest ports in America, and trade through its harbor was essential to the town's merchants, as well as the surrounding farmers, lumbermen, and a multitude of small businesses. The impact would be felt on patriots and loyalists alike.

The official reason Parliament enacted the Boston Port Bill, namely the unease the King felt about the seditious actions occurring in the American colonies, was stated in its first article, *"Whereas dangerous commotions and insurrections have been fermented and raised in the town of Boston, in the province of Massachusetts Bay, in New England, by diverse ill-affected persons, to the subversion of his Majesty's government, and to the utter destruction of the public peace, and good order of the said town."*

The port was to remain closed until several terms were met, specifically, *"until it shall sufficiently appear to his Majesty that full satisfaction hath been made by or on behalf of the inhabitants of said town of Boston to the united company of merchants of England trading to the east indies."* The value of the tea destroyed at the Boston Tea Party had to be paid in full to the East India Company. Also, reasonable satisfaction had to be made to the royal officers who had suffered by riots and insurrection.

Finally, and as objectionable to the colonists as paying for the tea, the King had to be assured Boston would obey all British Laws, pay all customs duties, and the citizens would be peaceful.

To enforce the closure of the port, General Thomas Gage was appointed to replace Thomas Hutchinson as the new royal governor; whereupon Gage would install martial law in the city. To support Gage, four regiments of British troops would be sent to Boston to prevent any insurrectional activity by the areas citizens. The setting governor, Thomas Hutchinson, was recalled to London to provide first-hand information to the King and his Ministers about conditions in the colony.

Thomas Gage, the son of a viscount, was not considered an aggressive military man by many who knew him. His military acumen was questioned during a skirmish in the French and Indian War when his regiment was defeated, suffering heavy casualties. He seemed wont to take the easiest paths; to rationalize actions so as to avoid conflicts. He was correct in manners and held a gentlemanly bearing. He enjoyed social affairs, but was considered dull socially. He was, of course, well versed in American affairs, having served extensively in the colonies. He had an American wife, Margret Kemble, from Brunswick, New Jersey, and had considerable land holdings in America. In his presentation to the King he asserted Britain must behave as lions, but whether he was up to being a British lion was far from certain.

As Gage made preparations to sail to America he received guidance from Lord Dartmouth, Minister of the American Colonies. First, instructed Dartmouth, he must make certain the port stays closed, and all royal government officers, including the customs commissioners, are obeyed. Dartmouth emphasized, *"the sovereignty of the King, in his Parliament, over the colonies requires a full and absolute submission."* Only if absolutely necessary, should soldiers be used against the colonials. The "absolute necessary" was defined as, "the madness of the people or the want of strength of the peace officers."

Gage arrived at the fort on Castle William Island in Boston's Harbor on May 13, 1774. The Massachusetts Governor he was replacing, Thomas Hutchinson, was waiting for him, before departing for London. Gage spent three days in consultation with Hutchinson. The General likely believed the advice he had given the King, and expected compliance from the populace, whether Hutchinson debased him of this naivety is uncertain.

In addition to having a new governor, the colony felt other changes. The Massachusetts capital was moved from Boston to Salem, the customs commissioners' office was moved to Plymouth, and all ships bringing supplies to Boston had to first stop at Marblehead for inspection.

Gage left the fort, and arrived at Boston's Long Wharf on May 17, 1774. He was received cordially. An Honor Guard of Cadets led by John Hancock provided military honors. It was an ironic reception, since Gage had been ordered to arrest the perpetrators of the Boston Tea Party, and John Hancock, along with Samuel Adams and Dr. Joseph Warren had been specifically mentioned. The General, however, took no notice of the prominent, supposedly rebellious, colonist. The evening ended with the reading of Gage's commission, and a formal dinner in Faneuil Hall.

The reaction in Massachusetts to the closure of Boston Harbor was, as expected, defiantly hostile to the British excursions into their government and livelihood. Coinciding with Gage's arrival, Samuel Adams had called a meeting in Boston on May 12 which was also attended by citizens of the surrounding towns of Dorchester, Roxbury, Brookline, Newton, Cambridge, Charlestown, Lynn, and Lexington. Although wanting to take strong action, Adams was wise enough not to breach any thoughts of independence, which would have caused concern, and possibly noncooperation from several of the other colonies.

The idea of independence was certainly bandied about throughout the American Colonies, but it was not thought practical by many. It was comforting, some contended, to have the support of British might, such as presently benefited Georgia, which was experiencing an Indian uprising. British arms and, if needed, troops, could provide vital support in times of crises. With independence, the new country would be vulnerable to threats from foreign powers which could compromise possession of adjacent territories, affect trading routes and ports, or force restrictions on trapping or fishing rights. The blanket of British laws, although some being presently repugnant, provided a consistency of government across all of the colonies. Independence was an attractive concept, but it came with its own set of problems which could be difficult.

The attendees of the Boston meeting were anxious to take immediate action to express their displeasure at Briton's closing of the port. They overwhelmingly approved a resolution calling for the non-consumption of British goods. The resolution implored the other colonies,

> Now is the time when all should be united in opposition to this violation of the liberties of all. The single question is, whether you consider Boston as suffering in the common cause, and sensibly feel and resent the injury and affront offered her? We cannot believe otherwise; assuring you that not in the least intimidated by this unhuman treatment, we are still determined to maintain to the utmost of our abilities the rights of America.

Paul Revere was dispatched to deliver a copy of the resolution to the committees of correspondence in the other colonies.

Vows of support came from most of the other towns in the Massachusetts Colony and from the other colonies. South Carolina offered 200 barrels of rice, Delaware, Maryland, and Virginia joined in promising aid to the beleaguered city. The small town of Brooklyn, Connecticut offered sheep and lambs which they volunteered to drive over land to Boston. Offers of grain, cattle, fish even money came from all over colonial America as its citizens defied the British oppression. Aid even came from the newly settled land in the west, as well as wheat from, French Quebec. It became apparent Boston was not going to suffer alone.

The King and his ministers were of the belief that if Boston were isolated and punished, the remaining colonies would be intimidated by the thought the same thing might happen to them. That if they acted insolently toward British rule, they could be disciplined in like manner, with their freedom and livelihood imperiled. It was thus important for the British rulers to ascertain how the remaining colonies reacted to this show of British might.

Virginia's brisk support of Boston, immediately upon learning of Parliament's action to close its port, was disheartening to the royal governor, Earl Dunmore. He immediately sent a report to Lord Dartmouth in London, alerting him to the sense of opposition to Britain's action he observed in the Virginia Assembly. Dartmouth's reply reflected the unease felt in Britain's Colonial Ministry,

> The information contained in your lordship's letter of the ninth of May of what passed in Virginia, in consequence of the measures passed in Parliament respecting the town of Boston has given me the greatest concern. There was reason to hope, from appearances in the other colonies, that the extravagant proposition of the people of Boston would have been everywhere disregarded; but it may now be well doubted whether the extraordinary conduct of the Burgesses of Virginia may not become an example to the other colonies.

Things were not progressing as the King and the Colonial Ministry had hoped.

The Boston Committee of Correspondence met again on May 30, at which time they wrote a more definitive proclamation called "a Solemn League and Covenant, respecting the disuse of British Manufactures." It was a call to all of the colonies to suspend all trade with Britain.

The covenant was not readily agreed to by many of the Boston merchants, who felt it would cause them more problems than it would to Britain. Other towns in the colony likewise felt the provisions of the covenant too strict in calling for a complete cessation of all trade with Britain, with no exceptions. They felt it was impractical and would not be effective at this time. The towns throughout the Massachusetts Colony, although active participants in the Massachusetts Assembly, were fervidly independent in matters directly affecting them; reflecting the heritage of their founders. They generally agreed with their fellow colonial citizens in Boston, but not necessarily in all cases. They strongly supported unity in opposition to Britain's obnoxious closing of Boston's harbor and the rewriting of the colony's charter. They would certainly come to Boston's aid in this time of this troubling vicissitude, but do so at their own volition.

The New York Committee of Correspondence, strongly influenced by their Sons of Liberty, was poised to accept Boston's call for a complete cessation of trade with Great Britain. However, before the Committee could make a formal declaration agreeing to a trade embargo on British goods, opposition to the Committee's decision arose. Not all in the colony agreed with the decision. At a general meeting in mid-May, it was decided to establish a new committee which would represent a wider spectrum of membership. Thus, a new committee of fifty-one was formed, its members selected by nomination from all citizens.

The membership of the new committee included a cross-section of the colony's populace, who held different views on their relationship with Britain. The irresolute Sons of Liberty were on one end, loyalists to Britain on the other, and a goodly number of undecided citizens in between. This new committee judged the cessation of all trade with Britain too severe at this time, as it would harm the colonies' merchants more than Britain. Instead, they proposed representatives from all of the American colonies meet in a Continental Congress, and discuss, in detail, what united actions they should take; including Boston's suggestion of a cessation of trade with Britain.

While Samuel Adams had proposed such a convention previously, he was disappointed in New York's proposal as he wanted something done immediately. He realized New York was of a different temper than Massachusetts, and it would be futile to press for stronger action at this time. He thus accepted the proposal.

The Pennsylvania committee, headed by "Farmer" Dickenson, and with its own cadre of moderates, including the conflict avoiding Quakers, agreed with the New York plan of a convention of the colonies, *"to state what we conceive our rights and to make a claim or petition of them to his Majesty, in firm, but descent and dutiful terms, so as that we may know by what lines to conduct ourselves in the future."* The Philadelphians wanted a sincere effort of *"reconciliation and future harmony with our mother country."*

Maryland, Connecticut, New Hampshire, New Jersey, South Carolina, quickly agreed with the call for a colonial congress, some even agreeing to an immediate cession of trade with Britain. In Virginia, a meeting of several of the colonial leaders in Williamsburg, including George Washington, declared June first, the day when Boston's port was to be closed, would be a day of fasting. Their resolve was dispatched throughout the colony. Upon learning of this action to support Boston, the royal governor, Dunmore, dissolved the House. Not to be deterred, the Virginia Burgesses moved to the nearby Raleigh tavern, and approved the call for a congress. In their discussions the attendees went so far as to declare they would, if required, defend their liberties with arms. It was becoming obvious, Boston would not be left to suffer Britain's wrath alone.

As the colonists were debating what course of action to take, and General Gage was settling into his new post, additional bills were being debated in Commons to further restrain the colonists in Massachusetts, actions which only further antagonized all of the colonies.

The first of these was the Massachusetts Government Act, which was designed, in effect, to rewrite the Massachusetts Charter it had received after the Glorious Revolution in 1691. The original charter had a Council of twenty-eight citizens to assist the governor in the running of the colony. The Council was elected annually by the members of the Massachusetts House, which meant they had an independence from Britain, and a strong allegiance to the colony. While Hutchinson, and Francis Bernard before him, had tried to restrict council membership to loyalists, it was still too independent for the ministries taste.

The new act mandated that the King would choose the members of Massachusetts' Council. It stated:

> That from and after August 1, 1774, so much of the charter granted by their majesties King William and Queen Mary to the inhabitants of the said province of the Massachusetts Bay, in New England, and all and every clause, matter, and thing, therein contained, which relates to the time and manner of electing the assistants or counselors for the said province, be revoked, and is hereby revoked and made void and of none effect; and that the offices of all counselors and assistants, elected and appointed in pursuance thereof, shall from thenceforth cease and determine: And that, from and after August 1, 1774, the council, or court assistants of the said province for the time being, shall be composed of such of the inhabitants or proprietors of lands within the same as shall be thereunto nominated and appointed by his Majesty, his heirs and successors.

Another provision of the new act was especially detested by the colonists. All of the judges of the superior and inferior courts, the attorney general, provosts, marshals, justices of the peace, and sheriffs would be appointed by the royal governor and serve at his pleasure. The procedure for selecting juries was to be changed to give the royally appointed sheriffs more control over who could serve on them. To stop Boston from conducting spurious meetings, all Town Meetings had to have the approval of the governor, and they could only be held once a year.

In total, it was a drastic revision of the Massachusetts Charter, taking all control from the elected representatives, and placing it completely under the King's representatives. It violated the primary reason many of the colony's ancestors had left England over a hundred years previously, and the original sentiments were not forgotten, entrenched in the animus of those now present.

The next penal bill, being discussed about the same time as the government act, and especially desired by the King, was the Administration of Justice Act. The British Ministry had been outraged as violators of the Stamp and Townshend Acts, tried in colonial courts, had routinely avoided conviction.

The new act gave the royal governor of Massachusetts the authority to move any trial to another colony or to Great Britain itself. It was also a way to protect royal officials or soldiers from being tried in colonial courts for actions incurred in suppressing uprisings by Massachusetts' citizens. Thus, if a trooper or law officer or agent of the customs commissioners killed or injured a colonial citizen, he had the assurance that any trial against him could be moved to London where he would be expected to be exonerated. The provisions of this act, to the Bostonians, were an excuse for the killing of citizens. It was so obnoxious to them it was given the sobriquet "The Murdering Act".

While there was more opposition to the these new acts than occurred with the Boston Port Act, in both Commons and the House of Lords, the prevailing mood was still strongly hostile against the New Englanders, and both acts passed easily, becoming law after being assented to by the King on May 20, 1774.

The passing of these acts were of great concern to all of the American Colonies, on whatever bases their governments were formed. The present Massachusetts Charter was granted by King William and Queen Mary, an eminently respected monarchy in British history, and, now, with a simple majority vote, and with no opportunity for the colonists to object or even be heard, it was drastically altered by Parliament. Could any of the colonies be safe from this incursion into the basic tenants of their governance? It was a drastic manifestation of the British Parliament legislating for the American Colonies where they had no representation or recourse, nor even an opportunity to partake in the discussions leading to its passage. It aroused extreme concern in all of the colonies.

The last of the four acts of Parliament which were called "Coercive Acts" in Britain, and "Intolerable Acts" in America, was passed on June 1, 1774. This last act, The Quartering Act, which was a revision of the earlier quartering law, was requested by the military as they were going to post additional regiments in the colonies, and needed assurance they could house them there. According to this new act, if any soldiers or officers were not provided with quarters twenty-four hours after the quarters had been requested from *"any town, township, city, district, or place within his Majesty's dominions in*

North America," then it would be lawful for the governor of the province *"to order and direct such and so many uninhabited houses, outhouses, barns, or other buildings, as he shall think necessary to be taken....for such time as he shall think proper."* It gave the royal governors greater power in finding quarters for the military, as what was deemed "uninhabited", was left up to him.

Britain's Parliament passed another act, which not usually identified as one of the Intolerable Acts, nevertheless, caused great concern in the American Colonies. The King assented to the Quebec Act on June 22, 1774 which had passed both houses of Parliament the previous month. The Quebec Act was an attempt by Britain to provide reassurances to the Catholics in Canada, who became citizens of Britain after the French and Indian War. Britain could not very well ignore the over sixty-five thousand Catholics, who were now subjects of the British Monarch, and who were deeply concerned with their freedom to practice their religion under protestant British rule. With the troubles Britain was experiencing in the American Colonies, they did not relish trouble in Canada. Thus, the act allowed the French-Canadians to continue practice of their Catholic faith.

In addition to granting Canada's Catholics freedom to practice their religion, the act also gave them property and civil rights, and allowed them the ability to serve in governmental positions. They were required to pledge allegiance to the King, but the oath was significantly different from the oath of allegiance written during the reign of Queen Elizabeth; the new oath they would use no longer referred to the Protestant faith.

The American Colonists, especially in the northern colonies, were very disturbed by the passage of the act. There were voices warning about the possibility of "Papists" joining with Indians, and causing havoc on the northern border, much as they had experienced in the French and Indian War. While this may not have been a serious threat, the change in Canada's border certainly was. The act gave much of the old Ohio Territory west of the Appalachians to Quebec. This was land the American Colonists were already sending settlers into to form new colonies. The settlers, like Daniel Boone, and land speculators, like George Washington, were aroused against the British action. If implemented, the new border would greatly hinder colonial America's growth.

There was no doubting the King's and Parliament's intent in taking harsh measures against the Americans, who challenged Britain's sovereignty over them. One Member of Parliament had asked the key question, *"Whether the Colonies are not the colonies of Great Britain."* The King, his Ministers, and Members of Parliament held the firm view that the colonies were indeed a part of the British Realm. Since, the British Parliament legislated for the entire realm, ergo; the British Parliament legislated for the American Colonies. It seemed to be a simple course of logic.

To the patriots in the American Colonies, however, there were fundamental rights granted by the British Constitution to all British subjects, and natural rights which were endowed on all, which overrode any rights of Parliament to tax and legislate for them. According to the constitution, British citizens could only be taxed with their consent, and laws made for them only by assemblies in which they were represented. And, to inhibit their freedom was a violation of natural law to which all men were subject. The two interpretations, one in Britain and one in America, were irreconcilable, so one side would have to be forced to submit to the other side's view. Or, as the King presciently observed upon the passage of the Boston Port Act, *"The die is now cast. The colonies must either submit or triumph."* Due to counsel given him from his Ministers, General Gage, and many others, the king was assured the colonists would submit, and sooner rather than later.

Chapter Twenty-Six

Approaching the Breaking Point

The first of the four British regiments sent to support Gage in his subjugation of the citizens of Massachusetts was the Fourth, an elite unit known as the "King's Own." It arrived on June 14, 1774, and was immediately encamped on Boston Common. The Fourth was followed shortly by the Forty-third and two companies of artillery. Together with the troops already stationed on Castle William Island in Boston Harbor, the British forces brandished a minatory presence.

These British troops were not here to protect against marauding Indians nor foreign invaders; they were not here merely to quell rioters and restore civil order. In a starkly sobering reality, these troops were here to subdue colonial citizens. These British troops were invaders whose aim was to force total, unrestrained submission to an external will. They were there to control the freedom of the populace, even to the extent of menacing the lives of those who openly resisted. It was an action that offended and alarmed the great majority of colonial citizenry.

The arrival of British troops did not intimidate Samuel Adams, as three days after the arrival of the imposing regiments, he called a, now illegal, meeting of the Massachusetts House. With the doors to the meeting chamber locked, and Gage's representatives unable to enter to read the general's order dissolving the assembly, the members in attendance set the date for the important Continental Congress. It was to be held on September 1, 1774 in Philadelphia, away from any interference by British troops. The assembly then chose as their delegates: Samuel Adams, John Adams, Thomas Cushing, James Bowdoin and Robert Trent Paine. The assembly members wanted their representatives to travel to and attend the congress in a proper manner, so the colony assessed itself a 500–pound tax to cover their expenses.

Later in the same month, June 27th, a unique Boston Town Meeting was held at which many of the town's British loyalists attended along with the usual number of patriots. The loyalists were emboldened by Gage's arrival, and installation as the colony's new royal governor, and by the arrival of the British troops. With the large contingent of protective British military encamped in the city, the loyalists felt secure enough to challenge the patriot-led town assembly.

Many references to the political leanings of the populace in both Britain and the American Colonies refer to "Tories" and "Whigs" as these were the labels given to the two main political parties in Britain at this time. The Tories tended to support a government led by a strong monarchy. The Whigs, on the other hand, advocated a reduced role for the monarch, and a greater role in government for Parliament. These political labels were well suited for the citizens of Great Britain, but became less representative of the feelings of the populace in the colonies. The two labels did not reflect how the colonists viewed both the Monarchy's and Parliament's role in their governance. A more appropriate term for those colonial citizenry, who wanted to maintain strong ties to Britain and the government there would be "Loyalists." For those who wanted little or no interference from Britain in their governance, the appellation "Patriots" better describes their persuasion. There were, of course, degrees of commitment to any general belief of government, but herein the terms "Patriot" and "Loyalist" will be used to describe the opposing factions of government advocates in the American Colonies rather than "Tory" and "Whig."

The meeting was a critical one for the Boston Committee of Correspondence as it tested the depth of their support in the town. The emboldened loyalists accused the committee, led by Samuel Adams, and populated with likeminded patriots, of not acting in the best interests of Boston's citizens, specifically in the passage of the Solemn Covenant, which called on all colonists to cease trade with Britain. The loyalists asserted the termination of all trade with the mother country would cause irreparable harm to many of Boston's merchants. One merchant, Samuel Eliot, stood at the meeting to bemoan he had ordered a large amount of goods from Britain which he could not stop. Enforcement of the covenant would cause him ruin he lamented. His sacrifice would be in vain, he maintained, as none of the other colonies had also agreed to the cessation of all British trade, and British goods would be available from them.

The loyalists present at the meeting fought forcefully to reduce the power of the committee or to eliminate it altogether. As reported in a letter by Bostonian Thomas Young, who attended the two-day meeting, *"Armory (lawyer John Armory, a loyalist)* "*had a long speech in writing in which he concluded with a Motion to remove Censure & annihilate the Committee of Corre-spondence, this was seconded by many Voices... There was a liberal flow of Sentiments & much Severity from the Tories (loyalists) upon the committee without any ill treatment."*

The loyalists were afforded a courteous opportunity to present their views, and Armory's motion for censure and annihilation was debated intensely. Ultimately, however, in a vote of the assembly, the motion lost by a great majority. An alternate motion was then entered, endorsing the committee, and expressing confidence in, and approval of, their actions. This motion passed, also by a great majority, estimated at four to one, af-firming strong support for the committee. It was a severe disappointment for the British loyalists as it became apparent they had only a modicum of support in Boston.

Thomas Hutchinson had left Boston on June 1, 1774 along with his son Elisha, daughter Peggy and several servants, on a delayed trip to London. Hutchinson's reason for sailing to London was, supposedly, to clear any dam-age to his reputation as a result of the embarrassing release of his letters, and the petition of the Massachusetts House to the King asking for his removal from the office of governor of the colony. He also had in mind to convince the Ministry and the King of his loyalty and devotion to serving Britain, and be awarded a significant pension.

Hutchinson had always suffered from seasickness, and the month-long passage left him comforted to finally land at Dover on the afternoon of June 29th. Early the next morning, he and his family set off for London, to lodging arranged by his youngest son Billy, who had migrated to England some years previous. Upon arrival at the spacious apartment on London's Parliament Street, he immediately sent a message to Lord Dartmouth acquainting him with his presence in the city. To his surprise, the Colonial Minister replied right back with a note asking him to come to Dartmouth's residence at noon the next day.

It was an apprehensive Hutchinson who made the short trip to the minis-ter's residence at noon the following day, July 1, 1774, where he met the man he had communicated with for several years only through official correspon-dence. After an exchange of pleasantries, and to his great surprise, Dartmouth informed him the King was anxious to see him, and they would meet with the monarch that very afternoon. Still unsettled from his voyage, and in travel clothes, he tried to put off the audience, but one does not turn down a King who was anxious to learn about conditions in his troubling domain from a person of authority. Thus, somewhat unnerved, and in awe of the being in the presence of the monarch, Thomas Hutchinson was ushered into the royal chambers.

The thirty-six year old monarch cordially asked after the well-being of the sixty-two year old royal official after his long voyage. Admitting to some seasickness during the voyage, Hutchinson apologized for his inappropriate appearance, but Lord Dartmouth, who was in attendance throughout the meeting, told the King he thought it was acceptable since he had just arrived. The King agreed, setting Hutchinson more at ease.

The King was renowned for his attention to detail, and he desired to learn all he could from this man about the present conditions in America. The King was very interested in how Parliament's Acts affected the colonials, and began by inquiring, *"How did the people receive the news of the late measures in Parliament?"*

Hutchinson had left Castle William Island on June first, so replied, *"When I left Boston we had no news of any Act of Parliament, except the one for shutting up the port, which was extensively alarming to the people."*

Lord Dartmouth interjected, *"I hear the people of Virginia have refused to comply with the request to shut up their ports, from the people of Boston, and Mr. Hutchinson seems to be of opinion that no colony will comply with that request."* Dartmouth and Hutchinson had obviously briefly discussed the subject before the meeting, but Hutchinson declined to provide any additional information concerning Virginia, saying he had only read something about it in a newspaper. He did, however, volunteer his opinion that Rhode Island would also consider action similar to Virginia's.

The King was aware of the difficulties Hutchinson had suffered during the Stamp Act riots, including the vandalization of his house, and inquired about the protection the former governor had to employ as safeguard from Boston's frenzied rabble, *"What guard had you?"* he asked.

Hutchinson realized his answer to the question could have an impact on how the King viewed him; and strove to present himself as one worthy of a significant pension. Intent on gaining the monarch's favor, he replied, *"I depended, Sir, on the protection of heaven,"* and continued with, a declaration of his character. He pointed out his honesty had never been challenged while he strove to do those things necessary to support the King's and Parliament's dictates.

The King desired to learn more about several of the leaders of the Massachusetts Colony such as John Hancock and Thomas Cushing, asking brief questions to which Hutchinson gave simple replies. The King asked what gave Samuel Adams the importance he seemed to carry. Hutchinson's biased, yet honest, answer, *"A great pretended zeal for Liberty, and a most inflexible natural temper."* He then volunteered, *"He was the first that publicly asserted the Independence of the colonies upon the Kingdom, or the supreme Authority of it."*

The King was familiar with the debates in Parliament in which great concern had been put forth from some members, concerned with how the citizens of Massachusetts would react to the new Parliamentary Act regarding the appointment of their Council by the royal governor instead of being elected by popular vote. The King asked, *"Pray Mr. Hutchinson, what is your opinion of the effect from the new regulations of the Council? Will it be agreeable to the people, and will the new appointed Councillors take the trust upon them."*

Hutchinson, of course, had not known of the Massachusetts Government Act since news of it had not reached Boston before he boarded ship for his voyage, and consequently, did not know which persons were being considered. He thus replied, *"I have not, may it please your Majesty, been able to inform myself who they are. I came to town last evening and seen nobody. I think much will depend upon the choice that has been made."*

The King assured his visitor that proper individuals were considered, *"Enquiry was made and pains taken that the most suitable persons should be appointed."* From the King's point of view, staunch loyalists would absolutely be needed in these important positions to assist in returning the colony to strict loyalty to Britain and the King.

Hutchinson felt obligated to explain the expected reaction of the majority Congregationalists, *"The body of the people are Dissenters from the Church of England, what are considered Congregationalists. If the Council shall have been generally selected from the Episcopalians, it will make the change more disagreeable."*

The King did not likely appreciate the significance of Hutchinson's observation. He was aware, as were most of the members of government in London, that the American Colonists strongly objected to Parliament taxing them or legislating for them, but he, like most of his ministers, did not realize the abhorrence of the New Englanders to perceived Kingly oppression, especially (real or imaginary) incursions by the Church of England into their communities. Ancestral lore, ingrained across the American Northeast, warned against such oppression, and amplified the dissatisfaction they felt across the entire colonial landscape.

The King probed the subject further, asking Hutchinson who his ancestors were, to which he replied, *"In general, Sir, Dissenters."* The King then asked what church Hutchinson attended. His reply was carefully crafted, *"With both, Sir, Sometimes at your Majesty's chapel (the Anglican King's Chapel in Boston), but more generally at a Congregational church, which has a very worthy minister, a friend of Government, who constantly prays for your Majesty, and all in authority under you."*

He was referring to Dr. Pemberton, and was pleased when the King replied, *"I have heard of Doctor Pemberton that he is a very good man."* It was not unusual for the King to be well acquainted with the minister's name, as he had a remarkable memory for people. He was reputed to know the names of every bishop in England, and even the towns they came from before being elevated.

In verification of his misunderstandings concerning the animosity of the Congregationalists, King George professed uncertainty as to why the ministers of the gospel in Massachusetts usually aligned with their congregations in opposing the British government. Hutchinson's reply was direct, *"They (the ministers) are, Sir, dependent upon the people. They are elected by the people, and when they are dissatisfied with them, they seldom leave till they get rid of them."* It is doubtful whether the King grasped the significance of Hutchinson's explanation that the congregational churches hired ministers they felt reflected their basic values, and would readily rid themselves of ministers of whom they felt otherwise.

After the meeting, Hutchinson went to his lodgings to write up every detail he could remember about the visit, and the words uttered between them. Also that evening, the King wrote a note to Lord North stating he felt certain Boston would soon submit to British rule. Placing words in Hutchinson's mouth he may not have said, the King wrote, *He owes the Boston Port Bill was the only wise effectual method that could have been suggested for bringing them to a speedy submission."* The King was making assumptions that verified Parliament's actions, but doing so with a very inaccurate understanding of the colonial mindset.

On July 4, 1774 the Fifth and Thirty-eighth British Regiments joined those in Boston, adding to the potency of the troops already encamped there. However, even this massive display of military might did not deter the patriots in their opposition to what they viewed as unjust British tyranny.

Before a continental congress could meet, and discuss a cessation of trade with Britain, Samuel Adams led the Massachusetts citizens in passing a proclamation enacting their own embargo on British goods. When General Gage learned of this defiant action, he forewarned that anyone who signed this provocative proclamation would be arrested. The General's influence was immediately felt as citizen after citizen hurried to sign the paper, including supporters in Connecticut and New Hampshire. The General was learning the extent of his influence over these defiant colonists. To comply with his warning the general would have to arrest a significant portion of New England's citizenry.

Gage was soon to learn even more of the impotency of his position. Under the provisions of the newly passed Massachusetts Government Act, the governor now appointed the members of the Massachusetts Council, the upper house of the General Court, the bicameral legislature of the colony. As the

King had told Hutchinson, Gage duly appointed citizens with proven loyalty to Britain. Almost immediately upon their names being announced, the appointees were harassed, and their lives threatened. Many resigned, others, who were living outside the city, moved into Boston where they were under the guardianship of the troops which had been sent to support Gage. The same fate befell other appointed officials such as judges and sheriffs.

In London, Minister Dartmouth was originally of the opinion that Boston's call for a September meeting of a Continental Congress was not being seriously considered by the other colonies. He had likely come to this conclusion because of letters from the royal governors in New York and Pennsylvania where the congress was a hotly debated issue without universal support. He was debased of this conviction by a letter from the royal governor of Virginia, Lord Dunmore, who had earlier alerted him to his colony's support of Boston after the British closed their port. Dunmore informed him of the willingness, even enthusiastic support by the Virginians, to participate in the congress.

Dartmouth replied to Dunmore on August 3rd, *"It remains to be seen whether the measures adopted by Parliament will or will not have the effect to restore peace and harmony between Great Britain and her colonies. The proceedings of the Burgesses of Virginia do not encourage me to hope for a speedy issue to the present discussion and we have seen too much of the prevalence of the example they have set to the other colonies not to be justly alarmed at what may be the result of the unconstitutional meeting they are endeavoring to promote."*

Dartmouth was not a strict hard liner, and had often searched for conciliatory means to ease the tension between Britain and her American Colonies. His efforts, however, were futile in the hostile, anti-American climate that pervaded Britain. He was in a difficult position, and would likely have resigned his position as Minister for the American Colonies, but his loyalty to his step-brother, Lord North, precluded him from doing so. His resignation would have reflected negatively on North, and could cause dissonance between North and the King.

By early summer of 1774, twelve of the thirteen colonies had agreed to meet in the first week of September in Philadelphia. Only Georgia, occupied with suppressing an uprising with the Creek Indians, demurred. After agreeing to attend the congress, the debate in the colonies shifted to naming delegates.

There were many in New York who wanted peace with Britain: some large merchants who traded extensively with the British government, significant landowners and others who coveted large land grants from the King, and those who received direct patronage from the crown, all favored close ties to the mother country. Opposed to these were the multitudes of citizens who were angered by Britain's imperious actions; especially with Parliament's insistence on the right to tax and legislate for them. The pro-British group, led by landowner John Jay, proposed a slate of delegates, most of whom favored close ties with Britain. However, many ordinary citizens objected to the proposed slate, and instead insisted New York hold a convention to elect the delegates by a majority vote. This proposal was not acceptable to the pro-British band, so the debate continued, often acrimoniously. Finally, as much in exhaustion as anything else, a slate of nine delegates with divergent views, was appointed.

As in New York, many of the elitist Members of the Pennsylvania colonial government had a definite preference for maintaining close ties to Britain. The Quakers, a large voting bloc, was known to oppose any actions that would provoke retaliation by Britain, as avoiding hostilities was ingrained into their beliefs. The vast majority of the colony's citizens, however, including many Quakers, objected strongly to Parliament's attempts to tax and legislate for them. The colony was thus internally conflicted in how their delegates should comport themselves during the congress's debates. In a compromise with the differing convictions of its members, the appointed delegates were given instructions to follow at the congress: *"to Form and adopt a plan which shall afford the best prospect of obtaining a redress of American grievances, ascertaining American rights, and establishing that union and harmony which is most essential to the welfare and happiness of both countries, to avoid everything indecent or disrespectful to the mother state."* It was an ambiguous yet narrow path for the delegates to follow.

In Virginia, during the debate on choosing delegates for the convention, George Washington stated concisely, *"The crisis is arrived when we must assert our rights, or submit to every imposition that can be heaped upon us, till custom and use shall make us tame and abject slaves."* It was the prevalent theme in the colony as seven delegates were named including, Washington and Patrick Henry.

In Charleston, South Caroline, in proceedings that were more typical of the remaining colonies, the conclave selected delegates, and instructed them to agree to the cessation of trade with Britain. Ratification of the action was approved just before the royal governor could dissolve the assembly.

In the time leading up to the congress, militias throughout the colonies increased their readiness. All able-bodied men sixteen and up were expected to serve. At the unit level the officers were elected by the men serving in them, based on their leadership abilities. It was in contrast to the British Military, where officers received their commissions based on family standing or bribes. Assemblies and drills, which the militias normally held quarterly, were increased, in many cases, to weekly. Having enough military supplies was a serious problem, and additional arms and powder were sought, while arms already in militias' possession were refurbished and secured. This increase in the militias' readiness was especially true in Massachusetts, angry with that strong contingent of British troops settled in their midst.

The strength of the militias in the Massachusetts colony was considerable. There were over a hundred and twenty thousand able bodied men, most of whom had their own rifles, and knew well how to use them. General Gage was continuously asked by the ministry in London why he had not yet arrested the perpetrators of the destruction of the tea. Realizing the depth of the widespread opposition to his rule, and the inadequacy of his army in the face of the potentially potent militias, he virtually ignored the inquiries. His only response was to revoke John Hancock's command of the Boston Cadets Corps, whereupon the cadets immediately voted to disband. The mighty British lion, vowing to the King he would turn the rebels into lambs, was only now realizing the scope of his assignment, and the difficulties he faced in carrying it out.

The anger felt in London against the American Colonies was more than matched by the anger and indignation felt by many in America. The intensity of their abhorrence to arbitrary British rule by the great majority of the colonists was echoed in the press, was heard in heated confabs in the taverns, and even preached from pulpits. The resolve to defend their liberties with indomitable fervor could be heard in all quarters.

The Americans' sentiments were fittingly articulated by a citizen of Pepperell, a district thirty-five miles northwest of Boston, up near the border with New Hampshire. William Prescott, an honored veteran of the 1745 siege of Louisbourg and the 1755 battle of Fort Beausejour put words to the Americans' convictions,

> if we submit to these regulations, all is gone. Our forefathers passed the vast Atlantic, spent their blood and treasure, that they might enjoy their liberties, both civil and religious, and transmit them to their posterity. Their children have waded through seas of difficulty, to leave us free and happy in the enjoyment of English privileges. Now if we should give them up, can our children rise up and call us blessed? Is a glorious death in defense of our liberties better than a short infamous life, and our memories to be had in detestation to the latest posterity? Let us all be of one heart, and stand fast in the liberties wherewith Christ has made us free; and may he of his infinite mercy grant us deliverance out of all our troubles.

They were uncompromising words that called on all Americans to rebel against the oppressive British laws, even with their lives.

In August, the official, royally directed government of Massachusetts attempted to operate under the new provisions dictated by Parliament, but all efforts to do so, except for a few agencies entirely within Boston, proved futile. The Chief Justice informed Gage they were unable to meet or to conduct business in the hostile environment. The General, with his new government at a standstill, and the courts closed, wrote to Lord Dartmouth, *"Conciliation, Moderation, Reasoning is over. Nothing can be done but by forcible means."* He then requested more troops, and put the onus for more desperate action back on the Ministry, stating he would follow London's guidance, *"to judge what is best to be done."* He was hardly behaving like the strong military commander the King had dispatched to quell the colony into submission, and many in London were becoming concerned the General was not up to the task he had assumed.

Chapter Twenty-Seven

First Continental Congress

In Mid-August of 1774 the Massachusetts delegates left Boston to begin their journey to Philadelphia, and the meeting of the anxiously awaited Continental Congress. Unfortunately, James Bowdoin was unable to join his fellow delegates due to an unfortunate illness in his family. The contingent left Boston in grand style in a fine coach flanked by servants and guards. The citizens of Boston had provided Samuel Adams with a new wardrobe as they were well aware he was wont to ignore his appearance, which he considered insignificant to the affairs of his office. The Bostonians wanted him to appear professional, and inspire confidence in his fellow delegates, who would soon learn firsthand of his strong opposition to British incursions into colonial affairs.

The Massachusetts delegates were feted all along the course of their trek to Philadelphia, with supporters encouraging them at every step. At the larger towns it was common for the local gentry to host a fine dinner in their honor. The Boston delegates were elevated in importance as it was their citizens who were face to face with British imperialism. While many cheered them on and vowed absolute support, others were concerned the rash New Englanders might initiate a violent confrontation with the British military, which could draw them into an armed conflict with unforeseen consequences.

Myriads of opinions swirled around taverns in every town and city in America. Some called for unyielding opposition to Britain, even to the use of force. Some worried the disciplined British troops would annihilate the inexperienced colonial militias, resulting in even more harsh British oppression. Others, along with King George himself, voiced the opinion the colonies were too independent to act with enough unity to be effective; with the possibility that colony would end up fighting against colony. It was an uncertain time, one that depended upon dedicated, inspired leaders pertinaciously holding to their beliefs, to divine a course of action leading to the freedom many desired.

All of the delegates to the congress were there to address what all felt were imperious, unjust actions taken by the British government against its American Colonies, but not all were in accordance concerning the actions to be taken to amend the British-Colonial relationship. The differences of opinion on an approach to be followed varied among the colonies, and even within individual colonies. There would be interesting and important discussions in the course of the congress which would have impacts far into the future.

Upon arrival, and prior to the commencement of any sessions, the Massachusetts delegation was counseled by a local Philadelphia physician, Dr. Benjamin Rush about the suspicions many of his fellow delegates harbored about the motives of the New Englanders. Dr. Rush advised them never to speak of independence as so many strongly objected to that option for dealing with the impasse that existed between Britain and her American Colonies. His message was given to the entire delegation, but was especially directed to Samuel Adams, who had accrued a reputation as being strongly anti-British. The delegates took the advice to heart, and demurred from mentioning the word, even though it was never far from intruding on all congressional discussions.

The first Continental Congress was supposed to have started on the first of September 1774, but as several delegates were late in arriving, the opening was put off until September 6th. Just as the delegates to the congress were getting settled an event occurred that had a profound effect in Massachusetts, Philadelphia, and even influenced attitudes in London.

General Gage had learned through spies the colonists had sequestered a significant amount of powder in Charlestown. In a bold, stealthy raid he sent Colonel Madison, and over two hundred soldiers to seize the powder, and return it to Boston. The well armed unit silently rowed up the Mystic River, then moved onshore, and into Charlestown, surprising the magazine's guards. It was a successful foray that netted two hundred and fifty barrels of powder, which Colonel Madison quickly moved to the safety of the fort at Castle William Island in Boston Harbor.

When news of the assault reached the surrounding towns, it included the erroneous assertion that the incursion included fighting in which several colonists were killed by the British troops. As a result, thousands of colonists from the surrounding towns turned out ready to confront the British. Fortunately, saner heads prevailed, and the farmers and merchants, who were ready for action, were convinced no colonists were harmed. They reluctantly returned to their homes, but vowed to react forcibly if British troops ventured into their land and injured any of their colonial neighbors.

The rapid reaction by the multitude of colonists, armed and ready to do battle made a startling impression on General Gage as he realized he had a grossly insufficient force with which to confront an aroused colonial militia, which potentially greatly outnumbered his forces. He informed London of his observation that this latest turnout of colonials wasn't just an unruly crowd of rouges and unemployed seamen as had been believed during the Stamp Act riots, but rather, these were freemen, responsible citizens who were willing to enter into combat against his army. He requested additional troops from Britain, and also took the precaution to fortify the land bridge at Boston's neck where an enemy could enter the city on foot. The event polarized feeling even more against British loyalists throughout Massachusetts; many more of whom felt it was prudent to move into Boston to be under the security of the troops stationed there.

In London, when the Earl of Sandwich heard the colonists could muster thousands to oppose British will, he opined the hope they would muster two hundred thousand so they could be extirpated all at once. In the Earl's opinion, which reflected the opinion of most Britons, the colonists were merely a bunch of country bumpkins, who would fall easily to British might. Others, such as Pitt-Chatham and Lord Rockingham were not so sanguine.

When news of the raid, complete with the erroneous assertion of colonial deaths reached Philadelphia, members of the congress were appalled. The differences between those supporting ties to Britain, and those opposing them seemed to disappear. They became united in their horror of the treacherous act, and all agreed it was a provocation by the British military against their sovereignty.

After learning the truth, tempers subsided, and the members eased back into their original sentiments. However, the united intensity that was aroused was a precursor of the feelings that could unite this divergent assembly.

Some resentment of the Massachusetts delegation was manifest in the perception their Puritan-Congregationalist religion was isolationist and intolerant. It was mentioned the Puritans had once tried Quakers, and why, one asked, were they so opposed to taxation without representation when they themselves had taxed other religions in their colony, yet gave them no say in the use of the funds.

It was surprising then, when Massachusetts delegate, Thomas Cushing made a motion to begin each daily session with a prayer. The motion was questioned as to how that would be possible since there were so diverse a roster of faiths including, Anglicans, Episcopalians, Quakers, Presbyterians, Anabaptists, as well as the Congregationalists. Cushing's motion, however, had been planned in advance, and during the debate, Samuel Adams rose and declared he would gladly pray with any pious man who also loved his country, no matter their faith. He then proposed that Jacob Duché, a rector at nearby Saint Peter's Episcopal Church be asked to honor them with his invocations. The reverend gracefully accepted the charge.

Samuel Adams thus diffused a matter which could have impeded the views of his colony in the debates. Actually, it was not difficult for Adams to accept an Episcopalian-led prayer as the Puritan-Congregationalist strict adherence to the demanding tenants of Calvinist predestination had been in the process of moderation for decades. Immigration into New England over the years included many honorable individuals with differing religious viewpoints, which tended to diminish the distrust of others felt by the older citizens of the colony. This alteration in religious views to a more liberating behavior was based partially on the writings of John Locke, who advocated an individual had natural, inherent rights. The changes in attitude had been hastened when Edward Holyoke was made president of Harvard College in 1737. The Harvard that John Adams had attended still confirmed the Congregationalist ministers, but Holyoke's convictions were now accepted theology. *"Ministers have no right to impose their interpretations of the laws of Christ upon their flocks,"* he wrote.

These fresh views, however, did not lessen the older Puritan convictions which deeply distrusted the English monarchs. While much of the older disciplines had moderated with the newer doctrine, the distrust of the English monarchy never abated.

The following morning, the Reverend Duché thus began the session with a reading of the 35th Psalm, which was seen as appropriate by the delegates. In a strong voice he read from his bible: *"Plead my cause O Lord, with them that strive with me: fight against them that fight against me. Take hold of shield and buckler, and stand up for mine help."* It was a call heeded by the delegates.

As the members of the Continental Congress began their deliberations in earnest within the main assembly room in Philadelphia's Carpenters Hall, other meetings were being conducted in Massachusetts as a number of counties prepared "Resolves" which documented their relationship to Britain, and opposition to the recent acts of Parliament.

The most significant of these meetings was one chaired by Dr. Joseph Warren in Milton, outside of Boston in Suffolk County. Warren had discussed the subject with Samuel Adams and others before the Massachusetts representatives left for the congress in Philadelphia, and they had agreed on the general content of any declarations to be presented to the county representatives for consideration. The Resolves approved at the meeting were an extended litany of statements which affirmed the King as sovereign, and entitled to their allegiance, but which also stated the colonies would not only not accept Parliament's laws, but asserted Massachusetts was a free state, which could enact their own laws, and assess their own taxes. Further, the colony could officially assemble their own militia and arm them.

The Resolves, referring to the recent acts of Parliament blocking Boston's Harbor and altering Massachusetts' charter and government, added, *"That no obedience is due from this province to either or any part of the acts above-mentioned, but that they are rejected as the attempts of a wicked administration to enslave America."* Upon passage of the resolves, Warren dispatched Paul Revere to Philadelphia with a copy of Suffolk's Resolves, to be given to the Continental Congress. Revere, making fifty miles a day, rode rapidly to Philadelphia.

It was no surprise Warren chose Paul Revere to deliver the extremely important resolves to the Continental Congress. Paul had the confidence of all of the patriot leaders in the Massachusetts Colony. The Reveres did not come to Boston in the same manner as most of Boston's citizens, but Paul was accepted and held in high regard by most of them. The path his family took to New England, at least on his father's side, was initiated by an action taken by the King of France almost ninety years earlier.

In 1685, a hundred and fifty years after Henry-VIII made life difficult for Catholics in England while promoting the Protestant Anglican Church; the French King Louis-XIV issued the Edict of Fontainebleau, which made life difficult for Protestants while promoting the Catholic Church. Both endeavors were designed to strengthen the ruling monarchy by aligning religious convictions with support for the government and its laws.

As a result of Louis-XIV's edict, hundreds of thousands of French men and women left the country to lands where they could freely follow their religious beliefs. The Protestant French, known as Huguenots, generally followed the teachings of Jean Cauvin (John Calvin in English), which were well accepted in various regions around the world such as the English settlements in New England.

One of the refugees who left France was young Apollos Rivoire. His family sent him to his uncle in Holland, who subsequently put the ten-year old boy on a ship bound for the New World. Uncle Simon had arranged for Apollos to be apprenticed to a successful Boston goldsmith, John Coney, for a ten-year commitment. The lad arrived in Boston in 1716.

When Coney died in 1722, twenty-year old Apollos, now called "Paul" with his last name modified to conform to English tongues as "Revere," paid off the three remaining years of his apprenticeship, and set out on his own. Apollos, now Paul, married Deborah Hitchbourn, daughter of a moderately prosperous property owner, whose family had settled in the colony some ninety-years earlier. Paul and Deborah's second child was born on New Year's Day in 1734, and named Paul after his father. The Hitchbourn's family harbored a somewhat rebellious nature, which was undoubtedly passed on to Deborah's son.

Growing up in the often hectic life in Boston, the boy was regaled with tales of adventure from the free-thinking relatives in his mother's clan. It is not surprising the young man was called "bold," a designation that followed him into adulthood. Paul Senior died in July 1754 when Paul was nineteen. He assumed the role of head of the household for two years, but then for some reason decided to join the army for a year. He went into a regiment headed to attack the French at their fort at Crown Point. The unit never did make it to their target, and Paul returned to Boston where he set up his own silversmith shop.

In August 1757 he married Sary Orne, and the couple immediately started a family. In 1759 Paul joined the Masons where he met a number of prominent Bostonians such as Dr. Joseph Warren. Paul had a sincere admiration for Warren, and thought his intelligence, character, and leadership qualities quite superior.

Paul became a member of the Whig Party and regularly attended meetings of the North Caucus where he met others objecting to the British controls being placed on their colony. In addition to Warren, Paul became acquainted with the more activist Bostonians such as Samuel Adams, Dr Benjamin Church, Benjamin Edes, publisher of the Boston Gazette, and others. The Stamp Act intensified the colonial Whigs' opposition to Britain's laws. Paul, as a member of the Sons of Liberty actively protested against the act.

After delivering the Suffolk Resolves to Samuel Adams in Philadelphia, Paul returned to Boston with letters and messages to the patriot leaders in Boston, ready to again to serve the patriot cause.

When the Congress finally started its proceedings on September 6th, the well respected Payton Randolph of Virginia, Thomas Jefferson's cousin, was elected chairman. The larger colonies wanted a colony's voting rights based on population, but this was opposed by the smaller colonies who felt they would have a greatly reduced impact on any decisions. When it was realized there was no accurate figures of a colony's population nor wealth on which to base a voting weight, it was finally agreed that, at the start, each colony would have one vote, but that the matter would be taken up again later.

As the congress began their sessions, the deliberations were polite and civil as the delegates took the measure of each other. John Adams was, at first, uncertain about the competency and dedication of the representatives from the other colonies, but he soon became convinced they were well-educated, and well-acquainted with the issues facing them. He did, however, observe any issue or proposition broached by a member would entail an incessant litany of speeches, which would cause debates to drag on for extended periods. This was not surprising since twenty-two of the fifty-six delegates were lawyers, the remainder being mainly merchants or farmers.

As the meetings progressed, John Adams became more vocal, and participated actively in the debates while Samuel Adams' influence was affected through more subtle means. There were many opportunities for the delegates to dine and socialize with one another, and the body soon became more open to discussion as personal relationships and mutual respect increased.

It soon became evident there were two opposing views for dealing with Britain. Some, such as those from Massachusetts and Virginia, were for strong action, while others, such as many in the New York and Pennsylvania delegations sought measures which would re-establish good relations between Britain and her American colonies, and were ambivalent regarding truculent actions. Or, as one author labeled the two factions: "loyalist moderates and radical separatists." There was, however, a broad spectrum of opinion between the two extremes.

One of the first issues to be discussed was the proposal for the cessation of trade with Great Britain. It was thought economic losses by British merchants would assist in forcing the government to repeal the Intolerable Acts. It became evident the majority of the colonies favored some sort of trade embargo, but the timing of its enforcement became an issue. Virginia, especially, had a concern their tobacco crop wouldn't be ready in time to be shipped if a trade embargo was imminent. South Carolina complained that while New England would see little impact of an embargo, the discontinuance of rice exports could well be disastrous for the colony. In compromise, a trade embargo was agreed to, which included provisions to insure compliance across all of the colonies. Termed the "Continental Association," it wouldn't take effect for another year, and the export of rice was to be allowed.

The Continental Association actually did more than just call for and establish means to enforce a boycott of British goods. The agreement called for the setting up committees of enforcement in colonial counties and cities to monitor compliance. Violators were to be identified and chastised in ways strict enough they usually repented, and ceased their unacceptable activity. In practice, the committees often went beyond just enforcing the boycott, and harassed royalists advocating allegiance to the crown.

With regard to the relationship with Britain and its Parliament making laws for the colonies, Joseph Galloway, the leader of the powerful Quaker bloc, who opposed the trade embargo, offered a unique procedure for a new legislative relationship between Britain and the Colonies which would sure to be acceptable to the King and Parliament. Galloway was known to favor close ties with the mother country, and his proposal did just that. He proposed the formation of a colonial-wide legislative assembly, called ostentatiously, the "American Grand Council." In Galloway's concept, this council would legislate for all of the American colonies in matters of common interest. It would have representatives from all of the colonies, and be led by a head (Resident General he called him) appointed by the King. All of the statues enacted by the council would be ratified by the British Parliament. John Jay of New York immediately seconded Galloway's motion.

The concept of an American Council subservient to Parliament was assailed by many, including Patrick Henry and Richard Lee of Virginia, who argued against the concept. True to the methods he employed successfully in his home colony, Samuel Adams worked behind the scenes, much of it in local taverns, a venue he knew well, to defeat the measure. He and others enraged the citizens of Philadelphia by asserting Galloway was giving away their freedoms. It was successful enough that Galloway felt threatened. The proposal was abandoned soon after Paul Revere arrived with the Suffolk Resolves which were soon a main topic for discussion.

It was proposed the congress adopt the Suffolk Resolves as their own since they addressed the issues they had with Britain. It was a hotly debated proposal as many felt Suffolk's resolves were too extreme; some alleging they were essentially a declaration of war which would cause a harsh reaction from Britain, destroying any possibility of reconciliation with the mother country. The Resolves were finally endorsed by the congress, and although the vote was recorded as unanimous, it was accepted only reluctantly by some.

The Continental Congress ended on October 14, 1774 with the issuance of a series of Declarations and Resolves issued by *"The good people of the several colonies of New-Hampshire, Massachusetts-Bay, Rhode Island and Providence Plantations, Connecticut, New York, New-Jersey, Pennsylvania, Newcastle, Kent, and Sussex on Delaware, Maryland, Virginia, North-Carolina and South-Carolina."* The declarations were not as strongly worded as those from Suffolk, but a similar message was evident. The tone of the final release was not belligerent, but was firm in alleging the recent British acts were illegal, and would not be accepted. The congress specifically disputed Parliament's authority to legislate for them or to tax them for the purpose of raising revenue. Britain was called on to repeal the illegal Coercive Acts immediately, as they were described as *"dangerous and destructive to the freedom of American legislation,"* and *"demonstrate a system formed to enslave America."*

A contentious issue debated intently during the congress was whether the British Parliament had the authority to enact ANY laws for the colonies, including navigation acts related to external trade. In a compromise between the disparate factions orchestrated by John Adams, Resolve Number Four condescendingly stated Parliament had the authority to legislate in matters *"restrained to the regulation of our external commerce for the pursuit of securing the commercial advantages of the whole empire."* However, to avoid any ambiguity, the resolve went on to state, *"excluding every idea of taxation internal or external, for raising revenue on the subjects of America, without their consent."*

With reference to the occupation of Boston by British troops, a resolve specifically stated *"that the keeping of a standing army in several of these colonies, in time of peace, without the consent of the legislature of that colony in which such army is kept, is against the law."*

Finally, the Congress composed an appeal to be given directly to King George which defined their disputes with Britain, and supplicated the King to grant them relief. Many still embraced the image of the King as a father figure who would only act in the best interests of his children. His only concern, they averred, was their welfare and happiness. Those exposing this perception did not know or would not accept the intractable position the King was taking to force their complete submission to British will.

The congress disbanded, and the delegates prepared to return to their respective colonies to report on what had been accomplished at the congress. They agreed to meet again in May of 1775. They left Philadelphia with a feeling of unity, and a sense of strength resulting from their certainty of purpose. Many of the more optimistic members believed their united front, and firm rejection of the Coercive Acts would cause the King and Parliament to accede to their call for the acts' repeal, repairing the breech with the mother country. They did not; however, appreciate the depth of the intransigence felt in London by the sovereign and most members of Parliament.

On October 5th, as the Massachusetts delegation was ending their participation in the congress in Philadelphia, and preparing to return home, the official Massachusetts Assembly was preparing to meet in Salem. However, when General Gage never appeared it became apparent he had effectively dissolved the Assembly. Not to be cowered by the British Governor, on October 7th the members of the assembly moved to Concord, and met as a Provincial Congress with John Hancock acting as president. The Provincial Congress assumed control of most government functions for the colony, excluding Boston.

Although the Provincial Congress was an illegal body in the eyes of the British, that did not constrain it from assuming the role of a legitimate government which could enact laws, collect taxes and prepare to defend their territory. A Committee of Safety was appointed to organize the militias, and prepare to oppose any military incursions from Gage's troops into their towns. The militias across America had already increased their training and readiness, but the stealthy attack on Charlestown, and the intermittent excursions outside of Boston by British troops, emphasized the need for a quick reaction capability. The towns in the province were directed to form elite units of the most able men in their ranks, which could react at a moment's notice to confront British aggression. These units were known as Minutemen.

The use of special units of younger, vigorous men to react rapidly to threats to a town or settlement went back to at least the Pequot War and, in fact, the concept was employed in the earliest settlements of the New World. The advantage accrued the colony was the ability to call for a sizeable contingent of defenders who could protect a valuable colonial asset such as a cache of weapons or powder. The disadvantage of the concept was that each town's militia acted independently, with little coordination of effort with the others.

Massachusetts was not the only colony who moved in the direction of setting up assemblies to govern, independent of British sanction. North Carolina acted similarly at about the same time as Massachusetts, and many of the others initiated processes which would result in their own provincial assemblies, governing without British approval.

At the South Carolina meeting a discussion was held concerning the exclusion of rice in the embargo with Britain. In their fervor to join with the other colonies in opposing British oppressions, and to subscribe to the intent of the embargo agreed to by the other colonies, the assembly explored the elimination of the exclusion on the exportation of rice, which would place a burden on the colony. However, the meeting ended without action on the matter so the original resolve would be maintained.

In New York, a motion was made in a meeting of the committee of correspondence, to approve of the actions taken at the Continental Congress. In the ensuing vote, the motion lost by one vote; the discord in the colony still evident. The majority of the ordinary citizens likely approved of the Congress's actions even if a cadre of its leaders did not, and the dissonance within the colony continued.

In Pennsylvania, the loyalists to Britain hoped to receive the support of the Quakers to continue opposition to the Congress's actions. While the Quakers reaffirmed their opposition to warfare, the assembly quickly assented to the Congress's proceedings. Joseph Galloway, who had proposed the "American Council," which would have given power to the King and Parliament, declined to serve in the next congress scheduled for the following May. The new Pennsylvania delegation would include patriot John Dickenson, noted for his "Letters from a Farmer" during the Stamp Act crisis.

About the time the Congress ended, Britain was again reminded the matter of tea, which chaffed British sensitivities, was not at an end. When a ship loaded with over two thousand pounds of tea docked at Annapolis, Maryland, the local citizenry were so inflamed against this overt attempt to land British tea to substantiate Parliament's right to enact laws for them, that the ship's owner was "persuaded" to burn the ship with the tea still aboard, which he did in full view of all.

General Gage felt more insecure in Boston, and again requested additional troops from Britain. About twenty-thousand would be needed he counseled. He also attempted to mobilize additional forces from Canada, including use of French citizens and Indians. Even though he was prodded to arrest the rebellious leaders in the colony, he hesitated to move against John Hancock, who continued to live at his estate on the edge of Boston Commons with his aunt Lydia. Gage also wrote to Lord Dartmouth recommending Britain temporarily suspend enforcement of the Coercive Acts to allow Britain time to strengthen her positions in the colonies to thwart any uprisings. The King thought the idea absurd.

Chapter Twenty-Eight

The Division Widens

In November of 1774 a newly elected British Parliament was seated in London. The King had carefully crafted early elections so the new assembly was of the same mind as the old one. The new Parliament thus still agreed with the King there could be no compromise with the American Colonies; they would have to be subjugated to British rule by whatever force was necessary. There could be no abatement of the acts Parliament passed in its last session regarding its control of the colonies, and no abandonment of Parliament's right to tax and to legislate for the Americans.

The Declarations and Resolves of the Continental Congress finally arrived in London in December 1774. In an attempt to gain a favorable response to the issues raised at the Congress, Ben Franklin, the colonial representative from Pennsylvania, but seen in London as the most important representative of the Americans, met with several prominent Britons including David Barclay and John Fothergill, who seemed to be favorably inclined to the petitions of the Congress. Franklin became hopeful something agreeable to both sides could be worked out to restore amiable relations between the colonies and Britain. Unfortunately, the King, and most of his ministers, found the congress's declarations and resolves insubordinate and insulting.

Lord North did not share the monarch's stern approach to subjugation of the colonies by force, and he searched for means to reconcile the British-Colonial divide. He realized the situation was rapidly spinning out of control, and could result in irrevocable actions which would forever blight the country's relations with its American brethren. However, since he always acceded to the Kings wishes, he was in a dilemma about what he could do to alleviate the situation. Along with Lord Dartmouth, he sought out Franklin to see if the distinguished American had any acceptable ideas for repairing the breech.

But, even at this high level, with the King's unbending attitude, no solutions could be found.

Franklin's hope for finding any positive responses to the Congress's resolutions in London was rapidly declining when he was called to a meeting with the eminent Pitt-Chatham, one of only a very few parliamentarians, who had long advocated the repeal the Coercive Acts. Pitt-Chatham, like the others who had approached Franklin, asked him what measures did he feel must be taken by Britain to satisfy the Americans. Franklin's initial response was that the occupation of Boston by British troops was the most unsettling, and their removal would greatly facilitate better dialogue.

In mid-January, Franklin received a message from Pitt-Chatham asking him to attend a session of the House of Lords at which time the renowned statesman would make an important speech. On January 20, 1775, Pitt-Chatham took the floor of the House of Lords to address his peers. He pleaded for *"immediate orders to remove the forces from the town of Boston as soon as possible."* He continued at length, extolling the righteousness of the American's petitions, *"When your lordships look at the papers transmitted us from America, when you consider their decency, firmness and wisdom, you cannot but respect their cause and wish to make it your own."* With regard to the Coercive Acts, he implored his countrymen; *"let us retract while we can, not when we must."* He warned his peers they could never subjugate the colonies.

While Lords Shelburne and Camden supported Pitt-Chatham, many other voices opposed him. Lord Lyttleton even accusing him of sedition in espousing the American's cause. When Pitt-Chatham then made a formal motion to repeal Parliament's oppressive acts, the vote failed by the large majority of 77 to 18. The vote was received by the King with elation as he felt the new Parliament was completely united with him in his goal of forcing the colonies to accept unconditional British rule. The House of Commons then voted to declare Massachusetts Bay in a state of rebellion. In a spiteful move, the king banned fishing by the colony in the North Atlantic waters from which they harvested one of their important sources of subsistence.

The King and his ministers were becoming more dissatisfied with General Gage and his docility with regard to enforcing British control, and especially his reluctance to arrest the leaders who instigated the dumping of British tea into Boston's Harbor, and the leaders of the illegal Massachusetts Provincial Assembly. Gage procrastinated and eschewed strong action as he was concerned arresting Hancock and Adams would precipitate hostilities against his outnumbered troops. The King, ever sensitive to the protocol of the aristocracy, was averse to outright replacing Gage as it would be a great embarrassment for the General and his family. Three other prominent Generals: William Howe, John Burgoyne, and Henry Clinton, were thus advised to prepare for assignment in America "advising" Gage.

In late January, Lord Dartmouth, desperate for action, sent General Gage a command to immediately move against the *"principal actors and abettors"* in Massachusetts. He promised additional troops would be sent, but opined, *"A smaller force now, if put to the test, would be able to encounter them with greater probability of success than might be expected from a greater army."* It was a strong directive, but, for some reason, the letter was not immediately dispatched to Gage.

In Massachusetts, relations between the British troops and the inhabitants of the province had become ever more tense; there was no recession from the stance each side had taken, and patience for some sort of resolution was waning. On February 26th, just before dawn, Gage sent two hundred troops to capture military stores he was informed were hidden at Salem. The contingent sailed from the fort at Castle William Island and landed at Marblehead, intending to march overland to Salem. As dawn broke, the citizens of the area became aware of the intrusion, and an alarm went out setting in motion an assemblage to challenge the soldiers. Facing a hostile gathering of armed patriots which outnumbered them, the British party retreated back to the safety of the fort.

On March 20, 1775, the Virginians who had attended the Continental Congress met in Richmond with the newly formed Virginia Revolutionary Council to present to their colonial compatriots what had been accomplished at the meetings in Philadelphia. They assembled without the permission of the Royal Governor, Lord Dunmore. Over 120 delegates from sixty-four counties and cities were represented at the meeting; the following day Augusta County, from west of the Alleghenies was also seated. The report from the Congress's delegates was optimistic; several of the delegates voiced the opinion the congress's firm stand would likely induce Britain to null the Intolerable Acts, or certainly to greatly reduce their more onerous provisions. This was a prevalent view even though just two weeks previously the King had extended the ban on fishing in Atlantic waters to include Maryland, New Jersey, Pennsylvania, South Carolina, and Virginia.

With Thomas Jefferson, who now felt well after recovering from dysentery, George Washington, Richard Henry Lee, Patrick Henry, and others in attendance at the meeting in Saint John's Church, the position of the Virginia Colony in its relationship to Britain was intensively debated. There was ambiguity in the minds of most of those in attendance regarding which specific actions needed to be taken to gain relief from the oppressive laws.

Independence, for many, was not thought the best approach as their long, historical dependence on Britain was deeply ingrained into their culture. How they would fare if left to their own resources actualized the apprehensions many felt with the concept. They were conflicted about what was reasonable and what was extreme. In an earlier debate after British troops occupied Boston, George Washington, who strongly objected to the British move, averred, *"I will raise a thousand men, subsist them at my own expense and march myself at their head for the relief of Boston."* It was a forceful declaration, pledging military action against the British. Yet, on a number of occasions Washington stated his opposition to independence from the mother country by the colonies. In the preceding October, he had stated, *"No such thing as independence is desired by any thinking man in America."* It was as if many were fearful of accepting the reality they faced. It was a frightening choice, submit or war.

On Wednesday, March 22, 1775, the Virginia convention voted on a motion to accept the Declarations and Resolves passed by the Congress:

> Resolved unanimously, that this Convention doth entirely and cordially approve the proceedings and resolutions of the American Continental Congress, and that they consider this whole continent as under the highest obligations to that very respectable body, for the wisdom of their counsels, and their unremitted endeavors to maintain and preserve inviolate the just rights and liberties of his Majesty's dutiful and loyal subjects in America.

The convention thanked their delegates to the Congress *"for their cheerful undertaking, and faithful discharge of, the very important trust reposed in them,"* and then adjourned for the day.

On Thursday, March 23, 1775 the session began, as usual with a reading by Reverend Miles Selden of Richmond's Saint John's Episcopal Church. The convention's delegates were somewhat in a state of indecision concerning what actions would be appropriate for the Colony to endorse. As the delegates sought to clarify their position, a speaker arose to present a clear exposition of the position in which the colonies found themselves, and what would be appropriate actions for them to take.

Patrick Henry was self-effacing concerning his education and abilities, but he harbored a confidence in his analytical mind and his ability to lucidly express his views. His veridical perception—to see things as they really were and not as one would like them to be—was a prominent attribute. Many remember the last sentence of Henry's speech, but it was his comprehensive, logical elucidation of the state of their affairs that ultimately moved many to seriously consider a conflict with Britain, and independence as a viable alternative. It was thus on the 23rd of March of 1775 that he rose and began his inspiring speech. Reproduced as well as possible long after the actual speech, it is still arousing.

No man thinks more highly than I do of the patriotism, as well as abilities, of the very worthy gentlemen who have just addressed the House. But different men often see the same subject in different lights; and therefore, I hope it will not be thought disrespectful to those gentlemen if, entertaining as I do opinions of a character very opposed to theirs, I shall speak forth my sentiments freely and without reserve. This is no time for ceremony. The question before the House is one of awful moment to this country. For my own part, I consider it as nothing less than a question of freedom or slavery; and in proportion to the magnitude of the subject ought to be the freedom of the debate. It is only in this way that we can hope to arrive at truth, and fulfill the great responsibility which we hold to God and our country. Should I keep back my opinions at such a time, through fear of giving offense, I should consider myself as guilty of treason towards my country, and of an act of disloyalty toward the Majesty of Heaven, which I revere above all earthly kings.

Mr. President, it is natural to man to indulge in the illusions of hope. We are apt to shut our eyes against a painful truth, and listen to the song of that siren till she transforms us into beasts. Is this the part of wise men, engaged in a great and arduous struggle for liberty? Are we disposed to be of the number of those who, having eyes, see not, and having ears, hear not, the things which so nearly concern their temporal salvation? For my part, whatever anguish of spirit it may cost, I am willing to know the whole truth; to know the worst, and to provide for it.

I have but one lamp by which my feet are guided, and that is the lamp of experience. I know of no way of judging of the future but by the past. And judging by the past, I wish to know what there has been in the conduct of the British ministry for the last ten years to justify those hopes with which gentlemen have been pleased to solace themselves and the House. Is it that insidious smile with which our petition has been received? Trust it not, sir; it will prove a snare to your feet. Suffer not yourselves to be betrayed with a kiss. Ask yourselves how this gracious reception of our petition comports with those warlike preparations which cover our waters and darken our land. Are fleets and armies necessary to a work of love and reconciliation? Have we shown ourselves so unwilling to be reconciled that force must be called in to win back our love? Let us not deceive ourselves, sir. These are the implements of war and subjugation; the last arguments to which kings resort. I ask gentlemen, sir, what means this martial array, if its purpose be not to force us to submission?

Can gentlemen assign any other possible motive for it? Has Great Britain any enemy, in this quarter of the world, to call for all this accumulation of navies and armies? No, sir, she has none. They are meant for us: they can be meant for no other. They are sent over to bind and rivet upon us those chains which the British ministry have been so long forging. And what have we to oppose them? Shall we try argument? Sir, we have been trying that for the last ten years. Have we anything new to offer upon the subject? Nothing. We have held the subject up in every light of which it is capable; but it has been all in vain. Shall we resort to entreaty and humble supplication? What terms shall we find which have not been already exhausted? Let us not, I beseech you, sir, deceive ourselves. Sir, we have done everything that could be done to avert the storm which is now coming on. We have petitioned; we have remonstrated; we have supplicated; we have prostrated ourselves before the throne, and have implored its interposition to arrest the tyrannical hands of the ministry and Parliament. Our petitions have been slighted; our remonstrances have produced additional violence and insult; our supplications have been disregarded; and we have been spurned, with contempt, from the foot of the throne! In vain, after these things, may we indulge the fond hope of peace and reconciliation. There is no longer any room for hope. If we wish to be free—if we mean to preserve inviolate those inestimable privileges for which we have been so long contending—if we mean not basely to abandon the noble struggle in which we have been so long engaged, and which we have pledged ourselves never to abandon until the glorious object of our contest shall be obtained—we must fight! I repeat it, sir, we must fight! An appeal to arms and to the God of hosts is all that is left us!

They tell us, sir, that we are weak; unable to cope with so formidable an adversary. But when shall we be stronger? Will it be the next week, or the next year? Will it be when we are totally disarmed, and when a British guard shall be stationed in every house? Shall we gather strength by irresolution and inaction? Shall we acquire the means of effectual resistance by lying supinely on our backs and hugging the delusive phantom of hope, until our enemies shall have bound us hand and foot? Sir, we are not weak if we make a proper use of those means which the God of nature hath placed in our power. The millions of people, armed in the holy cause of liberty, and in such a country as that which we possess, are invincible by any force which our enemy can send against us. Besides, sir, we shall not fight our battles alone. There is a just God who resides over the destinies of nations, and who will raise up friends to fight our battles for us. The battle, sir, is not to the strong alone; it is to the vigilant, the active, the brave. Besides, sir, we have no election. If we were base enough to desire it, it is now too late to retire from the contest. There is no retreat but in submission and slavery! Our chains are forged! Their clanking may be heard on the plains of Boston! The war is inevitable—and let it come! I repeat it, sir, let it come.

It is in vain, sir, to extenuate the matter. Gentlemen may cry, Peace, Peace— but there is no peace. The war is actually begun! The next gale that sweeps from the north will bring to our ears the clash of resounding arms! Our brethren are already in the field! Why stand we here idle? What is it that gentlemen wish? What would they have? Is life so dear, or peace so sweet, as to be purchased at the price of chains and slavery? Forbid it, Almighty God! I know not what course others may take; but as for me, give me liberty or give me death!

As the truth in Patrick Henry's words, which were published widely, swept into the consciousnesses of the Virginians and subsequently across all of the colonies, it became obvious they must act. The Virginia Council voted that same day for:

Resolved that a well regulated militia, composed of Gentlemen and Yeomen, is the natural strength, and only security, of a free government; that such a militia in this colony would for ever render it unnecessary for the Mother Country to keep among us, for the purpose of our defense, any standing army of mercenary forces, always subversive of the quiet and dangerous to the liberties of the people, and would obviate the pretext of taxing us for their support.

That the establishment of such a militia is at this time peculiarly necessary, by the state of our laws, for the protection and defense of the country, some of which are already expired, and others will shortly do so; and that the known remissness of government, in calling us together in a legislative capacity, render it too insecure, in this time of danger and distress, to rely that opportunity will be given of renewing them in General Assembly, or making any provision to secure our inestimable rights and liberties from those farther violations with which they are threatened.

Resolved therefore, that this colony immediately put into a posture of defense, and that Patrick Henry, Richard Henry Lee, Robert Carter Nicholas, Benjamin Harrison, Lemuel Riddick, George Washington, Adam Stephen, Andrew Lewis, William Christian, Edmund Pendleton, Thomas Jefferson, and Isaac Zane, Esqrs. Be a committee to prepare a plan for the embodying, arming, and disciplining such a number of men as many be sufficient for that purpose.

The convention went on to reaffirm its support of the citizens of Boston, and to describe how their militia should be organized and supported. It was a decisive alteration in outlook that occurred at the Virginia convention, a change strong enough to persist into the future.

Realizing his efforts in Britain were fruitless and pining for his wife who had died suddenly of a stroke in December, Benjamin Franklin left London to sail home to Pennsylvania. Just before leaving, however, he was presented with a bribe by Lord Hyde. Hyde hinted that Franklin would be rewarded beyond his expectations if he would only craft more reasonable terms for the colonial acceptance of British rule. Franklin was incensed by the offer. He wrote a note to Joseph Galloway in Pennsylvania espousing his disgust, *"When I consider the extreme corruption prevalent among all orders of men in this old, rotten state, and the glorious public virtue so predominant in our rising country, I cannot but apprehend more mischief than benefit from a closer union."*

In Boston, the troops were becoming more openly hostile to patriots advocating separation from British rule. Some of the more nefarious began vandalizing John Hancock's mansion, causing John's Aunt Lydia to leave and move to the old Hancock house in Lexington, where John had lived as a child with his grandfather, "Bishop" Hancock. The house was presently occupied by the new minister, Jonas Clarke, and his family; they welcomed Lydia and her charge, John's fiancé, Dorothy Quincy warmly.

As the fateful month of April 1775 arrived, the American Colonies had taken steps in their relations with the mother country which were decisive as seen from both perspectives. All of the colonies had agreed to the Continental Association approved by the Continental Congress, and a boycott of British goods began in earnest.

Of more significance, many of the colonies had, or were in the process, of forming their own legislatures, independent of British control. The riots during the Stamp Act, the dumping of tea, or even the boycott of British goods could be viewed as protests against the mother country's actions the colonies found oppressive. Setting up independent governments, however, was a patently rebellious act. Usurping British control in what the government in London viewed as nearly vassal settlements, hardened the positions of the King and Parliament. They chafed at the audacity of the colonies to assess and collect taxes, to control the selection of representatives, and to establish stronger militias. These were indeed provocative and grave deeds.

The king and his ministers now faced a difficult, essentially irreversible situation. Even if Parliament would now agree to repeal the Intolerable Acts, there was no certainty a colony would voluntarily give up its assumed government and revert back to British control. With no other viable course open at this point, Britain could only push ahead more strongly with their plan of subjugating the colonies, and forcing their submission to British domination.

Sensing the climate becoming more hazardous to their safety, John Hancock and Samuel Adams moved into the parsonage of Jonas Clarke and his wife Lucy. With the Clarke's large family of ten children, and with Aunt Lydia and her charge, Hancock and Adams moved into in a crowded residence. However, it seemed to work as there was a common agreement upon the purpose which they all pursued. Adams especially appreciated the counsel he received from Reverend Clarke, a strong patriot, who exhibited a unique combination of intelligence and practically.

John Hancock and Samuel Adams, although both believed strongly in the patriot cause, were different personalities. Adams was fiercely dedicated to separation from Britain, and used his cunning to mold opinions to that end. He was analytical and calculating in his approach. He was a master at political infighting, and, using any means available, influenced decisions made in local and now, colonial-wide assemblies. Hancock, in contrast, was urbane and forward in manner. He was intelligent, but not intellectual in approach. He had very much a what-you-see-is what you-have personality. As the richest man in the province, he was used to deference from others. He liked the spectacle of authority, taking great pride in his position as commander of the, now disbanded, Cadet Guard.

President of the Provincial Council meeting in Concord and Chairman of the Committee of Safety, Hancock was a strong, competent leader in a time of uncertainty. Like Adams, he was a target of the British, who wanted him arrested and returned to England where he would face certain execution. Both men were extremely important to the continuance of the patriot cause. Well aware of their vulnerability, they had begun to take steps to avoid capture.

It seemed to most there were two disparate outcomes to the crisis: submission or independence, or as Patrick Henry stated, slavery or war. King George had also described the options as submission or independence, but Adams knew there was a third option, and it worried him. The third option was an insidious occurrence in which one or more of the colonies would not agree to further confrontation with Britain, and independent of the others, agree to some sort of pact with Britain in which they would acknowledge British sovereignty over them for special favors. If even one colony took this path it could easily cause any attempt by the others to confront Britain militarily to fail.

New York, had not yet officially approved the Declarations and Resolves of the Continental Congress, nor selected delegates to the upcoming congress in May. Lord North attempted to seduce New York into supporting an accommodation with Britain independent of the other colonies. Although his plan was available to all of the colonies, he felt New York was not as intransigent in their opposition to the British acts as were the others. He proposed a method whereby a colony would assess taxes on itself to pay for British support, and, if the taxes were sufficient, Parliament would be restricted to assess taxes only for external commerce. The scheme, of course, did not address the basic question of whether Parliament had the right to legislate for and tax a colony.

The minister felt this approach would be acceptable to many in New York, and as a further show of good will, New York was excluded from the ban on fishing in Atlantic waters. New York was a divided colony, but the majority of its citizens did not agree with several of the prominent royalist-leaning leaders. The Dutch settlers certainly did not have any feelings of loyalty to an English King. Joining with the New York Sons of Liberty and others supporting the patriot position, they forced the selection of delegates to the May congress, and reaffirmed their accordance with the rest of colonial America.

The position of the patriots of Massachusetts to confront the mighty British Empire was dire. It was aptly described by George Bancroft in Volume Seven of his seventeenth-century epic work, History of the United States,

with no treasury but the good-will of the people; not a soldier in actual service; hardly ammunition enough for a parade day; as for artillery, having scarce more than ten cannon of iron, four of brass, and two cohorns; with no executive but the committee of safety; no internal government but by committees of correspondence; no visible centre of authority; and no distinguished general officer to take command of the provincial troops. Anarchy must prevail, unless there lives in the heart of the people an invisible, resistless, formative principle, that can organize and guide.

The patriot leaders knew they would be tested, and welcomed the trial.

Chapter Twenty-Nine

Confrontation in Lexington

The general mood of the British troops stationed in Boston was souring. An outbreak of smallpox in the city and several surrounding towns caused fear in the confines of the city where so many were closely congregated. They had been confined to Boston Common since their arrival last summer, and were bored with the endless routine of drills and weapon cleanings demanded by their officers. It was drudgery to repeat the same tasks day after day; work despised by armies everywhere, forced into inactivity with no battles to break the monotony.

There was a general dissatisfaction with their commander as well. Many felt Gage too easy on the colonials. Why, they grumbled, hadn't he arrested those trouble-making rebels as he was ordered to do? For professional soldiers, Gage's rule seemed too benevolent; permitting freedom of a press which often attacked British rule, and, except for the guarded gate at Boston Neck, allowed the Bostonians freedom of movement. In situations where disputes arose between the military and the citizenry, the soldiers felt Gage went out of his way to side with the Bostonians and against them.

That Gage had sympathy for the colonials, although not their cause is probable. He had lived in the New World for most of the last twenty years, had an American wife (who may have, from time to time, provided the patriots with useful information), and had large land holdings in the land. He was an army compatriot of George Washington, with whom he served in the French and Indian War, and counted many other Americans among his friends. He was, however, a dedicated military officer with loyalty to the King. Torn between his sympathies and his duty he was often slow to react to orders from the Provincial Minister in London.

Gage, on-site in the troubled province had his reasons for treading softly in relations with the Bostonians. As recently as March 25th he had written

Minister Dartmouth explaining his rationale. *"I have been at pains to prevent anything of consequence taking its rise from trifles and idle quarrels, and when the cause of Boston became the general concern of America, endeavored to manage that Administration might have an opening to negotiate if anything conciliatory should present itself or be in a condition to prosecute their plans with greater advantage."* The General still held hope that an amicable resolution to the disputes between the colonies and Britain could be worked out, and order restored peacefully.

Lord Dartmouth, thousands of miles away did not appreciate Gage's position. He couldn't understand why, with four thousand British troops at his disposal, Gage couldn't enforce any action he pleased. In London, Dartmouth, goaded by the King and other hard-liners, assured by the likes of ex-governor Hutchinson the colonists would cower when faced with British might, was frustrated with Gage's inactivity. He did not, of course, perceive the threat posed by over a hundred thousand armed and angry patriots ready to challenge Gage's army.

With the beneficence Gage was showing to the Citizens of Boston, and the lack of overt British actions, Samuel Adams felt the intensity of the dispute with Britain drifting. Some drastic action, rousing colonial emotions was needed to re-instill the fervor necessary to force British retraction of the oppressive acts, or to inspire a fight to gain outright independence. Efforts to establish a continental army at the last congress had gone nowhere, and, even in Massachusetts where they had the nascent beginnings of an army, many of the militias were not, in Adams' view, moving forcefully to strengthen their potency. At the meeting of the Provincial Congress in Concord at the end of March they had established "rules and regulations for a constitutional army," which defined the service's broad outlines, even naming several generals, but it was essentially a paper organization.

In the event military action did occur, Adams was concerned Gage would attempt to isolate New England by moving troops, maybe some from Canada, to the Hudson River, sealing the province's western boundary, cutting off any help from that direction. He sent Pittsfield patriot John Brown to scout out the province's western territory to determine how great the risk of envelopment really was.

Brown soon reported back with his disheartening observations. In the event hostilities broke out, he told Adams, it was critical the British stronghold at the south end of Lake Champlain, Fort Ticonderoga, be taken immediately. A short stretch of water to the south of the fort led to Lake George and from there directly into the Hudson River. Brown went further than just recommending an action against the fort; he had had contact with a rowdy bunch of New Hampshireites. These pioneer settlers were angry at the British monarch for siding with the colony of New York in a dispute over the ownership of land they had inhabited for years. The men, self-named the "Green Mountain Boys," were led by a bellicose leader named Ethan Allen, a flamboyant goliath of a man in terms of physical size and commanding personality. If Gage took action against the citizens of Massachusetts, Allen promised his men would capture Fort Ticonderoga and toss the British out.

There were spies working for both the British military and the Massachusetts Provincial Leaders. Within the city of Boston there were numerous patriot supporters. The most prominent patriot, and the acknowledged leader in the city, was Dr. Joseph Warren, who was the recipient of intelligence gathered by Paul Revere. Revere had thirty or so volunteers who, two at a time, would patrol the streets at all hours to monitor the British military. Their diligence around the clock was to detect any untoward activity. Meeting frequently in the Green Dragon Tavern, they would discuss any unusual action by the troops. Revere would assess the information, and pass it along to Warren, who would determine if the Provincial leaders such as John Hancock or Samuel Adams should be informed.

For his part, Gage often sent out-of-uniform soldiers into the countryside to assess the strength of the militias in the region, and to learn about military supplies stored by the patriots. Samuel Adams had long feared there was a high-level spy in the patriot ranks who provided information to Gage. His concern was well founded, as the respected physician, Dr. Benjamin Church, an avowed patriot, was providing information to the General for payment he used to support his Boston mistress, and Church did, in fact, provide valuable secrets to the British.

Church informed Gage of a store of supplies and fourteen cannon hidden in the town of Concord, even providing specific locations. In early April, the general decided to conduct a foray into the town and capture the stores, but he didn't want to suffer the fiasco of the previous venture to capture provincial supplies. At the end of February Gage had dispatched a small contingent of over two hundred troops to Salem to capture military stores supposedly secured there by the provincials. The unit was sent stealthily over water, but the raid did not go well as the invaders were discovered before they could reach their objective. The local patriots delayed the advance of the unit at a bridge while the stores were re-hidden. With a number of patriot militia now alerted against them, the British commander aborted his mission, and returned to the fort on Castle William Island in Boston Harbor empty-handed. For this mission to Concord, Gage planned to use a larger force. He also kept his plan a secret, not even telling the officer who was to lead the assault of where he would be going or what the objective of the mission would be.

The first hint the British were up to something occurred on Saturday night, April 15th, when patriot observers saw the British moving a number of boats capable of carrying troops being readied for use. The boats were being moved to the shore of the Back Bay. In addition, a number of the light infantry companies, along with some of the elite grenadiers, were taken off their regular duties, allowing them to prepare for some unknown mission. When Paul Revere assembled the information given to him by his sentries, he immediately reported it to Dr. Joseph Warren.

As the two men digested the intelligence they came to the conclusion the boats were being readied to take the soldiers across the Charles River to pass through Charlestown to—it could only be one of two places, they decided. Either Gage had finally decided to follow orders and arrest Hancock and Adams at Lexington, or to capture the military stores secreted at Concord. The following day, Sunday, April 16th, not knowing the actual intent of the British, but sensing it was of importance, Warren dispatched Revere to ride the nearly twenty miles to Lexington, and warn the two prominent Patriot leaders of the suspected activity. Arriving at the Clarke parsonage where Adams and Hancock were staying, Revere delivered his message.

John Hancock, head of the Committee of Safety, became concerned the locations of the provincial stores had been compromised, so he sent orders to Concord to re-hide the stores as well as they could in the short time available. A broader call went out to the militias in the surrounding towns to be in readiness for a possible confrontation with the British. Adams was invigorated, sensing an opportunity to revitalize the patriot cause.

With the information Dr. Church had provided, Gage knew exactly where the stores were hidden, and also knew the difficulties the Provincial Council was having in forming an effective army. On that same Sunday (the 16th), Gage finally received the letter Dartmouth had sent much earlier urging him to take action and arrest the colonial leaders. Rejecting Dartmouth's order to arrest the colonials as too risky a proposition, he pushed ahead with the mission to Concord, to capture the cannons, powder and other stores there. Capture of the patriot's military materials would greatly hamper any overt action by the provincials.

Gage thought the mission to Concord to be a simple one. He had sent out spies a month earlier to assess the conditions of the roads, and the layout of the town. While the General kept his intentions secret, the movement of the boats, and the readying of the grenadiers and light infantry were signs that were quickly picked up, not only by the patriot spies, but also by Gage's own troops.

By Tuesday, April 18th all was in readiness. Gage called his infantry commander Lieutenant Colonel Francis Smith to his quarters. He informed the officer he would be leading a raid, but still intent on maintaining tight security, did not tell him where it was to be or the intent of the mission. Instead, he gave Smith an envelope containing detailed written orders which were to be opened only after he had left Boston.

Lt. Col. Smith, a grossly overweight professional military man, was ponderously deliberate in his actions. If Gage wanted a rapid foray to capture the Concord stores, he could not have chosen a worse officer to carry out the raid.

The excursion Smith was to command consisted of seven hundred soldiers; ten light infantry companies and eleven of grenadiers. The light infantry was composed of strong able men who could move easily and rapidly. The grenadiers were chosen for their size, being taller and heavier than the average trooper. Supporting Smith as second in command was Major John Pitcairn, a respected officer, even by many patriots.

Tuesday was also a busy day for Dr. Joseph Warren, the patriot commander in Boston. Information coming to him ever more strongly indicated the British would be sending out a sortie that evening. Rumors of the mission were coming from a variety of sources, including British soldiers. Though not privy to any valid information, they were speculating about the upcoming exercise in their casual conversations with Boston merchants. Possible objectives of the expedition included a number of possible sites, but Lexington and Concord were mentioned predominantly. The arrest of Hancock and Adams or the stores at Concord were obvious targets; or even both in a single swoop into the countryside.

Warren felt assured Lexington and Concord were in the general's plans, but he was unsure of the path the British would take to march there. He was aware of Gage's reconnaissance to assess the condition of the roads, but it was unknown whether the troops would he take the long way around Boston's neck, a trip of over twenty miles, or ferry the troops over the bay landing them below Charlestown, saving about four miles, but complicating the mission. It was possible the readying of the boats was a ruse to throw the patriots off; the truth would become evident only with more intelligence.

Warren's chief rider, Paul Revere had already anticipated the dilemma, and had contacted the leader of the Charlestown Committee of Safety, Colonel Conant on his last incursion to Lexington, and had established a signal which would inform the Charlestown militia of the route actually being used. When the British started moving, expected that very night, the colonel was to watch the steeple of the North Church; if he saw two lanterns it would mean the British were taking boats across the bay, if one lamp, they were marching out the isthmus neck. Revere wanted to set up this signal in the event both the water and land routes out of the city were blocked when the British troops began their sortie. If no curriers from Boston could get free to warn Adams and Hancock, someone in Charlestown would have to undertake the task.

That afternoon, an observant eighteen year old from Lexington, Solomon Brown, was returning from a morning at the market in Boston, when he observed several British officers (nine he thought) on the road from Boston to Lexington. They wore heavy coats even though it was an especially fine spring day. The reason for the coats became obvious when he noticed they concealed side arms at their waists. It signified they were not just out for a pleasant, personal ride, but were up to something.

When he arrived in Lexington he informed William Monroe, a sergeant of the local minutemen of his observation. Concerned the officers were being sent to arrest Hancock and Adams, Monroe set up a guard around the parsonage where the two patriots were staying. The tension eased when in the early evening the British officers rode through town without stopping; continuing on the road to Concord.

While Gage may have thought his plan was secure, he was soon debased of this illusion. At nine o'clock Gage had confided his plan to his brigadier, Lord Percy, informing him that not even the mission's commander knew the ultimate objective of the expedition. After leaving Gage, Percy happened upon several of the town's citizens talking excitedly. In the dark, he sidled up unnoticed to the edge of the group. He was astonished to hear their discussing the British army's recent activity, and opining that they must be going to Concord to capture the military stores there, or, perhaps, to arrest Hancock and Adams. Percy quickly returned to Gage and informed him of what he had heard. Appalled, the General ordered all access out of the city halted.

It was about ten o'clock in the evening when the troops who would carry out the offensive were awakened, and led silently to the shore of the Back Bay where boats were waiting. The only noise, a barking dog, was silenced with a sharp bayonet.

As soon as knowledge of the troop's movement to the boats was known, the information was relayed to Warren. He immediately sent William Dawes to take the land route out Boston's neck, and Revere to row across the water to Charlestown. William Dawes' family had a long history in the province. An earlier William Dawes first came to the region with the Endicott fleet in 1628 to assess conditions in the area. He returned to England and reported what he observed to John Winthrop before he sailed in 1630 to establish the Massachusetts Bay Colony. In 1637, William's fifteen year old son, William, jr., sailed to America to start the Dawes clan in the new world. The present William Dawes jr, was thus a fifth-generation American member of the family, and a dedicated Son of Liberty.

Dawes ran into an immediate problem as the neck had a guard post which had to be passed to get out of the city, and security would be heightened. Dawes had previously befriended the guards as he had at several times over the past several weeks left and reentered the post on normal business, often using a ruse. When he arrived at the gate, although he was pleased to see the guard at the station was one of his acquaintances, he was apprehensive. Fortunately, as he arrived at the gate, a small routine patrol of British sentries was passing through. Dawes followed along with them, pretending to be interested in their gait. He was allowed to slip past the post, and was on his way out of Boston to begin his momentous ride.

For Paul Revere, circumstances weren't as easy. Now, knowing the British were going to use the water passage, he met with the sexton of the North Church, and informed him two lanterns should be displayed in the steeple for Conant in Charlestown to see; and the signal was given. He had arranged for two friends, Thomas Richardson and Joshua Bently, to row him across the short channel to Charlestown. Revere had a small skiff waiting at the water's edge near the Old Mill Pond at the northerly tip of Boston's peninsula. With a moon rising in the east to provide a hazy light, at about eleven o'clock, an hour after Dawes had left, and with oars muffled by soft cloths, they made their way silently across the water. They were well away from the British troops gathering at the shore of the Back Bay to the south, with the British man-o-war, the Somerset, watching over them.

Landing at Charlestown, Revere met Colonel Conant and another member of the Charlestown Committee of Safety, Richard Devens. Conant warned Revere there were British sentries stationed on the roads to intercept any messengers riding to alert the provincial militias in the surrounding countryside. Devens told Revere when they saw the two lantern signal they had dispatched a rider to Lexington, but did not know if he could get through (he did not).

Revere was given, in his own words, *"a very good horse"* by Deacon John Larkin. Lexington was now only eleven miles up the direct road, a trip of about an hour. With his good steed, Revere started out from Charlestown, but immediately passing the cutoff road to Medford, he spied two riders waiting under a tree, just up the road. He recognized them as British sentries, even being close enough to see the holsters at their waists.

One of the soldiers moved toward him somewhat deliberately, blocking his path. The other soldier moved slightly back on the road making it impossible to get by them on the direct road to Lexington. He quickly reined his horse turning it about, and retraced his path heading back to the Medford road. He began galloping faster, obviously trying to avoid the sentries. The sentry closest realized Revere was attempting to get to the Medford road, and he made a decision to cross a field just above the intersection of the two roads to cut Revere off. Fortunately for Revere, the field contained a hidden clay bog which mired the sentry's horse. Moving as fast as the horse could run, Revere sped up the Medford road. The other sentry attempted a chase, but soon realized his horse was no match for Revere's.

Revere's route would now be longer, requiring him to divert to Medford before continuing on to Lexington, but he and Dawes were well ahead of the British force. Both of the intrepid riders moved as swiftly as they could, shouting the dire warning to houses along their route, "The British Are Coming!"

Back at the shore of the Charles River on Boston's west side, the British were lumbering to get their troops organized and aboard the boats to cross the bay. Lt. Col. Smith was late to the poorly organized operation at the Back Bay, and it was some time before the boats were filled with troops, ferried across the Charles River, and landed at Lechmere Point, nearly a mile below the point where Revere had debarked.

Revere took advantage of his unexpected detour to stop briefly in Medford to alert the minutemen there. He didn't tarry long, however, as it was just past midnight when he arrived at the outskirts of Lexington. As word was spread by the two riders along their route, other riders from other towns were dispatched. It was a sort of geometric progression of horsemen, as an increasing multitude of riders took to the roads that night to warn of the British invasion.

When Revere arrived at the Clarke parsonage, the guards, led by Sergeant Monroe would not allow him to enter as he did not know him. The sergeant informed Revere everyone had retired for the night, and didn't want any noise. *"Noise,"* Revere exclaimed, *"You'll soon have noise enough before long. The regulars are coming out."* After being allowed in, Revere gave Hancock Dr. Warren's report, warning of an impending invasion of over a thousand men.

On hearing this news, Monroe sent a messenger to wake the captain of the Lexington minutemen. The Captain, forty-five year old John Parker, although weakened with tuberculosis, was aroused and arrived shortly. Dawes, although starting an hour before Revere, arrived a half an hour later due to the extra distance he had to travel. When he arrived, the two intrepid patriots rode past the Lexington Green, and set out together on the Concord road to alert the citizens of that town. Moving at an unhurried pace with their tired horses, they were confident they were well ahead of the Redcoats. They were soon overtaken by another rider. It was a well-known, Concord Son of Liberty, twenty-three year old physician Dr. Samuel Prescott, who had been courting the comely Lydia Mulliken of Lexington. When informed in Lexington of the British raid on his town, he had moved at a fast gallop to catch up to the two curriers.

The three riders continued on together, alerting households along the way of the impending British regulars. About three miles out of Lexington the three riders were stopped by four armed British officers who quickly surrounded them. Ordering the trio to a nearby pasture, the mounted patriots began to comply by passing through an opening in the rock wall at the edge of the road. After passing through the small opening, in a heroic move, Prescott spurred his horse, surprising the British. Leaping another wall he rode off furiously across the pasture. The startled regulars stayed with the two they had, and did not give chase as Prescott sped off to Concord to warn the patriots there.

Revere was secured by the officers, but Dawes, taking a cue from Prescott, also startled the British by racing off into the night in another direction. Feeling he was not a threat as he was riding away from Concord, they let him go. He rode quickly to a farmhouse in the area where he abandoned his horse and continued furtively on foot, headed back to Boston.

Now, with only Revere in their hands, the British officers demanded to know what he was doing out at night. Revere truthfully told his captors he was alerting provincials to the British raid. The provincial militias, Revere warned, would soon arrive in numbers. A major arrived, and was told by the troopers of their captors' assertion. The major menacingly placed a pistol to Revere's head, averring he would blow his brains out if he did not answer truthfully. Revere repeated the answers he had given previously.

Seemingly satisfied with his answers, the major ordered one of the soldiers to take the reins of Revere's horse. Almost immediately, several more soldiers arrived, leading four additional prisoners they had captured riding the roads. All were told to dismount, upon which the horses' reins of the newly arrived four were cut, and the horses driven away. Revere also dismounted, but his "very good Horse" was not driven off, but rather given to an overweight British grenadier whose own horse was fatigued. Revere walked back to the Clarke parsonage making his way through the cemetery and surrounding fields. It is apparent the British sentries were given orders to be firm in stopping provincial curriers, but to accord them respect without physical harm. Gage did not want an event which would rouse the provincials' ire, thus Revere and the other captured patriots were allowed to leave freely after their horses had been taken or chased away.

Ready to begin the incursion outside of Boston, Colonel Smith opened the secret orders he had been given by General Gage.

Lieut. Colonel Smith, 10th Regiment 'Foot,

Sir,

Having received intelligence, that a quantity of Ammunition, Provisions, Artillery, Tents and small Arms, have been collected at Concord, for the Avowed Purpose of raising and supporting a Rebellion against His Majesty, you will march with a Corps of Grenadiers and Light Infantry, put under your Command, with the utmost expedition and Secrecy to Concord, where you will seize and destroy all Artillery, Ammunition, Provisions, Tents, Small Arms, and all Military Stores whatever. But you will take care that the Soldiers do not plunder the Inhabitants, or hurt private property.

You have a Draught of Concord, on which is marked the Houses, Barns, &c,which contain the above military Stores. You will order a Trunion to be knocked off each Gun, but if its found impracticable on any, they must be spiked, and the Carriages destroyed. The Powder and flower must be shook out of the Barrels into the River, the Tents burnt, Pork and Beef destroyed in the best way you can devise. And the Men may put Balls of lead in their pockets, throwing them by degrees into Ponds, Ditches &c., but no Quantity together, so that they may be recovered afterwards. If you meet any Brass Artillery, you will order their muzzles to be beat in so as to render them useless.

You will observe by the Draught that it will be necessary to secure the two Bridges as soon as possible, you will therefore Order a party of the best Marchers, to go on with expedition for the purpose.

A small party of Horseback is ordered out to stop all advice of your March getting to Concord before you, and a small number of Artillery go out in Chaises to wait for you on the road, with Sledge Hammers, Spikes, &c.

You will open your business and return with the Troops, as soon as possible, with I must leave to your own Judgment and Discretion.

I am, Sir,
Your most obedient humble servant

Thos. Gage.

The plan Gage laid out, if conducted properly, allowed sufficient time for the troops to reach Concord just before daylight so they could initiate their raid in near darkness, hopefully surprising the town's citizens. With the lethargic Smith in command, however, everything was late. The troops were not ready to board the boats at ten; standing idly at the shore waiting for an order to begin. It wasn't until after midnight the boats ferried the now perturbed soldiers across the water, landing in the marshes at Lechmere Point below Charlestown. Standing in water for a period, the troops had to wait until two o'clock before they could begin their march up the road while supplies were ferried across. As one British soldier later wrote about their path after landing

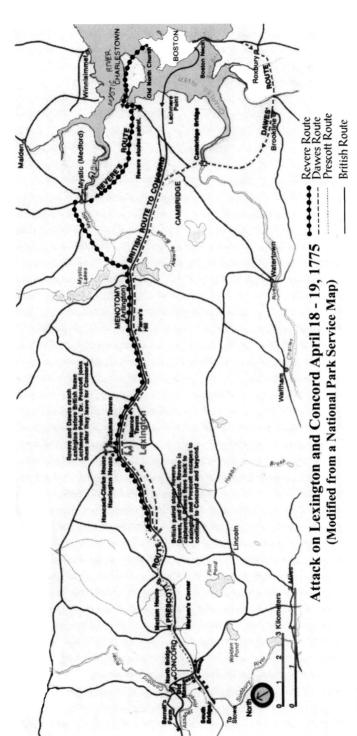

Attack on Lexington and Concord April 18 - 19, 1775
(Modified from a National Park Service Map)

Revere Route
Dawes Route
Prescott Route
British Route

Figure 29.1.

from the boats, *"through some swamps and slips of the sea till we got into the road leading to Lexington."* It wasn't until three am when they were noted by the citizens of Monotony passing through town.

Well over a hundred Lexington minutemen responded to Captain Parker's call, and assembled on the town green at about one o'clock in the morning, a representative turnout for the village of slightly over seven hundred. The men gathered together in the cool, clear night air, and discussed how they should react to a redcoat incursion into their town. It was an open discussion with all free to speak. Captain Parker was elected, not appointed, commander to lead the militia. Thus, any premeditated action the militia undertook was done in a more democratic rather than military manner. They had thought the arrival of the British troops was imminent, but, there were no redcoats in sight, and riders sent out to find them found none in the vicinity or didn't return. Seeing no immediate reason to be out in the middle of the night, the men began to disperse, some returning to their homes, and a number to nearby Buckman's tavern. Parker told them to reassemble if they heard the drum roll of young William Diamond.

Lexington's Common, also referred to as Lexington Green, is roughly in the form of a triangle. The apex of the triangle is formed by a fork in the road leading from Boston. One road goes off to the right leading to Bedford; the left road continues on to Concord. Near the front of the green on the left side, is the town's meeting house, a good sized three-story structure, which also serves as the town's church. Further on the left, about mid-length back, is a belfry, looking out of place setting alone on the grass instead of atop a church. Near the back of the green on the left is a small schoolhouse with a well nearby. The green is terminated over five hundred feet back from the fork by a small cross road, along which are several small residential houses. On the right, just past the fork, across the road from the Common, is Buckman's tavern, a landmark in the town since its construction way back in 1690. Stables were strung along its northerly side.

Past the stables, a rock wall boarders the road in front of a pasture, an arrangement typical of those found aside fields and pastures throughout New England. It is further down this road, slanting to the right, away from the Common, the Clarke parsonage stands; where Samuel Adams and John Hancock were staying.

At the Clarke parsonage, Adams and Hancock were convinced by Revere's encounter with the British patrol, a sortie by the regulars was definitely in progress, and heading in their direction. Hancock was reluctant to leave, vowing to personally encounter the British. After visiting the Common, site of the potential engagement, he was finally convinced by Adams their value to the cause was in their leadership roles, not as warriors; they departed Lexington heading eventually to Billerica. It is not known whether Hancock spoke with Captain Parker to discuss strategy, or even gave him any advice, but it is quite logical that he would.

Finally, at four-thirty, Captain Parker received word the British troops were nearing the town. He called young Diamond, who beat his drum in a call to arms, easily heard by the remnants of the minutemen in Buckman's tavern.

More than fifty of Lexington's minutemen responded quickly to this call, with others drifting in haphazardly. Parker's command, unlike the British, did not have definite orders defining what they were supposed to accomplish in their confrontation with the regulars. Parker lined his men up in two rows across the middle of the green so they would directly face the advancing British. They were, indeed, involved in the midst of world-changing events, but they saw it much more simply—to maintain the town's honor they were obligated to exhibit some sort of protest against this illegal excursion onto their soil by the British military.

As a small, lead contingent of the British force neared Lexington, the major who had interrogated Revere, raced up to meet them. He informed the lead officers, Lieutenants Jesse Adair and William Sutherland of Revere's allegation: five hundred armed provincial militia were waiting for his party, he told them. Moving forward, now with care, the officers gathered additional intelligence from a captured colonial that seemed to substantiate the warning, claiming the whole area was teeming with colonial militia, and even more militiamen were waiting for them than they were first told, perhaps a thousand! The report of activity by the provincial militias prompted Lt. Col. Smith to send a messenger back to General Gage requesting the promised reinforcements.

Lt. Sutherland was dismayed by this news and rode away from the road to look out into the dim countryside. What he saw seemed to add creditability to the warnings they had been given. He later testified he saw, *"a large number of the country militia going over the hill with their arms to Lexington."* The militias around Boston, he thought, were indeed out to assist in the confrontation with the British at Lexington and Concord.

Alarmed at the prospect of being overwhelmed, the two lieutenants decided to double back to merge with a larger force of six companies of infantry, about two-hundred men, led by Major John Pitcairn, following closely behind. This contingent was bound for the bridges in Concord. Their task was to secure the bridges, to prevent the militia from harassing the troops who were to search for and capture or destroy the provincial military stores.

After being briefed by the two lieutenants and now expecting a battle with a great number of armed militia, Pitcairn ordered his men to load their weapons, and be ready to use them. The British were concerned the provincial militias would fire upon them from concealed cover, a manner of fighting they were not used to, and feared. The soldiers were haggard from the long march, uncomfortable in wet boots, and with many likely harboring resentment at the insolence of these colonials for their defiance of legal British authority.

It was thus, in the dawning light of April 19, 1775, approximately seventy Lexington minutemen, with what muskets they could muster, lined up in two lines at the center of Lexington green to face two-hundred professional, angry redcoats. Additional militiamen were still straggling in, some bound for the meeting house to secure a weapon, others ambling to join the rows already lined up on the green. In their original plan, the British force would have marched past Lexington without stopping, and continued up the road to Concord. Now, however, it was not possible to do so as they would expose their right flank to any militia on Lexington's Common.

As he rode up to the fork in the road at the front of the Green, Major Pitcairn now saw there were fewer colonials than expected to oppose his troops. He testified later he initially thought there were about two hundred provincials there to oppose them With the poor light of the nearing dawn, Pitcairn had first mistaken the many villagers who had innocently come to the scene merely to watch, as being part of the militia.. As he got closer he saw the seventy-odd militiamen in the center of the green, armed with muskets, and fully realized the paucity of opposition they were actually facing.

As the disciplined British infantry moved off the road and onto the Common, Pitcairn either ordered the men to move forward at quick-time or ordered the formation of a battle-line. In forming a battle-line, the troops at the front of a column continue to move forward, but also move to one side while those to the rear move double-time to catch up, forming a wide row of infantry ready to fire a volley from across a broad front.

In either case, to the minutemen assembled on the Common to oppose the royal infantry, what they saw rushing rapidly toward them was the manifest reality of British military might: Well-armed professional soldiers marching at a quickened pace onto the green, and continuing menacingly toward the apprehensive farmers and merchants; most unsure of how they should react. These patriots, in age from the teens to sixties saw the fierce intensity in the eyes of soldiers ready for battle.

Who fired the first shot has been debated ever since. The witnesses' testimonies are ambiguous. It is possible, as Major Pitcairn states, one or more minutemen went behind the rock wall at the side of the Common and fired upon the British troops provoking their firing back. It is also possible, as several witnesses testified, a British officer told his men, "Fire, damned you Fire!" even though his troops had not been fired upon. It is also possible a late returning Lexington minuteman, or a militia man from another town, fired from a distance as he witnessed the Infantry charge the Lexington men.

The whole area was alarmed, and a number of militia were moving around the vicinity of Lexington Green.

Major Pitcairn angled his horse to the left of the meeting house while the troops advanced directly up the Green on its right. As Pitcairn passed by the meeting house, he was positioned to take in the whole scene. He called out harshly to the militiamen, *"Disperse ye villains, ye rebels. Disperse. Lay down your arms."* Pitcairn, by all accounts a descent man, wanted his men to surround and disarm the militia. They were, after all, British citizens, even though showing disrespect to the crown's authority.

Feeling his militia had made their point at being present on the Common in a defiant measure of resistance to British troops, but now facing an overwhelming force, Captain Parker ordered his men to hold their fire and disperse. Many of the men, obeying their captain, started to disperse, but kept their weapons. They moved in all directions in a random retreat away from the charging British, yielding the green to the British force. But Jonas Parker, the older cousin of the Captain, had vowed never to withdraw from a British incursion into his town, and so stood his ground, musket in hand.

The British infantry, yelling wildly, began a frenzied charge at the dispersing militia, most of whom were moving slowly at first, still retaining their weapons, but more rapidly as they felt shots from the infantry whistling about them. Old Jonas Parker, however, did in fact remain true to his vow to stand his ground, and not retreat from the British invaders. He placed his musket balls, flints and powder nearby and prepared to defend colonial honor. Before he could get off a shot he was hit and knocked to the ground. Lying prostrate he fired his musket awkwardly. Reaching for his powder to reload he was run through by a bayonet wielded by a charging soldier, dying with his honor intact.

Jonathan Harrington lived in one of the houses on the road at the back of the green, where he may have been headed as he left the Common. When he was hit he fell to the ground, and began crawling toward his home. Watched by his horrified wife and eight-year old son, he made it to his front step where he died. Isaac Muzzy and Robert Monroe, who had fought bravely with the British army at Louisburg during the French and Indian War, were killed in the initial charge. Caleb Harrington was caught in the Meeting House when the firing started. He tried running away hoping to make the safety of a house on the far side of the Common. Running virtually between British units he was hit and killed.

Two other Lexington militiamen were killed as they fled the Common, Samuel Hadley and John Brown suffering wounds in their back. A man from Woburn, Ashabel Porter, who the British had captured on the road that morning, decided now was the time to run from his captors. He too was slain with a round in his back. Nine other militia men were wounded in the battle, including Prince Estabrook, a black slave, serving in the Lexington militia, suffered a wound in his shoulder (Estabrook served in the colonial army throughout the war and eventually returned to his freedom).

For the British, Major Pitcairn's horse had sustained two wounds that were not serious enough to prevent the animal from continuing to carry the officer. A single British soldier suffered a minor wound to his leg, so mild it did not prevent him from continuing along with the rest of his company.

Lt. Col. Smith arrived on the scene with the grenadiers, and was disgusted at the scene before him. The riotous infantry were ignoring Major Pitcairn's orders to cease fire, and were chasing after the scattering colonials. He well remembered Gage's specific orders, *"But you will take care that the Soldiers do not plunder the Inhabitants, or hurt private property."* The infantry were running out of control, and could well break into houses or the tavern in their pursuit of rebels. He found Lt. Sutherland and ordered him to find a drummer to beat a call to order. He was successful; found a drummer whose cadence slowed the temper of the troops, who then ceased their rampage.

Off in the distance Hancock and Adams were making their way to safety when they heard the shots ring out from Lexington. Adams smiled and said quietly, *"O, what a glorious morning this is."* Noting Hancock did not grasp the significance of his comment, he amended, *"I mean what a glorious morning for America."* Adams knew he now had his provocation which would unite colonial opposition to British rule.

On April 25th, six days after the carnage on Lexington Green, militia Captain John Parker gave a sworn disposition describing the event as he saw it.

> I, John Parker, of lawful age, and commander of the Militia in Lexington, do testify and declare, that on the nineteenth instant, in the morning, about one of the clock, being informed that there were a number of Regular Officers riding up and down the road, stopping and insulting people as they passed the road, and also was informed that a number of regular troops were on their march from Boston, in order to take the Province stores at Concord, ordered our militia to meet on the Common in said Lexington, to consult what to do, and concluded not to be discovered, not meddle or make with said Regular Troops (if they should approach) unless they should insult us, and upon their sudden approach, I immediately ordered our Militia to disperse and not to fire. Immediately Said Troops made their appearance and rushed furiously, fired upon and killed eight of our party without receiving any provocation therefore from us.

There were a number of additional dispositions from other witnesses to the battle. While generally agreeing with Captain Parker, several others stated it was one of the British officers who first fired his pistol, which was followed by the musket barrage from the infantry. There is a possibility that Parker did indeed speak with Hancock, the Chairman of the Provincial Committee of Safety in the interim between the first alarm and the eventual arrival of the British, certainly there was enough time and opportunity. Some have postulated Parker received guidance from the chairman allowing, in the face of the vastly greater force, a defiant stand in the center of Lexington's Commons in front of the British troops, then dispersing without firing a shot, would be a sufficient statement of their rejection of British authority. That is a possibility, but it certainly was not agreed to by the likes of Jonas Parker.

An alternate version of the confrontation was written on April 26th by British Major John Pitcairn. It was contained in a report he wrote when back in Boston, to General Gage.

Sir, as you are anxious to know the particulars that happened near and at Lexington on the 19th instant. I will in as concise a manner as possible: state the facts. For my time at present is so much employed, as to prevent a more particular narrative of the occurrences of that day.

Six companies of Light Infantry were detached by Lt. Col. Smith to take possession of two bridges on the other side of Concord—near three in the morning when we are advanced within two miles of Lexington, intelligence was received that about 500 men in arms were assembled, determined to oppose the Kings Troops and retard them in their march—on this intelligence, I mounted my horse, and galloped up to the Six Light Companies—when I arrived at the head of the advance Company, two Officers came and informed me that a man of the rebels advanced from those assembled, had presented his musket and attempted to shoot them, but the piece flashed in the pan—On this I gave directions to the troops to move forward, but on no account to fire, or even attempt it without orders: When I arrived at the end of the Village, I observed dawn up upon the green near two hundred of the rebels. When I came within about one hundred yards of them, they began to file off towards some stone walls on our right flank—The Light Infantry observing this, ran after them—I instantly called to the soldiers not to fire, but surround them and disarm them and after several repetitions of these positive orders to the men, not to fire, etc.—some of the rebels who had jumped over the wall, fired four or five shots at the soldiers, which wounded a man of the Tenth, and my horse was wounded in two places, from some quarter or other and at the same time several shots were fired from a Meeting House on our left—upon this without any order or regularity, the Light Infantry began a scattered fire, and continued in that situation for some little time, contrary to the repeated orders both of me and other officers that were present. It will be needless to mention what happened after, as I suppose Colonel Smith hath given a particular account of it.

With the officers back in control of the troops, they were reorganized, and prepared to march down the road to Concord to compete their mission. Before departing, however, and to the disgusted horror of Parson Jonas Clarke, who had come to the green, The British troops, as was their custom, with the colonial dead still lying on the green, gave three cheers and fired a volley into the air to celebrate their victorious battle. To Clarke it was a sacrilegious salute to infamy.

The citizens of Lexington were left with the woeful duty to bury the dead and care for the wounded. Horrified, weeping women, joined by some disoriented men drifting back to the scene departed by the British, felt great sadness, mixed with anger, as they viewed the aftermath of the carnage. When the caskets of the dead were placed in the ground, the burial ground was covered with forest debris so the honored fallen would not be desecrated by British soldiers passing through on their return to Boston.

In a somber yet shining epilog to the battle, the remnants of Captain Parker's command, including several wounded, reassembled into a line, and began a resolute march up the road to Concord to continue the battle against the redcoats alongside many other freedom-loving militias.

Chapter Thirty

Concord—The Battle Begins

After escaping the British patrol, Dr. Samuel Prescott raced over familiar roads and fields. Taking a southerly route to alarm the people of Lincoln, he arrived in Concord slightly after one AM to sound the alarm. Concord's minutemen heard the ringing of the alarm bell, and quickly began arriving at Wright's Tavern to learn of the imminent arrival of British Regulars intent on capturing the provincial military stores.

Major John Buttrick, second in command of the town's militia, began assessing the situation as more of his charge convened on the inn. Concord, with a population of approximately fifteen hundred, twice that of Lexington, was as aroused as its sister village at the news. The attack wasn't entirely unexpected as Paul Revere had alerted them to the possibility several days ago. Fortunately, they had heeded the warning and moved the stores out of their original sites and scattered them to several surrounding towns.

After carrying the news to his home town, the aroused physician continued his ride westerly to alert the militias in nearby Acton and Stow. He also dispatched his younger brother, Abel, south to warn Sudbury and Framingham. As British Lieutenant Sutherland had observed on his march to Lexington, the roads were teeming with riders bringing news of the British invasion across a wide area. Riders were spreading the word of the British aggression throughout the colony, and even further to Connecticut, Rhode Island, New Hampshire and Maine.

At about the same time shots were being fired on Lexington Green, nearly a hundred and fifty Concord minutemen, along with several from nearby Lincoln, were awaiting orders from Major Buttrick to begin their confrontation with the redcoats. As was the routine throughout the day, the number of militia continued to increase as they awaited action. After several hours, with daylight now upon them, and with no Britons in sight, they were uneasy in the stillness of the morning. Out of anxiety with the unexplained calm, over two hundred minutemen decided to march down the Lexington road to ascertain where the British were presently located.

A mile and a half or so outside of town, the redcoats were spotted marching spiritedly toward them. Flush with their victory at Lexington, they advanced on Concord with drums and fifes playing a musical rhythmic cadence. Amos Barrett, who was with the reconnoitering minutemen, described the scene, *"We see them acommig, we halted and stayed till they got within about a 100 rods then we was ordered about face and marched before them with our Drums and fifes agoing and also the British. We had grand music."*

To young Concord minuteman, Thaddeus Blood it was an imposing sight. He was struck by the scene of the coordinated marching military; the British infantry and grenadiers clothed in their bright red jackets, white pants and black boots; toting clean, shiny muskets. The officers added to the flamboyance of the picture with gold or silver stitching emblazoned on their uniforms, announcing their rank. The young minuteman was impressed enough to remember later, *"The sun was rising and shined on their arms, and they made a noble appearance in their red coats and glistening arms."* The two separate aggregations, one with a mission to seize hidden stores, the other whose intent is was to stop them from carrying out their mission, marched magnificently toward Concord.

The Concord militia moving briskly in front of the British, dispersed and regrouped on a hill north of town, where they could watch the British as they entered Concord behind them. Knowing the British troop's arrival was imminent, Concord's citizens had moved rapidly to secure the hiding places of their stores, and to secret any valuables raiding soldiers might loot. At Barrett's farm, two miles up the road after crossing the North Bridge, the stores not yet spread to other surrounding towns were re-hidden in plowed fields.

A mile before Concord's town center, the seven hundred British troops passed over a small bridge spanning a swollen brook immediately before Meriam's Corner. At the corner, just past the bridge, a side road going north to Bedford went off to the right. It was at this point, where the Concord road took a slight turn to the left, there arose a series of steep hills on the north (right) side of the road. The hills provided an excellent perch for militiamen who were streaming in to join the fight against the invaders. Lt. Col. Smith sent some of his light infantry up the hills, chasing away any militia lookouts.

At Concord, the terrain was more hilly and varied than at Lexington Common; with a number of hills and rivers that affected military strategy. Less than a half-mile to the northwest of Concord's town center the Sudbury River, flowing from the south, joined the Assabet River coming from the west, to form the Concord River, which continued in a northeasterly direction to join the larger Merrimack River near Lowell outside of Boston.

There were two local bridges over the rivers. The South Bridge crossed the Sudbury a little more than a half-mile west of the town. The other bridge, the North Bridge, crossed the Concord River several hundred feet above the confluence of the Sudbury and Assebet. West of the North Bridge was an elevated ridge, snaking alongside the river about two hundred yards away. The elevated height of the ridge allowed a commanding view of the North Bridge and surrounding road. In April of 1775, after a mild winter, the spring runoff had raised the level of the river so that it overflowed its banks in several locations.

The British troops continued resolutely up the road recently left by the militiamen, the Britons marched past a broad plain containing the mill pond on the left, until near eight o'clock in the morning they reached the town's center. At Concord's town center stood the dominant Meeting House, Wright's Tavern, the jail, an inn, and a number of residential houses. A side road went off to the left leading to the South Bridge, while the original road continued on, eventually crossing the North Bridge, a half-mile away.

With the British force now emplaced in Concord, the militia held discussions about what to do next. Colonel James Barrett, the Concord militia commander, who had arrived to take command, held a consultation with his officers. The consensus' decision was to move over the North Bridge, and establish their force on the far ridge overlooking the bridge, river and surrounding roads. They had not yet received a definitive report on what had happened in Lexington, and so long as the British troops did minimal damage and not harm anyone, there was no strong compelling reason to start hostilities. It was one thing to talk about fighting and killing British oppressors, and quite another thing to actually do so.

Standing with the militia leaders was the Concord Minister, William Emerson. Emerson had served as Chaplin to the Provincial Congress at its recent meetings in Concord. He, like many other colonial ministers, often preached a message from the pulpit that equated worshiping and serving a divine god with striving for freedom from oppression. The message subtly equated fighting against the British with pleasing god, thus making the fight both secularly and religiously proper. Emerson angrily voiced the opinion; shared by several others who wanted to confront the British right there, *"Let us stand our ground. If we die, let us die here."* However the commander's decision prevailed, and they crossed over the bridge, and moved up onto the elevation on the other side. The decision to move across the bridge and to the higher ground was actually a good one, as their numbers were growing rapidly it would greatly facilitate the arriving militia coming from other towns west of the river.

In the center of the town, Lt. Col. Smith paused to begin deploying his troops to conduct their mission. One company of light infantry was moved to the South Bridge to secure the pathway from reinforcements joining the Concord militia from that direction. Six of the light infantry companies, slightly less than two hundred men, were dispatched to the North Bridge under Captain Parsons. His orders were to secure the bridge, and to send a contingent up the road to Barrett's farm to seek out and destroy the military stores suspected of being there.

Arriving at the North Bridge, Captain Parsons decided he could better secure the crossing with his men on the far side. After leading his men across the bridge, Captain Parsons took three of the companies with him, and moved up the road to Barrett's farm, two miles distant. He left a single company, about thirty men, posted on the far side of the bridge to stop any militia from using it, and spread the remaining two companies several hundred yards further along the road leading to Barrett's farm. The wisdom of this decision was questionable as this isolated company of British light infantry stood at the far end of the North Bridge under Captain Walter Laurie, gazing up at a ridge only two hundred yards distant, where now, over four hundred armed provincial militia were looking down at his meager force.

Back at Concord's center, the elite grenadiers, with Lt. Col. Smith and Major Pitcairn guiding them, began the search for military stores they knew were there. Using information provided by the traitor Dr. Church, they knew just where to look.

After the debacle at Lexington with the light infantry ignoring orders to cease fire, the grenadiers had received a strong directive not to antagonize Concord's citizens, now depleted of militiamen. In their effort to conform to their commanders' intent to act civilly, they often overlooked stores which a more aggressive approach would have discovered.

Timothy Wheeler's barn held a significant stash of flour intended for use by the provincial militia. Near the ample sacks of provincial grain Wheeler had carefully placed bags of his own grain. Thus when asked by an inspecting grenadier, the scrupulously honest Wheeler could place his hand on a sack near the front of several, and truthfully say, *"This is my flour, this is my wheat, this is my rye; this is mine."*

The cooperative grenadier inspectors took Wheeler at his own word and left his barn untouched, stating, *"We do not injure private property."* Not all of the provincial flour escaped detection as finding other casks; the soldiers threw them into the mill pond. The same fate was suffered by provincial musket and cannon balls, as the grenadiers took the easiest path of destruction and tossed them likewise into the mill pond, not following General Gage's written orders: *"And the Men may put Balls of lead in their pockets, throwing them by degrees into Ponds, Ditches &c., but no Quantity together, so that they may be recovered afterwards."*

Not all of the searches were done with cordially. When jail keeper Ephraim Jones refused to unlock a door which was suspected of hiding three canons, Major Pitcairn was called. The officer took out his pistol and threatened the colonial, who decided to unlock the doors and reveal the location of the cannon, which was summarily rendered unusable.

Learning Jones, in addition to being the town's jailer, ran a small inn, Pitcairn ordered his captive to prepare him breakfast there. After the meal the Major dutifully paid his bill. A number of other British soldiers received breakfast reluctantly at other houses they entered; including Colonel Barrett's where his wife, who, like the other women providing meals to the soldiers, did not want British money. While most of the grenadiers were polite and considerate in their intrusions into the colonial homes, some looting occurred during the searches.

The British might have thought the mission to this point was at least a partial success. It was, however, anything but. The canon found at the jail had been made unusable, and some damage was done to a miscellany of equipment, but nothing that couldn't be replaced. No treasure of stores had been found at Barrett's farm. Canon and musket balls had been thrown into the mill pond along with a number of casks of flour, but, after the British departed, the canon and musket balls were quickly retrieved from the water in perfect shape. Even the casks of flour were found to be mostly salvageable.

Toward the end of their searches, the grenadiers took an action that changed the day irrevocably. At several barns and stables, after cutting up harnesses and reins; they broke up several wooden carriages. Near the center of town they placed the broken carriages in a pile along with the liberty pole, wooden trenchants, gun stocks, even wooden spoons, and set fire to the heap of combustibles.

On the ridge overlooking the North Bridge, the four hundred militiamen from Concord, Lincoln, Acton and Sudbury were behaving with a mix of calmness and uncertainly. If the British troops had quietly gathered together and left peaceably the colonial militia might well have allowed them to go without a violent confrontation. It seemed at first none of the British really wanted a fight or to damage their town. However, it was at this time a militia member on the ridge saw the smoke from the fire the grenadiers had set. The source of the fire was not visible to the militia on the ridge due to distance and terrain, and they became agitated at what might be burning. *"They're burning the town,"* someone shouted.

One of Concord's militia officers, Joseph Hosmer, became alarmed as his family was still in his house in the town. *"Will you let them burn the town down?"* he pleaded emotionally. Colonel Barrett ordered the men to load their weapons, but with strict orders not to fire till the British fired first—then to fire as fast as we can. He ordered his force to descend down the ridge toward the greatly outnumbered British infantry directly at the front of the bridge.

The two British companies strung out along the road to Barrett's farm became concerned the advancing provincials would cut them off from the main British force if the militias took the bridge. They began a deliberate withdrawal from the posts assigned them by Captain Parsons to join the company at the bridge. As the provincial militias continued their advance, Captain Laurie, with his outnumbered infantry on the northerly side, felt threatened. He sent a messenger to request immediate reinforcements from Lt. Col. Smith.

The three infantry companies, about one hundred in all, were now together facing a force maybe four times their size. Behind them was the river with the narrow bridge the only means of escape. Seeing no alternative, Captain Laurie ordered his troops back over the span, and to take up defensive positions on the far side to stop the provincials from crossing. In an attempt to retard the colonials the British soldiers started to remove some of the bridge's deck planks. A warning shot convinced the British to stop their wreckage. Since the two forces were now so close, they stopped trying to destroy the bridge and fell back.

It was a perilous situation. British professional soldiers following orders to defend the bridge, and impassioned militiamen disturbed by what looked to them an attempt to burn down their town, and possibly harm their families. A British officer Lt. John Barker, who seemed to disapprove of the conduct of the whole operation, appraised the situation in a record he prepared later,

> Captain Laurie, who commanded then these companies, sent to Colonel Smith, begging he would send more troops to his assistance and informing him of his situation; the Colonel ordered two or three companies but put himself at their head, by which means stopped them from being time enough, for being a very fat heavy man he would not have reached the bridge in half an hour, though it was not half mile to it; in the meantime, the rebels marched into the road and were coming down upon us, when Captain Laurie made his men retire to this side of the bridge (which, by the bye, he ought to have done at first, and then he would have had time to make a good disposition, but at this time, he had not, for the rebels got so near him that his people were obliged to form at best way they could).

Captain Laurie, in an effort to control access across the bridge ordered one of the companies to form into a four-wide column at the end of the span, with ranks of additional four-wide behind them. In this arrangement the first rank could fire, and then retreat to the rear of the column to reload, while the next rank moved forward with loaded muskets to fire as necessary. It was a formation that could control access across the bridge, but as the road to the bridge was through a meadow, the column would be vulnerable to salvos from the side. Laurie additionally ordered another company to line up along the river's bank.

In the tension of the moment, with both sides fearful of the other, a shot was fired. As immortalized by Ralph Waldo Emerson in his epic poem "Concord Hymn."

> By the rude bridge that arched the flood,
> Their flag to April's breeze unfurled,
> Here once the embattled farmers stood,
> And fired the shot heard round the world.

Lt. Sutherland, who was at the river, stated the provincials fired first. His opinion was agreed to by British Ensign Jeremy Lister, also present. However, Captain Laurie later stated, *"I imagine myself that a man of my company did first fire his piece."*

With only about fifty yards separating the combatant groups, the firing exploded in intensity. Leading the provincial charge, Captain Isaac Davis, of the Acton militia and one of his men were killed in the first British volley. Major John Buttrick, of Concord yelled his now famous order, *"Fire fellow soldiers, for God's sake fire!"*

In the first withering salvo from the provincials, several British were killed or wounded. Fearing more fire from the larger provincial militia, the British infantry beat a hasty retreat away from the bridge, heading to Concord's town center where the rest of the British force was situated. Half way there, the retreating infantry ran into Lt. Col. Smith, who had brought some grenadiers as reinforcements. Smith realized quickly, however, that the size of the militia force had increased significantly, and he would be outnumbered at the bridge site, so he moved the retreating infantry and grenadiers back to the center of town.

The provincial militias did not pursue the retreating British as by this time the fire had died down, and, as they realized their houses were not burning, they had no compelling reason for continuing the fight, especially with the larger British force in the center of town. Instead they dispersed around the town, and up the hills to observe them at a distance. Back at the now nearly deserted bridge, an unfortunate incident occurred that would have an effect on British views of the battle. A severely wounded British soldier crawled onto the road as a young boy happened by. The lad was carrying an axe which he used to smash the unfortunate soldier in the head.

It was unfortunate, as when Captain Parsons returned across the bridge (unmolested) after his foray to Barrett's farm, he and his troops saw the mutilated soldier, and began the rumor the colonials were reverting to the barbaric savagery of the Indian wars, and were scalping dead and wounded British soldiers.

For over two hours the two sides were at a standoff. Lt. Col. Smith was apprehensive about marching his troops on the open roads back to Boston, and the provincial militias were bidding their time, uncertain how aggressive they should be in challenging the invading redcoats. While the militias waited, however, their numbers continued to swell.

As more militias from the surrounding towns arrived, Colonel Barrett's command was correspondingly diluted. Each militia unit had its own leader, and there had been little coordination between them. The provincial force consisted of essentially independent fighting units, and even within units, individual militiamen were deciding to do the fight as each thought best. Farmers, merchants, blacksmiths, hired hands, even parsons were in these fighting militias, determined to contest this British intrusion into their colony. The deeply ingrained mistrust, and outright dislike of illegally perceived British sovereignty, was anathema to their sense of freedom and law. Unseen to the British in the middle of Concord, hundreds more provincial fighters were descending on the town, and elsewhere along the road returning the British to Boston.

Close to midday, after a pleasant meal at the tavern by the officers, Smith realized his reinforcements were not imminent in coming to his aid, and decided he had to move his troops out of Concord, and march back to Boston. Captain Parson's infantry companies had arrived back without trouble, so perhaps they could just move out of town without any more fighting. The wounded were cared for, with several carts requisitioned for the more seriously injured. Two wounded Lieutenants, Gould and Hull, were each placed on a wagon, and set out on the road to Boston before the rest of Smith's command set forth.

The retreat from Concord was in stark contrast to its entrance. No fifes or drums beating a lively cadence, rather a somber procession of weary soldiers, unsure of what awaited them. To deter militiamen from firing at them from their flanks, Smith sent several infantry units to the higher ground at the side of the road, protecting the main convoy.

At first, the procession of weary redcoats moved out of Concord, and onto the road to Lexington without incident. Reaching the small bridge at Meriam's Corner, the flanking infantry had to come in to cross the span with the rest of the marchers. As the British force approached the bridge the militias from Billerica and Reading, who had recently arrived, were approaching the bridge down the Bedford road from the north. At the same time the Framingham and Sudbury militias were approaching from the south across a flat plain below the mill pond. The militias from the fight at the North Bridge were closing in from behind. All of the militias by this time knew of the killings on Lexington Green

The men of the militias harbored a visceral anger towards these British troops, seen as violent enforcers of British rule, who had attacked and slain their peaceful neighbors in Lexington. They represented Britain, which had taxed them illegally, taken away their government and courts, and closed their port cutting off their livelihood. These troops were the means by which Britain was forcing the colonial citizens into becoming vassals, slaves without the rights accorded free men. These militiamen, with the strength of mutual support, and a strong sense of common purpose, confronted their enemy, and initiated the stroke of defiance requisite to freedom.

As the British began crossing the narrow bridge, the militias, without the hesitation shown in Lexington and initially at the North Bridge, released a fierce fusillade of fire on the concentrated redcoats. Withering musket balls from three sides took immediate causalities. To the British it seemed the shots were coming from all sides from a massive unseen army. The British returned fire as well as they could, and accelerated their march across the bridge.

After passing over the bridge, the light infantry flankers were again deployed to provide a protective shield at the sides of the column, but the British soon realized this wasn't just an isolated ambush by provincial units waiting for them at the bridge, but, rather, rebels were strung all along the side of the road as far ahead as they could see.

The additional provincials could be seen in ever increasing numbers; jumping out from behind shelters, firing, then retreating. There was no let up in the attack as the British troops moved away from the bridge and continued up the road. The soldiers of Smith's contingent soon perceived this was to be their fate all the sixteen miles to Boston. There was no escape from the incessant fire. Any attempt to move off the road into the woods and fields would have been disastrous. The realization of their horrendous plight drove many to near panic. Lt. Col. Smith was wounded in the leg so Major Pitcairn assumed command, and with the other officers tried to bring a semblance of military discipline to the disrupted troops.

The flanking infantry did have some success as they had only to move out about fifty yards, the range of the muskets being used, to disrupt the lethality of the musket balls. They were able to route and kill the militiamen they were able to surprise in their cover, but it did little to hamper the relentless barrage. Any house, barn or shed along the road was potential shelter for the militia snipers, and each was searched, but the effort had a minor impact on the fire the British were receiving from the ever growing militia strength. Adding to the British plight, they were running out of ammunition.

With no alternative, the British force moved forward along the road as provincial militias moved along with them, firing from behind trees, walls and the occasional structure. This was not the sort of battle for which the British officers had been trained. They were familiar with warfare on open fields, with contesting armies facing each other using time-tested maneuvers, not the dishonorable conduct of rouge shooters hiding behind cover to fire at defenseless men in open exposure.

As the macabre parade approached Lexington, both sides felt the pain of fighting, but the battle did not lessen in intensity. As the beleaguered troops reached the fork in the road at the head of Lexington Green, many of the British troops could suffer the battle no longer and began to run in panic along the road in retreat. The British officers did what they could, but with little effect. One British officer thought it might be necessary to surrender or be annihilated.

At this dire moment for Smith's command, a horrific sound overwhelmed the sound of musket fire as a massive hole erupted in the Lexington Meeting House. A cannon ball had plowed through structure, causing little damage to the ground troops on either side, but getting their immediate attention. Realizing the shot was from a British cannon sited on a rise in the road on the far side of Lexington brought cheers from the besieged British troops, and caused the provincials to scatter for cover. Seeing the reinforcements brought new hope to Smith's force.

The reinforcements Smith had requested were very late, but welcome nevertheless. General Gage had given orders the night before to have a brigade, along with some mobile canon, and supported by a contingent of marines, a force of over twelve-hundred men, ready to move out under Lord Percy at four AM the next morning. This would allow time enough for the reinforcements to reach Concord as Smith was completing his mission there, and could secure their return to Boston. If the secrecy of the mission had been compromised, as he was told it might have been, it was possible the provincial militias were already preparing to oppose his force to Concord, and Smith might need assistance upon his return to Boston. With the plan for early deployment of the reinforcements made, and orders to carry it out issued, Gage went to bed on the evening of the eighteenth comfortable in the knowledge he had taken all necessary measures to insure the success of the operation.

However Gage's complacency was misplaced; consistent with the incompetence shown in earlier phases of the mission, Gage's orders never reached the officers necessary to carry them out. The major commanding the brigade was enjoying a social dinner out the evening of the eighteenth, and the orders to field the brigade were left in his quarters without any sense of urgency. Upon his return, the officer wasn't told of the orders waiting for him on his desk, so went to bed. The orders to the marines were delivered to the major in their charge, Pitcairn, who was serving as second-in-command to Lt. Col. Smith in Concord, and thus not present to receive them.

The next morning, Gage was awakened at five am by a messenger carrying Smith's request for reinforcements. He was enraged to discover, not only was the brigade or marines not yet moved out, they were all still asleep!

Events moved with rapidity in the military compound in Boston when the gaffe and delay in the reinforcement's readiness was discovered. The brigade was awakened, and was ready to march at eight when it was discovered the marine support was not present as they had also never received the orders. It wasn't until nine am when the whole body of reinforcements was finally ready to move out, which they did marching out Boston neck under Gage's brigadier, Lord Percy.

If Gage did one thing right it was in selecting Percy to lead the relief troops. Brigadier General Hugh Percy, the second Duke of Northumberland, was a competent military commander, who had the respect of the men in his charge. While he had Whig political leanings, and was no supporter of potent monarchial power, he had become disillusioned with the actions of the colonials.

After passing Roxbury without incident, his force encountered a short delay at the Cambridge Bridge over the Charles River as the provincials had removed the planks making up the roadbed. Fortunately the planks were piled up on the far side. Men were sent to retrieve and replace them on the bridges' stringers so the artillery and supply wagons could be wheeled across.

As Percy moved his troops past Cambridge he noted an unnatural quiescence all along his route, *"As all the houses were shut up, and there was not the appearance of a single inhabitant, I could get no intelligence."* To the astute commander, the eerie silence of the countryside portended danger. If the colonials were not in their villages or houses along the road, where were they?

When Percy reached Menotomy, the town before Lexington, his suspicion of serious trouble was confirmed. The two wagons carrying Lieutenants Gould and Hull, which had preceded Smith's force out of Concord, arrived at the front of Percy's brigade and related the events of the day. Alerted to the plight of Smith's troops, Percy quickened his march. On the outskirts of Lexington, at about two in the afternoon, Percy could hear musket fire coming from the town as the provincials continued to pound the desperate British troops. Coming into sight of the town on a slight rise, Percy could scarcely believe the scene before him. Out manned, out gunned British troops were cowering under the unrelenting provincial fire.

With Lexington's Meeting House in sight a half-mile distant, he ordered the cannons brought up, and fired a shot at the inert structure. It was this blast that scattered the militias and gave new hope to Smith's force. In his haste to rescue Smith's force he did not secure the rear of his brigade. At Monotony, the two wounded lieutenants were captured by provincials now descending on the entire area. More importantly, they also captured Percy's supply wagons, killing the driver of one and capturing the six grenadier guards.

Using his cannon sporadically to deter militia attacks, he was able to set up a defensive position allowing the two commands to merge and plan a retreat. Percy quickly perceived the difficulties he and Smith's forces were in as the militias' numbers continued to grow. Percy, taking command of the entire British force, set up a command post in the tavern of Lexington's militia officer Sergeant Monroe, located nearly a mile southeast of Lexington Green. Near the tavern were several residential houses which were burned to eliminate hiding places for militia shooters.

The combined British force of about eighteen hundred was a substantial part of Gage's whole army in Boston, and Percy was aware Gage would be reluctant to commit any additional strength to his aid, as they might be needed in a defense of the city itself. After a brief respite to rest Smith's troop, the British moved out again on the road to Boston, utilizing alternating companies to guard the rear and flanking infantry to guard their sides.

As the British were planning their next steps, a new leader of the provincial militias arrived at Lexington to assist in coordinating the militias' strategy. The Provincial Congress had appointed four men as generals reporting to the Committee of Safety. One of these, a farmer from Roxbury, William Heath, commissioned a Major General, was directed that morning by the Committee of Safety, who were in Monotony, to assume command of the provincial force. Heath had an interest in military affairs, and had been an officer in earlier provincial military units, but he never had had a wartime command.

Heath's first action was to send a militia unit back to the Cambridge Bridge over the Charles River, and remove the planks from the roadbed. This would impede, even stop, Percy if he led his army back along the same route he took leaving Boston. He also posted some militia at the bridge to guard it. He then moved to the site of fighting around Lexington. Heath tried to exert some measure of military order to the militias' actions, but their strategy remained more individualistic than structured, and he had little actual effect on the fighting.

At Lexington, Heath was joined by Dr. Joseph Warren, a prominent Committee of Safety member, who had left Boston to be where the fighting was occurring. Warren was a welcome addition by Heath as well as the troops. Extremely intelligent, well-liked, and decisive, Warren's presence provided stability and direction, as he was well known as a strong proponent of the Patriot cause.

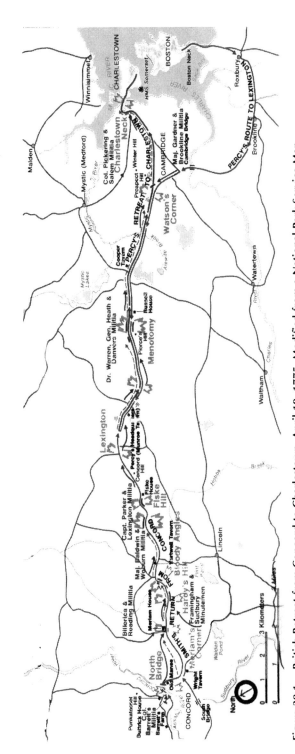

Figure 30.1.   British Retreat from Concord to Charlestown, April 19, 1775. Modified from a National Park Service Map.

It was near four o'clock when the British resumed their retreat, and the battle continued much as it had after Concord. Militias firing from concealed positions along the route, with infantry flankers attempting to find and slay any militiamen they found. Frustrated with the incessant fire from hidden shooters, the British became more active in raiding houses and killing any men they found inside—militiamen or innocent bystanders. Some of the flankers reverted to looting the houses they entered, taking advantage of the chaos. Percy's sporadic cannon firings would disperse groups of militias, but the effect was always short-lived as they quickly returned and resumed their barrages.

No tale of the fight could be complete without relating the episode of old, seventy-nine year old Samuel Whittemore, who, like Jonas Parker on Lexington Green, exhibited the determined fighting spirit of the provincials in their opposition to what they viewed as British oppression. Sam took his musket and pistols, and hid himself near a stone wall in the vicinity of Cooper's Tavern, waiting for the British to appear. When one finally did, Sam shot and killed him with his musket. The soldier, however, was not alone. Other flankers appeared and, using his pistol, Sam killed another. Before he could reload he was shot in the face and overwhelmed by additional soldiers, who, frustrated with snipers like Sam, attacked him and beat him viciously. Leaving the disfigured, bleeding and thoroughly thrashed old man for dead they left in the belief they had ended his life with severe pain. Tough old Samuel Whittemore, however, survived, and lived long enough to see the drastic changes coming to his colony. He died sixteen years later at ninety-six.

The plight of the British increased the closer they got to Boston as militias from the more populous towns near the city joined in the fray. Militias appeared from Essex, Danvers, Dorchester, Brookline, Roxbury, Dedham, even more distant Pepperell and Worcester arrived to join the fray. Over forty towns sent their militias to battle the invading British; almost four thousand men, all volunteers, in the fight for freedom.

As Percy neared the road to Cambridge, he faced a decision. He could attempt to return to Boston by retracing the path he took leaving Boston earlier. This would require a several long mile trek, including a crossing of the Cambridge Bridge over the Charles River, then continuing on through Roxbury to Boston neck.

The British commander did not relish that option. It was a long march, and he was running out of ammunition for his cannon. He was also aware the provincials may have rendered the Cambridge Bridge unusable, and the Charles River was too deep for his convoy to cross. If he took his troops that route, and could not use the bridge, he would be trapped. Instead, Percy made an inspired decision, and, instead of turning south on the road to the Cambridge

Bridge as was expected, he turned east and headed to Charlestown. That town could afford some protection for the British troops as they would be in the range of the guns on the large British man-o-war, the Somerset, at anchor near the north end of Boston.

In an effort to stop the British from crossing into Charlestown, several militiamen formed a line across the road, but Percy effectively utilized his remaining cannon balls to disperse them. The strong Salem and Marblehead militias were supposed to be at the road to stop the British if they took that route, but their commander, Timothy Pickering, delayed their arrival so the British were able to cross Charlestown neck and find safety. With great relief the weary British made it to sanctuary on the open land on Bunker Hill. The militia ceased their attack and both sides tended their slain and wounded. Over the next few days the British troops were ferried across the Charles River from Charlestown, and returned to their compound in Boston.

It was a disastrous day for the British, who suffered seventy-three killed and one hundred seventy-four wounded. An additional twenty-three were missing. The provincials saw forty-nine killed and thirty-nine wounded. In an effort to affect public opinion in both America and in Britain, each side issued erroneous or greatly exaggerated reports which demonized the other.

Ensign Jeremy Lister, in his official account of the battle, made a most outlandish claim. In referring to men killed in the fighting at the North Bridge, *"who was afterwards scalp'd their Eyes goug'd their Noses and Ears cutoff, such barbarity exercis'd upon the Corps could scarcely be paralelld by the most uncivilized Saveges."* A similar erroneous claim was also contained in Lord Percy's report to General Gage. It was cited extensively in British newspapers.

A report prepared by Dr. Warren, and later embellished by the colonial press, was also printed widely in the American newspapers. It claimed British soldiers, during the retreat to Boston, drove naked women from their childbed (where they had recently given birth) and into the cold so their houses could be burned down.

The whole mission was a serious setback for the British. Gage's mission had done little to reduce the supplies at Concord. Worse, it had demonstrated the vulnerability of sending even large numbers of troops out into the countryside. Lord Percy debased the myth believed by most loyalists in America, and governmental leaders in London, that the provincials were a ragtag mob, who would run at the approach of British military might. He stated later, *"Whoever looks upon them as an irregular mob, will find himself much mistaken; they have men amongst them who know very well what they are all about, having been employed as rangers against Indians and Canadians, and this country being much covered with wood and hilly, is very advantageous*

for their method of fighting. " He then added some words for the British leaders to ponder, *"You may depend upon it, that as the rebels have now had time
to prepare, they are determined to go through with it, nor will the insurrection here turn out so despicable as it is perhaps imagined at home. "*

General Gage was startled at the intensity of the militias fighting spirit, a
strength unexpected by him, *"The rebels are not the despicable rabble too
many have supposed them to be. "* With the new respect he had for the provincials' potency he now had to devise a defense of the city, a concept he would
not have thought necessary only recently.

For the provincials the turnout of so many ready to fight to the death was
an inspiring progression from the speeches, sermons and tavern talk that
proceeded. It meant the cause of the colonies was validated with the blood
of those left on the battlefield. The most significant and ultimately critical
impact of the whole episode is the effect it had on the formation of a colonial
army, and that effect, in turn, had on the road to independence.

Chapter Thirty-One

Militias to Army

The conflicts at Lexington and Concord had irrevocably changed things for nearly everyone involved. The men of the militia and the men of the provincial congress knew they had passed a point of no return with regard to their relationship with their mother country. While they could have claimed self-defense for the fighting at Lexington, that argument was no longer plausible now. The killing of British soldiers on an official mission to Concord was now either murder or insurrection; either charge punishable by death for the patriot leaders if Britain put down all resistance, and exerted firm control over the colonies.

Throughout the Massachusetts Bay Colony rumors were rampant. Many were panicked by untrue allegations of British troops seeking out patriots in a spate of violent revenge. Other vowed they had seen atrocities committed by British soldiers on innocent women and the elderly; these also were untrue. Citizens at some of the seashore towns did evacuate inland to escape any hostilities which could come from naval ships, whether landing troops or bombarding them with cannon.

With Adams, Hancock and the rest of the Massachusetts delegation bound for the Continental Congress in Philadelphia, the reins of coordinating the affairs of the colony, and especially protection from any additional escapades by the British army fell to the leaders remaining. The most prominent leader, the ranking member of the Committee of Safety, was Dr. Joseph Warren. Warren was seen as a person who could lead effectively; one whom men would follow. The personable Warren, held little personal pretense, and was respected and listened to by the entire strata of colonial Massachusetts. He had proven his courage by moving with the militias all the way from Lexington to Charlestown. On the route he was grazed by a musket ball, which he docilely ignored.

Warren held strong convictions the British were violating the precepts of the English Constitution in the hostile laws and proclamations they had issued to illegally govern the citizens of the Massachusetts Bay Colony. He was an active member of the patriot movement, often speaking out at formal assemblages such as the ceremonies honoring the victims of the Boston Massacre. But, even as he supported the military action directed against the King's troops, he, like many of the colonial leaders, still sought to find a means to breech the divide between the colonies and their mother country. Also, however, like many of the colonial leaders, he was beginning to realize the repair might not be possible. As he stated in the aftermath of Lexington and Concord, *"The next views from England must be conciliatory, or the connection between us ends."*

Warren had worked long enough, and closely enough, with Samuel Adams to learn the importance of public support. He crafted a message to the colony's citizens calling for support to battle Gage's troops. On April 20th he wrote and widely distributed a pamphlet throughout the colony, and beyond.

Gentlemen. The barbarous murders committed on our innocent brethren on Wednesday, the 19th instant, have made it absolutely necessary that we immediately raise an army to defend our wives and our children from the butchering hands of an inhuman soldiery, who, incensed at the obstacles they met with in their bloody progress, and enraged at being repulsed from the field of slaughter, will, without the least doubt, take the first opportunity in their power to ravage this devoted country with fire and sword.

Warren went on to ask for volunteers for the army. He implored for an immediate response. *"An hour lost may deluge your country in blood and entail perpetual slavery upon the few of your posterity who may survive the carnage."*

The immediate problem facing Warren and the provincial leaders was how to contain Gage's army within the confines of Boston. Joining Warren at the newly established provincial army headquarters in Cambridge was Artemas Ward, who had been appointed earlier by the provincial congress to head the army. He took over from William Heath, who had taken temporary command of the colonial forces in the fight with the British during their retreat from Concord, as he was the only general on the scene. Ward had risen from his sickbed, and marched with the militia from Shrewsbury to join the massive army being formed in Boston's environs. Ward had military experience, serving as a Colonel during the French and Indian War, and had gained the respect of the men serving under him.

Throughout April 20th, numerous militias and individuals descended on Cambridge to join the army battling the British. They left fields in the midst of plowing, left boats on the shore, said hastened goodbyes to families. Left with the clothes they had been wearing when the alarm reached them. An estimated twenty-thousand arrived to support the patriot cause. The volunteers came from across the Massachusetts Bay colony and from neighboring colonies of New Hampshire, Connecticut, and Rhode Island.

The entire area around Cambridge became essentially a sprawling military base. The students at Harvard were sent away to make room in the University's halls for the colonial troops massing there. Residences abandoned by British loyalists who moved to Boston were quickly filled by the military; the fine mansions taken by colonial officers and their staffs. Even the Anglican Christ Church was converted into a military barracks. Some of the soldiers encamped in tents, but there were not enough of them even though the Committee of Supplies was fabricating tents from ships sails, and many soldiers were forced to sleep in the open.

A large army was thus established with General Artemas Ward as commander, but with able officers from the entire New England area. While this army was preparing to confront the immediate threat posed by the encamped British, other militias from throughout colonial America were being prepared for action. In all of the other colonies men were being called to arms, and plans made to join those already at the field of action.

In Boston, Gage immediately grasped the seriousness of his position. He did not know how many militiamen were present to oppose him, but he knew there were many, and their numbers were increasing. He also now knew they would fight, and fight courageously. The patriot army took measures to surround Boston, necessitating Gage to take measures to protect the city. He kept all of his troops on alert, and posted sentries along Boston's shores where an invasion might take place. He also strengthened the guard at Boston Neck; the only land connection between the city and the mainland.

The British were now contained on the small peninsula containing the city of Boston (see the old *Plan of the Town and Harbor of Boston*—with some discrepancies). Boston's land mass was shaped somewhat like an oak leaf attached to the mainland by a tenuous stem, a narrow isthmus which, under the right conditions of tide and wind, could be under water. The northerly tip of the city was only a few hundred yards from the town of Charlestown, reachable by ferries normally streaming back and forth. There were several small rises on Boston's terrain, including one at the northwest corner called Copp's Hill, where admiral Graves had mounted several cannon which faced Charlestown.

Along the left (westerly) side of the peninsula ran the Charles River, whose waters widened and curved inward at the isthmus, creating the shallow Back Bay. Across the bay, opposite Boston, is where the Provincial army had set up its headquarters around Cambridge. On the peninsula's right side was Boston's Harbor, speckled with islands of various sizes. Many held provisions and livestock used by the city's inhabitants and Gage's troops. Castle William Island held the British fort where troops were stationed. The Long Wharf, built to facilitate maritime commerce, extended nearly a half-mile out into the harbor from the center of the right-hand shore.

A road over the isthmus ran from Boston to Roxbury, connecting Boston peninsula to a generally flat mainland. To the right of the isthmus, across a shallow bay, Dorchester Neck projected into the harbor's waters. At its end, the land took a right angle turn, and formed a small peninsula containing Dorchester Heights, which overlooked Boston and its Harbor.

On April 22nd the Provincial Congress first met at Concord as usual, but moved their session to Watertown to be closer to the army. Dr. Warren was elected temporary President to take the place of John Hancock, who was on his way to the Continental Congress in Philadelphia. The provincial leaders had not known Gage would provoke such a grave conflict, or that it would turn out as it did, but with the battle now an actual event, they prepared to advance their cause as quickly as possible.

A concerted effort was initiated to effect public opinion both throughout the colonies, but also in Great Britain. The Provincial Congress ordered dispositions taken from eyewitnesses to the battles at Lexington and Concord,

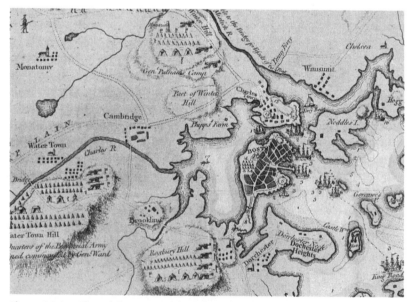

Figure 31.1. Plan of the Town and Harbor of Boston.

which would substantiate it was the British who fired first on innocent provincials, precipitating a defensive militia response. The witnesses' accounts, colonials as well as three British soldiers who had been captured, verified this version of events.

If enough of the British populace, including the members of Parliament, could be convinced the colonies were being maltreated, perhaps, Parliament might reconsider their passage of the Intolerable Acts, and some sort of accommodation could be developed the colonies could accept. However, as a practical matter, if the King remained intractably intent on total subservience of the colonies, it was a futile hope Parliament would oblige the colonials. The King still wielded too much power; with control of the Ministries and command of the disposition of patronages, not enough members of Parliament would dare oppose the King's wishes.

Gage meanwhile prepared his own version of the events in a report to London. The report was given to Lt. Nunn of the Royal Navy who boarded the next ship bound for London, the Sukey, and left Boston on April 25th. The Provincial Congress knew it was best to get their version of the battles to London before Gage's, and so commissioned Salem's John Derby to carry the report on his fast ship, Quero, which left on April 29th. Derby was aware his ship might be stopped by British authorities, and the report confiscated, if he went up the Thames directly to London, so, after a hurried passage across the ocean, he landed in Southern England, and the report sent overland, arriving in London on May 28th, over a week ahead of Gage's official report.

The provincial report describing the battles at Lexington and Concord was published quickly and extensively throughout Britain. This version of the events depicted the colonials as peaceful British citizens, who were unjustifiably assailed by British troops. It garnered much public sympathy for the patriots and their cause. However, when Gage's official report arrived, it was the one considered valid in London's governmental halls. The London Gazette published Gage's report in their edition of June 10, 1775. The report described the British troop's mission:

"upon their arrival at Lexington, found a body of the country people under arms, on a green close to the road; and upon the King's troops marching upon them, in order to inquire the reason of their being so assembled, they went off in great confusion, and several guns were fired upon the King's troops from behind a stone wall, and also from the meeting house and other houses, by which one man was wounded, and Major Pitcairn's horse was shot in two places. In consequence of this attack by the rebels, the troops returned the fire and killed several of them. After which, the detachment marched on to Concord without any further happening."

In London a great ferment arose over the bloody fighting at Lexington and Concord. British anxiety over the killing of British citizens by British troops evoked a number of opinions to be put forth about steps the government should take next. Pitt-Chatham and Lord Rockingham emphatically stated that now was the time to be conciliatory towards the American Colonies before it was too late. Parliament must repeal the Coercive Acts or the colonies will be lost. It is inexplicable, they advised, the colonies could be defeated militarily across the thousands of miles of ocean separating them.

The King, and the majority of the members of Parliament, did not share this view, and was ever more insistent the colonies must be subdued by force. Public opinion, though divided, agreed with their approach. The common belief in Britain was that the majority of British subjects in the colonies did not want a confrontation with the mother country. Only perhaps a third of the populace in America wanted to challenge British authority, but this aggressive minority was creating an atmosphere of hostility toward Britain, and intimidating the true loyal majority from speaking out. It was inconceivable to believe the majority in America would pursue such a defiant course.

With hostilities now actually occurring in New England, and the prospect of more in the future, the King, backed by his ministers and Parliament, felt it was time to mobilize the large military force necessary to quell this illegal rebellion. The British army had troops in garrisons around the world which could be called to service; in Gibraltar, Minorca, and at home in England, Scotland and Ireland. Britain could also, as they had done in past wars, rent mercenaries from the German princes. All of this might be needed to subdue the rebellious Americans.

The patriot leaders at Cambridge were aware they needed a more stable military force if they were to succeed. They had discussed earlier the formation of a 30,000–man New England army, of which 13,600 would come from Massachusetts, but, now, as the reality of their plight became apparent, they realized they didn't need all of the twenty-thousand presently encamped, but they did need a solid core of about eight thousand or so, on whom they could depend to be present, and willing to fight.

The Provincial Congress approved funds (in provincial script) to pay soldiers who would enlist until the end of the year. Ward and Warren, along with other officers, began to organize the loose conglomerations of independent militias into a hierarchal arrangement of regiments and companies, and appointed officers to lead them. It was important to organize into stable, effective units, which would be effective in carrying out strategies quickly and effectively. It was, however, a difficult matter to convince locally-formed militia to accept leadership from officers they did not know or personally respect.

Provisions for the mass of militias being remodeled into an army was also an immediate concern. Like the mass of men arriving for military duty, there arose a multitude of others, women, old men, some partially disabled, even children, who arrived with foodstuffs. Dried fruit, salted meat, smoked fish, hard breads, to keep the army fed. While the effort of these volunteers was useful, it was apparent there needed to be an ordered organization to support the army. It would, however, be some time before anything resembling an efficient supply organization was put in place.

A bit over a week into Boston's siege, a brash young officer named Benedict Arnold came before the Committee of Safety with a plan for them to consider. Husky, strong physically, and extremely confident and ambitious, Arnold had come to Cambridge as Captain of the New Haven Foot Guards. He told the committee he had been at Fort Ticonderoga while serving with the British army during the French and Indian War. He proposed the fort be attacked and, he believed, could be easily taken. Resplendent in a uniform his vanity had induced him to have tailored at his own expense, Arnold offered to recruit a cadre of men to undertake the task.

The Committee of Safety was unaware of the agreement Samuel Adams had made with Ethan Allen and the Green Mountain Boys for the same mission, and they readily agreed with Arnold's proposal. Warren was concerned, however, with offending the Colony of New York, on whose land the mission would take place, and so wrote a letter to them informing them of the venture. Like Samuel Adams, the committee was ready to expand the conflict with the British, and those armaments at the fort were badly needed by the colonial troops. Arnold was commissioned a Colonel in the Provincial Army. He was given orders to recruit enough men (400), to attack the fort as soon as possible. Arnold left Cambridge with two lieutenants, and headed to the western end of Massachusetts, enthusiastic with carrying out his plan.

A few days into his trek, Arnold learned the mission to capture the fort had previously been given to Ethan Allen. Not to be deterred, Arnold left the recruitment of additional men to his lieutenants, and began a hurried advance to catch up with Allen before he attacked the fort. He finally caught up with him at a tavern in Bennington of the New Hampshire Colony.

Allen had a hundred of his Green Mountain boys with him, and was supported by fifty Massachusetts militia from Berkshire under Colonel James Easton. The lawyer, John Brown, who Samuel Adams had first sent to the area, was also present. Arnold, still wearing his splendid uniform, informed Allen he had an official commission from the Massachusetts Committee of Safety to lead an attack on Fort Ticonderoga, and he and his men were welcome to serve under him in the fort's conquest.

The Green Mountain Boys were not enamored with the idea of serving under this pretty boy. They had signed up to follow Ethan Allen, and that is what they intended to do. If Allen wasn't leading the mission they were going home. The crisis was quelled when Allen agreed Arnold could come along with them, and call himself co-leader if that was what he wanted.

Shortly before dawn on May 10, the band reached the northern end of Lake George just a short distance below the fort at the southern end of Lake Champlain.They found enough small boats to carry the eighty-three man attack force across the water where they marched the short distance to the base of the fort as dawn was breaking. The sentry on duty at the gate, startled by this pack of disheveled men with weapons, at first raised his fusil (small musket), thought better of the idea of challenging them, and abandoned his post in haste.

With easy entry into the fort, Allen and his charges were confronted by a British officer, Lieutenant Jocelyn Feltham, who demanded what authority gave them the right to enter his fort. *"In the name of the Great Jehovah and the Continental Congress,"* Allen roared at the intimidated soldier. The colonial warriors quickly moved to disarm the forty or so British soldiers stationed there, after which Allen and Arnold roused the fort's commander, Captain William Delaplace, who quickly appraised the situation and surrendered.

The capture of Fort Ticonderoga was an immense morale boost for the Provincial Army. More importantly, was the great store of weapons found and taken; over a hundred iron cannon, two brass cannon, two large mortars, a substantial quantity of cannon and musket balls, and ten cases of greatly needed powder. The victory was especially gratifying to the Green Mountain Boys, who discovered the fort's rum supply which was immediately liberated.

A few days after the fort's capture, fifty men recruited by Arnold's lieutenants arrived, and Arnold officially took command of the fort in the name of the Provincial Congress. The forty captured British soldiers were sent back to Connecticut as prisoners-of-war. Seth Wagner, one of Arnold's lieutenants, along with a small detachment, went up the lake several miles and captured the small British fort at Crown's point, manned by only twelve men, but contained additional cannon the colonials could use.

The same date Fort Ticonderoga was captured, the Second Continental Congress began its sessions in the State House in Philadelphia. The Massachusetts delegates had been received as heroes in passing through New York. They were paraded through that city by a vast throng garnering encouragement for their fight with the British all along their route.

While Samuel Adams meant to exploit the massacre of colonial citizens at Lexington and Concord to incite strong antagonism against British rule, he soon found many of the delegates were of a different tenor. They sympathized with the situation in which the New Englanders found themselves, but were nowhere near concluding it was time for a rift with Britain, and especially were not considering declaring the colonies independent.

Near the end of May, the acting president, Peyton Randolph of Virginia was called back to his colony, being replaced as a Virginia delegate by Thomas Jefferson. Henry Middleton of South Carolina was asked to serve as president, but demurred, citing illness. John Hancock was then elected as president of the congress to preside over the sessions.

For those advocating a peaceful reconciliation with Britain, even the news that Fort Ticonderoga had fallen, elicited as much concern about protecting British assets at the fort as it inspired satisfaction with a military victory. In the ambiguous atmosphere of the colonial assembly, John Adams began the debate about what actions the Congress should take with regard to the situation at Boston. He urged the Congress to assume charge of the army assembled there; appoint a commander, and underwrite the costs of its operation.

It was a critical proposal, the implications, well understood by the delegates, horrified many. As things presently stood, there was a Massachusetts Bay Colony Provincial Army fighting the British army (although some considered it a New England Provincial Army) in deadly warfare. If the Congress should adopt the army, and appoint a commander, it would become an American Colonial Army fighting the King's troops; it would be a virtual declaration of war by the colonies as a whole, quite a different thing from a local uprising around Boston.

A definite majority of the delegates wanted to find a way to come to an accommodation with Great Britain which would be acceptable to both sides. John Dickenson, who had eloquently written the Letters from a Pennsylvania Farmer during the Stamp Act crisis strongly opposing that law, proposed instead the Congress attempt to negotiate with the crown's representatives.

Dickenson, and others like him, were as much against the oppressive acts Britain had passed as were any of those harboring thoughts of independence. They were searching, however, for means to abolish them without suffering additional causalities from conflicts. They had the belief the King, if he heard a sincere plea from them to repeal the laws, would at least open a dialog which could pave the way to a peaceful resolution of their anguish. It was a means the more aggressive of the colonials like Samuel Adams thought was a waste of time, but the patriots like Adams advocating a break with Britain realized, with the present mood of the congress, they would have to attempt to satisfy the peace-seeking members before all would agree on more aggressive action.

John Adams' instinct was to vocally oppose Dickenson's proposal, but he was told, and realized himself, the time was not yet sensible to oppose a sincere effort to bring peace to the land, and avoid the bloodshed which would surely follow any radical moves such as separation from the mother country. Accordingly, he voted for the measure. The resolution passed, and a conciliatory plea to the King was prepared. Termed "The Olive Branch Petition," it placed the onus of the troubles between the colonies and Britain on the King's ministers and Parliament, removing the King himself from accountability for the discord.

The petition, obsequious in tone, was carefully written, but not officially sent until July 8, 1775. It proffered allegiance to the King stating, *with the utmost deference for your Majesty; and we therefore pray, that your Majesty's royal magnanimity and benevolence may make the most favorable constructions of our expressions on so uncommon an occasion.*" The petition, signed by the delegates, emphatically stated the desire of the colonies to resume peaceful relations with Britain. It promised devotion to the crown, but also asked the statutes that caused to distress to the colonies be repealed.

Back in Cambridge outside of Boston, Joseph Warren dispatched Dr. Benjamin Church (whose duplicity in providing intelligence to General Gage had not yet been discovered) to the Continental Congress with several requests. Arriving on June 1st, he read Warren's well-written request to the congress, pleading for guidance in setting up a provincial government for the Massachusetts Bay Colony; and reiterating his desire for the congress to take responsibility for the army now encamped outside of Boston, and appoint a commander. Acting positively on either of these actions would signify the congress was assuming a leadership role in the battle with the British.

Warren's request was substantiated by information British troops were continuously arriving to reinforce Gage's force. On May 14th six-hundred marines had landed and on May 25th the HMS Cerberus docked with Major Generals William Howe, Henry Clinton, and John Burgoyne aboard.

The generals had been sent to assist Gage as the King and his ministers were dissatisfied with Gage's reluctance to take aggressive action. These new generals were of a definitely different mindset than the general they were helping.

Forty-six year old William Howe was the highest ranking of the three. He was an extremely competent leader, who had gain plaudits for leading troops in the scaling of the cliffs at the edge of the Plains of Abraham during the French and Indian War; a feat which led to the fall of Quebec. He was somewhat conflicted with his assignment to America. He had recently been elected to Parliament as a Whig, and had promised during his election campaign he would not fight against the colonials. However, when the King ordered him to command in Boston, like the good soldier he was, he relented, and obeyed the King's wishes (he also needed the added active duty salary to pay his extensive gambling debts).

Henry Clinton, at thirty-seven the youngest of the new generals, was known for fastidious attention to detail, and his dogged pursuit to achieve his military goals. Of a short, portly structure, he was known to be overly sensitive to criticism, and required careful handling.

John Burgoyne, although the oldest of the three at age fifty-three, was the lowest in rank, having interrupted his army career for a time to pursue other callings. Flamboyant, he was well-liked by troops serving under him as he eschewed the corporal punishment widely used within the British army for infractions. When he learned Gage's force was under siege in Boston, he exclaimed, *"What, ten thousand peasants keep five thousand King's troops shut up? Well, let us get in and we'll soon find elbowroom."* The boast was widely circulated.

While nothing of a major episode had occurred as the new generals were arriving, there had been several small encounters between the two forces. The British schooner, Diana, had run aground and became stranded near Noddle's Island. The patriots attacked the hapless vessel, which led to its burning. Included in the patriot ranks was the ever active General Israel Putnam from Connecticut. Another encounter occurred when the British attempted to gather some bales of hay for their livestock from Grape Island, near the shore at Weymouth in the eastern harbor. The British troops were driven off by a provincial squad ordered to the scene by General John Thomas, commander of the army at Roxbury. The provincial patrol possibly included Dr. Joseph Warren, who seemed to gravitate to wherever fighting occurred.

On June 7th, the Continental Congress acceded to Warren's request and directed the Massachusetts Provincial Congress to set up a civil government, independent of the government directed by Parliament's Massachusetts Government Act. The issue of a continental commander of the army was still undecided.

The wording of the directions the Continental Congress sent to Massachusetts was ambiguous with regard to what they were actually approving. It stated,

> no obedience being due to the Act of Parliament for altering the charter of the Colony of Massachusetts Bay, nor to a Governor or Lieutenant-Governor who will not observe the directions of, but endeavor to support, that charter. The Governor and Lieutenant-Governor of that colony are to be considered as absent, and their offices vacant; and as there is no Council there, and the inconveniences arising from the suspension of the powers of government are intolerable, especially at a time when General Gage hath actually levied war and is carrying on hostilities against his Majesty's peaceable and loyal subjects of that Colony; that, in order to conform as near as may be to the spirit and substance of the charter, it is recommended to the Provincial Convention to write letters to

the inhabitants of the several places, which are entitled to representation in Assembly, requesting them to choose such representatives, and that the Assembly when chosen do elect Counsellors; and that such assembly or Council exercise the powers of government, until a Governor of His Majesty's appointment will consent to govern the Colony according to its charter.

The guidance given to Massachusetts by the Continental Congress, while clouded with words implying loyalty to the King, nevertheless assumed an authority reserved to the monarch. Those continental delegates still attempting to effect reconciliation with Britain likely rationalized their directive to Massachusetts was a temporary measure which would be abrogated when reconciliation finally occurred. It only theoretically negated the King's legal prerogatives as it was a temporary measure. In fact, no matter how they couched the wording, they were replacing the King's authority with their own. This authority they were assuming was not granted to them by any other body or entity, they were just taking it. The action was a significant movement to self-government, even if many did not see it at the time.

With the delegates to the Continental Congress somewhat mollified by the passage of the Olive Branch Petition to the King, John Adams detected a slight change in the delegates' opinion regarding more aggressive action. He felt it was time to move on the issue of a commander of the army. On July 14th Adams took the floor. In an animated speech he warned of the devastation that would accrue if the British troops gained enough strength to break out of their Boston enclave and attack innocent colonials. He ended his speech stating it was now time for military leadership, and the one man who could undertake such a difficult task was the gentleman from Virginia, George Washington. To John's satisfaction, second-cousin Samuel rose to second the motion.

When his name was placed in nomination to become the commander of the colonial army, Washington, who had attended the sessions in his military uniform, stepped out of the room so the debate could continue with his presence not affecting the discussions. Washington had been the choice of many in Massachusetts, although both Adams' knew John Hancock coveted the position. They did not feel Hancock could do the job as well as Washington, and both were well aware there were many in the congress who were suspicious of New England and its objectives. Hancock, might have been upset at not being the cousins' choice, but showed no disquiet.

Several delegates rose to oppose Washington's nomination. To Adams' consternation his fellow Massachusetts delegates, Thomas Cushing and Robert Trent Paine, voiced concerns a commander from Virginia might not be acceptable to the present troops, as they usually selected their own officers. And, why? Asked Edmund Pendleton, a delegate from Virginia, would another commander be needed when there seemed to be a competent commander in place. Artemas Ward seemed to be doing a satisfactory job of keeping the British confined in Boston. Ward was well acquainted with the present officer corps, and had detailed knowledge of the land and its people. With objections raised to the nomination, it was tabled for the day.

That night John Adams and other supporters of Washington politicked for his appointment, outlining their rationale for their choice. Having units choose their own officers, while a democratic thing to do, often meant the officers were beholden to the men under their command, and could be reluctant to order them into unpleasant or dangerous situations. Artemas Ward was a competent general, but he has been ill, and did not have the experience or standing of General Washington.

The next morning, Thomas Johnson of Maryland re-introduced Washington's name. The vote was unanimous; George Washington was elected as commander-in-chief of the now American Colonial Army, with all of the implications of united colonies fighting against the British military. On June 16th Washington accepted the responsibility of his charge with his usual humility. In his acceptance statement he promised to serve to the best of his ability, but he also voiced concerns about what posterity might think of him if he failed. He also stated he did not want pay for his services, only for the Congress to cover his expenses.

Mr. President: Tho' I am truly sensible of the High Honour done me in this Appointment, yet I feel great distress from a consciousness that my abilities and Military experience may not be equal to the extensive and important Trust: However, as the Congress desires I will enter upon the momentous duty, and exert every power I Posses In their Service for the Support of the glorious Cause: I beg they will accept my most cordial thanks for this distinguished testimony of their Approbation.

But lest some unlucky event should happen unfavorable to my reputation, I beg it may be remembered by every Gentn. In the room, that I this day declare with the utmost sincerity, I do not think my self equal to the Command I am honoured with.

As to pay, Sir, I beg leave to Assure the Congress that as no pecuniary consideration could have tempted me to have accepted this Ardous employment [at the expense of my domestt. Ease and happiness] I do not wish to make any profit from it: I will keep an exact Account of my expenses; those I doubt not they will discharge and that is all I desire.

Chapter Thirty-Two

Bunker and Breed's Hills

On the evening of June 16th, the day Washington addressed the delegates in Philadelphia accepting the responsibility of leading the Continental Army, Colonel William Prescott of the Massachusetts militia assembled slightly over a thousand men at the colonial encampment in Cambridge. Equipped with picks and shovels, Prescott marched his command over the narrow width of land connecting the mainland to the Charlestown peninsula to conduct a clandestine, nighttime mission to challenge the British army. Prescott's contingent was manned by three regiments of the Massachusetts militia, two hundred militiamen from Putnam's Connecticut regiment under Captain Thomas Knowlton, and a battalion of artillery under Colonel Richard Gridley, the army's chief of engineering and artillery.

The colonials were undertaking this bold mission because they had received unexpected and disturbing intelligence from the New Hampshire Committee of Safety. The intelligence revealed General Gage, commander of the British army occupying Boston, had made plans for an operation to break out of the city and attack colonial territory. According to a trusted source who had acquired details of the planned British operation, General Howe was to command a force to sieze the high ground on the Charlestown Peninsula, while other units under the command of Generals Clinton or Burgoyne, first attacked Roxbury, and then moved on to take Dorchester Heights. If conditions proved favorable after occupying Dorchester; a foray would be made against the Provincial Army Headquarters in Cambridge. It was an ambitious plan; one Gage was likely coerced into approving by the new generals, who had arrived the previous month, and were impatient to take more aggressive action. The attack was supposedly set for June 18th.

In earlier discussions of what steps needed to be taken to keep Gage and his troops confined in Boston, the colonial military leaders had discussed a number of options. The recommendation most favored by Artemas Ward, the colonial commander, and several others on the Committee of Safety, was to first build a breastwork on the mainland side of Charlestown Neck, and, later, add another on Bunker Hill, just across the neck on Charlestown's peninsula. It was a conservative strategy favored by Ward because the colonial army was poorly equipped, and, he believed, not yet ready for major conflicts—not all of the colonial soldiers had muskets and there was a severe shortage of powder. However, upon learning of this inimical British plan, the Massachusetts Committee of Safety felt they were forced to move onto the Charlestown Peninsula at once, and prepared an order sent to the provincial generals: *"Whereas, it appears of Importance to the Safety of this Colony, that possession of the Hill called Bunker's Hill in Charlestown, be securely kept and defended; and also someone hill or hills on Dorchester Neck be likewise Secured."*

The Charlestown Peninsula, like Boston, extended out from the mainland over a narrow neck of land. On maps, the land gave the impression of an irregular bell hanging by a strap at its narrow northwest corner, with its wide end abutting the waters of Boston Harbor. The distance from the strap (neck) at the mainland to the shore at Boston's Harbor was approximately a mile. The land at the neck was level and just slightly above sea level. About five-hundred yards out on the peninsula, the land rose to Bunker Hill, topping at an elevation of one hundred and ten feet. Descending down the back slope of Bunker Hill, out another five hundred yards, and slightly to the right, the land rose again at Breed's Hill, its elevation of sixty-some feet, about fifty feet lower than Bunker Hill.

There was a gradual slope to the land from Breed's Hill to the wide end of the bell-shaped peninsula next to the water. The shore here was only five hundred yards from Boston's docks. In more peaceful times ferries routinely plied the gap between the two land masses. On the westerly side of the wide end of the peninsula, the town of Charlestown was situated; it's two hundred plus houses now abandoned by its populace. The shore here was bordered by the shallow waters of the Charles River, with a Mill Pond at Charlestown Neck. Opposite the town on the broad water end was another small rise called Moulton's Hill, setting at the entrance to the Mystic River, which ran along the easterly side of the peninsula. A small escarpment about eight-feet high traced along the river, bordering a level shore, which here was accessible for walking.

Marching his men up the incline to Bunker Hill, they passed the small, now abandoned, fort-like structure Lord Percy had built near the entrance to the peninsula to protect his retreat after the battle of Concord. Prescott stopped at the broad elevation of the hill to hold a conference with his fellow officers. It is possible General Israel Putnam of Connecticut was with Prescott at this time as he was very active in maneuvering the colonial troops to oppose the British, but his presence is only inferred, as history is silent on the matter.

The only information about this conference came from a second-hand report that "two generals went on to the hill at night and reconnoitered the grounds." An argument supposedly ensued in which one of the generals and Colonel Gridley proposed putting up a defensive post on Bunker Hill, but the other general argued forcefully to emplace the post on Breed's Hill. It is unknown who these "generals" were, although the teller was likely referring to Colonel Prescott as one, the other never identified.

The selection of a site on which to construct a small fortress, a redoubt, was based on the site's vulnerability and effectiveness. Bunker Hill was the safer choice, but Breed's Hill afforded a better view of the city and harbor. Breed's Hill, however, was closer to the British ships-of-war, and would be within range of their cannon, and the added distance to Charlestown's Neck could be a problem. If a battle ensued, the neck would have to be used by reinforcing troops to aid those at the redoubt, or for a retreat if that became necessary. Retreating from Breed's Hill would leave departing troops exposed to enemy ground fire from charging British regulars. The Breed's Hill site, it was certain, would provoke a response from Gage's forces, diverting them from their planned attack on Roxbury and Dorchester. After a pause, a decision was reached, and the contingent of soldiers, construction tools in hand, proceeded down the far slope of Bunker Hill, and up another rise to Breed's Hill. There, construction was started on a roughly square earthen redoubt.

William Prescott, commander of the militia from Pepperell, Massachusetts, was an experienced and extremely well-regarded leader. He served so well at the battle of Fort Beausejour during the French and Indian War, the British wanted him to join their army. He declined, and later returned home. When the disputes between the colonies and Britain became more serious, and the colonials began to mobilize, he was chosen as head of his town's militia. After Lexington and Concord, he had brought his militia company to Cambridge to join the Continental Army.

The fortress, laid out by sixty-five year old Colonel Gridley, was finally started about midnight. It was to be a square, 136 feet on a side, one corner overlooking Boston. The earth was piled up six feet, with an interior platform on which soldiers could stand and fire over the earthen shield. A narrow opening was provided in the back to provide entry and egress.

It was a rigorous undertaking by the colonial militiamen as they worked through the night without stopping for food or sleep, neither of which they had had before embarking on the mission since the day before.

The work did not go unnoticed by the British. General Clinton in Boston heard the noise of shovels and picks working the earth during the night, and realized at once what the colonials were up to. He rushed to inform Gage. With backing from Howe, he recommended an attack at the first light of sunrise. Gage was more cautious after the beating his troops had suffered at Lexington and Concord, and deferred action until the next morning when they could see what was actually being done. It wouldn't do to send troops into Charlestown to what could be a deception, exposing Boston itself to attack. Clinton strongly disagreed with the delay, and so wrote to a friend in London.

As the diffused light from the early morning sky dimly illuminated the peninsula, Prescott realized, with the redoubt on Breed's Hill, they were critically exposed on the sides to flanking maneuvers by British infantry. The redoubt had a field of fire on the right covering the slopes going down to the Charles River, but that was only marginally sufficient, and additional troops would be needed there if the British moved through the town of Charlestown, and up the slopes, or if they attempted to reach Charlestown's neck from that side. The left side, however, was the more serious problem. The redcoats could proceed up the gradual slope on the left where no colonial troops were posted, or British infantry could move along the shore of the Mystic River on the left, and come up behind the colonial fortification. Either option would trap the defenders in the redoubt.

The four AM morning light also alerted the crew of the British ship, Lively, one of several war ships in the Harbor to the activity on the hill. The ship moved closer to the waters off Charlestown, turned to set its cannon facing toward the redoubt, and commenced firing its twenty cannon. The sound of the blasts was heard throughout the area, alerting everyone something significant was occurring. Admiral Graves, head of the British navy at Boston, ordered the firing stopped until a more coordinated plan could be developed.

At this respite, Prescott had his fatigued troops extend the security of the redoubt by constructing a breastwork, running a hundred and sixty-five feet from the left side of the redoubt to the road from Bunker Hill. It ended behind swampy ground which would delay, but not stop, a British attack. It wasn't the best in terms of protection against a charging enemy, but it would have to do.

As other British ships, Glasgow, Symmetry, and Spitfire were moved to join the Lively, the shelling resumed. The roar of many cannons reverberated loudly and now incessantly. For many in the colonial militia this was the first taste of battle they had ever witnessed, and were tensed at the bombardment. Even though the cannon balls did little real damage it was unnerving for the men on the hill as plumes of dirt were raised around the makeshift fort as the heavy cannon balls plowed into the earth with thunder-like thuds. Prescott was concerned with panic and desertions by his soldiers, and moved visibly among them with words of encouragement. They were further unnerved

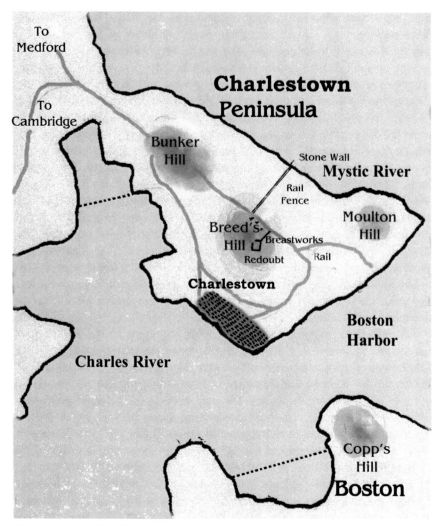

Figure 32.1.   Battle of Bunker/Breed's Hills.

when a colonial soldier, working in front of the redoubt, was decapitated by a stray cannon ball, but after a quick burial and service, Prescott kept his men to their task in spite of the grizzly sight they just witnessed.

At Gage's headquarters, Clinton was anxious for action. He too had observed the weakness at the colonial's flanks, and aspired to attack immediately. Gage, however, maintained his resolve for a more deliberate approach. He knew he had to take action against this rebel provocation, but was angry his master plan of an attack on Charlestown and Dorchester had been preempted by this bold colonial maneuver, and wanted to be certain his response would crush the rebels.

The plan finally agreed to by Gage, assigned to Howe a frontal attack on the left side of the colonial fort (the right side from the British point-of-view). Howe was confident his forces could easily overrun the redoubt by breeching the left flank of the colonial line. An assault by bayonet wielding infantry would quickly seal these undisciplined, cowardly rebels' fate. He selected Moulton's point as the place to land his troops, but that choice meant he would have to wait until three in the afternoon before the tide would permit the soldier-laden boats to land there. The extra time was used by the British to provide provisions for their soldiers as Howe wanted them prepared to stay three days without resupply. This meant they would have to carry additional provisions and equipment.

This upcoming battle between the British troops and the colonial militia was of a different sense than the fighting at Lexington and Concord. Those previous encounters could be viewed as spontaneous reactions to an insulting British disparagement of colonial rights. An unplanned, unexpected confrontation that turned deadly for both sides. This upcoming battle, however, was a clear, premeditated act of war.

As daylight brightened, and the details of the colonials' defense exposed, the British generals were confident they could easily defeat them. One mighty frontal attack would be a dramatic display of British military might, which would let the brash rebels know what they were facing, and could discourage them fatally. These were the rabble who had fought with the British during the French and Indian War, most of whom were considered far below British military standards. It they did not run, they would be destroyed upon the first attack.

General Israel Putnam, the energetic leader of the Connecticut militia had been in and out of Charlestown Peninsula during the night and into the morning. He also periodically checked on his men in Charlestown, trying to ascertain if they would be needed if Gage attempted to move against Roxbury or Cambridge. If not there he wanted them to move to support Prescott.

Putnam was a fearless, adventurous sort, who, like Prescott, had fought with the British during the French and Indian War. He had fought at Fort Ticonderoga and Montreal where his demonstrated abilities eventually earned him the rank of Major. After the war, he eventually settled at his farm in Connecticut. A vocal opponent of the imposition of the Stamp and Intolerable Acts, he became a dedicated member of the Sons-of-Liberty. He was made a commander in the Connecticut militia, and after the confrontations at Lexington and Concord, he moved quickly to bring his militia to Cambridge to join the Colonial Army where he was made a General (he supposedly moved so rapidly to Cambridge, he left the plow he was using in the middle of his farm field).

After assessing the situation at the redoubt in the morning light, Putnam rode to Cambridge and told Artemas Ward reinforcements were badly needed on Charlestown peninsula. Ward had only a few aides, such as one young volunteer; a bookseller from Boston named Henry Knox, who had recently slipped out of the city with his sweetheart, the daughter of a prominent loyalist. Thus, Ward lacked continuing, current information on the preparations for the upcoming battle, and was thus unsure of his decisions. Ward was reluctant to send reinforcements to the hill as he was concerned Gage would use the opportunity to send troops across the Back Bay, and attack the colonial headquarters at Cambridge. However, he partially relented and agreed to send two hundred men from John Stark's New Hampshire regiment at Medford to aid Prescott.

In mid-morning the large twenty-four pound naval cannon, which had been installed on Copp's Hill at Boston's northwest corner, began firing. Copp's Hill was at about the same elevation as Breed's Hill, and the cannon balls from Copp's could reach Charlestown Neck, discouraging passage by the colonial troops. The bombardment discouraged, but did not stop, the colonials from moving across the neck.

About this time, Gage ventured to a spot where he could view the newly erected rebel fort. In scanning the redoubt with his spyglass he spotted a tall figure moving actively, giving orders. Gage asked his aide, Abijah Willard, a Bostonian, if he recognized the man, the obvious leader at the site. Willard did indeed recognize the rebel leader. *"Will he fight?"* Gage inquired.

"I cannot answer for his men," Willard answered, *"but Prescott will fight you to the gates of Hell."* Willard well knew the man, as Prescott was his brother-in-law, one of many families split by the Colonial-British dispute.

The artillery brought to the redoubt the night before, was not fully functional. Gridley had not provided supporting platforms for the big guns nor even openings in the redoubt for them to fire through, and Gridley himself had disappeared. Colonel Gridley's son, Captain Samuel Gridley, one of two Captains commanding the artillery unit, solved one of the omissions by blasting openings in the earthen walls.

At nearly ten in the morning Prescott realized his men were so badly fatigued after the work expended building the redoubt they may not be up to extended fighting. Without sleep nor a meal for nearly twenty-four hours their compromised condition was readily evident, and fresh troops would be needed. Prescott dispatched Major Brooks to Cambridge to request additional reinforcements. At the same time he sent one of his captains with a small squad down to Charlestown to watch for any British activity which would require a response.

Brooks wanted to use one of the horses the artillery used to haul their cannons for his trip to Cambridge, but the artillery captains would not relinquish any. They declared the horses would be needed if they had to move the field pieces, thus Brooks had to make the three-miles to Cambridge on foot, delaying the dispatching of reinforcements to aid Prescott.

When Brooks arrived at Ward's headquarters, the Commanding General of the Colonial Army was suffering from a gall bladder attack, and yet not sure of his decisions. He was still concerned about an attack on Cambridge, but had the acumen to realize the situation was perilous. Fortunately the Committee of Safety was meeting nearby, so he sent Brooks with Prescott's request to them. The committee immediately ordered the rest of John Stark's regiment along with James Reed's New Hampshire regiment; both units bivouacked at Medford, to aid Prescott. Upon receiving the orders the troops were provisioned, and began the three-mile march to the Charlestown Peninsula.

About noon, the masses of British regulars began congregating at the wharves at Boston's north end. It was the verification the colonials had been waiting for—the British were not going to attack Roxbury or Cambridge, their objective was clearly Charlestown. However with the continued cannon bombardment of Roxbury, General Thomas kept his troops alert, and improved his defenses opposite the isthmus to Boston.

General Putnam now had no doubt about where the British troops were headed, and rode to Cambridge to order the rest of his Connecticut regiment to aid Prescott on Breed's Hill. In the confusion of the moment, not all of the Connecticut militia made it to the Charlestown peninsula; some were left still backing up the troops at Roxbury.

An hour after the British soldiers began assembling at the wharves, they began loading onto boats to carry them the short passing to Charlestown. It was a formidable looking British force: ten companies of mobile light infantry, ten companies of grenadiers, and two full regiments of foot soldiers supported by artillery and marines. In a softening up strategy preceding the attack, the British cannons increased their fire on Breed's Hill. There were several causalities among the colonials, but most remained steadfast in the redoubt.

With British troops heading to Moulton's Point, Prescott recognized Howe's obvious strategy was to attack the colonials' left flank, which was not fully manned. To counter the threat, he ordered two cannon to move to the left of the redoubt to oppose the anticipated British onslaught there, and directed thirty-five year old Captain Knowlton to take his two-hundred Connecticut militia, to provide cover for the cannon. Knowlton, an Indian fighter as a teenager, was as competent and brave an officer the army had.

The move Prescott ordered would have helped defense of their position, but the artillery captains, Samuel Gridley and John Callender instead of going to where Prescott had ordered, moved their cannon from the redoubt to Bunker Hill, well behind the front lines. There, they ran into General Putnam who ordered them back. They told the General they were out of ammunition, and could fire no more. When Putnam opened the boxes on their cart he discovered they still had plenty of balls and powder. He again angrily ordered them back. In the confusion after Putnam left to attend other problems, the artillery men decided the British threat too menacing, and left across Charlestown Neck.

Back at the redoubt's left flank Knowlton, however, understood the problem and took his Connecticut militia to the left of the breastworks where a rail fence extended from the Bunker Hill Road nearly to the Mystic River. It wasn't much, two wooden rails over a short stone hedge. Knowlton's men gathered rails from other, unused fences in the area, and set up another, lighter fence several yards in front of the first. The troops worked hastily to add grass and anything else they could find to the median between the two fences as well as on the fences themselves. It wasn't much protection from cannon or musket balls, but it was concealment the troops could use to hide behind until ready to fire. The fence line now extended from the Bunker Hill road, to the drop-off at the Mystic River.

The New Hampshire regiments under Stark and Reed, bravely crossed Charlestown Neck under continuous cannon fire and stopped on Bunker Hill. Both commanders saw the weakened position on the left flank, and moved their troops to support Knowlton along the rail fence.

At the Mystic River itself, the shore was about eight feet down the escarpment. Even with the high tide, the width of the shore was such the British could march along it concealed beneath the level land before coming up onto the peninsula behind colonial lines. Stark's troops began construction of a low stone wall from the left end of the rail fence down to the Mystic River. Upon Completion of the hastily constructed deterrent to attack, the men spread along the rail fence and stone wall to await the British charge.

Stark used his experience from his time serving with the British army during the French and Indian War, to position his men in a manner to withstand the British charge along the level shore where the attackers could move more rapidly. He was familiar with how the British attack would progress; the British would vigorously charge with bayonets in a tiered column four or five abreast. If after the first volley, the defenders stopped to reload their weapons after disabling the first rank, the following ranks would move quickly to overwhelm the defenders.

Stark skillfully arranged his defenders behind the rock wall at the shore in three ranks, one behind the other. The front rank was ordered to fire only when ordered, then to immediately fall back behind the third to reload their muskets. The second rank would then step forward and fire, repeating the stratagem. Using this tactic the British would be subject to nearly continuous volleys of musket balls.

The resistance at the rail fence was enhanced when Samuel Trevett of the Marblehead Massachusetts militia dragged two cannon to the line replacing the artillery from Gridley's battalion which was ordered there, but never made it.

The line to the left was now complete except for a small gap along the Bunker Hill road from the breastworks Prescott had added to the left of the redoubt, to the start of the rail fence two hundred yards behind. Fortunately, the gap faced swampy ground, but the colonials added several small v-shaped ditches, or fleches, to afford some protection for militiamen who moved there.

To the right of the redoubt, Prescott had moved three companies down the slope to Charlestown, and into the town itself where they could find firing positions behind whatever shelter they could find.

In the redoubt, Colonel Prescott received an unexpected visitor. Dr. Joseph Warren arrived with musket in hand, ready to do battle. Warren had been commissioned a Major General a few days before, and Prescott immediately deferred to Warren, asking for orders. Warren, however, said he was not there to command (he had not yet formally received his commission). He told Prescott he was there as an ordinary soldier, and would fight like one.

Warren was not alone in this show of humble patriotism. Seventy-year old Seth Pomeroy of Northampton, an honored veteran of both King George's and the French and Indian Wars, had like Warren, recently been commissioned a General in the Colonial army, and also like Warren, had not yet officially received it. After crossing Charlestown Neck he ran into General Putnam, who like Prescott at the redoubt, offered to take orders from him. Pomeroy declined the offer. Cradling his old musket, he made his way down to the front lines at the rail fence.

Shortly before the three-o'clock high tide, twenty-eight long boats started to ferry Howe's men, fifty to a boat, to Moulton's Point. With synchronous oars plying the waters, the boats moved over a thousand soldiers and supporting cannon ever closer to their objective. Landing the troops at Moulton's Point, the boats returned to Boston to fetch additional men along with the leader of the assault, General William Howe. From his observation point, Gage had observed the growing colonial activities, and ordered additional reinforcements ready to support Howe's attack.

The British were concerned there may be snipers hidden in the houses in the abandoned town of Charlestown (they were in fact there), so Gage ordered the town burned. Incendiary shells from the cannon started the fires, and a patrol of marines landed on shore, and made sure the conflagration was complete.

After all of the British troops were landed, Howe had over two-thousand British regulars plus supporting artillery. He spread his soldiers out from the base of Moulton's Hill, and paused to allow his men to eat lunch before battle. His plan was conventional British tactics; he would lead the main attack at the colonial's left side (the British right side) with his grenadiers, while General Pigot would move on a broad front on the colonial right, which included the redoubt. As an added thrust, Howe was sending the mobile light infantry along the shore of the Mystic River where they would penetrate behind enemy lines, and come up behind them. He was confident his plan would succeed quickly and easily.

In the early afternoon, after their lunch, the British Attack began, supported by cannon from the naval ships, Copp's Hill in Boston, and two guns recently emplaced on Moulton's Hill. The British troops, carrying heavy provisions and equipment for a three-day siege, spread out along the bottom of Charlestown Peninsula in a typical double line. With General Howe leading the front ranks, and drummers beating a steady cadence which reverberated over the field of battle, they proceeded ominously up the hill.

The march up the open slope to the rail fence was not as facile as originally thought. The fields had not been tended by Charlestown's farmers, and the grass was waist high. The high grass hid low stone walls marking pasture borders, and the ever present boulders strewn about. The yielding marshy ground also hindered the charge. Along the shore of the Mystic River, the light infantry moved quickly.

Howe had concluded he could overwhelm the disorganized rebels with his men using glistening bayonets to create fear and panic in these untested soldiers. With his preconceived opinion of the colonial's fighting ability, he was convinced an all-out charge would cause them to run, and the battle would be over quickly.

As the colonial troops watched the British advance, the patriot leaders harbored a deep concern: they had only a limited amount of powder and musket balls. As the British closed, the patriot officers cautioned their charges to wait until the British were very close before firing. "Not until you see the whites of their eyes," was a command, which might have been issued, but there is no assured historical record of who gave that command. But, the meaning was clear, wait until you had a good shot and don't waste ammunition.

Along the shore of the Mystic River, the light infantry, led by the Welsh Fusiliers, advanced in a four-wide column. Within fifty yards of the small stone barricade, the colonials rose from behind the barrier, shouldered their muskets and unleashed a furious volley. The leading column was dropped quickly. The rank that followed stepped over their fallen comrades, to continue the charge, and also quickly succumbed to the hail of musket balls as each succeeding rank of militiamen moved forward to fire in their turn. The rebel resistance was so intense, and the causalities so complete, the remaining infantry turned, and retreated in a disorganized run, making it all the way to the boats that had bought them there; some even attempting to reboard them.

On the open ground along the front of the rail fence, the British line, moving more deliberately than the charge at the river, was within fifty yards when they too felt the concentrated fire of the colonial army. The result on the field was the same as it had been at the shore. As many fell, the British line broke, and the soldiers retreated. After the British retreat, Colonel Stark went forward from his post behind the stone wall to assess the toll the British suffered, and counted ninety-six fallen.

Pigot's charge on the colonial right didn't fare any better than Howe's. Firings from the redoubt, and by snipers near the burning Charlestown, forced his troops to retreat. The colonial front-line patriot defenders had repelled the first British charge at great cost to the imperial army.

British officers worked feverously to regroup their troops back into line. After much cajoling, they succeeded, and the British line reformed and resumed moving up the hill, their intent again to overwhelm the rebels. At the second attack, the British felt the same withering fire that so depleted the charging line at the first assault, they again were obliged to fall back. Howe could not obtain the bayonet charge into the American lines he had envisioned as there were too many killed or wounded to sustain a charge.

As the British tended their wounded and shocked survivors, Howe requested reinforcements from Gage. General Clinton could no longer stay outside the battle, and joined the boats bringing the reinforcements. While the British reinforcements were being rowed to support Howe, the colonials were discovering what the battle had cost them so far. There were a number of casualties among the troops, but most importantly, they were nearly out of ammunition and powder; certainly not enough to sustain another fusillade like they had used to successfully repel the first two British charges.

Disorder, too, was occurring with the militia. A conglomeration of soldiers was gathered on Bunker Hill; some were fragments of units separated from their commanders, others newly arrived volunteers. In the confusion of battle and lacking competent officers to lead them, they were reluctant to move down from Bunker Hill to the intense battle at the front lines. A number of the front-line troops were too exhausted to fight (over twenty-four hours without sleep) and retreated to safety. Many others, however, braved the conditions, and went to the aid of those in the redoubt, and along the breastworks and rail fence.

Critically missing from the American side was an overall battlefield commander who had the authority and knowledge to maneuver men and cannon where it would be most effective. General Ward, weakened by illness, remained in Charlestown worried about other British attacks, and never ventured to the battle site. The only on-site general, Israel Putnam, was never given overall battlefield command, and was doing whatever he felt important at any moment. Besides, he was head of the Connecticut Militia, and had no real authority over the militias from the other colonies. It was a deficiency as severe as the lack of powder.

The British, on the other hand, held a significant advantage in their command structure. It was Howe's responsibility to conduct and win this battle, and all on the British side knew it. With that well-defined responsibility and command came resolve, and Howe had resolved he would not lose. The rebels' intent to aim at officers had a serious effect on the British command leadership as a disproportionate share of the killed and wounded occurred with the officer corps, but Howe made the necessary adjustments, and his force was still functional.

With the arrival of four hundred healthy and fit reinforcements in place, his officers replaced where critical, and his cannon moved up and repositioned to sweep the defenders at the breastworks with grapeshot, the British began their third charge up the hill. The British troops discarded the heavy provisions they originally had been ordered to carry, so their movement was much facilitated. This time the main thrust would be against the redoubt and the breastworks. Prescott had about five hundred able defenders in the redoubt and along the breastworks, while there were more at the fleches and rail fences to his left. Even though continuing to take heavy causalities, the British resolutely continued to advance. The Americans were running out of powder and ammunition, and could not sustain the heavy salvos necessary to stop the assault.

As the defense at the breastworks began to collapse due to the effective cannon fire, the British climbed over the earthen shields penetrating the defenses at the breastworks, and began climbing into redoubt itself. Many of the militiamen continued to fire what they had, but as more redcoats poured into the fort, bayonets forward, Prescott ordered a retreat. The interior of the redoubt was obscured by smoke and dust. It was difficult to determine friend from foe. The militia began to exit through the small opening in the rear, but British soldiers were moving in and around the small fort engaging the defenders in hand-to-hand fighting.

It was at this point in the intense engagement two warriors were slain. British Major John Pitcairn, who had led the charge at Lexington Green was mortally wounded by a shot from Salem Prince, one of several freed slaves who fought bravely for the patriots.

The American cause was dealt a devastating blow when Dr. Joseph Warren was hit with a musket ball in the back of his head and died instantly. As the colonial survivors moved away from the redoubt, they were under continuous fire from British muskets and cannon. Colonel Prescott, his coat tattered by bayonet rips, using only his sword to parry the British bayonets, was the last to leave through the narrow rear opening. As the survivors from the redoubt and breastworks clamored down the back slope of Breed's Hill, up the front slope of Bunker Hill, and to safety across Charlestown Neck, they suffered many causalities.

The carnage of the colonials would have been much greater, but the troops at the rail fence held their ground prohibiting a large British flanking maneuver at the side of the retreating militia. Seeing the failure of the redoubt and breastworks, the troops at the rail fence began an orderly withdrawal rather than a panic-driven retreat. This action saved many colonial lives. They even dragged one of the valued cannons with them. The British made an effort to capture the prize, but the New Hampshire militia kept them at bay, and the big gun was moved over Charlestown Neck to safety. General Burgoyne, observing the colonial retreat from the rail fence from his observation perch in Boston, observed (their), *"retreat was no flight; it was even covered with bravery and military skill."*

Charlestown Neck was crowded with the retreating colonial army. The British continued to bombard the area with cannon from their ships and from Copp's Hill. Clinton, who had joined the infantry in the attack at the redoubt, was pleading with General Howe to continue the attack on what he described as the disorganized colonial army. Howe, however, would not order it. The majority of his troops were exhausted from three ascents up the hills, and had sustained considerable losses.

The last colonial troops to leave the peninsula were the company of militia from burned out Charlestown, motivated by the destruction of their town to fight the British to the last. As the colonial soldiers passed over the small land bridge, Putnam was at work directing the digging of entrenchments on the mainland side of the neck opposing any attempt by the British to cross it.

Clinton satisfied himself by setting up a defensive position on Bunker Hill opposite the colonial army on the mainland. Upon further reflection, he observed, *"A dear bought victory, another such would have ruined us."* The same thought was repeated by the fallen British Colonel James Abercromby, who wrote from his deathbed after the battle, *"A few such victories would ruin the Army."*

Night brought medical men on both sides to care for the wounded. One British doctor noted the effect of the ammunition used by the rebels when out of musket balls, *"their muskets were charged with old nails and angular pieces of iron."* He opined it was done deliberately to wound rather than kill. He was, of course, incorrect, but the story was repeated in the British press, again attempting to demonize the rebels and their cause.

The battle was considered to be a victory for the British and a defeat by the colonials as holding the land was the measure used, but the combat demonstrated one overriding fact that was not lost on the British: These rebels would fight, and do so effectively and with ardor. Beating them would not be an easy task.

In the days following, the cost of the battle was found severe for both antagonists. On the British side there were 1054 causalities; 226 killed and 828 wounded, almost fifty-percent of the British soldiers actually engaged. Of more immediate import was the extremely high casualty rate among the officer corps.

On the colonial side, later counts revealed a total of 450 killed, wounded or missing. Equally concerning was the depletion of powder and shells. The colonial war machine was seriously weakened.

As time went by, Gage and Howe discussed what options were open to them. Additional troops were on the way, but supplies were running low, and resupply by ships only barely sufficient. All of Boston was feeling the effects of the colonial siege. The ever aggressive Clinton wanted to attack someplace, Dorchester, he argued, was an enticing target, but he was not allowed to do so as priority was placed on solidifying the defenses of Boston itself.

The idea of abandoning Boston by the British army was discussed at length in both London and Boston. It didn't seem the place where a massive British army could be assembled to fight the rebels on a much broader scale. The harbor was not all that amenable to assembling a large army, and then there were those extremely hostile natives.

Recriminations were rampant in the colonial camp. Why construct the fort on Breed's Hill where retreat was difficult instead of Bunker Hill which could have been defended? Colonel Prescott was furious he did not receive more reinforcements—why, he asked, did those soldiers on Bunker Hill not come down to the front lines? Why was there not enough powder and ammunition? Several officers were cited for "misdeeds." The artillery officers John Callender and Scarborough Gridley were tried and dismissed from the army. Scarborough Gridley, another of Colonel Gridley's sons, had kept his cannon on the mainland side of Charlestown Neck, avoiding exposure to British fire.

(Callender later fought bravely in future battles, and his record of dismissal was expunged by George Washington, who reinstated him as an officer).

However, even with these self-criticisms, and the disappointment of being routed from Charlestown Peninsula, no one denied the exemplary bravery, and deep-belief in the patriot cause exhibited by the patriot soldiers who so bravely fought there. It was the first major battle which set inexperienced colonial militia against well-trained, well-provisioned, well commanded British regulars. Although the field was lost, the British were harmed and humbled. Talk of other attacks by Royal forces were quickly dismissed by most of the British military leaders, knowing it would not be easy, and could even be fatal to them. The British boast that "a force of five thousand regulars would be sufficient to rout the whole of the American Colonies," now rang hallow.

The greatest deficiency faced by the patriots in the battle was lack of a formal command structure, led by a respected, competent leader. That was about to change as General George Washington began making his way to Cambridge to assume command of the now, Colonial army.

Chapter Thirty-Three

The Patriots Declare

On July 5th 1775, the Continental Congress had passed the Olive Branch Petition to King George III, respectfully requesting the monarch to consider mitigating the effects of the recent acts of Parliament. Signed by 49 members of the congress it was dispatched to London on July 8th. The petition approved by the Continental Congress finally reached London in early August. It was carried there by two prominent colonials; Arthur Lee of Virginia, the younger brother of Richard Lee, a congressional delegate and one of the signers of the petition, and Richard Penn of Pennsylvania, the grandson of William Penn, the first proprietor of the Pennsylvania Colony.

The petition was filled with fawning verbiage, vowing loyalty to the King, *"Attached to your Majestys person, family and government with all the devotion that principal and affection can inspire, connected with the Great Britain by the strongest ties that can unite society....and to transmit your Majestys name to posterity adorned with that signal and lasting glory... "*

However, it still put forward a relationship with Britain which gave the American Colonies a great deal of autonomy. While not advocating outright independence, it ordained the intolerable acts be repealed. This implied the colonies would not accept all of Parliament's Laws or accede to taxation. While there was some acceptance of Parliament's and the King's right to regulate trade by the colonists, this was a minor concession that did not assuage the powers in London. The petition may have sounded reasonable to the colonists, but it did not to the King and his ministers in London.

Lee and Penn took the petition to Lord Dartmouth for presentation to the King, but the King was adamant in his refusal to even see it. Dartmouth informed the two colonists, *"As His Majesty did not receive the petition on the throne, no answer would be given."* The King later formally rejected the petition stating it was an illegal petition written by an illegal Congress.

The King's refusal was a severe disappointment to the two hopeful patriots who had carried it across the ocean to present it to his majesty personally. Returning to Philadelphia the next month, they reported on their unsuccessful attempt to a disappointed congress.

On August 23, 1775, the King issued a Proclamation declaring the Colonies were in a state of rebellion *"misled by dangerous and ill-designing men"*, and required all civil and military offices *"to exert their utmost endeavourers to suppress such rebellion, and to bring the traitors to justice."*

In London, the great majority of the government's ministers, members of Parliament, and the general public, supported the King's position. There was, however, a minority in Parliament who were disturbed by the King's stance on aggrieving the colonies. Lord Camden, who had opposed the taxation of the colonies, observed, *"Who could have imagined that the ministry could have become so popular by forcing this country into a destructive war and advancing the power of the Crown to a state of despotism."*

Those congressional members in Philadelphia hoping for reconciliation with Britain, now had no real prospect of a peaceful accommodation with the mother country, and that comment about bringing traitors to justice in the King's proclamation was a personal threat. They were faced with the options so eloquently articulated earlier by Patrick Henry: they would have to submit (to slavery) or fight. Aversion to submission to Britain became ever more widespread throughout the colonies. For many, this was the moment of truth: independence became the only viable alternative.

When George Washington had arrived in Cambridge, Massachusetts, on July 3, 1775, he set up his headquarters in the resplendent mansion of Colonel John Vassall, a loyalist who had fled to Boston. He soon discovered the army he was to command was seriously under-manned and under-provisioned. Supplies were deficient across the board, especially powder and ammunition, which was so low Washington kept the deficiency a secret, even from his officers, lest word be leaked of their precarious position. Of perhaps more importance, the troop level needed to keep Gage penned up in Boston was falling. Many of the soldiers had enlisted only until the end of last year, and local re-enlistments were not sufficient to maintain a strong army. Efforts were made to recruit men from throughout the colonies to augment the New Englanders leaving to return to their farms. Especially welcome were riflemen from Virginia and Pennsylvania, whose weapon spanned a much greater range than the muskets in general use by the New Englanders.

To support Washington, the congress had appointed as generals, Charles Lee of Virginia, to serve as second in rank to Washington, and Philip Schuyler of New York. Artemas Ward, Israel Putman and several other Generals were retained to assist in the continuance of command, and the formation of a navy was authorized.

In September, Washington was faced with an incident which greatly disturbed the Massachusetts patriots. Dr. Benjamin Church's spying activities for the British army was discovered. Always thought to be one of the most trusted and committed of the patriots, his traitorous actions was deeply distressing to all, especially to Samuel Adams, who had considered him one of his protégés. Washington directed a trial which convicted the doctor, and sent him to prison. The event troubled many who raised thoughts, could anyone be trusted? Fortunately, Church's defection was not a wide-spread problem.

Washington's main mission was to keep British troops confined to Boston's and Charlestown's peninsulas. Gage, out of favor with the King, was replaced and left for London in October, turning over command of the British army in America to General Howe. In London Lord Dartmouth had had enough and resigned in November, being replaced as Minister for the American Colonies by George Germain, a military man thought to be more aggressive in subduing the rebellious colonists. His attitude towards the colonists was a disparaging *"these country clowns cannot whip us."*

The replacements didn't change anything for Washington around Boston, but seeking an opportunity in the north he had sent Brigadier General Richard Montgomery on a mission to Canada. To support him, Benedict Arnold was sent via the sea and then overland along the Kennebec River to assist in the capture of Quebec. Only a moderate number of troops (about two thousand) were deemed necessary. It was believed by many of the American colonists that the French settlers would join them in opposing the British. While there may have been some of that mindset among the French in Canada, most were apathetic to the Americans' cause. Britain had allowed the French settlers in Canada to keep their priests and practice the Catholic religion freely. There had also been inferences of future settlement opportunities in the Ohio Territory.

The attack on a reinforced and resupplied Quebec at the end of 1775 subsequently failed miserably. General Montgomery was killed and Arnold wounded; the defeated soldiers, many suffering from smallpox and other maladies, straggled back to colonial territory.

General Burgoyne had left in December 1775 as the King had promised him he could return to London if he did not receive a substantial command. General Clinton, always anxious for action, had taken some troops and ships in a failed attempt to attack Charlestown, South Carolina, so it was General Howe alone who commanded the forces in Boston.

Earlier in the fall of 1775, spies had told the patriot military leaders of the hardships in Boston. Supply by ships in the fall and winter was not sufficient to keep the troops and populace in the city well-fed and comfortable. With the deteriorating conditions in Boston, there was concern Howe would undertake an imprudent maneuver to break out of the city's confines. Many in the patriot ranks felt some action must be taken against the British before they could be resupplied and troops added in the coming spring and summer. Washington considered an attack on Boston using boats to cross the Charles River, but was again dissuaded from an invasion by his War Council.

It was at this time an extraordinary individual undertook a formidable mission which changed things considerably. Henry Knox, Artemas Ward's aide during the battle on Charlestown Peninsula, had become an officer in the Rhode Island Guards. He had met Washington the last summer, and a mutual respect bonded the two. In this fall of 1775 Knox went to Washington with an audacious plan: retrieve the heavy cannon from the forts at Ticonderoga and Crown Point, and bring them back for use by the colonial army at Boston. It was an extremely difficult and hazardous undertaking Knox was proposing. Moving down the Hudson River and over the Berkshire mountains in the middle of winter was thought well-nigh impossible.

With Washington's assent, in mid-November 1775, the intrepid twenty-five year old Knox left Cambridge with his younger brother (16) and a supporting contingent to begin the arduous mission. He was authorized to expend funds for the construction of boats for the voyage down Lake George, sleds and carts for the overland passage; horses and oxen to pull them, and for recruiting men to assist in the journey.

Knox arrived at Fort Ticonderoga the first week of December. Winter had arrived in full, but ice on parts of Lake George was not thick enough for sleds, boats would have to be used. After examining the weapons, both cannon and several mortars at the forts, Knox selected twenty-nine of the weapons from the fort at Crown Point and thirty from Ticonderoga. The weapons were all bulky, with the huge brass twenty-four pound cannon the heaviest at two and a half tons; the rest at a ton or less each were still difficult to handle and move. Knox and his men would have to go two hundred miles south before turning east for another hundred miles to Cambridge, a daunting three hundred miles in all.

Securing the weapons on boats, movement down the lake began. Hampered by a strong north wind making rowing laborious, movement south was grudgingly gained. One of the boats sank, dumping its cannon into the icy waters. With great difficulty it was retrieved, and, in the frosty coldness of winter, the progression continued. After about thirty miles the caravan reached the southern end of Lake George. Moving the weapons to forty-two sleds pulled by eighty oxen, the train of men, animals and weapons slowly continued south aside the Hudson River. The terrain dictated several crossing of the river, and during one such, the ice gave way dumping another cannon in the brink, only to again be rescued and replaced upon a sled.

At the southern end of the trek near Albany the party turned east facing the daunting hundred mile trek through the Berkshire Mountains of western Massachusetts. Over hill and valley they trudged; many times seemingly facing an impassible obstacle, only to be galvanized by Knox's implacable resolve. Passing through the mountainous country, the transport crew was often aided by the locals, and feted with warm drinks and hospitality.

Finally, near the end of January, 1776, the incredible mission ended with the delivery of all of the cannon and mortars (not one was lost) to an astonished and delighted Washington and his troops. Knox had fulfilled Washington's confidence in him. He had proven himself an exceptional officer whose talents would well serve the colonial army.

Washington now had the means to attack the British. Supported by cannon, the colonials could mount a conventional attack on Boston over the land bridge at Boston Neck and across the ice on the Charles River. The city, however, was now well entrenched, and an attack could be disastrous if it failed. Washington's war council could not support such a direct approach. However, if the cannon could be located on Dorchester Heights, which overlooked the city and its harbor, the British would be gravely threatened. But, to begin fortifications on Dorchester Heights would certainly force Howe to respond; the outcome of which would be uncertain.

At this time, an ingenious plan was formulated to create a surprise for Howe by emplacing the cannon behind a fortress on Dorchester Heights in a single night! Israel Putnam's cousin, Rufus Putnam, had been studying ways that had been used by past armies to quickly construct fortifications, and suggested building pre-fabricated protective structures of wood and hay, which could be installed rapidly. The plan was adopted and detailed planning began.

On March 2, 1776, a bombardment of Boston was commenced by several of Knox's cannon dispersed around the city to provide a distraction to allow the piling of hay bales around the base of Dorchester Heights to hide the colonials' activity. Washington selected March fifth, the date of the Boston Massacre, still celebrated by the patriots, as the day of occupation. On the night of March fourth, the fortifications on Dorchester Heights began. As night descended on the scene, three thousand men, hundreds of oxen and horses, and multitudes of wagon moved and emplaced the prefabricated timber chandeliers, earth-filled barrels, and twenty of the cannon, on the 110–foot elevation of Dorchester Heights. It was a formidable undertaking creating an oppressive fortress.

Several of the British sentries, hearing activity across the water during the night, informed their superiors the rebels were up to something on Dorchester, but it was not thought meaningful, and no actions were taken.

As the morning sun rose in the east illuminating Dorchester Heights, the British were astounded. Howe, viewing the fortress with its cannon exclaimed, *"My God, these fellows have done more work in one night than I could make my army do in three months!"* Howe reported to London the colonies employed 14,000 men in fabricating the fort.

The British at first tried their cannon against the emplacement, but they proved futile in reaching the higher elevations of the heights. Howe's initial, angry reaction at being shown up was to prepare for a frontal assault against the site, but a storm delayed his plan. During the hiatus, he was talked out of what would have most likely been a stinging defeat for his army, as Washington's troops were well entrenched behind the steep slopes up to the heights, and those earth-filled barrels Washington had insisted on were to be rolled down the slopes, disrupting a charge at the colonial stronghold. Washington was disappointed the British did not attack as he was confident they would have suffered a resounding defeat.

The British army, all of Boston, and ships in the harbor now lay helpless under the menacing colonial cannons. Howe realized he had no real option of maintaining his force in Boston, and sent an unofficial message to Washington agreeing not to burn the city if his army was allowed to leave unmolested. Even though no formal compact was reached, that is what occurred. Loading his troops and loyalists civilians aboard 120 ships, they left Boston nearly intact. After a delay in the harbor to repair several of the ships, on March 17, 1776, the British abandoned Boston, bound for Halifax in Nova Scotia.

Washington correctly perceived the British would move the greater part of their army to New York, if not immediately, then soon. He made plans to move the bulk of his army south to confront them when they arrived. He left General Artemas Ward in charge of a reduced contingent in Boston, and moved with the main force of his army to New York.

In Philadelphia in the spring of 1776, the intensity and purpose of debate within the Continental Congress shifted considerably from those of a year before. When the King refused to even look at the Olive Branch Petition, those in the Continental Congress who had strongly advocating some sort of reconciliation with Britain, were deflated. It had been their fervent contention the King would accede to an honest, sincere plea for the relief desired so intently by the colonials. Now, with his abrupt, insolent refusal to even hear their plea, they began to see the monarchy and Britain's governance in a different light. King George III seemed to take the rebellion as a personal affront, and was demanding servile obedience from his colonial subjects, by force if necessary; nothing else would do.

Last winter the Congress had formed the Committee of Secret Correspondence to explore the attitudes of foreign governments toward them. In December, 1775 several of the committee's members, led by Benjamin Franklin, had met with an "unofficial" French diplomat to determine the views each government had of the other.

The meeting was a sensitive one for each side. Seeking aid from France, Briton's historical enemy, was sure to displease those citizens of Britain who were sympatric to the colonial cause. At the same time, France was leery about any support they would provide to the colonists; where would they be if they agreed to help only to have the Americans achieve some sort of reconciliation with King George III? The discussions proceeded with caution on both sides, but the French representative, Julien Achard de Bonvouloir, was captivated by the Americans and the intensity with which they pursued their cause. He had reported to Paris the Americans would certainly achieve independence, perhaps soon. It began a dialogue between the continental congress and France which would prove valuable to both sides.

It was about this time another view of the monarchy was being widely read throughout the colonies. Written by a recent British immigrant, Thomas Paine, the ideas presented in his pamphlet, *Common Sense*; objected to the concept of a hereditary monarchy on both religious and logical grounds. He wrote, *"a long habit of not thinking a thing wrong, gives it the superficial appearance of being right, and raises at first a formidable outcry in defense of custom."* The monarchy wasn't ordained by God, he asserted, but invented by men who sustained its continuance to maintain power by a hereditary elite. The monarchy and system of peers, Paine pointed out, *"by being hereditary are independent of the people; wherefore in a constitutional sense they contribute nothing towards the freedom of the state."*

Many were being influenced by the work. George Washington observed, *"I find Common Sense is working a powerful change in the minds of many men."*

John Adams met with Paine, and while he disagreed with some of the precepts in the publication relating to religious objections to the monarchy, he had similar views of government. As Adams, and others, examined the concept of authority, they became convinced the purist form of government was one in which the people being governed were the source of that authority. It wasn't just with taxation, as in their present state, but it was with ALL aspects of government. The concept that authority was vested in an ancestral chain was exposed in their minds to be factious and outdated. While Britain was enmeshed in ancestral linkages in monarchs, earls, viscounts, and the like, the colonies, if they were to become independent, would suffer little of the corruptive pressures associated with this type of influence on their government.

The British system of government and laws had served the empire well. British citizens accepted and obeyed the hierarchy of control over them as it was deemed necessary for their common good. However, acceptance of the government's laws and controls were conditioned on the primacy of individual rights. The British constitution, that assemblage of laws, compacts and judicial decisions, gave individuals certain rights and privileges which were an essential ingredient in the acceptance of government. As far back as the 1215 Magna Carta, rights were granted to protect individuals from the capricious oppression by ruling Monarchs. The revision of this agreement, written in 1297, entitled *"The Great Charter of the Liberties of England, and of the Liberties of the Forest"* remains the law in England. Over the intervening almost six hundred years individual rights had been more precisely defined, and accepted by the rulers and the ruled.

Now, the citizens of Colonial America could no longer tolerate the abrogation of their precious rights upon which was based their valued freedom. For many, the present provisions of the laws forced a choice: freedom or slavery, and these proud people, with a society hewn from what was to them a wild land, with the blood of generations past, could not acquiesce to the form of slavery imposed by their mother country.

While individual and collective attitudes within the colonies varied by region, one could reasonably conclude that a wide spread sense of unjust mistreatment at the hands of the Crown was prevalent throughout most of the colonial population regardless of region or class. The Stamp Act, and the following Intolerable Acts, affected all Colonies and was resented and resisted by nearly every British subject in North America, even amongst most loyalists.

It was becoming apparent many, and most likely a majority, in the Continental Congress now favored independence over reconciliation. While there were differences of opinion in the various sectors of Colonial America, there was overriding agreement among them that to continue in the present relationship with Britain was not acceptable.

In New England, first settled by Puritans from East Anglia, and later augmented by immigrants from throughout England, Scotland, Ireland, and a scattering of French Huguenots, the population had a custom of descent, and a sense of personal freedom and independence that was uncommon in England at the time of their emigration. Those attitudes still remained strong in the colony in 1776.

In the New York colony, and similarly in New Jersey, a more polyglot population composed of English, Dutch, French, German and others lived in a liberal culture highly tolerant of diverse views and values, and dedicated to trade. There were generally no intense emotional imperatives over moral values as found in New England, but there was still a cadre of average citizens who were repelled by British actions that affected them, and who were willing to fight to keep their perceived freedom.

The Pennsylvania and Delaware Colonies had large Quaker populations, mostly English, but with a large and growing German/Dutch element. Among this segment of the population, agriculture was the main occupation; with only a perfunctory interest in politics. There was sentiment to be left alone to have peace and freedom of worship. They were willing to seek compromise to avoid open conflict, but there were limits for many to the oppression they would tolerate from the King and Parliament. In Pennsylvania's western mountain frontier area, occupied predominately by English and Welsh settlers, there was a passive anti-Crown culture, which arose from their strong sense of independence.

In Virginia, and to a degree Maryland, the politics was dominated by large plantation owners in the tide water areas who were dependent on English and European markets for their products. However, from this area emerged the most eloquent, dedicated champions of colonial rights and opposition to absolute British rule. Though dependent on England in many key areas, and likely to suffer severely in any open conflict, individuals from these colonies provided leadership critical to forming a strong, organized resistance to Britain.

North and South Carolina, and emerging Georgia, was similar in outlook to Virginia, but on a smaller scale. They were geographically removed from the center of political and economic conflict, but shared the same reluctance to docilely accede to Britain's oppressive acts.

Since the start of the new congress in January, the subject of independence was becoming the main focus of debate within the Congress. John Adams of Massachusetts and John Dickinson of Pennsylvania spared often over the matter, with others offering a variety of opinions. The issue was finally forcefully addressed on a fateful June 7, 1776 when Richard Henry Lee of Virginia rose and offered his momentous motion: *"That these United Colonies are, and of right ought to be, free and independent States, that they are absolved from all allegiance to the British Crown, and that all political connection between them and the State of Great Britain is, and ought to be totally dissolved."*

John Dickinson of Pennsylvania and Edward Rutledge of South Carolina argued it was not yet time for so momentous a decision; where would they be if Washington was hastily defeated by British might? After three-days of contentious debate and back-room bargaining, the delegates voted to postpone a vote on the motion until July. Approval was given to study three facets of consequence in Lee's motion: preparation of a confederation agreement between the colonies, the establishment of treaties with foreign powers (support from France was deemed essential), and, importantly, the writing and approval of a Declaration of Independence which would publically announce their intention. Committees were formed to address each of these points.

The committee on writing the declaration included John Adams of Massachusetts, Thomas Jefferson of Virginia, Benjamin Franklin of Pennsylvania, Robert Livingston of New York, and Roger Sherman of Connecticut. At the committee's first meeting Jefferson proposed John Adams should write the declaration as he had been the delegate most aggressive in supporting independence. Adams, however, thought the popular Jefferson, as a Virginian should write the document since he (Adams) had antagonized so many of the delegates with his forceful speeches. Besides, he famously quipped, *"you can write ten times better than I can."*

Thus, in June of 1776, thirty-three year old Thomas Jefferson began the serious task of writing the declaration which would define what the American Colonies were undertaking and why. His wordsmanship, as Adams had pointed out, was masterful. For example, he altered an older version of rights from "life, liberty and property," to "life, liberty and the pursuit of happiness," thus including all citizens whether they owned property or not. He eruditely covered the source of authority of government—"from the consent of the governed." He listed the abuses the King and Parliament inflected on the colonies, and explicitly stated their total independence from Great Britain.

At the end of June the committee gave copies of Jefferson's declaration to the congresses' delegates for review. One aspect of the wording of the document Jefferson prepared bothered some. Although a long-time slave owner, Jefferson recognized the practice of slavery contrasted incongruously with the concept "all men were created equal." Jefferson had placed words blaming the King for prosecuting slavery in the colonies, thus marking it as an injustice, but opposition from both the north and south arose, and the King's actions were rewritten and defined more innocuously, removing any reference to slavery. The final draft of the declaration was finally agreed to by the congressional delegates.

On July 1, 1776, Richard Henry Lee again rose and remade the motion the American Colonies declare themselves to be independent states with no tie to Great Britain. The vote for approval of the motion was, as usual, one in which each colony would cast one vote, a majority of the colonies favoring the motion needed for it to pass. It was left to each colony to determine individually, within their colony, what their vote would be.

John Dickinson of Pennsylvania did not oppose the colonies seeking independence, but voiced concern such an act was not prudent now. Wait, he advised, until we have established the confederation amongst ourselves, and have secured encouragement and support from France.

In the uncertainty of the moment the certainty of the motion was not assured, and the delegates wanted to find out how each of the colonies would vote before making a final commitment. Thus, it was agreed that after the initial cast of votes on July 1st, another formal casting of votes would occur the following day, July 2nd.

The first tally of votes ended with a majority of nine colonies voting for the motion and independence. Opposing were North Carolina, Delaware, Pennsylvania and New York. It was that very afternoon the congress received a report from George Washington stating he expected the British to attack the colonial army in New York. The message of impending aggression from the colonial commander effected South Carolina and Delaware to aver they would switch their vote to approval. The Pennsylvania delegates held a meeting to reconsider their position. John Dickinson and his supporters removed themselves from the meeting so those remaining, who favored independence, could direct their vote be changed to approval. The New York delegation was in a quandary as the British threat on their colony had disrupted the local meeting there and the delegates in Philadelphia could not receive instructions from their home colony concerning how they should vote.

On July 2, 1776, the vote was again called for. The final tally was twelve for approval, one (New York) abstaining (but approving). Two days later, on July 4, 1776, Jefferson's amended Declaration of Independence was approved, the preamble of which follows:

Declaration of Independence

When in the course of human events, it becomes necessary for one people to dissolve the political bands which have connected them with another, and to assume among the powers of the earth, the separate and equal station to which the laws of nature and of nature's God entitle them, a decent respect to the opinions of mankind requires that they should declare the causes which impel them to the separation.

We hold these truths to be self-evident:

That all men are created equal; that they are endowed by their Creator with certain unalienable rights; that among these are life, liberty, and the pursuit of happiness; that, to secure these rights, governments are instituted among men, deriving their just powers from the consent of the governed; that whenever any form of government becomes destructive of these ends, it is the right of the people to alter or to abolish it, and to institute new government, laying its foundation on such principles, and organizing its powers in such form, as to them shall seem most likely to effect their safety and happiness. Prudence, indeed, will dictate that governments long established should not be changed for light and transient causes; and accordingly all experience hath shown that mankind are more disposed to suffer, while evils are sufferable than to right themselves by abolishing the forms to which they are accustomed. But when a long train of abuses and usurpations, pursuing invariably the same object, evinces a design to reduce them under absolute despotism, it is their right, it is their duty, to throw off such government, and to provide new guards for their future security. Such has been the patient sufferance of these colonies; and such is now the necessity which constrains them to alter their former systems of government. The history of the present King of Great Britain is a history of repeated injuries and usurpations, all having in direct object the establishment of an absolute tyranny over these states. To prove this, let facts be submitted to a candid world.

Additional words were added to the declaration outlining the British actions which forced the colonists to become *FREE AND INDEPENDENT STATES*; the document was signed by 56 of the delegates to the Continental Congress.

Up until the colonies declared their independence from Britain they were fighting to resist Britain's enforcement of the Intolerable Acts. It was a nebulous sort of motivation for most of the fighters in the army. After declaring independence, however, the soldiers were fighting for their own country, a decidedly different mindset. The declaration also made it more uncomfortable for those American colonists who had not yet decided which side they would support. Many undecided were measuring which side they believed would prevail in the upcoming conflict, and refrained from choosing until they could be more confident in picking a winner. But with passage of the declaration, the populace became polarized, and individuals were essentially required to state their allegiance.

As the colonial delegates were concluding their debates and voting on independence in Philadelphia, an immense British naval armada under Admiral Richard Howe was sailing into New York Harbor. The ships carried over thirty-thousand troops of the British army along with thousands of German mercenaries. This mighty land force was under the leadership of General William Howe, the admiral's brother. They had come to America to subdue the colonies, and bring them back under the dominion and control of King George III and the British Parliament.

Efforts at a negotiated peace would fail as the Americans adamantly refused to give up their, now treasured, Declaration. The war to follow would be difficult and expensive for both sides. The colonial army under General George Washington would suffer defeats and victories in five long years of often brutal and bloody conflicts. Finally, at Yorktown, Virginia in October 1781, Washington's army, supported by the French Fleet, forced over eight thousand British troops under British General Charles Cornwallis to surrender, effectively ending Britain's hopes to crush the colonies' rebellion. Four months later, with war weary Britain suffering severe financial hardships, the

British House of Commons voted to end all hostilities. Lord North was compelled to resign as Prime Minister, and was replaced by Lord Rockingham who began efforts for peace, leading to a formal treaty on February 4, 1783 in which Britain officially accepted the colonies' independence.

The war of independence, which began with a minor disturbance between British regulars and a local militia on the common green of a small village on April 19, 1775, was now successfully concluded with the defeat of the most powerful nation on earth. The delegates to the continental congress then set about defining and building a new nation, to be called, "The United States of America."

Bibliography

BOOKS

Anderson, Fred, *The War That Made America, A short history of the French and Indian war*, 2005, Penguin Books, NY, NY.

Anderson, Virginia DeJohn, *New England's Generation, The Great Migration, Society and Culture in the Seventeenth Century*, 1991, Cambridge University Press, UK.

Axelrod, Alan, *Blooding at Great Meadow, Young Geor4ge Washington and the Battle that Shaped the Man*, 2007, Running Press, Philadelphia, PA.

Bailyn, Bernard, *The Ideological Origins of the American Revolution*, 1967, Harvard University Press, Cambridge, MA.

———, *The Peopling of British North America*, 1986, Vintage Books, NY, NY.

Baker, C. Alice, *True Stories of New England Captives*, 1897, Published in 1990 by Heritage Books, Inc., Westminster, MD.

Bancroft, George, *History of the United States*, A monumental history written in the mid- and late- nineteenth century in eight volumes, Available from the University of Michigan Library, Ann Arbor, MI.

Bargar, B. D., *Lord Dartmouth and the American Revolution*, 1965, The University of South Carolina Press, Columbia, SC.

Barone, Michael, *Our First Revolution*, 2001, Three Rivers Press, NY, NY.

Bremer, Francis J., *The Puritan Experiment*, 1995, University Press of New England, Lebanon, NH.

———, *John Winthrop*, 2003, Oxford University Press, NY, NY.

Brewer, J. S. (Revised by), *A History of England*, 1902, Published by John Murray, Out of Print.

Brown, Richard D., *Revolutionary Politics in Massachusetts, The Boston Committee of Correspondence and the Towns, 1772–1774*, 1970, W.W. Norton & Co, NY, NY.

Chacksfield, K. Merle, *Glorious Revolution 1688*, Dorset Publishing Company, Dorset MA.

Cook, Don, *The long Fuse How England Lost the American Colonies, 1760–1785*, 1995, Atlantic Monthly Press, NY, NY.

Dawes, C. Burr (Compiled by), *William Dawes First Rider for Revolution*, Historic Garden Press, 1976, Unknown.

Delbanco, Andrew, *The Puritan Ordeal*, 1989, Harvard University Press, Boston, MA.

Dorson, Richard M. (Editor), *Patriots of the American Revolution*, 1953, Gramercy Books, NY, NY.

Dunn, Richard S. and Yeandle, Laetitia, editors, *The Journal of John Winthrop 1630 -1649*, 1996, Harvard University Press, Cambridge, MA.

Egerton, Hugh Edward, *The Origin & Growth of the English Colonies and of Their System of Government*, Replica of the 1903 publication by Claredon Press, UK.

Fischer, David Hackett, *Albion's Seed Four British Folkways in America*, 1989, Oxford University Press, NY, NY.

———, *Paul Revere' Ride, 1994, Oxford University Press*, NY, NY.

Forbes, Esther, *Paul Revere and the World He Lived In*, 1999, Houghton Mifflin, NY, NY.

Fowler, William M., *The Baron of Beacon Hill, A Biography of John Hancock*, 1980, Houghton Mifflin Company, Boston, MA.

Fradin, Dennis, *Samuel Adams, The Father of American Independence*, 1988, Clarion Books, NY, NY.

Frothingham, Richard, *History of the Siege of Boston And Of The Battles of Lexington, Concord And Bunker Hill*, 1872, Kissinger Publishing Legacy Reprints (www.kissinger.net).

———, *Life and Times of Joseph Warren*, Kissinger Publishing Legacy Reprints (www.kissinger.net).

Graham, Judith S., *Puritan Family Life*, 2000, Northeastern University Press, Boston, MA.

Grant, James, *John Adams, Party of One*, 2005, Farrar, Straus and Giroux, NY, NY.

Green, Evarts Boutell, *The Provincial Governor*, Longmans, Green, and Co., 1898, Harvard University Doctoral Dissertation, Cambridge, MA.

Gross, Robert A., *The Minute Men and Their World*, 1976, Hill and Wang, NY, NY.

Higginson, Thomas Wentworth, *Life of Francis Higginson*, 1891, Dodd, Mead and Co., NY, NY. First Minister in the Massachusetts Bay Colony and author of "New England's Plantation (1630)."

Innes, Stephen, *Creating the Commonwealth, The Economic Culture of Puritan New England*, 1995, W. W. Norton & Company, NY, NY.

Lacey, Robert, *Great Tales From English History*, 2006, Little Brown and Company, NY, NY.

Langguth, A. J., *Patriots The Men Who Started the American Revolution*, 1988, Touchtone Books, Simon & Schuster, Inc. NY, NY.

Lapore, Jill, *The Name of War (King Philips War)*, 1998, Vintage Books, NY, NY.

Maier, Pauline, *American Scripture, Making the Declaration of Independence*, 1997, Vintage Books, NY, NY.

Marshall, Dorothy, *Eighteenth Century England*, 1962, The Chaucer Press, UK.

Marston, Daniel, *The French-Indian War 1754–1760*, 2002, Routledge, London, UK.

———, *The American Revolution 1774–1783*, 2002, Osprey Publishing, Oxford, UK.

McFarland, Philip, *The Brave Bostonians*, 1998, Perseus Books Group, NY, NY.

Meiklejohn, J. M. D., *A New History of England and Great Britain*, 1899, Alfred M. Holden, London, UK.

Meinig, D. W., *The Shaping of America, Volume 1, Atlantic America 1492–1800*, 1986, Yale University Press, New Haven, CT.

Middlekauff, Robert, *The Glorious Cause The American Revolution, 1763–1789*, 1982, Oxford University Press, NY, NY.

Middleton, Richard, *Colonial America A History, 1565–1776*, 1992 Blackwell Publishing, Victoria, Australia.

Morgan, Edmund S. & Morgan, Helen, M., *The Stamp Act Crisis*, 1953, The University of North Carolina Press, Chapel Hill, NC.

Morgan, Edmund S., *The Birth of the Republic 1763–89*, 1956, The University of Chicago Press, Chicago, IL (third edition in 1992).

———, *The Puritan Dilemma, The Story of John Winthrop*, 1958, Little Brown and Company, Boston, MA.

———, *Prologue to Revolution—Sources and Documents of the Stamp Act Crisis, 1764–1766*, 1959, The University of North Carolina Press, Chapel Hill, NC.

———, *American Slavery American Freedom, The Ordeal of Colonial Virginia*, 1975, W. W. Norton & Company, NY, NY.

———, *The Meaning of Independence*, 1976, University of Virginia Press, Charlottesville, VA.

———, *The Challenge of the American Revolution*, 1976, W. W. Norton Company, NY, NY.

———, *Inventing the People*, 1988, W. W. Norton & Company, NY, NY.

———, *Benjamin Franklin*, Yale University Press, New Haven, CT.

———, *The Genuine Article, A Historian Looks at Early America*, 2004, W. W. Norton & Company, NY, NY.

Hall, David D., editor, *Puritans in the New World*, 2004, Princeton University Press, Princeton, NJ.

Hawke, David Freeman, *Everyday Life in Early America*, 1988, Harper Collins, NY, NY.

Hibbert, Chistopher, *Redcoats And Rebels The American Revolution Through British Eyes*, 1990, W. W. Norton & Company, NY, NY.

———, *George III*, 1998, Basic Books, NY, NY.

Hosmer, James K., *The Life of Thomas Hutchinson*, (Reproduction of 1896 publication by Bibliolife, Lexington, KY).

Hutchinson, Peter Orlando, Editor, *The Diary and Letters of His Excellency Thomas Hutchinson, Esq.*, (University of Michigan reprint of an 1884 edition), University of Michigan Library.

Ketchum, Richard M., *Decision Day, The Battle for Bunker Hill*, 1962, Henry Holt and Company, NY, NY.

Knollenberg, Bernhard, *Origin of the American Revolution: 1759–1766*, 1960, Liberty Fund, Indianapolis, IN.

———, *Growth of the American Revolution: 1766–1775*, 1975, The Free Press (MacMillian), NY, NY.

Nash, Gary B., *The Urban Crucible The Northern Seaports and the Origins of the American Revolution*, 1979, Harvard University Press, Cambridge, MA.

O'Brien, Cormac, *The Forgotten History of America*, 2008, Quayside Publishing Group, Beverly, MA.

Padget, Howard (rendered by), *William Bradford, Of Plymouth Plantation*, 1920, E. P. Dutton, NY, NY.

Patterson, Stephen E., *Political Parties in Revolutionary Massachusetts*, 1973, University of Wisconsin Press, Madison, WI.

Pearson, Michael, *Those Damned Rebels, The American Revolution as Seen Through British Eyes*, 1972, De Capo Press, Perseus Group, NY, NY.

Pestana, Carla Gardina, *Quakers and Baptists in Colonial Massachusetts*, 1991, Cambridge University Press, Cambridge, UK.

Philbrick, Nathaniel, *Mayflower*, 2006, Viking Press, NY, NY.

Philips, Kevin, *The Cousins War*, 1999, Basic Books of the Perseus Group, NY, NY.

Puls, Mark, *Samuel Adams Father of the American Revolution*, 2006, Pulgrave MacMillan, NY, NY.

Quincy, Josiah, *A Municipal History of the Town and City of Boston, 1630–1830*, Originally published in 1852, available as a reprint from the University of Michigan Library.

Raphael, Ray, *The First American Revolution*, 2002, The New Press, NY, NY.

Reid, Stewart, *British Redcoat 1740–93*, 1996, Osprey publishing, UK.

Rose-Troup, Francis, *The Massachusetts Bay Company and Its Predecessors*, 1930, Sentry Press, NY, NY.

Russel, Howard S., *Indian New England Before the Mayflower*, 1980, University Press of New England, Lebanon, NH.

Schlesinger, Arthur Meier, *The Colonial Merchants And The American Revolution 1763–1776*, 1918, Facsimile Library, NY, NY.

Schlesinger, Arthur M., *Prelude to Independence, The Newspaper War on Britain 1764–1776*, 1980, Northeastern University Press, Boston, MA.

Several Contributors, *Paul Revere's Boston: 1735–1818*, 1975, Museum of Fine Arts, Boston, MA.

Shy, John, *Toward Lexington, The Role of the British Army in the Coming of the American Revolution*, 1965, Princeton University Press, Princeton, NJ.

Stoll, Ira, *Samuel Adams, A Life*, 2008, Free Press, NY, NY.

Taylor, Alan, *American Colonies, The Settling of North America*, 2001, Penguin Books, NY, NY.

Taylor, Dale, *Everyday Life in Colonial America*, 1997, Writer's Digest Books, Cincinnati, OH.

Thomas, I. D. E., *A Puritan Golden Treasury*, 1975, Versa Press, East Peoria, IL.

Thompson, C. Bradley (selected by), *The Revolutionary Writings of John Adams*, 2000, Liberty Fund, Inc., Indianapolis, IN.

Tourtellot, Arthur B., *Lexington and Concord*, 1959, W. W. Norton & Company, NY, NY.

Wade, Herbert Treadwell, *A Brief History of the Colonial Wars in America*, 1948, Society of Colonial Wars, NY, NY.

Waters, John J., Jr., *The Otis Family in Provincial and Revolutionary Massachusetts*, 1968, University of North Carolina Press, Chapel Hill, NC.

Winslow, Edward, *Good News from New England*, First Published in 1624, Reproduction by Applewood Books, Bedford, MA.

Wood, W. J., *Battles of the Revolutionary War 1775–1781*, 1990, Da Capo Press (Perseus Group), Cambridge, MA.

Wood, Gordon S., *The American Revolution*, 2002, Modern Library, Random House, NY, NY.

Zannieri, Nina, Director, Paul Revere Memorial Association, *Paul Revere—Artisan, Businessman, and Patriot*, 1987, Boston, MA.

Zobel, Hiller B., *The Boston Massacre*, 1970, W. W. Norton & Company, NY, NY.

PAMPHLETS

Common Sense by Thomas Paine, 1776, Available from Penguin Books, NY, NY.

Heros of the Battle Road, 1775, by Frank Wilson Cheney Hersey, 1930, Printed by the Anderson Co., Inc., West Concord, MA.

The Journal of Major George Washington, 1754, by William Hunter, Published by Colonial Williamsburg Foundation, Williamsburg, VA.

The Nineteenth of April, 1775, A Collection of First Hand Accounts, 1968, Originally Published by Sawtells of Somerset, Lincoln, MA, Now Available from The National Park Service.

A Narrative of the Excursion and Ravages of the Kings Troops on the nineteenth of April, 1775, Available from the New England & Virginia Co, Salem, MA.

A Particular Account of the Battle of Bunker Or Breed's Hill On The June 17, 1775, by Alden Bradford, Available from Kessinger Publishing (www.kessinger.net).

INTERNET SITES

Not all of the Internet sites visited in the preparation of this book are listed below. Internet sites are helpful as a subject can be entered into a search engine and a number of sites relevant to the subject are then identified. For example, the two sites following provide useful information.

The first lists Great Britain's Prime Ministers: http://en.wikipedia.org/wiki/List_of_Prime_Ministers_of_the_United_Kingdom.

The second, a site at Colonial Williamsburg, is one of several to display Patrick Henry's "Liberty-or-Death" Speech. http://www.history.org/almanack/life/politics/giveme.cfm.

However, Internet sites cannot be depended upon for accuracy and care must be used when extracting information from them. For example, Wikipedia sites, which have a great deal of information in an extremely broad vista of relevant subjects, are not peer reviewed, and facts and data must be verified by alternate means. In addition, sites are continually updated and replaced with successor sites which make reference to them difficult. With that caveat, the Internet Sites listed below are representative of useful sites which were used in this book:

Historic Documents at the Lillian Goldman Law Library of the Yale Law School (Declarations, Charters, Bills, Proclamations, etc.—separated by century) http://avalon.law.yale.edu/subject_menus/17th.asp.

Historical Documents ordered by date (e.g. Magna Carta) http://odur.let.rug.nl/usa/D/index.htm.

Documents, Resolves, Treaties, etc. by Ashland Un9iversity http://www.bostonhistory.org/.

Massachusetts Historical Society Site. The home site is http://www.masshist.org/. The home site leads to numerous other useful sites, for example, small volumes written by John Adams is found at http://www.masshist.org/digitaladams/aea/diary/.

Useful information and data are found at the Boston Historical Society http://www.bostonhistory.org/.

Accounts of Early Exploration and Settlements from the Wisconsin Historical Society http://www.americanjourneys.org/.

Index

Lightning Source UK Ltd.
Milton Keynes UK
UKOW05n0731221213

223469UK00007B/184/P